The Defense Industry

The Defense Industry

Jacques S. Gansler

The MIT Press
Cambridge, Massachusetts
London, England

Third printing, April 1981
Second printing, December 1980
© 1980 by
The Massachusetts Institute of Technology

This book was set in English Times by A & B Typesetters, Inc., Concord, N.H. and printed and bound by Halliday Lithograph in the United States of America.

Library of Congress Cataloging in Publication Data

Gansler, Jacques S
  The defense industry.

  Bibliography: p. 321
  Includes index.
  1. War—Economic aspects—United States. I. Title.
HC110.D4G36   338.4′76234′0973   80-23647
ISBN 0-262-07078-2

Contents

List of Figures

List of Tables

Preface

This book, which is based on nearly three years of intensive research and twenty-five years of firsthand exposure, is the first serious effort to investigate the total U.S. defense industry with a focus on the post-Vietnam era. Exploring this major sector of the American economy from both economic and strategic perspectives, it concludes that the industrial base of defense is becoming economically inefficient and unresponsive to a potential strategic emergency. Specific factors in the defense industry that will result in a significant weakening of the security posture of this country in the coming years are identified and quantified.

The book also proposes explicit policy changes aimed at improving the future security position of the United States. If these corrective actions were to be initiated soon, the Department of Defense would be able to buy well over $3 billion worth of additional equipment each year without any budgetary increases and the defense industry would be far more responsive to future demands for rapid increases in the production of military goods. Without these changes America's defense problems will grow far worse: The overall defense posture will weaken seriously while defense budgets increase greatly. It is not inconceivable that the United States will follow the path taken by Western Europe—nationalization of the defense industry—unless the undesirable economic and strategic trends are corrected soon.

While I assume full responsibility for all of the findings and recommendations presented in this study, I acknowledge Professors Walter Adams of Michigan State University, Rayford Boddy of American University, J. Ronald Fox of Harvard University, Ronald Müller of American University, Merton J. Peck of Yale University, and Judith Reppy of Cornell University for their evaluations of the various drafts; Major Orville Collins (U.S. Air Force) and Colonel Ralph Luther (U.S. Army) for their assistance with the research; Leah Cabezas, Lawrence T. Friend, Dr. Karen Koenigs, and Eugene Spangenberger for their editorial assistance; and Sylvia Hubbard, Norma Whited, and A. Lillian Tibbetts for their infinite patience in preparing the manuscript. All have worked with great dedication to make this book possible.

The Defense Industry

Introduction

The free-market system is not operating to achieve economically efficient or strategically responsive behavior in the area frequently referred to as the "military-industrial complex."

Not only do the data presented herein confirm this, but the trends in these data clearly indicate that the economic and strategic problems in the defense industry are getting far worse. In terms of the traditional economic criteria for industrial organizations—structure, conduct, and performance—it is clear that the business operations between the defense industry and the U.S. government deviate widely from the conventional wisdom of free-market theory and that many of the results are not in the public interest. It also can be seen that the resources of the defense industry (labor, capital, and materials) are not being used efficiently or effectively.

In addition, the data reveal many specific and critical conflicts between free-market theory (and the corresponding assumptions of the policymakers) and the reality within various elements of the defense industry.

For example, the structure of the industry and the planning of both the government and the industry are based on the assumption that the demand for defense equipment will remain relatively constant (except for the need for wartime production increases), yet American history has shown this demand to be extremely cyclic and likely to continue as such. Also, it is assumed that prime contractors have a competitive and viable base of parts suppliers and subcontractors (as the large commercial firms do in the civilian sector), but the data show that critical high-technology parts usually come from sole-source suppliers, that many of these small suppliers are facing unhealthy financial conditions, and that this segment of the defense economy is shrinking.

It is a basic strategic tenet that the U.S. defense industry must be self-sufficient. Yet today that industry is significantly dependent on sales to other countries and on the supply of parts and materials from foreign sources. Current U.S. government policy is leading to even greater dependency. Similarly, it is assumed that the U.S. defense industry, through the excess capacity it maintains, has the ability to respond rapidly and at high rates of production whenever the military demand so requires. However, this response time always has been unacceptably long, and is becoming longer because of inadequate planning and preparation and the increased complexity of military equipment.

In the area of legislation, it is argued that the government should have uniform procurement practices to achieve "fairness" in awards and equality of profits throughout the defense industry. But the structures of the various parts of the defense industry (for example, aircraft, shipbuilding, and munitions) are so diverse that uniform government policies tend to exaggerate the differences, resulting in grossly nonuniform and often undesirable performance in the various sectors. Also, the "fairness" theory and the relevant federal laws and regulations say that competition should be the required method of procurement; however, most defense-contract money is awarded on a sole-source basis, and less than 8 percent is awarded solely on the basis of price competition.

Essentially, there is a gap between what the structure, conduct, and performance of the defense-industry market require to achieve economic efficiency and strategic-production responsiveness and the actual laws, regulations, policies, and practices that are used to control this market. The government policymakers fail to recognize, or refuse to look at, this gross difference. As a result, far less military equipment (with lower overall military performance) has been produced than could have been produced at the same levels of defense expenditures, short-term military effectiveness has declined (because of lesser quantities of equipment), longer-term military effectiveness in support of combat forces has decreased (because of the lack of production responsiveness to crisis-period demands), and military budgets have gone up to compensate for economic inefficiencies.

Without corrective steps in the near future, these problems will have even greater impact on national defense objectives. This can lead only to drastic political and economic action by the federal government—that is, nationalization. This book offers a set of policy-oriented solutions directed at averting such an impasse. These corrective actions can be implemented within the current economic and political structure because they maximize the use and benefits of the capitalistic private-enterprise system. In essence, this work is a plea for more efficient and effective use of a critical national resource and a presentation of specific steps to achieve this objective.

In view of the importance of the defense industry to America's overall strategic and economic posture, there is a surprising dearth of quantitative and scholarly research on the subject. What does exist (for example, the work of Peck, Scherer, and Fox[1]) is primarily directed toward the way in which the Department of Defense does its business, rather than toward the impact these practices have on the defense industry, which is the focus of this study.

However, some data are available in the Congressional Record and in a few government-funded reports, and considerable historic and current information is obtainable from Department of Defense sources. This data base has been complemented by personal interviews and extensive analyses at both the prime-contractor and subcontractor levels. In addition, I have drawn heavily on personal experience from the twenty years during which I worked for three corporations in the defense industry and from my subsequent five years as an official in the Department of Defense.

Figure 1 illustrates the scope of this study. In reality, there are no clear lines separating any of these blocks. A prime contractor in the aerospace sector may well be concurrently a subcontractor in some ship programs and a parts supplier in the military electronics business. (In fact, there has been an increasing tendency toward vertical integration over the last few years.) Similarly, ownership is often a gray area. In the aircraft industry about one-third of the plant space and equipment is government-owned—and often located in the same area with privately owned plants and equipment.

Oligopoly (if not monopoly or government ownership) is the rule in most supplier areas. The federal government is clearly a monopsonistic (single) buyer, yet historically it never has been concerned about how the diverse parts of its supplier base fit (or should fit) together. No coherent national leadership has addressed the problems of the defense industry in

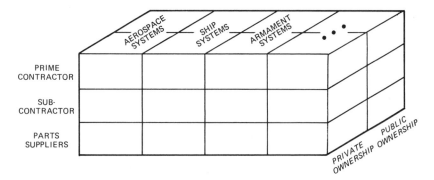

Figure 1
The composition of the defense industrial base.

an attempt to bring about efficiencies where the industry has been inefficient, to inject vitality where the industry may have become ineffective, or to keep the industry from eroding or disappearing altogether.

Clearly, the U.S. defense industry is a significant factor in the American economy and in the nation's strategic posture. It provides more than $50 billion worth of goods and services per year to the Department of Defense alone. It employs between one-third and one-fifth of all American scientists and engineers, and between one-tenth and one-twelfth of the manufacturing labor force. In time of war or national emergency it is critical to America's defensive strength.

The overriding conclusion of this book is that the industrial base of U.S. defense is becoming both economically inefficient in the production of defense materiel and strategically unresponsive in terms of the production speedup required to meet an emergency. Evidence of economic, political, and strategic problems in the defense industrial base has been present in peacetime periods throughout the history of the United States; however, in the post-Vietnam period rapid domestic and international changes amplified normal peacetime problems and may have created significant new ones. One change that highlighted the structural problems in the defense industrial base was the dramatic post-Vietnam reduction in defense procurements. In the seven years following the war's peak, procurements dropped from $44 billion to $17 billion (in constant dollars). This was the lowest level of real purchasing power since just after World War II. A second significant change was the dramatic trend toward selling more and better military equipment to other countries, which was a direct result of the major shifts in the world's geopolitical and economic structure. These rapid changes, combined with the historical conditions in the defense industrial base that had evolved over 200 years, have led to a current state of considerable weakness—and to trends that indicate even greater problems. Perhaps the last time the U.S. defense industry evidenced problems of this magnitude was immediately after World War II, when the industry was almost completely dismantled. But then the United States was clearly the most powerful nation in the world, and there were no other countries with comparable military might. This certainly is not the case today, and it is not likely to be the case in the future. Therefore, the problems of the U.S. defense industry must be addressed now.

These problems must be considered at the prime-contractor level and at the subcontractor-and-parts-supplier level.[2]

Many large prime contractors are sustaining considerable excess capacity, and many are in unhealthy financial positions, with aging plants and equipment. An added complication is the formidable government-created "barriers to exit" for these corporations. At this level there is ample production surge capacity; not so at the subcontractor level. Current planning for the likely scenarios of the nuclear era indicates that conflicts may be too short for the industrial base to respond with significant quantities of major weapons systems, such as ships and aircraft. For the potentially longer conflicts, bottlenecks will occur at the parts level rather than because of a lack of prime-contractor plants and equipment. We are paying for this excess prime-contractor capacity, although it is unlikely that it will ever be utilized effectively.

Further investigation shows that at the prime-contractor level only a few companies are doing a major share of the business, and these are using large amounts of government-supplied funds, plant space, and equipment. Additionally, most of the government procurement regulations and oversight practices are widely applied to this sector (although these regulations were written mostly for small, conventional procurements, such as food and clothing). Thus, this prime-contractor level appears to already have almost total government involvement. The Department of Defense is the regulator, the specifier of new products, the "banker," the judge of claims, and almost the sole buyer. Data indicate that this detailed government intervention is grossly inefficient and frequently self-defeating, yet a free-market economy does not and probably cannot exist in this environment of a single buyer and a small number of suppliers.

The opposite problem exists at the lower levels of the defense industry, among the subcontractors and parts suppliers. The smaller contractors (those remaining after the giants have achieved a large amount of vertical integration) are required to supply their own plants, equipment, and money. Also, because of the way the government and the prime contractors do business, these smaller contractors are realizing a relatively low return on investment in comparison with the prime contractors and with small contractors in the civilian sector—frequently at a level where bankruptcy is common. Furthermore, with the rapid drop in defense procurements, the prime contractors and the government began bringing more of their business "in house," so the defense-market dollars available were shrinking even faster for the smaller companies than for the prime contractors. As a result, large numbers of lower-level defense suppliers have been either going bankrupt or purposely leaving the defense business for the growing and financially more attractive civilian and foreign markets. Finally, weapons systems are becoming extremely complex, and this has brought about high-technology, capital-intensive specialization among subcontractors and parts suppliers. The combination of these trends has significantly reduced the number of suppliers of critical parts. In many important areas, the remaining suppliers are in monopolistic positions and are therefore able to raise prices rapidly and dictate long delivery times. These large price increases[3] should, by traditional economic theory, attract large numbers of companies to this market. However, no such rush has occurred. This is attributable to the "barriers to entry" created by the Department of Defense through such procurement practices as the use of unduly specialized military specifications; "preferred parts" lists; the purchase of small quantites; the annual nature of procurements; and the high uncertainty of continued project fundings. Other barriers to entry are the length of gestation periods, the likelihood that profits will be low, and the highly specialized, unique nature of military research and development that prohibits entry by technologically advanced consumer-goods producers.

This shrinkage of suppliers at the parts level not only affects the production efficiency of defense procurements, but also creates significant industrial bottlenecks threatening production surge capability in times of national crisis. A simple example of this was the 1974 request by the Congress for the Department of Defense to increase tank production as a result of the 1973 Mideast War. The industrial base was unable to respond—not because of a shortage of tank-building capacity by the prime contractor (a government-owned plant operated by Chrysler Corporation), but because of the inability to get steel castings of a certain type from a sole-source supplier that preferred to do civilian business.

Dramatic changes taking place in the worldwide economic and political environment overlay these domestic problems of the U.S. defense industrial base at all levels. The once bipolar power structure is now multipolar, and less-developed countries are wielding the power of oil and scarce materials. The long-standing American supremacy in technology is dwindling. Large U.S. defense-oriented corporations are exhibiting a transnational mentality. These changes, alone and collectively, have had a significant impact on the area of foreign military assistance. Specifically, in the mid-1970s annual foreign military sales grew from $1.5 billion worth of older-generation equipment to \$14 billion in advanced equipment. Recent sales have stressed the overseas transfer of manufacturing technology and equipment, as well as engineering, training, and complete factories. In many cases the U.S. firm does not even obtain an equity position in these foreign plants.

These worldwide changes are making the large prime contractors dependent on foreign military sales—not only to maintain volume and profits, but in some cases[4] for survival. In addition, the United States is rapidly becoming dependent on foreign sources for many critical parts as well as for critical materials. This problem is amplified by foreign governments' recent emphasis on agreements for joint production and "offset" arrangements (by which they supply parts to the United States in exchange for weapons systems and advanced technology). These significant changes in international military assistance will have long-term implications for America's overall economic and political comparative advantage, as well as for our strategic posture.

Here, as with the domestic problems in the defense industry, the U.S. government has claimed a *laissez faire* position. However, the government actually has been playing a dominant role in aggressively pursuing short-term political and economic objectives—perhaps at the expense of long-term results in these same areas. In the interest of increased exports (and even of "détente"), and at the urging of some defense firms, the U.S. government frequently has allowed or encouraged the overseas sale of sophisticated manufacturing equipment and even entire plants capable of producing highly advanced weapons systems. In addition, most of the U.S. government's laws, regulations, practices, policies, and organizations are geared not to the present but rather to the international conditions of twenty years ago. This structural lag must be overcome.

To attack all of these problems, the government must implement a set of coordinated policies aimed at creating a viable market economy in each sector of the defense industry. In fact, the solutions must begin with a clear recognition that each sector has unique problems requiring special corrective actions.

The last chapter proposes a seven-point plan of coordinated policy actions whose proper implementation realistically can be expected to result in the annual availability of billions of dollars' worth of additional military equipment from current defense budget levels. Most military analysts believe this equipment is badly needed. In the long run, the policy actions advanced in this study will provide a greatly strengthened military posture at reduced expenditure levels, prevent a drastic restructuring of the defense industry (with the possibility of nationalization), and preclude large increases in peacetime defense expenditures.

1 The Defense Industry and the U.S. Economy

From pre-Revolutionary times America has had a defense industry to provide the weapons of war. Today that industry remains a major factor as a deterrent. In times of crisis the defense industrial base has required the full support of the nation's research and industrial genius and productivity, and throughout America's history it has often made the difference between victory and defeat on the battlefield. While these strategic considerations often are paramount, the economic importance of this major sector of the U.S. economy should not be overlooked. All through our history defense spending has been an important variable affecting the level of overall national economic activity and employment—particularly in the twentieth century. The economic efficiency with which this industry operates during peacetime certainly bears directly on the strength and capability of the military in relation to the funds authorized annually by Congress. All these aspects of the U.S. defense industrial base—its strategic responsiveness, its significance to the economy, and its own economic efficiency—will be considered in this chapter.

1.1 Historical Overview

The major focus here is the U.S. defense industry in the post-Vietnam period. However, many of the current undesirable characteristics and problems of the defense industrial base owe their origin directly to the historical evolution of this portion of the U.S. economy. Over 200 years, the following eight features stand out.[1] Each can be seen as a significant problem and also as a potential area for corrective action.

The extremely cyclic nature of defense procurements Since 1776 the nation has gone through periods of large increases in defense expenditures in times of crisis or apparent crisis and then followed these with almost total dismemberment of the defense industrial base. If these cycles are likely to continue, action should be taken to reduce the inefficiencies they create. Instead, what one finds is a lack of industrial-base planning for even year-to-year fluctuations in the demand for military equipment.

The lack of structural planning From the inception of the defense industrial base until the present, its evolution and status at any point (for example, the mix between government-owned and privately owned plants) has been largely based on chance.[2] This has been justified by total confidence in the operation of the free-market economy. However, recognition of the fact that such a free market generally does not exist for defense procurements might yield a recommendation for more structural planning. Planning in such areas as the number of firms, the ability of the government to create competition, and the mix of government and private ownership and work might prove much more efficient and effective—both economically and in terms of production response to sudden demands.

The inadequacy of industrial-preparedness planning   As noted above, in 1974 the United States tried to exercise its industrial-preparedness planning program to buy more tanks quickly and was foiled by a lack of castings. This is not atypical in the history of the defense industrial base. In fact, this history has been marked by an absence of peacetime planning for meeting future crises; when emergencies developed, no plans were available to cope with them. Preparing for such emergencies is relatively inexpensive and can have a very significant impact on response time when a crisis occurs. In the case of the tanks, simply having ordered one or two years' worth of castings in advance would not have added to the expense, but would have resulted in an important surge capability for tank production.

The lack of actual industrial readiness   In all wars over the history of the United States we have been able to mobilize men much more rapidly than we have been able to equip them. Because of the increased sophistication of equipment today, lead times are far longer. Thus, without proper planning, our response to a crisis now will be far slower than it ever was in the past, despite America's increased overall industrial strength.

The importance of technology and research in defense   Throughout America's history, military crises have led to technological advances. Often these came too late for the military encounters for which they were developed, but they created whole new civilian industries once the emergency had passed.[3] Although of limited military value, these developments clearly strengthened the overall U.S. economy. Therefore they often have been used to justify an extremely large defense research and development (R&D) budget, especially in the post–World War II era. However, a stronger argument for the importance of defense R&D is the need to maintain technological superiority (especially when, as today, the

United States lacks numerical superiority) and to avoid technological sur-
prises that, if developed by potential adversaries, could affect significantly the balance of power. Regardless of the justification, history shows that
the U.S. defense industry has been driven by technology (rather than by
costs). This has resulted in an extremely heavy emphasis on R&D funding,
often at the expense of production funding. Greater emphasis has often
been placed on systems under development than on those deployed.

**The differences among the industries that make up the defense industrial
base** Primarily because of their different historical evolutions, the
various sectors (such as shipbuilding, aircraft construction, and munitions manufacturing) are significantly different today. These differences
range from percent of government ownership to diverse ways of doing
business. Yet the government continues to pursue (and the Congress insists upon) "uniform procurement practices" across all of these sectors.
The application of the same "corrective actions" to sectors having different structural characteristics actually amplifies these differences.

The high concentration within industries Each rapid buildup and rapid
"selloff" has increased the concentration of the share of the business in a
few large firms. This was particularly true after World War II.[4] The
highly sophisticated nature and high capital intensiveness of modern
technology (both in R&D and in production) have contributed further to
this concentration.

The heavy dependence on international military assistance Foreign military aid has always played a major role in American policy. Thus, while
one normally would think of defense as a problem that can be considered
in a closed domestic economic system, the facts indicate the contrary. Today the defense industrial base is becoming increasingly dependent on the
level of our foreign military sales, as well as on the shipments from
foreign countries of critical components and materials for U.S. military
equipment.

The significance of the repetition of each of these historical patterns is
clearly evident when we look at the current impact of defense expenditures on the U.S. economy and at specific trends and problems in the
post-Vietnam period.

1.2 The Impact of Defense Expenditures on the U.S. Economy

As is evident from the level of defense procurements (figure 1.1), the
post–World War II period has been one of almost continuous crisis (or
apparent crisis). During this period the United States has maintained a
significant budget for the purchase of military equipment. As in the past,
there have been major peaks and valleys, but the high level of average expenditures is something new. This could be due to a number of causes: the
cold war, the involvement in conflicts such as those in Korea and Vietnam, and the fact that the oceans no longer provide physical security. The
appetite for high technology not only proved to be expensive but also required continuous "feeding" with the rapidly evolving new technologies.
The other significant change that has occurred in the post–World War II

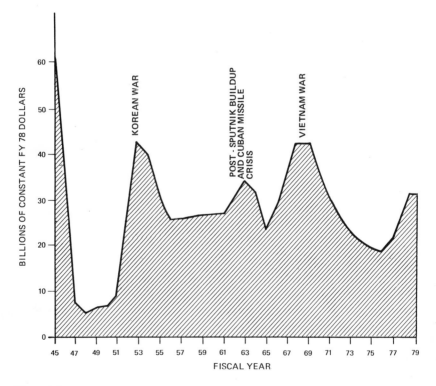

Figure 1.1
Defense procurements since World War II.

era was that the United States decided that, even in crisis periods, it wanted both "guns and butter." The civilian sector would not be mobilized to produce military goods in crisis periods; rather, these crises would be met from within the defense industry. It has been believed that the United States could afford to do this while maintaining its civilian economy as though the country were not engaged in military conflict.

The question of large defense expenditures during peacetime raises the macroeconomic question of whether the effect of such expenditures on the U.S. economy is positive or negative. This question is not academic; it is highly relevant to such issues as the impact of arms-control agreements and the stimulative or inflationary effects of the arms race. The question is extremely difficult to answer. There are experts and data to support both arguments, and the answers seem highly dependent upon such factors as the overall national economic conditions, the type of alternative expenditures or fiscal policies with which the military spending is compared, the economic and social objectives of the policies, and the structure of and the conditions within the defense industry.

It is often pointed out that since 1929 the United States has utilized its full production capacity only during periods of armed conflict.[5] (The argument that capitalistic systems need war to create demand sufficient to absorb the excess goods produced, but not normally consumed, was raised almost 200 years ago by Malthus, and was a major point of Marx's theories.) With peacetime defense expenditures responsible for more than 7 million jobs[6] and an annual defense budget of far more than $100 billion, it is natural that many look to defense policy as a possible source of stimulation for the overall economy, as well as for employment in defense-related areas. However, comparing the effects of such peacetime stimulation with those of other government fiscal or monetary alternatives is highly ambiguous. For example, defense expenditures may be a more effective stimulant than expenditures in other areas of government, because defense is more capital-intensive[7] and thus creates a greater economic multiplier for the dollars invested. However, a tax cut might be an even more effective stimulant (this depends on the form of the cut and the state of the economy at the time of the cut). Similarly, the public-policy objective of the economic stimulant is very important. For example, while the creation of jobs may be an objective, the defense sector affects hard-core unemployment very little because of its high skill requirements and high salaries. (One analysis has shown that, per dollar, military expenditures generate half as many jobs as, but 20 percent more salary dollars than,[8] civilian expenditures).

It would be possible to go on citing theories of macroeconomic impacts of defense expenditures;[9] however, perhaps a statement by former Federal Reserve Chairman Arthur Burns is the best summary: "If the defense sector has stimulated economic development in some directions, it has retarded growth in others."[10] Much more study in this macroeconomic area is warranted. Now that congressional budget committees are required to assess the relative expenditure for each of the government agencies (and their economic impacts), more light may be shed. However, with or without these studies, it is important to realize that Congress' relative willingness to spend money for "national security" always makes defense spending the most obvious candidate for economic stimulation whenever the need arises—and particularly in periods of perceived national-security crises. As Galbraith has stated, defense is one of the easiest ways to generate government budgeting for reduced unemployment, even in periods of relative peace.[11]

The year 1980 was one of perceived national security crisis. The revolutionaries in Iran held 50 Americans captive in the embassy. The Soviet Union had moved troops into Afghanistan. The SALT II treaty ratification had been put aside by Congress and the administration. The nation had begun to realize how far behind the Soviet Union it was in quantities of military equipment. It was an election year, and both parties were advocating significant increases in annual defense expenditures for the coming years. The relevant question was what the impact of these expenditures would be on an economy that already had an inflation rate approaching 20% per year.

Many argued, using selected portions of the above data, that such increased defense expenditures would reduce unemployment and provide the necessary military equipment to restore a strong military posture. Others argued—often with reference to the inflationary effects of the Vietnam War—that these defense expenditures would further increase inflation and would have to come at the expense of urgent social-welfare programs.

It is my position that proponents of both these arguments were taking the wrong perspective in analyzing the macroeconomic effects of defense expenditures. Instead of looking at the total U.S. economy and assuming it to be so uniform that all dollars spent create jobs and that all employees are essentially equally qualified for all jobs, it is necessary to look at the specific structure and condition of the defense industry in order to see what the economic effects of such increased defense expenditures are likely to be. For example, in 1980 the U.S. defense industry had just experienced a period of rapidly increasing defense expenditures (at the end of the 1970s). Simultaneously, there was a significant increase in the demand for commercial aircraft. Defense production competes with commercial-aircraft production for engineers,[12] skilled laborers, the use of certain production machinery, and many critical parts.[13] Although there were many badly underutilized plants and redundant employees, it was highly likely that greatly increased defense funds, spent on the present products with the present contractors, would not yield significantly more military equipment but would only raise the prices. The existing bottlenecks of labor, parts, and production machinery would not be removed, and the few firms doing the business on the increased demand would simply pay more for the scarce parts and labor and charge the government more for the equipment produced. The impact would be inflationary, with little benefit in terms of either employment or national security. This is an extreme position, but it certainly makes the point that structural analyses of the details of the defense industry and of the specific budgetary items are necessary before one can predict the macroeconomic impacts of increased or reduced defense expenditures.

Beyond these macroeconomic issues lies another important economic consideration that has received insufficient notice: the inflationary impact of military spending at the microeconomic level, not just in terms of program inefficiencies but also in terms of the high cost of the equipment. The latter results from the continuous demand for increasing performance at almost any cost. To counter an increasingly dangerous perceived threat, or to gain advantage over potential adversaries, each new generation of weapons has been driven to the "state of the art" in performance. The result has been rising unit production costs (figure 1.2) in almost all classes of weapons.[14] Thus, keeping a constant-strength military force (in size, age, and capability relative to assumed increases in potential adversaries' performance) requires additional defense procurements on the order of 5 percent each year (excluding inflation).

To understand figure 1.2, consider the case of the tanks. The data show that an XM-1 tank costs about three times as much as the M60 tank it is replacing (excluding inflation and assuming one-for-one replacement).

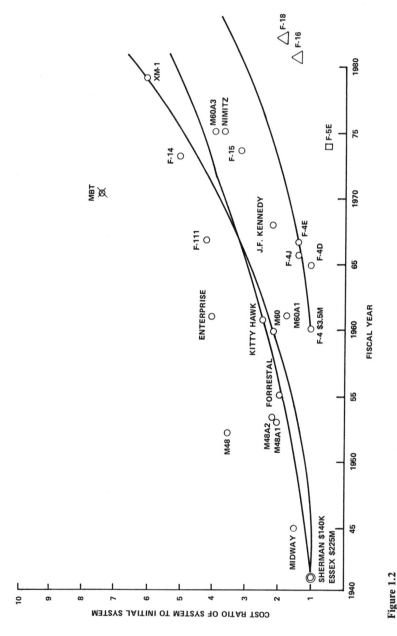

Figure 1.2

The trend in procurement costs of weapons systems. Examples used are aircraft carriers (indicated by names), tanks (Sherman and M numbers), and fighter aircraft (F numbers). Tank data are for 1,000th unit, aircraft data for 100th unit. All data are normalized to remove the costs of inflation and quantity changes.

The XM-1 performs much better than the M60—perhaps even three times as well—so on a one-for-one replacement basis it is worth the money. But it still costs three times as much, so if the United States wants to keep the same number of tanks it has to triple its procurement expenditures.

The effect of the increasing unit cost of defense equipment is not only felt in the defense sector of the U.S. economy, but also is reflected in some of the civilian sectors. The degree of this impact is a function of how widely one believes the effects of defense expenditures permeate the rest of the U.S. economy,[15] but clearly the impact is felt directly by the Department of Defense—in terms of reduced quantities of military equipment. A significant amount of this cost increase could have been avoided. For example, a comparison of the cost growth of military systems with the cost trends for high-technology civilian products (figure 1.3) shows just the opposite trends. Excluding inflation, prices of electronics products have been driven down while product performance has been improved. Figure 1.3 represents a valid comparison with defense expenditures; these electronics products are technologically similar to defense electronics, which account for about one-third of the total cost of modern defense systems.[16] I would use the data in figure 1.3 both to question the influence of "defense philosophy" on the operation of the other parts of the U.S. economy and to argue that the costs of individual pieces of military equipment could be significantly lower.

Regardless of whether or not one concludes that past defense expenditures have had a significant impact on the U.S. economy, it is clear that in the post–World War II period, in spite of the almost continuous state of perceived worldwide crisis, the significance of defense expenditures in the national economy has lessened. This is shown in figure 1.4 in terms of a comparison between defense outlays and the gross national product and as a percentage of the total federal budget.[17] (The percentage of defense expenditures is even lower when the rising state and local government budgets are included.) Figure 1.5 shows the economic impact of defense spending in terms of the relative amounts of U.S. government expenditures. Even within the defense community, major changes in the capital and labor structure have been occurring. Personnel costs have risen sharply while procurement dollars have decreased. The only answer to the problems of declining overall real procurement dollars and increasing costs of weapons systems has been for the Department of Defense to buy fewer weapons. For example, the United States bought about 3,000 tac-

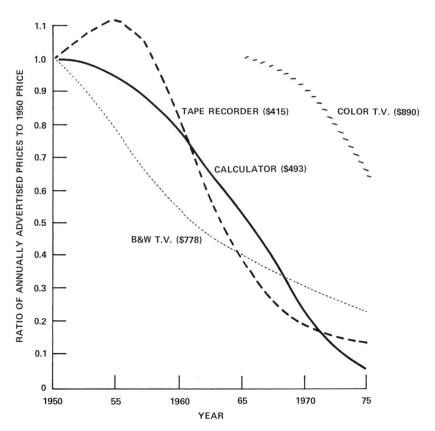

Figure 1.3
Cost trends for high-technology civilian electronic products, 1950–1975. Bracketed figures
are 1950 prices in constant FY 1977 dollars (color T.V. figure is 1965 price in constant FY
1977 dollars).

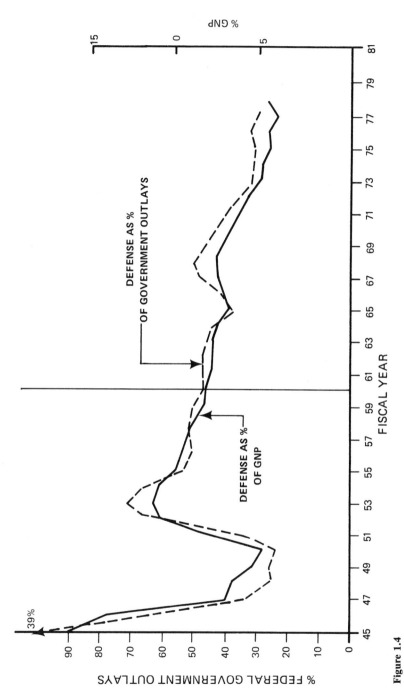

Figure 1.4
Defense outlays as percentages of gross national product and of total federal outlays, 1945–1978.

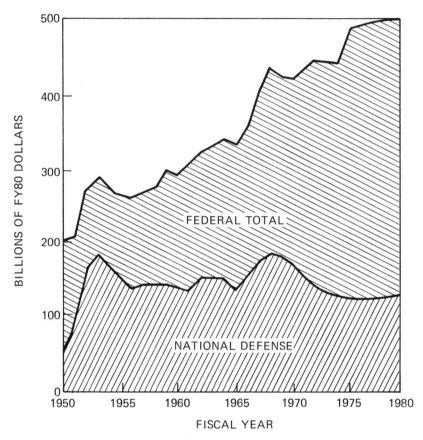

Figure 1.5
Total federal outlays compared with defense outlays, 1950–1980. Source: Assistant
Secretary of Defense (Comptroller).

tical military aircraft per year in the 1950s, about 1,000 per year in the 1960s, and about 300 per year in the 1970s.[18] The result of buying fewer, more expensive systems is that the peacetime defense industrial base cannot achieve high production rates or be easily maintained for future emergency surge demands.

One final point about the post–World War II period is that military technology has brought about the creation of new civilian industries: computers, jet aircraft, nuclear power, and space communication. In each case, development began with a perceived military need and Department of Defense R&D money brought these industries along until civilian markets were created. Undoubtedly, without defense expenditures these industries would have developed at some future date, but the earlier availability of these totally new and geopolitically significant civilian industries must be considered a major legacy of the post–World War II period.

1.3 The Post-Vietnam Period

National attitudes shaped by the Vietnam War led to significant changes in a number of important defense areas. The most obvious was the sharp drop in defense procurements to a level not seen since immediately after World War II. The reasons were many. The military felt that it did not need to buy a lot of older-generation equipment; what it needed was to acquire new families of weapons to replace the rapidly aging inventory used in Vietnam. Initially, there was a far greater need for R&D dollars than for procurement dollars. At the same time, military pay and allowances increased dramatically, first for comparability with civilian pay, then with the institution of the all-volunteer services. As a result, the average military pay doubled (including the effect of inflation) from 1968 to 1975, from an average of $5,500 to $11,000. In order for the Department of Defense to live within the shrinking total defense budget, research and development remained almost constant while procurement was rapidly reduced. In real dollars, procurement outlays for 1976 were the lowest since 1951. Conversely, the average weapons system continued to increase in cost by 5 percent a year (in real, noninflation dollars). Thus, the buying power for defense was reduced significantly.

Some questioned the nation's ability to afford the sophisticated equipment being designed. Congress, particularly, questioned the affordability of maintaining a high level of defense expenditures, and cut more deeply into the procurement account than any of the other budget accounts submitted during the post-Vietnam years.[19] These cuts, combined with the executive branch's reductions in the procurement account (in favor of R&D spending), rising equipment costs, military pay increases, and the cost of maintaining rapidly aging military equipment, worked to erode defense buying power.

The congressional cuts were not made in a vacuum. The will of the people, who were fed up with the war in Vietnam, was to devote all available resources toward improving the peacetime life of the nation. The environment and energy were new issues for the nation to address, and the people wanted to enjoy more of the fruits of their labor. The sense of Congress was a reflection of the sense of the people. The result was that, in relation to the gross national product, defense was the only major sector that was shrinking (figure 1.6). In the typical postwar pattern, defense was not a good area for an industrial firm looking for growth.

However, these priorities apparently were not being shared by the Union of Soviet Socialist Republics. The Soviets were estimated to be spending 12 percent of their gross national product on defense[20] (compared with 6 percent for the United States), and were building up their forces and increasing expenditures for research and development while America was spending less and less (figure 1.7).[21] By the end of the 1970s the Soviet Union was estimated to be spending 50 percent more on military outlays than the United States.[22] Even by 1974, the Soviet Union appeared to have more systems fielded and more coming off the production lines than the United States (table 1.1).[23] More important, Soviet systems had improved significantly—and, on the basis of expenditures for research and development, could be expected to continue improving. Thus, the Soviet Union's military systems were frequently on a par with, and in some cases better than, those of the United States. With comparable quality, numbers of systems became far more important; however, not enough procurement dollars were being allocated to U.S. defense.

The fact that the leaders of the United States now were arguing whether or not America was behind the Soviets or had parity with them was a new condition for our country to face. The United States clearly was no longer the single, dominant military force in the world. This new environment demanded more serious attention to arms control and defense planning, both in terms of equipment in the field and in terms of future materiel.

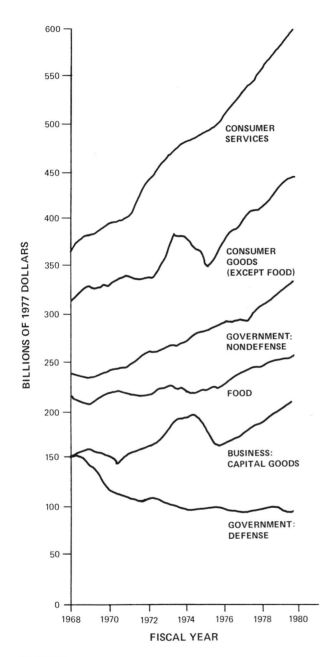

Figure 1.6
The course of spending (by sector) of the gross national product.

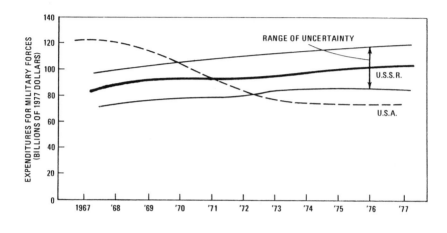

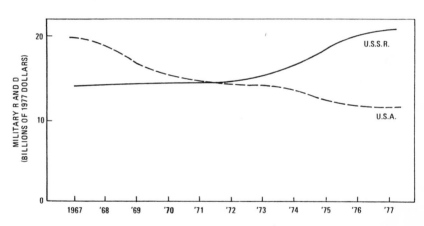

Figure 1.7
U.S. and Soviet defense expenditures, 1967–1977.

Table 1.1
U.S. and Soviet Inventories and Production Rates

	U.S.		U.S.S.R.	
	Total Inventory[a]	Production per year[b]	Total Inventory[a]	Production per year[b]
Ships (major combatants)	161	11	225	39
Tanks (all types)	10,000	462	48,000	3,000
Tactical aircraft	4,800	540	5,100	930
Helicopters	9,000	920	2,100	710
Artillery (ground support)	4,695	170	22,000	1,200
Submarines (attack and ballistic-missile)	116	3	350	11

a. Inventory as of fiscal year 1974.
b. Average annual production from 1972 through 1974.
Source: Joint Chiefs of Staff, U.S. Military Posture Statement for 1976.

The United States and the Soviet Union recognize their relative strengths and weaknesses for the variety of possible war scenarios. The Soviets have overwhelming superiority in the quantities of conventional forces and in the current production rates of their new systems. Thus, they appear to be in a far superior position for a war that lasts only a few months, or even one to two years.[24] They clearly recognize the overwhelming long-term superiority of U.S. industrial strength if two or three years are available for America to "gear up." Thus, in the tactical area, if there is to be a war it is clearly in the Soviet interest to have a "short" war, or at least an "intermediate-length" war (one lasting less than two years), and, in either case, to go to war without an extended period of warning, which would give U.S. industry time to shift into military production.

There are two courses of action the United States can take to provide a more credible deterrent to any Soviet threat: to strengthen conventional forces or to shorten greatly the industrial response time. Both actions would increase significantly the viability of America's deterrent for conventional warfare. The only alternative, should tactical warfare begin, is to make credible the threat to escalate to nuclear warfare, since the United States clearly is outgunned in conventional equipment. To make such a response believable the United States would have to increase significantly its planning for tactical nuclear warfare, and make this known to the Soviets. Additionally, the United States must convince the U.S.S.R. that it believes strategic nuclear warfare is possible. Apparently the Soviets do believe this, for they take significant action to disperse their plants, harden their equipment, and prepare their civilian population.[25] The United States takes no similar actions. To the Soviets, therefore, it appears as though the United States does not believe that nuclear war is possible—or, if it is possible, that there would not be a "winner."

Given these conditions, the most likely scenario for a future war would be the short, high-intensity war fought with highly sophisticated tactical weapons—with the threat of nuclear escalation always present. Thus, it behooves the United States to strengthen its deterrent credibility by increasing its tactical forces and/or broadening arms-control agreements, and by improving its industrial planning to ensure military responsiveness.

No summary of post-Vietnam changes in the defense area would be complete without noting the significant shift toward foreign military sales, especially since 1973. While U.S. defense procurements in the post-Vietnam period dropped from a 1968 high of $44 billion to a 1975 low of $17 billion (in constant dollars), foreign military sales jumped in the first half of the 1970s from about $1.5 billion to over $14 billion a year. Additionally, there was a qualitative shift in sales, from old equipment to first-line equipment and manufacturing capability (even complete plants). Thus, the U.S. defense industry became dependent on foreign military sales, since their magnitude was comparable to that of U.S. expenditures and, in many sectors, even larger. (In 1976 the Army Missile Command bought 70 percent of its procurements for foreign military sales, and in the same year U.S. military aircraft production was greater for foreign sales than for domestic military needs.)

Finally, during the post-Vietnam period the United States began to recognize that many structural problems were developing within its defense industry.[26] For example, only around 50 percent of available aircraft plant space and equipment was being utilized. Shipbuilders were having significant financial and labor problems, with billions of dollars in claims pending. In addition, parts suppliers and subcontractors were rapidly leaving the defense industry for the more attractive civilian sector. Partly in an attempt at a short-term correction of these problems, but largely in recognition of the weakening relative military position of the United States, the defense procurement budget began to increase substantially in the second half of the 1970s.[27] From a military perspective this action was necessary, but it had the added and undesirable effect of masking the problems within the defense industry (particularly when combined with the short-term surge in the replacement of an aging commercial aircraft fleet and the high level of foreign military sales). The problems of the defense industry would have been more likely to receive greater government attention had it not been for this large infusion of funds. However, their presence allowed the economic inefficiencies and strategic unresponsiveness of the defense industry to continue without correction.

For 200 years the United States has not treated its defense industrial base as the vital national resource it is. Clearly this base has been a significant part of the nation's historical defense posture, and yet the defense industry is not considered when the Department of Defense sits down to plan its overall deterrent and war posture. Similarly, from an economic perspective, considerable care is given to the planning and management of each individual weapons system, yet the economic efficiency of the overall defense industry is rarely if ever considered.

Two opposing myths exist about the overall defense industry. The first is that the market is taking care of optimal allocation of resources. Yet there really is no free market at work. In this unique environment, the proper question is not whether the government should get involved (it already is), but rather how it should most efficiently utilize the defense industry for the realization of its needs, which are low-cost production to achieve the largest quantity of systems for the dollars available, creation of a timely industrial response for crisis demands, and maintenance of a significant research and development establishment to take full advantage of the evolving technology for future military needs.

The alternate myth, still held by many, is represented by the statement of Heilbroner and Thurow that "the Department of Defense is the largest planned economy outside the Soviet Union."[28] This belief assumes that the Department of Defense actually selects its contractors on the basis of optimal utilization of defense resources, and that it effectively plans its industrial-preparedness activities for crisis situations.

Those familiar with defense procurement practices would recognize that neither the way in which source selections are made for new weapons systems nor the totally isolated program-by-program decision-making process includes any consideration of the overall defense industry.[29] What many people have noted is that large numbers of small government actions are being taken and new micropolicies continually being made without consideration of their overall impact.

American history clearly indicates that war is a very real possibility for every generation. Thus, there must be systematic planning for the efficient use of the resources spent on procuring defense equipment, and for making the defense industrial base strategically responsive. Only in this way can the Department of Defense present the strongest deterrent possible for the dollars available. This book calls for more coordinated government actions at the macro level and far fewer detailed government involvements at the micro level.

2 Underlying Economic Factors

"It is a dangerous delusion to keep mumbling the old myths of free enterprise when they are irrelevant. Ethics requires calling a spade a spade. If we are to save the noblest and best of free enterprise and strengthen the force of market competition, we must be clear about where it is relevant and where it is not."[1] George C. Lodge of the Harvard Graduate School of Business Administration made this statement in 1976 in connection with the government's role in saving the Lockheed Corporation. However, as we will see, the relationship between the government and the defense industry is not a normal free market, and recognition of this fact is an essential first step in any possible corrective actions.

Table 2.1 presents a long list of examples of the "imperfections and failures" of the defense industry in relation to traditional free-market theory. This table alone gives over thirty important assumptions of free-market economic theory that are completely countered by what actually takes place in the defense market. The defense market also differs significantly from traditional oligopoly and monopoly markets, in which the buyer and the seller are still essentially in adversary bargaining positions. In the defense market, the buyer and seller have a far greater mutuality of interest; price plays a relatively minor role.

The absence of the "invisible hand" of the free market does not mean that we simply must throw out all economic theory in establishing defense policy. Rather, the "theory of the second best" should be applied.[2] In simple terms, this theory says that if some conditions for the traditional free market (the "first best") do not apply and cannot be created, then creating some additional free-market conditions or moving more in the direction of free-market conditions may actually result in reduced efficiency in the allocation of resources. Since it is clear that in the case of the defense industry some of the constraints to free-market operation cannot be removed, it follows that all policy actions in the defense sector must be made with the "theory of the second best" clearly in mind.

That the free market is not operating effectively in the defense industry and that the "theory of the second best" should apply is not universally accepted. For example, a U.S. senator commented at a 1976 public meeting that there was a dangerous story going around Washington to the effect that it would be a good idea to close some aircraft plants.[3] He noted that this would clearly reduce competition and capacity, therefore, it must be wrong. This speech, based upon traditional free-market economic

Table 2.1
Some Examples of "Market Imperfections and Failures" in Defense

Free-Market Theory	Defense Market
Many small buyers.	One buyer (DoD).
Many small suppliers.	Very few, large suppliers of a given item.
All items small, perfectly divisible, and in large quantities.	One ship built every few years, for hundreds of millions of dollars each.
Market sets prices.	Monopoly or oligopoly pricing—or "buy in" to "available" dollars.
Free movement in and out of market.	Extensive barriers to entry and exit.
Prices set by marginal costs.	Prices proportional to total costs.
Prices set by marginal utility.	Any price paid for the desired military performance.
Prices fall with reduced demand.	Prices rise with reduced demand.
Supply adjusts to demand.	Large excess capacity.
Labor highly mobile.	Greatly diminishing labor mobility.
Decreasing or constant returns to scale.	Increasing returns to scale in region of interest.
Market shifts rapidly to changes in supply and demand.	7–10 years to develop a new system, then 3–5 years to produce it.
Market smoothly reaches equilibrium.	Erratic behavior from year to year.
General equilibrium—assumes prices will return to their equilibrium value.	Costs have been rising at approximately 5% per year (excluding inflation).
Profits equalized across the economy.	Wide and consistent profit variations between sectors; even wider between firms.
Perfect mobility of capital (money).	Heavy debt, difficulty in borrowing.
Mobility of capital (equipment) to changing demand.	Large and old capital equipment "locks in" companies.
No government involvement.	Government is regulator, specifier, banker, judge of claims, etc.
Selection based on price.	Selection often based on politics, or sole source, or "negotiation"; only 8% of dollars awarded on price competition.
No externalities.	All businesses working for DoD must satisfy requirements of OSHA, EEO, awards to areas of high unemployment, small business set-aides, etc.
Prices fixed by market.	Most business, with any risk, is for "cost plus fee."
All products of a given type are the same.	Essentially, each producer's products are different.
Competition is for share of market.	Competition is frequently for all or none of a given market.

Table 2.1 (continued)

Free-Market Theory	Defense Market
Production is for inventory.	Production occurs after sale is made.
Size of market established by the buyers and sellers.	Size of market established by "third party" (Congress) through annual budget.
Demand sensitive to price.	Demand "threat"-sensitive, or responds to availability of new technology; almost never price-sensitive.
Equal technology throughout industry.	Competitive technologies.
Relatively stable, multiyear commitments.	Annual commitments, with frequent changes.
Benefits of the purchase go to the buyer.	A "public good."
Buyer has the choice of spending now or saving for a later purchase.	DoD must spend its annual congressional authorization.

theory (mixed with politics), neglected the applicability of the "theory of the second best" to this case, in which less competition and less capacity would still be sufficient and would result in a more efficient overall industry.

The "theory of the second best" suggests that, given the structure of the defense industry and its non-free-market operation, it is proper to question policies that attempt to impose optimal free-market conditions piecemeal in individual cases or individual sectors—unless it can be demonstrated that their overall effect (in combination) will result in improvements. Yet through its various regulations and micro policies the Department of Defense has been applying small adjustments here and there in an attempt to create conditions closer to optimal free-market conditions, with neither an overall (sector by sector) policy coordination effort nor a recognition that these actions might be making things worse.

The approach taken throughout this book is that it is the structure of an industry, combined with considerations of the factors of production for that industry (money, equipment, materials, and labor), that determines the conduct and thus the performance of the market.[4] Therefore, rather than beginning with a discussion of such performance parameters as profit and productivity, we will first look at the structure of the defense industry, recognizing that significant improvements in the performance of the industry can only come through addressing its basic structure.

2.1 The Structure of the Defense Industry

2.1.1 The Nature of the Buyer

Since the government, as the buyer, greatly influences the structure of the defense industry (through the way it does business), it is desirable for us to look at the demand side of the market and highlight two characteristics of this buyer: insensitivity to price and the tendency to concentrate procurements into a very few programs. To a large extent, these two characteristics, along with the research and development process and the highly specialized way in which the government contracts for its products, dictate the structure of the U.S. defense industry.

Weapons programs arise from one of two sources: a military "requirement" for a more advanced weapons system or a new technological "opportunity" that promises greater military capability. In either case, the military performance of the new weapons system is the characteristic that will be pushed during the system's evolution. The overall U.S. defense posture is to maintain technological superiority over the Soviet Union. Thus, equipment price is not the primary design characteristic, as it might be in a civilian application or if quantity of equipment were to be stressed equally. Rather, it is assumed that each individual system must be the very "best," and that Congress will provide sufficient funds to buy enough of these systems to provide the best possible total defense posture.

In this case, it is neither the buyer nor the seller that establishes the annual expenditure level—it is Congress. Thus, the mood of the country, affected as it is by domestic and international events, establishes the amount of military equipment to be bought each year.[5] This annual budget process creates considerable uncertainty in the defense industry's long-term planning, and demands strong lobbying efforts by the Department of Defense and its industrial contractors.

Figure 2.1 shows the very large increase in program concentration that has taken place over the last few years. Note that only 20 programs now consume over 40 percent of the Department of Defense's procurement dollars each year. Table 2.2 presents this concentration from a different perspective by showing the breakdown in projected cost of the top 33 of the 107 major weapon systems reported to Congress in 1975. The top 12 alone represent 50 percent of the total estimated major-program cost of $200 billion. Also, of these 33 programs, 17 are valued at over $3 billion

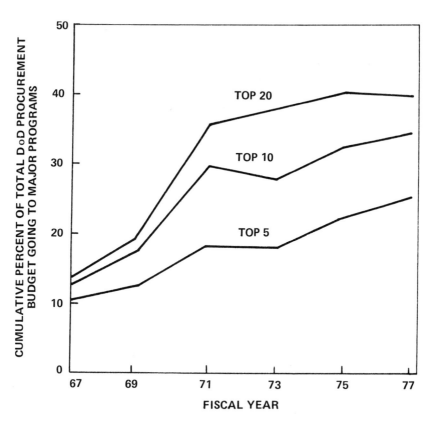

Figure 2.1
The trend toward concentration of procurement funds in major weapons-system programs.
Source: Office of the Assistant Secretary of Defense (Comptroller).

Table 2.2
Costs of Thirty-Three Major Weapons Systems

Navy ($64.2 billion total)		Army ($27.0 billion total)	
A-7E aircraft	$ 2.6 billion	Lance missile	$ 0.9 billion
E-2C aircraft	$ 1.0 billion	Improved Hawk missile	$ 0.9 billion
F-14A aircraft	$ 6.3 billion	Safeguard ABM system	$ 5.4 billion
P-3C aircraft	$ 2.7 billion	SAM-D missile	$ 6.7 billion
S-3A aircraft	$ 3.3 billion	UTTAS helicopter	$ 4.0 billion
Harpoon missile	$ 1.2 billion	AAH helicopter	$ 2.9 billion
Phoenix missile	$ 1.2 billion	XM-1 tank	$ 6.2 billion
Poseidon missile	$ 4.8 billion		
Sparrow III F missile[a]	$ 0.8 billion		
Trident missile and submarine	$15.4 billion	**Air Force ($53.2 billion total)**	
		A-7D aircraft	$ 1.6 billion
MK-48 torpedo	$ 1.6 billion	A-10 aircraft	$ 3.1 billion
SSN-668 submarine	$ 7.9 billion	B-1 aircraft	$18.6 billion
DD-963 destroyer	$ 3.6 billion	F-15 aircraft	$10.9 billion
DLGN-38 frigate	$ 1.6 billion	F-111 aircraft	$ 7.3 billion
LHA helicopter carrier	$ 1.2 billion	AWACS aircraft	$ 3.0 billion
Patrol frigate	$ 5.3 billion	Minuteman III missile	$ 7.0 billion
PHM patrol hydrofoil	$ 1.1 billion	SRAM missile	$ 1.2 billion
CVAN carriers	$ 2.6 billion	Sparrow III missile[a]	$ 0.5 billion

a. Combined Navy–Air Force program.
Source: Systems Acquisition Reports submitted by DoD to Congress.

each! For any business, these numbers are staggering. The large magnitude of these individual programs results in the very severe and unique form of oligopoly competition (or rivalry) that is evident in the defense market. There is no "share of the market" in the traditional sense; a contractor is either a winner or completely out of competition.

Some argue that the selection of winning firms is planned explicitly—that people in the Department of Defense simply say "it is the XYZ company's turn."[6] But this is not the case. The appearance of such planning may be the indirect result of people in the DoD "worrying" about the XYZ company, and of the company (which is in the position of being forced out of the defense business if it doesn't win a big contract) making the most attractive proposal on the next competition—that is, "buying in."

A unique characteristic of the government as buyer in the defense area is that it has its own factories, which compete directly in many cases with those of its industrial suppliers.[7] Historically the evolution of the mix between the public and private sectors, has been largely *ad hoc,* and has varied widely among industries.[8] In order to achieve efficiency and to justify the work force, the government tends to keep its plants busy, which makes the competition in these cases somewhat biased. For some examples, table 2.3 is a breakdown of some aircraft modification programs accomplished in fiscal year 1975. The list is split between government-owned-and-operated facilities and contractors' facilities (which may also be partly government-owned). In each of these programs there was the clear choice between which facilities should perform the work, and in many cases the work was split between the public and private sectors. If such work were competitively awarded, on a purely price-sensitive basis, this mixture might be very desirable as a way to increase the competition in the defense industry. However, what actually happens is that the in-house bids are significantly lower because of the government's way of bookkeeping, which does not consider depreciation of plant and facilities, retirement pay, or, or course, profit. One might expect Congress to resolve the issue of public versus private ownership; however,

Table 2.3
Examples of Distribution of Defense Work Between Government Facilities and Contractors: Aircraft Modification Programs in Fiscal 1975

	Amount Awarded (Millions of Dollars)	
Aircraft	Government Facilities	Contractors
AH-1	0.0	77.5
A-6	6.9	62.0
A-7	11.9	27.4
B-52	71.6	30.8
CH-47C	7.5	2.0
C-5	22.9	11.7
F-4 (Navy)	55.4	0.6
F-4/RF-4 (USAF)	48.1	28.4
F-111	26.5	0.1
OV-1	0.0	17.0

legislation in this area is sufficiently ambiguous to justify actions in either direction.[9]

Another form of unique buyer competition in defense is that among the three armed services. In many small ways, each of the services tailors systems to its unique needs. Thus, for many reasons (pride, belief in their differences, desire for greater control over the contractors or over testing, and so on), the services try to maximize the differences between the products they use and those their sister services buy. Similarly, each service prefers to have its own "captive" suppliers, and this leads to the development of contractor communities aligned with individual services. One company will be considered a Navy supplier and will have great difficulty supplying products to the Air Force. As a result, if there are two suppliers of a particular product, one may become a Navy supplier and the other an Air Force supplier, and the small amount of supplier competition that might have existed is eliminated. (An example of this is the fact that Lockheed became the strategic-missile supplier for the Navy and Boeing for the Air Force.) This is another reason for the lack of price sensitivity in the defense market.

2.1.2 The Characteristics of the Suppliers

We have recognized that the various levels (prime contractors, subcontractors, and parts suppliers) of the defense industry naturally have significantly different characteristics, but what common traits define the separation between defense and nondefense firms? Perhaps the most obvious trait is the heavy involvement of the government in the operation of the firm. This naturally leads to a great deal of specialization, since few firms are familiar with the government's unique way of doing business. When this specialization is combined with the large size of individual programs, a great deal of concentration in the defense industry results. A look at the aggregate defense industry (figure 2.2) shows that the top 100 defense companies obtain 70 percent of the total business, while 25 companies alone control 50 percent of the business and the top 5 control 20 percent. This concentration, by itself, is not unusual; in all of U.S. industry the top 500 companies control 70 percent,[10] and only 111 firms control more than half of the total U.S. sales.[11] Thus, at the aggregate level defense is not an especially highly concentrated industry.

As figure 2.3 shows, a significant increase in concentration has been

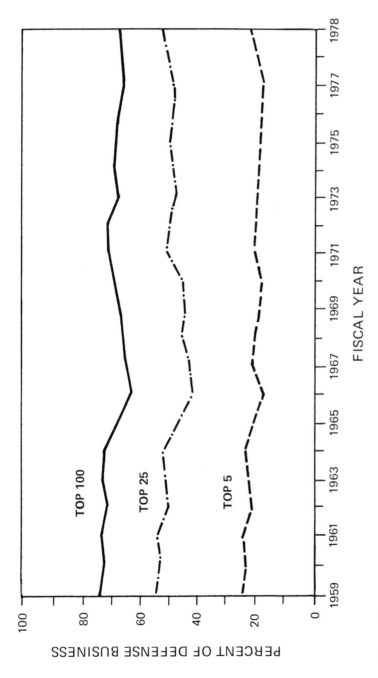

Figure 2.2
Percentages of total Department of Defense business done by largest prime contractors.

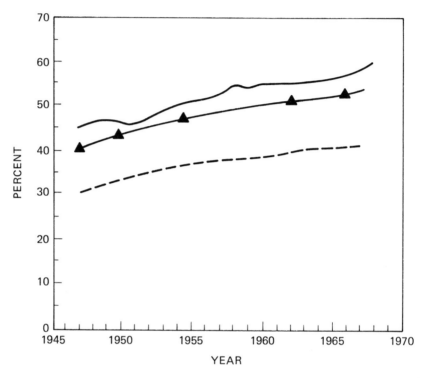

Figure 2.3
Long-term trend of aggregate concentration in total U.S. industry. ————: Total
manufacturing assets of the 200 largest manufacturing firms (source: Federal Trade Commission, "Economic Report on Corporation Mergers," p. 173). ▲————▲: Percent of
total manufacturer's assets controlled by the 100 largest firms (source: Scherer, *Industrial
Market Structure and Economic Performance*, p. 43). — — — : Value added by
manufacture, 200 largest manufacturing firms (source: Bureau of the Census, "Concentration Ratios in Manufacturing," part I, table 1).

taking place in the civilian sector.[12] Yet even in the post-Vietnam 1970s, when defense expenditures dropped rapidly and the concentration of total dollars into a few programs increased, defense-industry concentration has not increased significantly. Two facts can account for this. First, each of the contractors is able to maintain its share of the business through the government's unique system of military-product competition. Second, the major firms have been acquiring other defense companies, both vertically and horizontally, and thereby maintaining their shares. Unless the Department of Defense significantly increases procurement budgets (as happened in the second half of the 1970s), this constant share of the business, reflected in figure 2.2, will become more difficult to maintain. If procurement budgets do not increase much, eventually the pressures for concentration will build and there will be a pattern in the defense area more similar to that of the civilian sector. This may be very desirable, because of the unique methods of defense's operation and because of the current large amounts of excess capacity.[13] However, if not properly anticipated and implemented, further concentration will have considerable negative economic and strategic consequences.

So far, in terms of their defense business, the large firms have been able to maintain their positions despite the declining procurements of the post-Vietnam years (table 2.4).[14] They were maintaining their shares of the defense business while each plant was getting less and less business. This is not the expected behavior for an efficient market operation, wherein the fully utilized and modernized plants would be expected to take more of the business and the older, underutilized plants would be expected to be forced to close.

In order to maintain their overall corporate growth, the firms are shifting heavily into the civilian area. The giants of the defense industry are becoming less and less dependent upon defense business.[15] In fact, the top 25 defense contractors went from almost 40 percent of their business in the defense area in 1958 to under 10 percent of their business coming from defense by 1975.[16]

In general, this diversification from dependency on defense is a very desirable trend from the firms' perspective. However, to be acceptable from the viewpoint of defense economics and strategic responsiveness, the diversification must take place at the plant level—the defense and the

Table 2.4
The twenty top defense contractors of 1977 (ranked in terms of dollars awarded)

	1967	1969	1971	1973	1975	1977
McDonnell Douglas	1	4	7	4	4	1
Lockheed	3	1	1	1	1	2
United Technologies	5	5	8	3	3	3
Boeing	6	9	9	2	2	4
General Electric	4	2	5	—	7	5
Rockwell International	7	8	13	10	10	6
Grumman	12	17	4	5	5	7
General Dynamics	2	3	2	9	6	8
Hughes Aircraft	17	14	12	12	9	9
Northrop	21	36	34	15	12	10
Raytheon	19	11	14	11	11	11
Westinghouse Electric	15	15	15	13	21	12
Tenneco	—	30	6	25	28	13
Sperry Rand	13	12	16	14	15	14
Chrysler	40	53	33	30	26	15
Litton Industries	36	21	11	16	8	16
IBM	34	27	19	18	18	17
Todd Shipyards	—	—	—	—	—	18
AT&T	8	6	3	6	14	19
Honeywell	20	18	22	19	23	20

nondefense work must use common facilities and common labor pools. Because of the specialized nature of the defense work, firms have not been able to achieve such internal diversification. The defense divisions of most of the large defense contractors have stayed exclusively in the defense area, and the diversification to the civilian sector has been achieved almost exclusively through separate acquisitions.[17]

Since the defense firms are no longer essentially captive suppliers,[18] this corporate diversification significantly reduces the bargaining power of the Department of Defense. The refusal of some of the shipyards to build Navy ships after they had been taken over by conglomerates is an example of the exercise of the contractors' new bargaining power. A second effect of this conglomerate takeover, the ability of the large firms to "cross-subsidize" their defense business in order to get a foothold in a new defense program, again distorts the market behavior.[19]

Why are the large conglomerates interested in getting into the defense area, with all its problems? The replies of a number of corporate executives fit into the following five categories, which are ranked in order of importance to the responders. (The overwhelming emphasis was on the first item.)

- *Government funding of research and development*   The R&D is paid for by the government, and there is the possibility of transferring the technology into the civilian sector.
- *The large volume of business*   The business base and the cash flow of billions of dollars is a very important consideration from a "power" (total sales and borrowing) viewpoint. The emphasis on volume here reflects a primary orientation toward sales rather than profit.
- *The experience of managing large, high-technology programs*   This is viewed as one of the most difficult management challenges, and many of the present top managers of the conglomerates come from defense backgrounds.
- *Long-term "runs"*   This response—surprising in view of the instability in the business—is based on the fact that, once awarded a development contract, the contractor can usually be assured of a five- to ten-year development program and then at least five years of production and additional years of support, if the program has any national priority and is at all well run.

Table 2.5
Concentration Ratios in the Military Market, Fiscal 1967

	Contract Awards (Millions of Dollars)	Percentage of Contracts	
		Top 4 firms	Top 8 firms
Surveillance and detection satellites	$ 236	100	100
Nuclear submarines	211	99	99
Space boosters	263	97	100
Fighter aircraft	2,164	97	100
Attack aircraft	570	97	100
Missile inertial guidance systems	539	97	99
Inertial navigation systems	201	96	99
Missile reentry vehicles	278	95	99
Aircraft fire-control systems	414	95	98
Transport and tanker aircraft	1,003	94	99
Helicopters	1,208	93	99
Jet aircraft engines	1,892	93	99
Data-processing systems	336	83	93
Missile solid-rocket propulsion systems	356	81	90
Combat vehicles	256	74	91
Ships and parts	1,391	67	77
Surface-based sonar systems	278	63	82
Countermeasures systems	209	63	76
Surface radar systems	215	62	81
Missile systems	2,119	59	82
Drones	224	59	72
Communications systems	224	56	81
Navy power systems	877	50	59

Source: Computed by Weidenbaum (note 22) from data supplied by Frost and Sullivan, Inc. (Defense Market Measures System).

- *Countercyclical balance for the civilian business* This balance, of course, includes the opportunity to take part in the wartime spending that often occurs during international crises.

Though a typical military product will have a single prime contractor, one of that firm's major jobs is the management of a highly sophisticated industrial team made up of the suppliers of the thousands of parts. (For example, on the Minuteman program there were 40,000 suppliers to Boeing.) Between 40 and 70 percent of the total business is subcontracted,[20] with the nominal value 50–60 percent. (The automobile industry also subcontracts in the range of 50 to 60 percent; the highly competitive food business subcontracts in the 80 percent range.) The percentage of subcontracting is frequently used as a measure of the degree of vertical integration of a firm, as well as an indicator of the degree of price sensitivity in an industry (here again defense shows its relative price insensitivity).

Aggregate business concentration was discussed in terms of the overall defense industry. However, price sensitivity must be considered in terms of the degree of concentration in particular product areas, at the prime-contractor level and at lower levels.[21] Table 2.5 presents data for fiscal 1967, the peak of the Vietnam War. As expenditures have dropped since that time, one would expect 1967 to show one of the lowest concentrations in recent years. However, even according to the extremely high concentration criterion suggested by Blair as a measure of non-free-market behavior (that the top eight firms account for 70 percent or more of the sales[23]), the data for the majority of the products in this table indicate such behavior and generally exceed the concentration characteristics of American manufacturing.[24] Certainly, if we use the Kaysen-Turner criterion for a heavily concentrated industry ("one in which the largest eight firms make at least 50 percent of the industry's shipments"[25]) there can be no question but that all sectors of the defense industry are very heavily concentrated. The difference between moderately and heavily concentrated industries is an important one, according to Bain,[26] since the moderately concentrated oligopolies tend to have the desirably competitive performance characteristics of the relatively atomistic structure, while this is not the case for the heavily concentrated industries. In fact, Bain notes that in areas of extremely high seller concentration "there is a fundamental impossibility of securing a market structure which is conducive to good performance in all important respects."

Of critical significance for the defense industry is the fact that even the concentration ratios shown in table 2.5 are greatly exceeded at the next lowest level of defense suppliers. For example, consider the concentration of the top four suppliers in fiscal 1966 in propellers (97.9 percent), turbines (92.2 percent), special dyes and tools (97.4 percent), and gas cylinders (100 percent.)[27] In some cases, there are monopolies at the component level—especially for individual products.

There is considerable controversy over the meaning of concentration ratios when the numbers get this large. They are, of course, an attempt to measure the degree of competition and the sensitivity to prices in the market, but clearly they do not reveal the severity of competition that might still take place over individual contracts—even between the only two competitors—when there is a monopsony buyer who has only a small, infrequent demand.[28] Nonetheless, these extremely high concentration figures certainly suggest that the usual models of free-market relationships are inadequate for analyzing the economics of defense markets.

There are actually two forms of vertical integration in the defense industry. In one, the same firm will do both the R&D and the production on a given program; in the other (which has been on the increase over the last ten years) the prime contractor buys up both large and small subcontractors. When Weidenbaum studied the aerospace mergers by industry and company size in the mid-1960s, he found that the largest number of acquisitions were in the electronics companies, and that the firms being acquired were the medium-sized and large ones, those with over $200 million per year in sales.[29] This trend continued over the next ten years, and seems to be accelerating as prime contractors struggle to maintain their share of the business. (Examples of this trend are the acquisition of Collins Radio by North American–Rockwell and the acquisition of Hoffman Electronics by Gould.)

In addition, horizontal integration has increased in the defense industry—again, out of the attempt to maintain market shares. For instance, General Dynamics, which used to be almost exclusively in the aircraft business, is now heavily into shipbuilding and electronics, having acquired Electric Boat and Stromberg-Carlson.

The effects of both forms of integration on the defense industry are to reduce competition and economic efficiency. The competition impact occurs for two reasons. First, a subcontractor (now a division) belonging to a prime contractor certainly has a favored bidding position, in relation to the parent corporation, over an outside subcontractor. However, this is a two-edged sword, since a subcontractor division may be at a disadvantage in bidding to a competing prime contractor. The other impact on competition is achieved through cross-subsidization from the parent firm to the competing division, which is becoming more common in the defense industry.

In the civilian economy vertical integration appears to be decreasing, according to Blair, who attributes this to the greater economic efficiency associated with specialization.[30] In the defense industry, by contrast, not only is vertical integration taking place through acquisitions, but many firms are doing it through internal development. For example, in the aircraft industry it appears as though all firms are setting up the capability for doing fabrication work on composite materials and thus keeping out the specialized producer. These aircraft firms feel partly that they need this capability to make their proposals look attractive, and partly that it offers an opportunity to increase their share of a particular program and thus reduce their overhead. Similarly, many defense electronics firms have set up their own facilities for manufacturing integrated circuits and printed interconnection boards. Such facilities are both very expensive and often grossly underutilized. These actions are only achievable because of the market power these large firms possess. In view of the low total volume of aircraft composite material required by the entire industry, and the large capital investment required, two or three independent firms specializing in composite materials would be far more economically efficient and could easily satisfy the overall industry's demands—and with competitive pricing. Thus, this tendency towards far greater vertical integration by the defense companies can be viewed as further evidence that the industry is not very price-sensitive and is becoming less economically efficient.

In any discussion about concentration and integration in the defense industry it is critically important to distinguish between number of firms and number of plants. Both are important, but in the defense area there is a tendency for a plant to be the equivalent of a "firm"—to have its own engineering, marketing, management, and so on. Thus, eliminating a firm without eliminating a plant may reduce competition without reducing excess capacity or redundant labor. For example, when McDonnell of

St. Louis took over Douglas of California the two continued to operate essentially as two separate, vertically integrated "firms," with the exception that competition was reduced and McDonnell's St. Louis defense operation was required to absorb some of the overhead of Douglas' civilian operation in California.[31] Thus, the defense industry's efficiency went further down.

One final aspect of concentration that must be noted is geographical distribution. California receives over 20 percent of the defense dollars (because of that state's preeminence in aerospace and electronics), while Texas and New York together get another 15 percent (again primarily in aerospace and electronics). Ten states get over two-thirds of the defense dollars. Obviously, defense makes a major contribution to the economies of these states. In fact, there are eleven states in which defense accounts for at least 10 percent of the state's income.[32] Certainly this contributes to the strong congressional interest in defense expenditures.[33]

The extremely high "barriers to entry and exit" that exist in the defense industry[34] greatly reduce free-market conditions. The thirteen factors that follow are barriers to entry, which keep firms from getting into defense business (including firms coming from comparable civilian areas).

- *Marketing problems* The defense marketplace is unique. There is no advertising of any significance, and most selling is done directly. The customer, though a single organization, is extremely diverse and constantly changing its personnel. Understanding the way in which the government operates and does business, and how to sell to this market, requires extremely specialized talents and a large marketing organization with great resources.

- *Inelastic demand* A firm entering the defense market cannot assume that, after it makes the investment to build a new plant, its output can be bought along with that of the other suppliers—even if the new firm lowers prices—since the total number of units demanded is established by a combination of the number of troops and the budget available. Notice that this inelastic demand—as a barrier to entry—is reinforced by the fact that most defense products require large capital investments in production equipment, which yield economic savings ("economies of scale") to the existing large defense suppliers.

- *"Brand loyalty"* The military services recognize the support that critical defense contractors have provided to them, particularly during prior wartime periods. This support, significant by any measure, has in some cases had a major impact on the war effort and on the success of an individual service. There is clearly a great deal of allegiance between the services and these old defense firms.

- *Demand for higher performance* Since the awarding of defense contracts is based primarily on improved performance rather than on price, a firm entering the market cannot simply duplicate an existing product at a lower price, but must offer an improved product as well.

- *Need for great engineering and scientific capability* Since the competition in the defense area is for the research and development contract (the production contract follows automatically), in order to compete a firm must not only have production capability but must also have a large R&D establishment.

- *Existence of expensive, specialized equipment* In any industry, the competitors' ownership of resources, particularly those that are rare or specialized, is a significant barrier. In defense, much of the very special equipment required (for example, large presses) has been bought by the Department of Defense and supplied to individual contractors. This makes it especially difficult for new firms to enter the market.

- *Need for capital* To write a proposal might cost millions of dollars. (North American–Rockwell is alleged to have spent $40 million in pursuing the Space Shuttle contract.) Such funds can only be available to a few large firms. The financial community looks with great disfavor on the defense market, and therefore getting capital for such investments becomes very difficult for small companies.

- *Reporting and other overhead requirements* To operate in the defense area a firm must be willing to establish systems compatible with defense requirements for accounting, management, drawing, inspection, welding, and so forth. Many of these standards are unique to defense, and require extensive background and experience.

- *Market environment* Certainly the shrinking market, the existing excess capacity, and the instability all discourage new entrants.

- *Political considerations* Congressmen try very hard to keep contractors in their districts in the defense business, against those who might choose to enter—for example, by passing legislation that no new munitions plants can be built in areas that are not adjacent to current munitions plants.

- *Federal regulations*   All requirements, such as those of OSHA, EEO, the Small Business Administration, Unemployment Areas Assistance, and environmental controls, are much more rigidly applied to firms doing work with the federal government than in the commercial sector. Thus, if these are not satisfied by a firm's normal practices, they represent a very significant barrier to entry into defense business.
- *Security clearance*   Most defense business requires both the workers and the plant to be "cleared," which is expensive and time-consuming. Thus, the lack of prior security clearance often makes it impossible to do defense business.
- *Social stigma*   During the mid-1960s it was a stigma to be in the defense business. Dupont was only one of the firms that chose to leave defense because of the social stigma (in Dupont's case the issue was napalm). In such a social climate the disincentive to defense work is especially strong if the major share of a company's business is in the civilian sector.

Numerous barriers discourage or prevent firms from leaving the defense business[35]—even when the market has shrunk drastically in an area where a comeback is unlikely, as is today the case in many segments where there are considerable excesses of plant space, equipment, and labor. Many of these exit barriers are mirror images of the barriers to entry.

- *Financial reasons*   The Department of Defense's monthly payments for work in progress provide a very favorable cash-flow situation, encouraging financially weak companies to stay in, while the heavy debt structure that many defense firms have makes it difficult for them to raise capital for new ventures in order to get out.
- *Research and development*   Government sponsorship of research and development (especially on cost-reimbursement contracts) encourages firms to stay in defense, sometimes in the hope of developing commercial products. It also encourages firms to give defense "just one more try," since the risk of defense research and development is low.
- *Overhead*   The large overhead required for defense work makes a company's prices unattractive in the commercial world.
- *Capital equipment*   Much of the special capital equipment required for defense lacks flexibility for diversification. Additionally, the Department of Defense pays firms to maintain even unused or old

capital equipment and unused plant space so that it is available for mobilization. This discourages even the partial closing of plants, and hinders diversification.

- *Contract awards* History shows that whenever a company has been in bad shape and about to go out of the defense business, it has received the next award—through a combination of desire, low bids, political reasons, and a good proposal effort.

- *Specialization of labor* A large percentage of the scientific and engineering labor characteristic of defense business is very difficult to apply directly to civilian products.

- *Specialization of marketing* The sales force required for defense business is not, for the most part, suited to the civilian market. (However, it may be transferable to other government markets, such as energy and transportation, and some firms have chosen this route.)

- *Military specifications* The use of military standards and specifications throughout the defense industry makes it very difficult to convert engineering and manufacturing forces to the lower-cost practices of the commercial world.

- *Unfilled orders* The business backlog of a defense firm is extremely difficult to sell to a competitor, because of the highly differentiated nature of the products. Because product developments are seven to ten years long, and a company at any given time may be in various stages on different programs, there is still a long-term commitment required, if one chooses to exit.

- *Emphasis on quality over quantity* The defense industry tends toward a relatively low rate of production with very high quality, as contrasted with most commercial areas, where high production rates and increased efficiency are the goal and slightly reduced quality is acceptable.

- *Foreign sales* Many firms have been kept in the defense area because of their foreign military sales. Thus, even though a firm may be at a low point in U.S. defense sales and might therefore tend to leave the industry, it is kept in by the lucrative foreign military market. It may then use its profits from this foreign market for proposal activities to get back into the U.S. market.

- *Market cycles* History has shown that the defense business is highly cyclical. Many firms stay in defense even when their own fortunes are low, with the expectation of "catching" the next cycle.

- *Profits*   The high level of return on investment realized by many firms using government-owned plants and equipment leads to structural rigidity.
- *Patriotism*   There is a sincere patriotic commitment on the part of those firms that have for a number of years been in the defense business. This feeling extends into the corporate structure of many of the conglomerates. In some cases it is expressed as "duty to the nation."

For an effective market to operate in the defense industry arena, many of these barriers to entry and exit must be reduced greatly or eliminated. We will address how this can be accomplished, and the difficulties involved, in chapter 12.

2.2 Production Factors

To fully understand the structure of any industry it is necessary to look at the "factors of production"—labor, equipment, money, and material.[36] Each of these factors affects the structure of an industry and is, in turn, influenced by that structure. For each of these factors of production there are characteristics unique to the defense industry.

2.2.1 Labor
Perhaps the most significant characteristic of the defense labor market is its extreme long-term instability. Figure 2.4 compares the long-term growth of nonagricultural employment in the U.S. labor force with the highly cyclical characteristics of the labor force in the aircraft industry. Similar (perhaps even greater) long-term instability is seen for individual defense plants, as shown in figure 2.5. This large variation from year to year in a given plant is quite typical. It is driven by the combination of the cyclical characteristics of the overall industry in response to varying domestic and worldwide conditions and the variation of business from firm to firm as contracts for major weapons systems are awarded. (The latter effect can be seen clearly in figure 2.5). In some segments of the defense industry this labor instability even appears over the short term—for example, in shipbuilding there is an annual turnover of approximately 75 percent of the labor force.[37] The other area of significant instability in the defense industry's labor force is the senior management

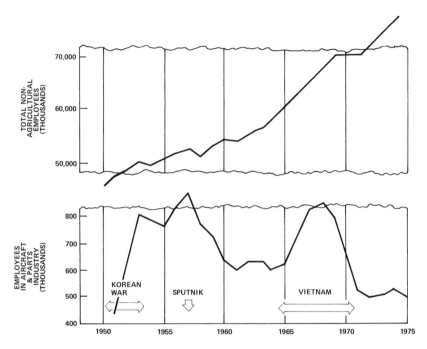

Figure 2.4
National employment trends. Source: U.S. Department of Labor, Bureau of Labor
Statistics.

level. The instability here is a direct result of the extremely cyclic nature of
the business.[38]

Because of training costs and because of the lack of "learning,"[39]
group unity, and supervisory continuity, such significant labor instabilities, which appear to occur throughout the defense industry, result
in great economic inefficiencies. Even among engineers there seems to be
great mobility, as firms "raid" each other for people in good times or
when one firm has recently won a big contract.[40]

A second major characteristic of the labor force in the defense industry
is its high cost, which is due to the very high skill levels required both in
manufacturing and in engineering, the long-term instability of the industry, and the fact that the industry is not price-sensitive.

Table 2.6 presents data that reflect the labor skill requirements in some
major defense industries. In all cases the ratio of production workers to

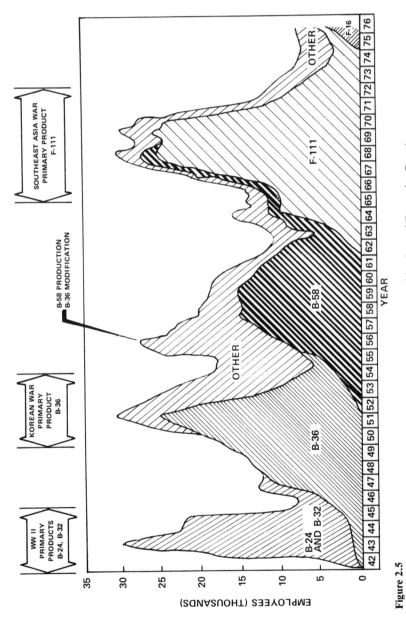

Figure 2.5
Employment history of Air Force Plant 4, Fort Worth, Texas (operated by General Dynamics Corp.).

Table 2.6
Wage-Rate Ranking and Percentage of Production Employees in
Selected Defense Industries

	Rank in Hourly Wage Rate[a]	Ratio of Production to Total Employees
Aircraft and parts	4	53.8%
Complete guided missiles	5	27.8
Shipbuilding and repair	9	79.1
Communications equipment	11	50.0
Ordnance and accessories	10	47.3
Motor vehicles	1	73.5
Electronic computing equipment	12	34.2
Average for U.S. industry	14	89.9

a. This ranking means that motor vehicles has the highest average hourly wage rate and that the average for each of the industries shown is higher than the rank of what would be the average industry (14).
Source: National Commission on Materials Policy, final report (Washington, D.C.: U.S. Government Printing Office, 1972).

total employees is considerably less for the defense industry than for the average industry, and in some cases (for example, guided missiles) fewer than one-third of workers are production workers.[41] Table 2.6 also shows that these defense industries have higher average wages than U.S. industry in general.[42]

A final structural characteristic of defense-industry labor is the aging of the work force, which appears to be caused by a combination of the shrinking market (which leads firms to keep employees with seniority and let go of those who are younger) and the fact that, despite the higher wage rates, defense does not appear to be an attractive business to many young workers, because of its inherent long-term instability.[43] In 1976 the average age of aerospace engineers was 43,[44] which is extremely old considering the rapid changes in engineering over the 20 years since the majority of these engineers had graduated. Thus, the designs being produced today are most likely not taking full advantage of modern engineering design techniques such as computer-aided design and manufacturing, and are therefore likely to be less efficient than their commercial counterparts. A 1976 study of the average age of production workers in the aircraft plants found the following: Lockheed (California division)–age 55;

Lockheed (Marietta, Georgia division)-age 62; Fairchild (Long Island, N.Y. division)-age 56.[45] Thus, most of these production workers were hired during World War II. Their experience is more suitable to older, less efficient manufacturing techniques. Another very significant strategic implication to this age distribution is that as older employees begin to retire, there are no new workers trained to replace them. This study revealed that in some parts of the aircraft industry (for example, among model and tool shop workers) problems due to a lack of skilled workers are already beginning to arise.

In light of the special labor considerations in the defense industry (high skills, low stability, high wages, old age, lack of production-rate "learning," and low productivity), it is shocking to realize how little attention is paid to this labor market—especially when one considers that 20–30 percent of all U.S. scientists and engineers and 8–10 percent of all factory workers belong in the defense categories.

2.2.2. Plants and Equipment

Some of these labor problems are amplified by the old age and low productivity of defense plants and equipment. In part, the problems are caused by the mixture of government and private ownership. The important issue is not who owns the equipment, but the fact that so large a share of the plants and equipment is government-owned tends to make the system far less price-sensitive.[46] Additionally, it tends to take much of the equipment out of possible use by the civilian sector. Rarely does lowest cost to the government turn out to be the criterion for the proper mixture of government and private plants and equipment. Other reasons—such as the unwillingness of a sole-source contractor to make the investment, or the government's belief that it will have greater control over equipment in times of emergency—become the overriding considerations. The U.S. government has invested about $18 billion in plants and equipment (which has a replacement value today of perhaps $100 billion). This includes 146 plants (mostly production plants for munitions, propellant, aircraft, and missiles and maintenance facilities for aircraft, ships, weapons, and vehicles).[47] It also includes around 500,000 items of industrial plant and equipment and large numbers of miscellaneous "other plant and equipment" items (work tables, test stands, carts, and such) having an acquisition value of almost $10 billion. Much of this equipment resides in government arsenals, but 60 percent of the real property and almost half of the equipment is in the hands of contractors. In any given plant, the public- and private-sector equipment will be totally intermixed. This has, of course, led to frequent recommendations for requiring the contractors to buy all of the government equipment in their possession or for government takeover of the facilities. The advocates of each choice claim that their solution would make better use of the resources than the current mix. However, the magnitude of the cost of some of the sites can be a deterrent. It is certainly a major consideration to take over facilities that are worth well over $100 million each[48] and have huge operating costs. (Government-owned plants and equipment have an annual operating cost of more than $7.1 billion.[49])

In addition, many of these facilities (particularly the munitions plants) are being run at extremely low levels of production, and a large number are inactive. It is extremely disturbing how many tax dollars are tied up in inactive or very little-used production facilities. For example, consider three inactive munitions production plants and their acquisition costs: Sunflower–$117 million; Ravena–$146 million; Badger–$131 million. Or some active plants running at very low levels: Joliet–$165 million; Indiana–$158 million; Lake City–$105 million; Holston–$141 million; Radford–$142 million. There is no easy answer to the problem presented by these very large investments in essentially special-purpose plants and equipment. The above are all "sunk costs," but the same problem is raised when new munitions plants are considered. Future thought should be given to alternative, civilian products that could be built in these facilities when they are not required for military use. As we go more and more to computer-controlled, automated machinery, such general-purpose production operations should become possible.

Placing government-owned facilities only with giant firms is a criticism often aimed at the Department of Defense. After each of the world wars, when government equipment was sold off (often at very low prices) much of it was purchased by the larger defense firms.[50] The use of these government-provided facilities is what allows the large firms to achieve such a high return on investment in their defense work. It also clearly represents a significant barrier to exit for these firms.[51]

What would be the optimal mixture of government and private ownership, in terms of improving the use of resources, remains an unanswered question.[52] The shipbuilding industry (which is all privately owned) is having significant capital-equipment problems, while the Army's tank and munitions industries (in which almost all the equipment is government-owned) are also saddled with very old and underutilized equipment. In the aircraft industry capital-equipment problems appear for those firms which have more government-owned equipment as well as for those which have less, although those with less government-owned equipment seem today to be in somewhat better shape. The government should search harder for alternative techniques to assist industry in making investments, relying more on the profit motive in capital utilization. However, this step alone is not sufficient; it must be coupled with a large number of additional actions in other areas.

An additional factor that is often said to be unique to defense plant and equipment requirements is the excess capacity that must be established and maintained in order to provide "surge" or mobilization capability. Because of this requirement the Department of Defense often argues that it is necessary to build in extra capacity when a production line is being set up, or to retain much of the unused plant space and equipment after a production run has been completed. They argue that it is far more expensive to tear down and sell equipment than to simply maintain it in place, and they hope that Congress will allocate funds in the next year's budget for the reinitiation of production. As long as the maintenance costs for such lines are considered allowable overhead on a company's charges against its defense contracts, the desire to maintain this equipment is completely compatible with the firm's desires as well. From the firm's viewpoint, "once investment has been made and business is established, the process of reducing productive capacity is slow and painful."[53] The firms and the government thus view a reduction in production as a temporary action, and use "projected increased production" and "retention for surge and mobilization" as arguments for keeping the production line going at a low level or even in a "ready condition."[54]

The Department of Defense issues no guidelines on capacity utilization or allowable percentage of excess capacity. In fact, there are no guidelines for measuring such parameters. However, in the civilian sector, an efficient operation appears to require about 93 percent utilization,[55] and the data indicate that in periods of relatively high demand most sectors of the

U.S. economy stay at such levels—with the exception of the defense industry.[56]

Whether or not this large excess capacity (ranging from over 90 percent in the munitions industry to between 30 percent and 50 percent in most other segments of the defense industry) is needed or even useful in terms of production surge capability will be treated in subsequent chapters. However, this extra capacity clearly raises the cost of defense production,[57] and its availability is a distinct discouragement to firms who wish to modernize the capacity actually in use. Of the DoD-owned plants currently in use, only about one-third were built since World War II. The vast majority were built during the war, and a few even earlier (four of them were built in the nineteenth century, and the oldest plants currently in use were built in 1813 and 1816). Much of the equipment in these plants is of Korean War vintage (1950–1955). Only the electrical and electronic equipment, mostly bought in the 1960s, keeps the average age of the overall industrial plant equipment in the current inventory under 20 years. Still, the majority of it exceeds 15 years of age, and 45 percent is at least 20 years old. Two important points result from the comparison of these numbers with the average age of equipment in the civilian sector: U.S. defense equipment is much older than the average American manufacturing equipment, which itself appears to be considerably older than that in other developed nations.[58] (The age of the total American equipment is reflected by the low relative productivity growth of overall U.S. manufacturing[59] [table 2.7]—and the U.S. defense industry is even worse.) Second,

Table 2.7
Average Annual Increase in Productivity
Per Man-Hour in Manufacturing, 1960–1974,
for Seven Nations

Japan	10.0%
Italy	6.3%
France	5.7%
W. Germany	5.6%
Canada	4.2%
United Kingdom	3.8%
United States	3.6%

Source: U.S. Department of Labor.

the relatively low investment being made in modernization of defense plants and equipment (around 50 percent less that being made by other comparable sectors of American industry) is one of the most striking characteristics about the current U.S. defense industry.[60]

There has been considerable concern on the part of the Department of Defense about the low levels of investment in modernization and the resulting low productivity—particularly in view of the high wages. However, it has been difficult for the DoD to address the causes of this low investment, since they are inherent in the basic structural problems and operational methods of the total defense industry and in the DoD's own acquisition practices. Specifically, there are fourteen causes—both recent and long-standing—for this low investment:

- A contractor can win a development program without a significant new investment because his production costs are not part of the development bid. Then, when he is in a sole-source position, he finds that higher costs for production actually mean more profit.
- Future business is very uncertain, because of such factors as the one-year budget cycle and the "all or nothing" nature of the competitions.
- There is little profit incentive; in fact, until the profit-policy change in 1977 a contractor was rewarded with increased profits if he used existing (old) government equipment.
- The low profit on sales realized by defense contractors limits the dollars available.
- Because of the poor view the investment community has about defense as a business area, it is very difficult and expensive for the defense companies to raise either equity or debt money.
- The cyclic sales and employment characteristics of the defense business make fixed investment unattractive.
- Considerable excess capacity exists.
- The total defense market is not expected to grow, and is in fact considered more likely to shrink over the long run.
- The Cost Accounting Standards Board, which controls how defense contractors do their bookkeeping, has decided that depreciation allowances must be based on the "estimated service life" rather than the shorter time allowed for tax purposes.
- The acquisition costs of new plants and equipment far exceed the depreciation allowances, because of the complexity of modern ma-

chinery as well as the significant levels of inflation that have been common since the mid-1970s. Thus, even the current level of defense-industry investment—which equals the depreciation allowances—is not keeping a constant modernization level, because of the higher replacement costs.

- The heavy, high-cost debt of many defense companies consumes much of the cash they can generate.
- Those companies that do have some extra cash are finding it far more profitable to put it into new external (nondefense) acquisitions.
- Many in industry claim that the severe environmental and safety regulations imposed on them in the post-Vietnam era have greatly drained capital. One estimate says that total expenditures for controlling air and water pollution in the United States for the ten-year period from 1974 through 1983 will average between $6 billion and $7 billion per year. These costs are not unique to the defense industry, but because no government contract can be awarded to a firm that does not conform to all governmental regulations there is probably more of a direct impact on the defense industry than on other manufacturers.
- Finally, it appears as though the defense firms' traditional primary criterion for investment has been mere survival rather than increasing the return on investment. The defense firms have thus far been able to maintain their positions in the industry without having to make significant capital investments.

2.2.3 Money
The problem of capital investment must be addressed simultaneously with the question of available money. The normal pattern is for the government to supply funds through "progress payments" of 80 percent to large contractors and 85 percent to small ones. These funds, supplied as work progresses (essentially, as costs are incurred), are an attractive way for the defense companies to do business. However, in spite of progress payments, the defense industry has very severe financial problems. These problems began with the great increase in debt that took place during the Vietnam-era expansion.

Figure 2.6 shows the debt trend for eight major aerospace companies. (This figure intentionally ignores some of the anomalies of the debt situation of three of the largest aerospace companies; the actual case is even

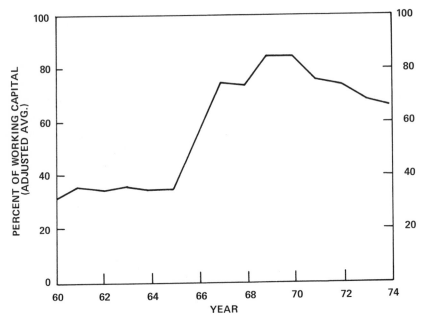

Figure 2.6
Long-term debt trend for eight major aerospace firms. Source: Investment Management Sciences, Inc., "The Need for Equity Capital."

worse.) In the period going into the peak of the Vietnam expenditures, the defense contractors borrowed heavily in order to increase their plant and equipment capacities for the expected increase in production. During this same period the civilian companies were also switching from equity to debt, making this form of borrowing characteristic of the whole financial picture in the United States. However, in the post-Vietnam period the overall defense market fell significantly, in contrast to the civilian market, so while the civilian world was borrowing against future growth (a relatively safe investment) the defense industry was borrowing against a shrinking market. This caused the major financial problems that exist today in the defense industry—problems of the sort that resulted in Lockheed having to be bailed out by the U.S. government, Grumman having to be saved by the Shah of Iran, and a number of other aerospace companies being in very dangerous financial positions. (Some writers have been calling this "welfare capitalism."[61]) Many of the leading conglomerates also went heavily into defense (frequently for the combination of high technology, good cash flow from progress payments, and large dollar sales). When the defense market started to shrink, they were trapped within a heavy debt structure and suffered considerably as a result of their defense holdings (an example is Litton's experience in ship-building). Not only did it cause them significant loss of borrowing power; it also greatly reduced their flexibility in management decisions—often to the disadvantage of the best interests of the Department of Defense.

To make matters worse, other cash demands were placed on the defense industry during this same period; for example, the significantly higher rate of interest, the rising fuel costs (which particularly hurt those on fixed-price contracts), the more numerous and expensive proposals competing for a smaller number of awards, and the fact that even in this shrinking environment the Department of Defense was often short of money to carry out its own programs and asked the contractors for help.[62] Furthermore, the significantly inflated cost of replacement equipment increased the demand for money, while the Cost Accounting Standards Board stretched the depreciation period. One estimate said that the overall cash-flow requirements for the total defense business would rise from the 1975 figure of $7.3 billion to a 1985 figure of 9.6 billion 1975 dollars.[63]

The basic problem is the extreme difficulty the defense firms face in raising money. Their price-to-earnings ratio and their bond rating are low (about half as good as those of their civilian counterparts), and therefore most investment houses are very reluctant to put their money into the defense sector. The financial community's pessimism with regard to the defense industry appears to rest mostly in its belief that profits are too low in comparison with the risks (which is countered by a Rand Corporation report that aerospace rate of return, even with risk taken into account, was still the second highest of a large number of industries surveyed[64]). Because of the financial institutions' reluctance, most of the funding comes from commercial banks in short-term (90-day) loans.[65]

To better understand the seriousness of the problems encountered by defense contractors in obtaining money, and to gain some insight into potential corrective actions, the DoD in 1975 commissioned The Conference Board (an independent, business-oriented organization) to survey the leading investment firms in the United States, and their views toward the defense industry.[66] The study, which questioned officials from thirty-four banking and other financial institutions, found unanimous concern about the low profits and high risks considered characteristic of the industry and concluded that the industry "is likely to find it increasingly difficult to secure both the short-term and the long-term financing it requires,"[67] The executives of major commercial banks, life insurance companies, investment banking firms, and public accounting firms emphasized the following four major points about defense business:

"Profits are too low for the risks faced and their long-term viability, compared with the profits of industries oriented to commercial markets."

"Uncertainty is the principal risk perceived by the survey participants—uncertainty both as to fulfillment of present contracts and winning future contracts."

"Other 'negatives' seen include limited product line and overreliance on a single customer; poor management practices and the propensity to 'buy-in' to programs; certain Defense Department policies, tactics, and administrative practices such as excessive management and policy changes, a propensity to alter specifications in mid-contract, and adoption of an adversary posture towards suppliers."

"The perhaps inevitable, but nonetheless deplorable injection of politics into defense contracting."

In general, the Conference Board study concluded that defense contractors are "not considered credit worthy." It also noted that "defense subcontractors are in a more perilous situation than the primes."

The findings of this DoD-funded study are fully in accord with the recommendations of this book. It seems surprising to find that the first recommendation made by the leaders of the American financial community was that "the Department of Defense should determine the make-up of the defense industrial base that is desirable, and take steps to achieve and sustain this base." Greater governmental policy coordination and planning at the aggregate, sectoral level can significantly reduce the risks associated with defense business and improve the industry's economic efficiency. Such planning, complemented with other governmental actions such as steps to improve industry profit and proper incentives for modernization, can make the industry much healthier and thus able to attract far more private financing. The resulting private investments would serve as a balance to the government's role in sectoral planning, thus preventing as the otherwise likely alternative solution to the financial problems of the defense industry: nationalization.

2.2.4 Materials and Energy

As with labor and manufacturing equipment, little concern is usually given to raw materials and energy by the Department of Defense, since all of its acquisition policies focus on the final product. However, it is at the level of raw materials and energy that the two primary concerns of this book—the economic and strategic viability of the defense industry—come directly together. The rapidly rising prices of imported raw materials and energy cannot be separated from the strategic issue of accessibility and dependency.

Figure 2.7 shows the percentages of raw materials consumed in the United States in 1975 that were foreign-supplied. As the report of the National Commission on Materials Policy stated, "it is clearly evident . . . that our reliance on foreign [materials] suppliers is steadily increasing."[68] Not only are we heavily dependent on foreign supplies, but, as with energy, there are a very limited number of suppliers, and they are able to control access and price quite easily. For example, chromium is a critical ingredient in steel (to prevent rust), and there is no substitute available. However, the primary sources of chromium are Rhodesia, South Africa, the U.S.S.R., and Turkey. In today's world political environment, these countries cannot always be counted upon to act in the best interests of the U.S. defense industry. The largest single source of high-quality titanium sponge (the processed form of titanium metal required for many military applications, such as high-performance aircraft) is the Soviet Union. For an extended period in the early 1970s the Soviet Union simply stopped supplying titanium sponge to the United States; then they condescended to reinstitute the supply at a much higher price. Clearly, such acts affect the economic and strategic viability of the U.S. defense industry significantly. This problem is bound to grow worse, not only because of the increasing U.S. demand but also because of the shrinking world supply of many materials. In fact, as Barnet and Müller have stated, "the realization that the world's long-term supply of critical materials [and energy], for the support of human life and modern industry, is limited, may be the single most revolutionary idea in economics since Adam Smith. Neither Marx nor Keynes doubted the infinite availability of the earth's resources to feed economic growth."[69]

The dependency issue is currently being complicted by the fact that, for a variety of "comparative advantage" reasons, including labor costs, en-

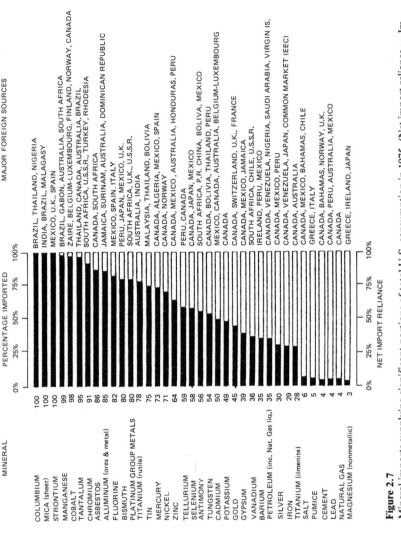

Figure 2.7

Mineral imports supplying significant portions of total U.S. consumption in 1975. (Net import reliance = Imports − Exports + Government stockpile releases ± Industry stock changes.) Sources: Bureau of Mines; Bureau of the Census (import − export data).

vironmental standards, taxes, and transportation costs, many U.S. firms are setting up plants in other countries for processing of the raw materials. If this trend continues, it will certainly increase the dependency problem.

To date, the problem of materials and energy has manifested itself less in an inability to obtain supplies (except under political circumstances, such as the Soviet stoppage of titanium sponge and the 1973 OPEC oil embargo) than in cost increases and longer lead times. However, its effects are not limited to foreign-produced parts and material, but are being seen across the board, owing to both foreign dependency and shrinking numbers of U.S. sources. Table 2.8 shows an example of the large price increases in one year in which the demand was actually slackening. Clearly the United States is suffering from the suppliers' "monopoly pricing."

Table 2.8
Material Price Increases Between
January 1, 1974 and January 1, 1975

Sheet and plate	
Aluminum	25%
Steel and stainless steel	30%
Titanium	30%
Extrusions	
Aluminum	25%
Steel and stainless steel	30%
Titanium	30%
Billets/forgings	
Aluminum	15%
Steel	20%
Titanium	30%
Plastics	35–50%
Fiberglass	25%
Paint	30%
Bearings	26%

This monopoly power is also demonstrated by table 2.9, which shows that from 1975 to 1979 lead times for obtaining basic materials increased dramatically.[68] Again, over the long period shown here one would have expected additional suppliers to enter (if there had been a competitive environment) and thereby reduce the prohibitive response times. The fact that none did is further proof of the monopoly position of the suppliers.

The increase in lead times has also been seen in the area of subsystems. For example, aircraft landing gear between 1973 and 1974 increased from a lead time of 60 weeks to 84 weeks; wheels and brakes from 52 weeks to 88 weeks. This delay in delivery of subsystems and parts has direct impact on the lead time for the delivery of the completed weapons system,[70] and thus on its cumulative cost. These long lead times have a "multiplier effect" on the basic price increases shown in table 2.8, because most defense firms are time-oriented; that is, there are many people on a program (for

Table 2.9
Increasing Lead Times (in Weeks) for Selected Critical Components

	Dec. 1975	Dec. 1977	Aug. 1979[a]
Aluminum extrusions (sheets, plates)	12–16	18–26	68–73
Bearings	16–20	20–26	46–55
Castings, large	30–32	38–40	46–62
Cobalt/Molysteel Bar	12–18	24–30	44–50*
Electrical connectors	16–24	20–28	47
Fasteners	6–8	6–8	39–54
Forgings, large			
Aluminum, steel	48–50	34–40	78–89
Titanium	50–55	40–46	99–105
Hinges	50–52	56–60	72–90*
Hydraulic fittings	36–38	32–34	80–84*
Titanium sheets and plates	12–18	14–20	76–77

Source: Air Force and Joint Logistics Commanders Data, July 1979.
a. Asterisk indicates April 1979 data.

example, program managers and production engineers) who will remain for its duration, no matter how long. Thus, the long lead time for the raw materials, parts, and subsystems increases the total cost of the weapons system significantly.

With the increased defense procurement budgets of the late 1970s, lead times did not go down but continued to lengthen (table 2.9); this was further proof of the lack of an effective market. By the end of the decade, lead times for critical materials and parts had gotten extreme (in some cases exceeding two years[71]), no new firms were entering the defense market, and prices continued to rise rapidly.

An extensive discussion of the energy problem faced by the Department of Defense is unnecessary here. However, it must be pointed out that the list of major suppliers of defense purchases grows each year with the names of leading oil companies.[72]

Congress has recognized some of the problems regarding materials and energy, and has taken actions to address at least the strategic impacts. To offset competition for critical materials between the defense-related industries and the commercial industries under conditions of short supply, Congress established (in 1950) the Defense Priorities and Allocation provisions of the Defense Production Act, which provide the government with two capabilities: the defense priorities system, which not only requires a contractor's acceptance and performance of a "defense-rated" contract order but also provides a means for expediting all phases of the contract work by assigning priority to defense work within a contractor's, subcontractor's, or parts supplier's production facility; and a defense material system requiring producers of selected essential materials to set aside each month a portion of their production which may be claimed by authorized contractors when needed to complete defense or defense-related orders.[73]

The original intent of the Defense Production Act was to provide a priority system to be exercised during peacetime but intended primarily for periods of national emergency (during or before wars). However, it has also been used during peacetime to assist the Department of Defense in getting parts as rapidly as possible, and thus minimizing peacetime defense costs. More recently, Congress has given similar priorities to the Alaskan petroleum and natural gas pipeline projects, to materials for large oil tankers, and to other energy-related projects.

The Congress showed its clear recognition of the strategic dependence of the United States on foreign raw materials right after World War II by passing the Strategic and Critical Material Stockpiling Act of 1946. The purpose of this act was to allow the United States to stockpile critical and strategic materials for use in time of national emergency. As of June 1975, the estimated value of the 91 strategic materials being held in government inventories amounted to around $8 billion (compared with the acquisition cost of around $4 billion, mostly spent before 1962).[74] The materials stockpiled range from chrome and titanium through duck feathers and castor oil.

The size and contents of these stockpiles must be based on specific war scenarios. For example, the differences between assuming a very short conflict (in which stockpiles would be of no value), a one-year conflict (chosen by President Nixon in order to minimize the amount of material required in the stockpile), or a three-year conflict (preferred by some members of Congress and requiring significant quantities of material in the stockpile) obviously make a difference of billions of dollars in the budget,[75] as well as in the types of materials to be stockpiled.

The predominant potential user of stockpiled parts and materials is not the Department of Defense, but rather the overall national economy—even in the case of war. Thus, great flexibility exists as to what "necessary" civilian sectors are to be maintained during emergency conditions. In the past, the need for stockpiles has been used in peacetime to maintain U.S. suppliers when they were not economically competitive on a world-wide basis.[76] The stockpiles have also often been used for political and individual gain.[77] These stockpiles, therefore, have become significant political issues. Additionally, because of the sensitivity of stockpiling to war scenarios, the stockpiles are subject to budgetary manipulation and are frequently proposed as offering a way to balance the federal budget.[78] Finally, because of the lessons learned from OPEC, there is considerable interest in the United States in the use of the strategic-materials stockpiles as "economic stockpiles"—as diplomatic rather than solely strategic resources. In 1976 and 1977 a Commission on Supplies and Shortages was chartered by Congress to consider such possibilities as economic stockpiles and the legislation and institutional changes required. The commission recommended three specific corrective actions:[79] that the government should directly address problems of this nature in the future, that there is a need for a central agency for the collection of sectoral data, and that this central data repository should be separated from the policymaking actions so that policy considerations would not influence the presentation of the data. To date there has been essentially no implementation of the recommendations of this commission.

While more and more people in the defense industry and in the Department of Defense have begun to recognize the obvious material and energy problems, they have done very little about them—and the problems are bound to get worse in the future. There is a lack of initiative in developing substitutes, in planning for the long term, and even in designing weapons systems that economize on critical materials and energy. Yet this may be an area in which the "long term" is only a few decades away. Considering the lead times required to take many of the necessary actions, the DoD and the rest of the U.S. government should act now, before the problems develop into major crises.[80]

2.3 Summary

In order to understand the economic operation of the U.S. defense industry, it is first absolutely essential to recognize that there is no free market at work in this area and that there likely cannot be one because of the dominant role played by the federal government. The combination of a single buyer, a few very large firms in each segment of the industry, and a small number of extremely expensive weapons programs constitutes a unique structure for doing business.

This unique structure and the government's unique way of doing business (described in the next chapter) have created large barriers to entry and exit. These barriers result in each firm managing to keep its share of the business—even in a shrinking market. They also keep defense firms from diversifying into the civilian sector, and prevent firms operating effectively in the civilian sector from entering the defense arena.

This very limited market is further constrained by a very large amount of vertical integration. This appears in two forms: when the firm that wins the competition for the research and development program is selected as the sole producer of the production equipment, and when the prime contractor supplies its own parts and subassemblies (either through acquisition of lower-tier firms or through a decision to "make" rather than "buy").

Under such a unique industry structure, the factors of production (labor, plant and equipment, money, parts, and materials) have many special characteristics. For example, in spite of the fact that defense is a labor-intensive industry, one finds extremely high turnover (especially at the plant level, where it is due to the win-or-lose nature of the business on the few large contracts). This significantly raises the cost of building defense equipment—not only because workers do not learn to improve their efficiency, but also because a wage premium must be paid to a skilled worker in order to get him to accept a job with a very uncertain future. Similarly, because of the highly technical nature of the work and the lack of normal price competition there is a very high and quickly climbing ratio of nonproduction workers to production workers. This, combined with the increasing number of support people, results in a high and growing overhead rate, which also contributes to rising equipment costs.

Old, inefficient, oversized, and often unnecessary plant space and equipment contribute to the costs of defense materiel. There has been very little investment in the defense industry for modernization of plants and equipment, and the existing incentives appear to be exactly in the opposite direction: Firms that invest in modernization often get a lower overall return on investment. Another reason for the lack of investment is the heavy debt that already exists in much of the defense industry and which is made much more burdensome for the firms by their inability to raise money from the financial community. Thus, the defense firms are largely dependent upon the U.S. government as their source of both operating capital and long-term investments.

Even at the raw material and parts levels economic inefficiency appears to be increasing. For example, although the defense industry has always been dependent on foreign sources for its raw materials, this dependency has been growing because of the need for exotic materials (such as titanium). This is occurring at a time when the foreign countries, developed and underdeveloped, have become more aware of their economic power and have been standing together to drive prices rapidly upward. These problems have been growing in both the civilian and defense sectors, but the defense industry has been feeling the impact much more, because it is considered a "bad customer" owing to its highly cyclic nature, its very low volume, and its dependence on the annual congressional budget. Thus, defense has been seeing rapidly rising material and parts costs, great increases in lead times for these items, and increasing dependency on often undependable foreign sources.

3 The Market and its Results

3.1 The Conduct of the Market

It is in the relationship between the buyer and the seller that the most interesting differences between defense and other sectors of the U.S. economy emerge. This unique relationship has been described from a variety of perspectives. Walter Adams called it "a closed system of buyer and seller, interrelated for common interests" that "defies analysis by conventional economic tools."[1] James McKee said that "it is a relationship of 'participation' " in which "the large buyer has a direct influence on the policies and decisions of the large seller," and that "what we observe is a kind of behavior that is not adequately described by any of the commonly employed 'models' of market relationships in economics."[2] Ralph Nader has emphasized "the institutionalized fusion of corporate desires with public bureaucracy, where the national security is synonymous with the state of Lockheed and Litton."[3]

In spite of this acknowledged commonality of interest and this close relationship between government and industry at the aggregate level, on individual programs the situation is closer to an adversary relationship than to a mutually beneficial joint effort. The latter situation is normally found in the civilian market,[4] but in the highly visible defense market there is a fear that the appearance of joint efforts might be misinterpreted as indicating abuse of public funds. Therefore, the government and the contractors' representatives go too far in the other direction. Similarly, because there are usually only a few firms involved in any particular award competition, there is often concern over the opportunity for collusion. However, none of the serious studies of the defense industry[5] has ever yielded any data to show that there is any form of conspiracy among the suppliers.[6]

Perhaps the two characteristics that most distinguish the defense-industry market are the interrelated areas of public accountability and regulation. All of the government's decisionmaking and all of the industry's records are subject to review by the Congress, the public, and authorized examiners.[7] Also, in recognition of the fact that this market does not involve open and free price competition, a series of policy substitutes—ranging from regulation through management controls—have developed to either replace or correct for the lack of a free market.

There is no question that the government is intimately involved in the operation of the defense market. It controls almost all of the research and development, and it provides most of the money (through progress payments) and much of the critical plant space and equipment. But it is in the day-to-day operating details of the firms that the government's involvement is so great that the defense market becomes unique and in fact ceases to be a market in any traditional sense.

The legal basis for this involvement comes from congressional legislation and the subsequent Department of Defense procurement regulations (over 16,000 pages of text, plus hundreds of pages of appendixes).[8] These regulations provide detailed information on exactly how defense business is to be conducted,[9] and are the reason why firms doing business with the DoD have special accounting systems, special quality-control procedures, special drawings, special soldering techniques, and so on.[10]

Many of these regulations are the result of congressional hearings into the activities of the defense industry. When a specific example of abuse is found, another regulation is added—to be universally applied. For the single case involved, the corrective action may or may not work; the cumulative impact of these actions is rarely considered, nor is their interrelation. Thus, the specific problem in the individual firm may be corrected, but the impact of the regulation on the overall industry is likely to be negative and expensive.

The defense industry is never listed as a regulated industry (even though it clearly is), since the way in which it is controlled is unique—the regulator and the buyer are one and the same. Since the government decisionmakers and regulators tend to focus on individual programs and specific, detailed regulations, there is no natural tendency on their part to consider the structure of the industry in implementing policy or regulatory decisions. As Larry Ellsworth points out, "the Department of Defense determines, by its procurement decisions, whether there will be more or less concentration,"[11] and yet there is no regulation relating to the allowable degree of concentration. In fact, as Adams noted, "the Pentagon creates more monopoly in one day than the Anti-Trust Division can undo in a year."[12]

To understand how such total regulation without an industrywide perspective could exist, it is necessary to look at how the Department of Defense goes about selecting its suppliers and contracting with them.[13] Here, two widespread beliefs exist—both wrong. The first says that the decisionmakers in the DoD consciously decide whose turn it is to receive the next contract[14] (thus allowing the firms in the business to maintain their position and allowing the DoD to maintain its industrial base). Actually, the detailed proposal and source-selection activities preclude such a simplistic process—but because of the oligopoly rivalry that takes place, the final result (the award to the selected firm, which is often the one that needs the business) may be the same as if "turns" had been taken. The second false belief is that the normal free market is at work (as required by procurement legislation), and that the selection of the supplier of the next weapons system is based on the lowest cost.

Actually, the acquisition of a major new weapons system usually begins with competition for a research and development contract. This award is based primarily on promised technical capability, with price playing a minor part. Often the only price even used in the selection process is the development cost, while the big dollars associated with the production program are ignored. Thousands of industry people are involved in writing a proposal.[15] Frequently, demonstration equipment is also built and tested as part of the proposal effort. The cost of such a proposal often runs into the millions of dollars.[16]

These proposals are then evaluated by the government in a very detailed source-selection process, which involves hundreds of employees and takes at least six months and often over a year. Since very few programs are initiated in any given decade, the competition is vicious. In essence, the government is making an "all or nothing" choice. Scherer has described this form of extreme competition as "rivalry."[17] Clearly, such competition is limited to a few large firms that have the resources and the time to compete.[18]

The government's budget for a development program is published well in advance (as part of the budget submitted to Congress two years before the program is to be initiated). Thus, the government is searching for the best performance a given design can offer for a given number of development dollars. However, because of the severe competition for the few large programs, there is a significant tendency for firms to "buy in"—that is, bid low. This is especially true of "hungry" companies (those who have not recently won a contract).[19] They believe that if their promised performance satisfies the government and if their development bid is the lowest, they will win the development contract—and they usually do. They are willing to take a loss on the smaller development contract in order to secure a sole-source position on the large production contract that is likely to follow. (In reality, since the development contracts almost always contain cost-reimbursement provisions, the only dollars at risk are the percentage of profit; all costs, including overruns, will be paid by the government.) The bidders on these development contracts also believe that the scope of the program will change significantly during the five to ten years of the program's development—so that they can rebid at a later date, but on a sole-source basis. Their confidence in this likelihood is based on the fact that the cost of a typical program is likely to grow by at least 45 percent during its duration—and a development program by much more.[20] Also, they know that the pricing of the thousands of changes causing this cost growth will be done after the competition has ended.[21]

This process of change and cost growth during a contract leads to much negotiation, and even litigation, over the cost impact of a change.[22] It also encourages the contractor to propose a large number of changes to the program and/or to the weapons system, causing continuous program revisions and redirections.[23] These changes usually continue right through the production program, prohibiting the smooth operation of the production line. The result is a very significant reduction in the economic efficiency with which defense materiel is developed and produced. In fact, the change process encourages the contractor to be inefficient.

Since almost all of the production awards go to the contractor who receives the development contract, and since most of the development work comes either from "follow-on" to the initial contract award or from changes that take place during the development program itself—and contracts for all this work are awarded on a sole-source basis—it is not surprising to find that a major share of the total Department of Defense contract dollars are not awarded on the basis of competition. In fact, this is an area of major difference between the legislative myth perpetuated by the existing regulations and the reality of the defense market. The regulations state explicitly the intent of the DoD to do its business by way of formal price competitions. However, as the data in figure 3.1 show, only around 8 percent of DoD business is done through formally advertised price competitions. Most of the other 92 percent fits under regulation 3-214, which allows for exceptions to the general rule under a variety of conditions, such as national security needs, critical schedule, prior investment, and unique tools.[24]

Figure 3.1 shows that of the over 90 percent of the total dollars "negotiated," about 30 percent were negotiated competitively. This

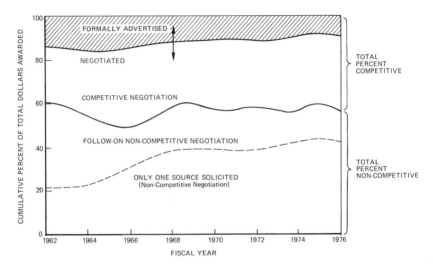

Figure 3.1
Trends in the awarding of Department of Defense contracts.

means that technical and cost proposals are received from various bidders
and a source-selection board evaluates the relative merits of these alternatives. A common case in these programs is for the government to base
the selection primarily on the technical evaluation. But the government
will still usually "negotiate" with the contractors in order to get the
lowest promised initial cost. Some refer to this as the "auction." The
figure also shows that most of the DoD dollars (over 60 percent) are
awarded on a noncompetitive, single-source basis—either as "follow-on"
to current business[25] or after a single-source solicitation. The price is
"negotiated" between the government and the sole supplier, but the supplier can effectively name his price. Also, the larger the dollar value of the
contract, the more likely it is that the awards will be made on a noncompetitive basis.[26]

When over 90 percent of the business is done under "exceptions" to the
normal practices, it is appropriate to consider alternative regulations
rather than to continue to believe that the normal practice is in operation.
In fact, the data appear to indicate that probably the "second best" solution, given the nature of the defense market, would be to have "limited
competition" on a far larger amount of the defense dollars (in contrast to
the classical argument that it is better to have more competitors). Scherer

pointed out that, in this unique form of oligopoly competition, the larger the number of competitors the less effort a company will make in the competition (owing to the reduced probability of success in single-winner, all-or-nothing competition).[27] There is clearly a great deal of randomness in the selection of a winner. It is a case of a number of large, highly qualified firms bidding against each other with differentiated products at essentially the price previously established by the defense budget.[28] Thus, when only two or three firms are bidding on a particular effort there is far more true competition present in terms of creative design, top performers being put on the proposal effort, and large-company investment in the proposal activity.[29] Scherer even found that "competition in the limiting case of only two rivals may be just as effective from a behavioral standpoint as competiton among a few firms."[30]

An attractive way of increasing competition on defense programs would be to establish two sources for production on large-quantity programs. This leads to the issues of economic efficiency associated with economies of scale, and the price and cost impacts of competition versus cost reduction through "labor learning" on greater quantitites. Here the data are very ambiguous, and each case must be separately analyzed under its "second best" conditions.[31] Sometimes the volume will be sufficiently small and the capital intensity of the manufacturing process sufficiently high that a monopoly condition will be justified;[32] however, even here competition may well be warranted at the lower tiers. In general, the benefits from competition appear to be far greater for most of the labor-intensive production on defense products, and thus competition would be warranted for the majority of the programs.[33]

Because fewer and fewer major weapons systems are being developed, a number of the prime contractors are teaming together in order to share both the costs and the rewards on these large competitive procurements[34]—and simultaneously gaining the increased congressional support of the representatives from both firms' districts. However, once the award is made to a team, even though two or more major prime contractors are involved, competition has been effectively eliminated. Clearly, two sources of a product do not automatically make for competition—unless the procurement has been so structured. Thus, it is up to the government to restructure the program in such a fashion that when the program goes into production the team members do, in fact, end up competing.[35]

The long time the government takes to make decisions constitutes another unique characteristic of the defense market. The delay is due partly to the lengthy bureaucratic process and partly to the sophistication and complexity of modern weapons systems. A typical program may have an initial ten-year planning and technology evolution (from research through exploratory and advanced development) and then a ten-year cycle of full-scale weapons-system acquisition (from prototyping through engineering development, operational test and evaluation, and initial production release). Thus, each of the major firms involved in the all-or-nothing struggle for the award of the next major weapons system will have not only a very cyclic behavior (based on winning or losing), but also a great deal of long-term uncertainty. In fact, the only way a firm can play the game is to assume that it will win the one or two big competitions in which it is involved over, say, five years. This is in contrast to a typical civilian market in which a firm assumes that it will get a certain share. This means that, in planning for labor, facilities, and such, each firm assumes—falsely, except for the winner—that it will be getting the next big program.[36] Each of the large firms believes that, as part of its proposal effort, it needs to show available, unutilized capacity in all areas, or else it will be marked down in some part of the competition and have no chance of winning. It is a perfect case of "Catch 22." Perhaps the government, having insight into both its own future needs and the conditions of each of the firms, is in a better position to do some of the long-range, aggregate industry planning, and to create a form of limited competition to take advantage of the unique characteristics of the defense market.

An additional aspect of the defense market's uniqueness is the dramatic shift that takes place in relative bargaining power of industry and government once a commitment to a single supplier has been made. As long as the program remains competitive, the government, being a monopsony buyer, is in a strong bargaining position and can play the contractors against each other to extract promises of high performance, low cost, and early delivery. But once the winning development contractor is announced, the tables are turned and the sole-source supplier is in an increasingly powerful position. As time goes on, the government becomes more and more dependent upon this contractor for a product that is (or is believed to be) badly needed and for which no substitute could be developed in less than seven to ten years. From this point on, the contractor is in a position to go to the government with "explanations" of "government-introduced'' problems that are increasing costs, causing delivery delays, and so forth, and to bargain for increased prices.[37] Again, this overall process is a great inducement for the firms to "buy in" (bid low initially), and then, after they are in a sole-source position and the government is dependent upon them, figure out ways to get their contracts changed.

Up to this point the discussion has been limited to the Department of Defense and the defense industry. However, the actual sphere of the "military-industrial complex" is far larger. In fact, Sidney Lens properly defines it to include a large group of legislators, other government officials (in more than fifty agencies), the labor hierarchy, and an important segment of academia.[38] Of these, undoubtedly the group with the greatest influence is the Congress. Here there have been two significant changes in the post-Vietnam period that greatly affect the operation of the defense market. First, the positions of Congressmen on major defense issues are much less predictable. In the past, the defense-oriented Congressmen were frequently the very senior committee chairmen (often from the South) who were strong supporters of the DoD and whose positions were relatively well known (both to the DoD, which tried to "sell" to them, and to fellow Congressmen who tried to oppose them). Today there is a far greater diversity of views in the Congress. Major debates often take place—with unpredictable outcomes—over individual weapons systems, such as the anti-ballistic missile and the B-1 bomber. This diversity of views within the Congress, though desirable from some viewpoints, increases uncertainty and instability on the "demand" side of the defense market. The second major change in the post-Vietnam Congress is the significant increase in the staffs of those committees involved with the DoD. For example, in the eight years following Vietnam, the staffs of the four committees specifically responsible for defense appropriations and authorizations more than doubled while the DoD was drastically reducing its fighting forces as well as its Pentagon staff. In addition, during the mid-1970s, the House and Senate budget committees were formed, and the joint budget office was staffed. Since defense represents a significant portion of the dollars reviewed by these new committees, they, in fact, added a third level of congressional review of the annual defense budget.[39]

A high level of congressional access and review is both desirable and necessary in a democratic society. However, Congress does its review on an annual basis, and introduces extreme "micro management" into the process by emphasizing the details of each project rather than the concept's overall merit. (It is only at the project level that individual districts and states—and therefore voters—actually become involved.) This raises the question of whether the detailed dollar-by-dollar and project-by-project annual congressional review is the most efficient or effective process for establishing the proper level and nature of the defense posture of the United States. Specific actions of the Congress make this question even more pertinent. For example, since Congressmen rarely gain votes by canceling or reducing programs and have the potential to gain significant numbers of votes by adding programs, the defense budget is often increased beyond the level requested by the Department of Defense in many areas. Some of the additions are made by an individual member because a particular plant in his district would profit from a specific program. Others are more generic in nature[40] and are added by a committee chairman or an individual Congressman out of a belief in the importance of one committee's area of concern, or occasionally for other political reasons. The nature of the committees themselves has a significant impact on the DoD budget. For example, it is more than a coincidence that there is a Sea Power Committee and an Air Power Committee, but no land power committee, and that there have been far greater budget authorizations for Navy and Air Force sea- and air-based procurements than for Army land-based procurements.

Many of the congressional additions are relatively small (in the millions of dollars), but others reach up into the hundreds of millions or the billions.[41] Of course, not all are undesirable or unnecessary simply because they were not included within the submitted presidential budget. Frequently the budget itself has been cut back because of the president's political or economic considerations, and sometimes he drops important programs intentionally, knowing full well they will be put back by the Congress when the budget goes to Capitol Hill. Similarly, since the DoD itself must often acknowledge internal political considerations, some of the judgments made by Congress—for example, on whether programs should be approved—are better than those made by the DoD when it submits its budget.

The Congress has its critics of the Department of Defense, many of whom play a positive role in controlling programs and in pointing out shortcomings and practices. In fact, there are times when programs get canceled by the Congress because the DoD lacked either the courage or the political strength to cancel them.[42] But in the majority of the cases the Congress makes its cuts "across the board"—as a fixed percentage of all programs. This is far easier politically, but much less effective. Additionally, in the post-Vietnam period the Congress chose to make more significant cuts in procurement and R&D than in the military or civilian personnel areas,[43] thus redistributing the resource requirements as submitted by the Pentagon—keeping the men, but not equipping them to fight. Such congressional actions have a large effect on the defense industry and introduce considerable uncertainty in the planning process. Once the Congress agrees to a cut in the procurement budget, the DoD must then go back and reshuffle hundreds (if not thousands) of individual programs.

A discussion of the congressional role could not be completed without mentioning the activity of lobbying, by industry, labor,[44] and the Department of Defense (DoD lobbying is specifically excluded by law, but does take place in the form of "dialog" between the two branches of the government). With multi-billion-dollar programs at stake during the annual congressional deliberations, there are bound to be very powerful efforts made to present the vested interests of the firms, the workers, and the armed services. Naturally, when the budget calls for an increase, the desires of these three groups will be in agreement, and thus they can put very significant pressure on Congress to go along with the increase. However, when a decrease is proposed by the executive branch, the groups come into conflict. It appears as though the executive branch has had more success with Congress in this area than have the industry and labor groups. Figure 3.2 shows an amazingly high correlation between executive-branch budget submittals and congressional appropriations. It clearly indicates that when budget increases were requested the Congress normally agreed to them (after appropriate reductions), and that budget reductions submitted by the executive branch have similarly been agreed to by the Congress.

In summary: The Congress plays a unique role in the operation of the U.S. military equipment market. However, the impact of the Congress is but one of many special considerations that make the defense market deviate from the operation and structure of traditional free-market economic theory and even from most of the economic theory of industrial

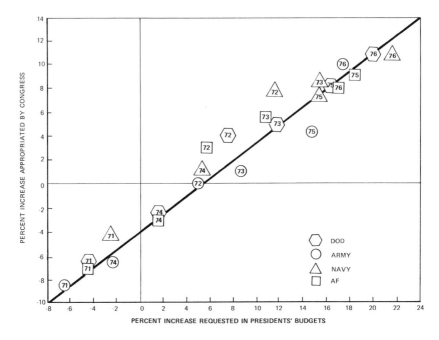

Figure 3.2
Percent increases for defense appropriated by Congress and requested in presidents'
budgets, 1971–1976. Source: former Undersecretary of the Army Norman Augustine.

organizations (including that covering oligopoly markets).[45] On the basis
of the characteristics of the supply and the demand sides, and the complex
relations between them, one is forced to conclude that this market is clearly a special case and must therefore be analyzed as such.

3.2 The Performance of the Market

Ronald Fox of the Harvard Graduate School of Business wrote the
following after serving for seven years in high levels of the Department of
Defense:

What seldom distinguishes any phase of the [weapons] acquisition process
is a genuine commitment to the most efficient and effective management
of resources—people, money, materials, facilities, and time. The current
relationships between Congress and the Defense Department, among
governmental defense agencies, and between government and industry effectively prevent the system from functioning to its best advantage.

Although weapons and equipment are, in fact, produced, the United States is paying an inordinate share of its federal budget to satisfy the needs of an inflexible bureaucracy, an over-extended industry, and the desires of the military establishment.[46]

The most obvious result of the failure of the market in the case of defense is the high and rising price of defense equipment. As shown in figure 1.2, even after inflation is removed and the unit costs have been adjusted for the reduced quantities procured, the cost of military equipment has been rising at about 5 percent per year. Thus, one generation of equipment costs three to five times as much as the prior one, and so significantly lower quantities of military equipment are being procured today. The result is not only reduced military capability, but also low and inefficient production rates.

By contrast, commercial equipment has been going down in constant-dollar price, while its performance has been going up. It is frequently argued that these defense-equipment cost increases are necessary in order to achieve the very high performance required of American military systems to match the increasing performance of Soviet systems. However, a 1976 study comparing U.S. and Soviet jet engines of similar performance found that the Soviet engines were inherently less costly (between one-third and one-half the cost of the "comparable" U.S. engine), even if they were to be built by U.S. personnel, in U.S. factories, and with U.S. material.[47] The reasons for the far lower cost of the Soviet engines were "design differences, maintenance philosophy differences, and specification differences."

The high prices of U.S. defense systems are not inevitable, but result from the way in which defense business is done—for example, the total emphasis upon performance, and the resultant neglect of cost and producibility as design criteria. The fact that there is almost no competition over defense systems—especially their production—not only allows the direct costs to rise, but also allows the overhead costs to become much larger.[48]

In the absence of competition there is an actual incentive for a firm to raise its costs (in order to raise its total profits, which are usually given as a percentage of its costs). This can be seen clearly from figure 3.3. To combat this negative incentive the DoD often awards its contracts with an "incentive fee"; that is, the final fee percentage is based on the actual costs realized. (Realized performance and delivery schedule also often receive

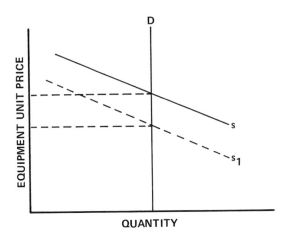

Figure 3.3
The incentive for price hikes in the absence of competition. With D (quantity of equipment demanded) fixed
by the size of the military force, and with supply fixed
by the production "learning curve" of the single firm
building the equipment, the shift from s to s_1, due to a
firm's increased productivity, will simply lower the
firm's sales; and, since price and profits are based on
costs, will lower the firm's profits (at least on follow-on
business). If the firm became less efficient, its production curve would move up—and prices and profits
would rise.

incentive fees.) However, the data appear to show that defense firms do
not see the small differences in projected fee provided by this form of contract as much of an incentive.[49] Rather, the driving factor in defense
business appears to be sales volume—the higher the volume, the greater
the total profit.

The lack of competition in defense procurements also allows a large
amount of excess capacity to remain and to be charged against contracts.
Many of these unnecessary charges are for redundant labor (especially in
the engineering and "overhead" categories), which is fully chargeable to
government contracts but is not truly required for the efficient ac-
complishment of current production and/or R&D work and would not be
kept if the work were being done within a price-sensitive competitive
market. In addition, there are significant costs for idle plant space and
equipment. The aircraft industry is operating at only 55 percent of capac-

ity. Across the defense industry there appears to be more than 30 percent idle capacity, whereas the desired level (on the basis of economic efficiency of production) is about 7 percent.[50] Chapter 5 will deal in depth with the argument that this extra capacity is desirable for possible mobilization. However, the capacity utilization referred to here is based on normal, one-shift production. In the event of multishift operation, considerable extra production potential would exist—even if the industry was operating at an economically efficient plant and equipment utilization level. The industry's production surge capability is limited by the availability of parts and critical production labor skills, not by a lack of plant capacity or design engineers. Thus, from an economic perspective, what is happening is a failure of the market to eliminate the "weak sisters." Scherer has defined a "sick industry" as one having "capacity much in excess of current and probable future needs, and rigidities which retard the reallocation of capital and/or labor toward growth industries."[51] The data in this book make it clear that the U.S. defense industry today fits well within this definition.

As Bain (and others) would argue, the high prices are directly attributable to the high concentration in the defense industry. This is also certainly the case in many areas of subcontracting and parts supply where there is essentially a single source, and thus very high prices.

In general, it would appear that each of these reasons alone is a factor in the high cost of defense equipment and that it is the combination of these causes that is making prices so exceptionally high.

Consider next the profit of each firm as a measure of the market's effectiveness. The criterion used by the Department of Defense for its profit negotiations—return on sales[52]—indicates that the negotiated, pretax profit rate (depending upon the type of contract and the overall defense economic conditions) ranges from a high (such as at the peak of the Vietnam War) for a "firm, fixed-price contract" level of over 11 percent down to a "cost-plus-fixed-fee" contract level of around 6.5 percent.[53] Though these negotiated levels are often cited by the DoD, they are largely meaningless. What matters to industry is the actual results achieved at the end of the contract period. The realized return-on-sales rate for the same Vietnam War period was around 4.9 percent;[54] it dropped to about 4.7 percent for the post-Vietnam period.[55] The realized profits were about half the negotiated profits.

This difference can be attributed to the responsibility of the contractor

for his "buy-in" or for technical or schedule problems that developed
during the contract, to "changes" imposed by the government but not
fully compensated, or to costs disallowed after the fact through government auditing (typically there is a 2 percent disallowance for
"unallowable expenses"). When compared with the profit for manufacturing industries in the civilian sector having high concentration ratios
and similar types of products, the return on sales for the defense industry
is about one-half that achieved in the commercial world by "defense-
oriented" companies and around one-third that of purely civilian firms.[56]
The lack of regulation, public visibility, accountability, and renegotiation
partly explains the difference between the civilian and the defense profits.
However, Baumol presents another explanation, more structural in
nature: A monopsonistic buyer can control the seller's profit to be under
that which would come from a market economy.[57] Most likely, the actual
cause is a combination of both explanations. In any case, it is clear that
the high profit Bain expects[58] for a highly concentrated industry does not
materialize in the defense industry, at least in terms of the criterion
(return on sales) which the government uses in measuring defense-
industry profits.

The low return on sales gives the government's contract negotiators
considerable pride. They feel that this low profit rate indicates that they
have done a good job in protecting the public's interests. A 1976 survey
confirmed that the contract negotiators consider it their job to attack the
profits of the defense suppliers.[59] This is the wrong perspective for these
negotiators to have; rather, they should attempt to reduce the total price
of the equipment, of which profit is only a small percentage. If the cost
base could be reduced significantly, perhaps even by allowing a slightly
higher profit, the government (and therefore the public) would be far better off—particularly if this increased profit could be reinvested to achieve
higher productivity and if its presence resulted in healthier, more effective
defense-industry suppliers.

Next, consider return on investment, the primary profit criterion by
which industry assesses the success of an operation. Here the picture is
much less clear. A Government Accounting Office (GAO) study showed a
slightly lower return on total capital invested by defense contractors versus comparable civilian-oriented contractors (11.2 percent versus 15.4
percent).[60] However, it was clear from this study that the top 12 firms had
a higher return on investment for their defense business (12.9 percent).

Another study of 145 major contracts at 37 major contractor facilities showed a 26 percent return on total capital invested.[61] Thus, the difference appears to depend on the corporation's size. The problems of profit for the small contractors and subcontractors will be discussed later; however, it is appropriate to note here that the high profits of the large firms are due not only to their bargaining power, but also to the fact that they often are utilizing a considerable amount of government-owned plant space and equipment. Additionally, these large firms are receiving government money (progress payments), which makes their capital needs relatively low and thus their return on investment quite high.

A Forbes Magazine study showed the "aerospace" and "defense industry" return on equity and return on total capital to be higher than the total U.S. industry levels (16.5 percent to 12.9 percent and 11.3 percent to 9.7 percent, respectively).[62] However, a 1969 study by the Logistics Management Institute (LMI) concluded that the average defense firm's return on investment is lower than that of a comparable civilian business.[63] In fact, that study went so far as to recommend a significant increase in profits in order to bring about the necessary investment in the defense area. The methods and the data of the GAO and LMI studies have been attacked. For example, Douglas Bohi showed significant problems with both of these analyses and concluded that there is no clear distinction between profits in the defense area and profits in the civilian sector.[64] Perhaps most important, the profit issue was considered in some depth by the Department of Defense in the mid-1970s (the "Profit '76" study). Here, for the first time, individual defense profit centers within large corporations were looked at, and the data were "cleansed" by certified public accountants. The indications were the same: Defense showed a significantly lower return on sales, but appeared to have a comparable or perhaps slightly higher return on investment, compared with the civilian sector.[65] These data confirmed two very significant points: that the profit for small defense companies was much less than for large ones and that there were very wide variations among segments of the defense industry.

The first conclusion one reaches (from the above studies) is that the return-on-investment figure for the defense industry depends on what data base is used—a few large firms that dominate the industry will show very high returns on investment, while the majority of the firms will appear to have relatively low returns. In some segments (such as shipbuilding) even the large firms have low returns on investment because (among other reasons) the firms are expected to buy their own equipment and facilities.

One frequent recommendation for improving the defense industry is that, since by using sales as the criterion for profit the Department of Defense is ignoring the investment criterion that industry uses, it would be far wiser for the DoD to base its profit negotiations and contracts on return on investment. This recommendation was made by Goodhue in 1972,[66] after the first round of profit studies, and was again made in the "Profit '76" study. In fact, because of this latter study, a new DoD profit policy was implemented in which 10 percent of the allowable profit is based upon a contractor's investment in plant and equipment. (Previously a contractor had been rewarded, by up to 5 percent of his profit, for his use of government equipment.) This is a step in the right direction, but still 50 percent of the profit is based upon sales (the remaining 40 percent is based on "risk"). Basing a larger percentage on investment seems to be called for.

This brings up the question of risk in the defense industry. The large prime contractors have frequently used risk as the rationale for the high profit they make on a relatively small investment. In 1968 Fisher and Hall looked at the rate of return in the aerospace industry (which in their analysis was second only to that in drugs, and exceeded that in automotives, chemicals, petroleum, rubber, steel, and other industries).[67] These investigators found that, even after adjustment for relative risk, the large aerospace companies had the second highest rate of return. They measured risk as the difficulty of forecasting future profits (the uncertainty or spread in the rate of return), and found that defense was a slightly higher risk than drugs, petroleum, rubber, food, steel, or textiles but a significantly lower risk than electrical machinery, automotive, office machinery, or chemicals. Thus, overall, they give the impression that the high profit of the large aerospace contractors is not, in fact, justified by the relative risk, but is more typical of the result of "monopolistic" pricing in the drug, chemical, petroleum, and rubber industries. Because of oligopoly, these high-profit civilian industries are able to mark up their prices greatly (far above a small percentage over costs), thus achieving a high return on their sales and therefore on their investments, whereas in defense the power of the monopsonistic buyer keeps the return on sales very low. However, many of the large defense firms can still achieve a high return on investment through the unique advantage of having a great deal of government plant space, equipment, and money, which means that they must invest very little.

Another argument in favor of increasing the return on investment in defense is the higher risk associated with the cyclic nature of the business. Scherer found that "the risk premium needed to lure capital into cyclically volatile industries does not, in fact, appear to be very large—not more than two to three percentage points on invested capital."[68] Thus, raising the defense industry's return on investment a few points might be justified. However, for many of the large firms the percentage already appears to be much higher than Scherer's figure.

As a final point in considering profits, it is important to look at the post-Vietnam trend toward increases in foreign military sales. Overall aerospace-industry earnings, after taxes, were 1.8 percent of sales in 1971; by 1974 the figure was up to 3.4 percent.[69] Certainly a significant part of this increase in earnings can be attributed to the increase in foreign military sales over this period. The "Profit '76" data showed that foreign military sales are about 2.5 times as profitable as military sales to the U.S. government. This is not primarily because the allowable profit is more than twice as much, but rather because the costs are significantly inflated by the contractors (since pricing is usually noncompetitive). With foreign military sales expected to be high for some years, and with the significant increase in defense production dollars that were available in the second half of the 1970s, it would be expected that defense-industry profits would rise accordingly. The important question is whether or not these profits are reinvested to improve economic efficiency in the development and production of defense goods. There is considerable concern about the likelihood of such reinvestment, not only because of the available excess capacity and the lack of price sensitivity in the industry but also because of the heavy debt of the large defense contractors.

The overall picture is not very bright. It is a combination of a weak market, heavy debt, inability to borrow, excess capacity, low profit on sales, perceived high risk, lack of capital investment, low productivity, and rising prices. To date the U.S. government has been the only source of help. (Besides raising the budget, it has already come to the aid of McDonnell-Douglas, General Dynamics, and Lockheed). Aerospace companies frequently complain that if they don't get the next contract they will be wiped out.

All of these "failures of the market" are rarely dealt with in Department of Defense discussions of weapons systems. Rather, the area that gets the most "management attention"—as well as speeches, headlines, and congressional hearings—is program overruns. Figure 3.4 shows the results of a GAO study of cost growth in selected major weapons programs. It shows an average growth, from program initiation through production, of approximately 90 percent. Since this study was done (in 1972), the DoD has initiated a number of major management improvements in its acquisition process, aimed specifically at reducing overruns. Some of these include such obvious steps as better initial cost estimating; others go to the heart of the issue by discussing such things as designing the equipment to be low in cost (not just designing it to a performance objective and then calculating what it will cost). Whether these actions have taken hold is an issue of debate. A DoD study on 1972 cost overruns showed a result similar to that of the GAO study: After adjustments for inflation and quantity changes (which the GAO study did not include) the DoD data showed a cost increase on an average program of over 6 percent per year. A similar analysis of the four subsequent years indicated that this percentage cost overrun was reduced by almost half, and that the 1976

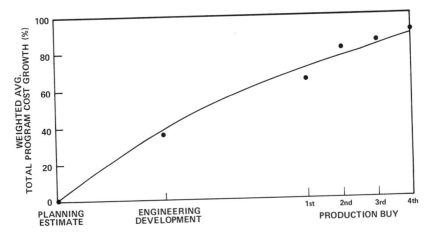

Figure 3.4
Total growth (not adjusted for inflation or change in quantity) of selected weapons-system programs: EA-6B, A-7E, Minuteman II and III, F-111, improved Hawk, M-60A2, TOW, and Mark-48 (total value approximately $30 billion).
Source: Comptroller General of the United States, "Acquisition of Major Weapon Systems," DoD report B-163058, July 1972.

level was approximately 3 percent per year—still not acceptable, but far better than it was less than five years before.

However, in 1979 the GAO issued a report stating the following:

Since 1969 the initial (planning) estimate (submitted by the DoD) has turned out to be approximately 100 percent below the actual costs of major systems. The later, more refined, development cost estimate given Congress prior to full-scale development has proven to be approximately 50 percent below actual procurement costs. The review . . . failed to find one example where the Department of Defense accurately estimated or overestimated the cost of any major weapon system. And once initial funds have been provided, it was found that a program is terminated only when the most extreme cost increases have occurred.[70]

In responding to this analysis the Department of Defense observed that, of these increases, 30 percent were due to inflation and 28 percent to quantity changes. The rest were acknowledged to be due to more "controllable" items. The results of the 1976 DoD study of annual overrun rates and the 1972 and 1979 GAO studies of total program overruns appear to indicate that the DoD is doing somewhat better in managing weapons-system development (after adjustments are made for the effects of inflation), but still has a long way to go towards achieving a desirable level of cost control.

Nonetheless, a 1976 comparison with other government programs (done in similar fashion to the above-noted DoD study) shows that the DoD does a far better job of managing complex, high-risk, interdisciplinary programs than most other government agencies.[71] For example, it notes that the Department of Transportation's urban mass transit program, the Energy Research and Development Administration's programs, the Veterans' Administration's programs, and the Washington Metro transit system had percentage overruns more than twice as large as that of the Department of Defense. The Federal Highway Administration had five times as large and the Appalachian Regional Commission ten times as large a percentage overrun. A query to the *New York Times'* Information Bank about "non-defense government program overruns" resulted in a 44-page list of citations of news coverage in this category for 1976 and the first half of 1977. Defense is not unique in having program overruns. They appear to be symptomatic of the government's way of doing business—specifically, of the budget process, in which the requestor is better off coming in with a low budget estimate[72] to get his program started and asking for additional funds if problems develop than he would be submitting a realistic budget and/or contingencies for likely problems, which he will be unable to defend at the program's initiation. (Contingencies shown in initial planning always look like "poor management" to the reviewer, who assumes that if a problem is foreseeable it should be avoidable. Actually, of course, rarely is a program completed at a cost below that budgeted. Thus, there is a systematic bias, which should be planned for, in the direction of overruns. The task of the Department of Defense in this area is to minimize these cost overruns. A combination of better budgeting (covering likely costs and likely contingencies), improved management of individual programs, and corrective actions in the overall defense industry (such as those suggested in chapter 12) would have the desired effect.

3.3 Summary

In considering the conduct and performance of the defense industry it is critically important that one recognize the great degree of regulation present, in spite of the fact that defense is not normally listed as a regulated industry. This regulation is unique in kind, in that the regulator is also the buyer. With so much involvement on the part of the buyer in the operation of the supplier, there can be no free market at work. Yet the Department of Defense, the defense industry, and the Congress continue to perpetuate the myth that a free market is in operation, and count on the invisible hand of this market to produce economic efficiency.[73]

Perhaps the dominant characteristic of the conduct of defense business is the lack of competition for most of the dollars involved. Yet this is often hard to understand in view of the fierce rivalry that takes place between a few firms when the DoD initiates competitive bidding for the development of a new generation of weapons. During this early research-and-development phase of a program, a few very large firms (often only two or three) are competing for a program that will eventually be worth billions of dollars (over many years) during its development and production phases. Thus, millions are often spent on the proposal activities for these few initial contract awards. The DoD picks up proposal costs as overhead expenses, so this is also inefficient use of defense money, since most of the proposal dollars are spent not on clever designs but on enhancing the proposal. These proposal efforts often drag on for years, during which the high uncertainty of the firm's future business forces it to take extreme risks in the "all or nothing" environment and discourages long-term planning.

Once the selection for this initial development effort has been made, the remainder of the program—product development, which may last over ten years, and then long-term production and product support—is normally conducted in a sole-source environment, where the contractor is in essentially a monopoly position and the government is dependent upon that producer for military equipment that it badly wants and for which it will usually pay whatever is asked. This distinction between the competition for an award and the competition during the execution of the program is the primary difference between military acquisitions and civilian business. It is a point frequently missed by those who argue that defense has a large amount of competition. The data clearly confirm this absence of competition on defense procurements. Even the DoD acknowledges that over 60 percent of defense dollars are awarded on a sole-source basis, and that the share of the dollars in this category has been increasing. However, even when an award was initially made on a competitive basis, once the DoD is "locked into" a sole source, that producer immediately begins to make changes to the program—all of which are "in the government's interests," but are bid under sole-source conditions. As a result of these "changes," the average contract grows by at least 45 percent, thus increasing the total dollars awarded in noncompetitive fashion. Even for the majority of the dollars awarded on a "competitive basis" the criterion normally used is not price, but technical performance. Less than 8 percent of the total DoD dollars are awarded solely on the basis of price competition.

Because of this fact (that almost all of the defense acquisition dollars are awarded as a result of technical competitions, changes to a single firm's contract after it has won the original competition, or sole-source awards to the only firm involved in a particular project), and since the majority of the subcontract dollars are similarly awarded to sole-source producers or to a firm's sister divisions (as a result of vertical integration), well over 90 percent of the defense contract dollars are not awarded on the basis of price competition or in the presence of any incentives that would drive down the costs.

The result is that equipment costs rise continuously, significantly above the rate attributable to inflation. After corrections for inflation and reduced quantities, the unit cost for defense equipment has been rising at an exponential rate—in most cases, over 5 percent per year. Thus, with decreasing total procurement dollars available, the quantities of military equipment procured each year have gone down significantly. Associated with these reduced quantities are very low production rates in the factories—in many cases down to almost zero, and in some extreme cases (for example, munitions plants) *actually* zero. There low rates keep the DoD from realizing economies of scale and production "labor learning." Thus, there is a "feedback system" in operation, wherein the high unit costs mean lower quantities and therefore still higher unit costs.

At the same time, increased performance is demanded of each new generation of equipment, which raises unit cost still farther. Since performance has been the primary goal of new systems and new technology, equipment cost has until very recently not been a design criterion for equipment in the defense sector. It is still a very minor consideration. Systems are not designed primarily to be produced in large quantities, but rather to achieve state-of-the-art technical performance. Thus, they are difficult and expensive to reproduce (even in comparison with Soviet systems, which have been designed for producibility). This high production cost is further compounded by frequent technical and quantity changes, which wreak havoc with production plans and result in continuous modification, expediting, and cost increases. Overall, the defense industry has low and decreasing productivity.

Not only is there a lack of cost-reducing incentives, but even the normal defense contracting incentives are cost-maximizing (for example, cost-plus-fee contracts for development, and production contract awards based upon the cost of the prior production program). With such incentives there is a lack of pressure to keep down labor and material costs—these can simply be passed on to the Department of Defense, and, because of the increased cost base, cause profits to rise directly (since contract fees are awarded as a percentage of total cost).

The Department of Defense negotiates profit rate with its contractors on the basis of sales. These negotiated profit rates tend to be low, thus generating very little cash for the large sales dollars and discouraging investment. However, the important parameter for industry is actually return on investment. In the defense industry we find very wide differences in return on investment, both by size of firm and by segment of the industry. Profits are far greater for the larger firms, which have both bargaining power and the use of a large amount of government plant space and equipment. In spite of "uniform profit policies" on the part of the government, some industry segments (for example, shipbuilding) have a very low return on investment and others (such as missiles) have a very high return. (This, too, may be largely attributable to the amount of government plant space and equipment.) Where the return on investment is low there are significant problems in even getting contractors to work for the defense industry. During the 1970s, almost every major ship-builder had the Navy in court with large "claims" against the government because of disagreements on contracts, and in some cases ships were built under injunction—certainly not an environment that leads to efficient operation. Similarly, among smaller firms, such as the subcontractors and parts suppliers, one finds a rapidly diminishing interest in defense business and therefore an erosion of the competitive nature of the business at this level as well.

The net result of this lack of price competition (especially after the initial R&D award) and the presence of incentives for cost increases throughout the defense market is significant cost growth in defense procurements. This is seen on almost all contracts. The cost growth comes primarily from negotiated changes to the contract, under a sole-source environment, and through overruns on contracts that have intentionally been bid very low (when there was competition at the initial stages of the program, and with the contractor knowing that he will later be reimbursed by the government under cost-based contract terms).

In spite of the obvious evidence of economic inefficiencies in defense acquisition, there is an almost total absence of any consideration of the industry's overall efficiency on the part of the Department of Defense or the U.S. government in general—again, because of the assumption that the free market is operating and achieving economic efficiency. The absence of an organization concerning itself with the overall problems of the defense industrial base, combined with the rigid application of uniform rules to nonuniform cases, exaggerates the differences among the segments of the industry and results in continued and growing inefficiencies. Individual programs are optimized in terms of their own production rates, timing, and other such factors, but no consideration is given to what these will do in combination with other programs to the overall economic efficiency of the defense industry. Similarly, no consideration is given to the effects of wide cycles in demand—at both the industry level and the plant level—on labor efficiency. In fact, although cyclic behavior in the defense industry has been the case for over two hundred years, it is always treated as unexpected.

What is most surprising, perhaps, is that although the Department of Defense does a great amount of planning in its budget process and in its force structure, and although it is the only buyer in an extremely concentrated industry, it makes no use of its position to achieve overall efficiency in its supplier base. Rather, it encourages only initial, "all or nothing" competition on programs, and the losers become dependent upon the government for their survival.

Clearly, traditional theory of economic behavior in a free market does not apply to the defense industry, and thus many of the actions that have been taken under the assumption that the theory is applicable have not had the desired effects. Today there are very serious economic problems and dangerous economic trends in the defense industry. Their combined impact is weakening the military posture of the United States, and has the potential to become even more critical in the years ahead unless significant changes are brought about.

4 Research and Development

The Department of Defense supports between one-third and one-fourth of all the scientists and engineers in the United States,[1] and has commensurate power in influencing the types of research to be performed and the products to be developed.[2] Over half of the approximately $40 billion spent in the United States each year on research and development comes from the federal government, and of this national defense accounts for more than half.[3]

This $10 billion or more spent yearly by the Department of Defense is not by itself what makes defense research and development so critically important. Rather, it is the fact that the United States bases its overall defense posture almost entirely on "technological superiority" that makes R&D a central focus for the DoD and therefore for the defense industrial base.

For military reasons, much of the technology being explored in defense R&D is on the very leading edge. Because of the high technical risk and the large expenditures required, the government tends to pay for all military R&D work—usually on a cost-reimbursement basis. Thus, there is the opportunity for firms to take part in this work with essentially no risk. The federal government makes defense R&D even more attractive by allowing a firm to retain patent rights for any potential civilian work, while the government retains only the rights for government use.[4] This has the desirable feature of encouraging transfer of government-sponsored R&D into the civilian sector. The advanced nature, the large dollar value, and the low risk of defense R&D are often cited as major inducements for firms to show interest in defense business.

Table 4.1 gives a product breakdown of the defense R&D budget, and table 4.2 shows the distribution by mission areas. Notice that about 60 percent of the dollars go for full-scale development of tactical and strategic systems. In this phase, designs that have been demonstrated to be feasible are readied for full testing and production. Much of the money spent here is for routine items such as drawings and data rather than major technological breakthroughs. To make matters worse, the cost of an individual weapon system's full-scale development has been growing significantly in the post-Vietnam era. Thus there have been fewer new systems developed and less technological innovation. Less than 20 percent of the total R&D money is going for "research and advanced development" (the so-called technology base), which is the critical area of really new ideas and feasibility demonstrations. Here too there are some

Table 4.1
Distribution of R&D Funds by Program Area, 1975

Aerospace:	
Missile programs	22.4%
Aircraft programs	17.1%
Space programs	5.5%
Ships[a]	7.0%
Ordnance and combat vehicles	5.5%
Management and support	10.0%
Other equipment	19.3%
Basic research and technical development	13.2%

a. The fact that the first ship of any class is funded not by R&D money but by production money artificially lowers the data in this category by a substantial amount.

Table 4.2
Distribution of R&D Funds by Mission Area, 1976

Research and advanced development	19%
Strategic programs (full-scale development)	24%
General-purpose programs (full-scale development)	36%
Intelligence and communications	7%
Management and support (including test ranges)	14%

Source: Former Secretary of Defense Donald Rumsfeld, Budget Committee testimony on 1977 defense budget.

undesirable trends, such as the percentage of dollars going to government laboratories (up from 23 percent in 1968 to 43 percent by 1971, and staying at that level through the 1970s).[5] In view of the impact of these expenditures on future U.S. technological superiority, if a large share of this work is to be done in government laboratories then methods must be devised for measuring the quality of the work. Perhaps more of this work should be done in industry, where the incentives are greater and effectiveness is easier to measure.[6]

The shifting of more funds into routine full-scale development work and the reduction of basic research and advanced technology efforts are but two of the many negative post-Vietnam trends in defense research and development. Four other such negative trends follow.

- The development time has lengthened for each succeeding generation of weapons system. (For example, the Polaris A-1 took five years, the Polaris A-3 took six years, the Poseidon C-3 over nine years, and the Trident C-4 was projected to take over eleven years.)[7] This results in higher program costs and the deployment of obsolete equipment.
- The large expenditures on engineering of complete weapons systems (especially in full-scale development) result in significantly less money going to the critical advancement of new components and materials—which have traditionally been the basis for the invention of really new military systems.
- There has been a clear shift of R&D funding from the small, inventor-led companies to the large firms. The latter are the only ones capable of the very large efforts associated with full-scale development of weapons systems, but they are certainly not the only sources of new inventions.
- The extreme R&D emphasis on equipment performance has rapidly increased the cost of military equipment (figure 4.1 gives an example) and thus greatly reduced the quantities of equipment procured. Performance has been increased, but at too high a cost. By contrast, in the civilian world R&D is used to reduce cost and improve performance simultaneously.

4.1 The Impact of Industrial Structure

The structure of the defense industry, combined with the way in which the Department of Defense does its business, has created undesirable trends

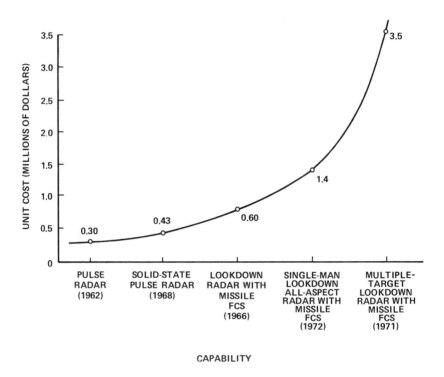

Figure 4.1
Unit cost versus performance increase: air-to-air radars. Cost represents investment cost for radar and fire-control system (FCS) per aircraft. Dates of implementation are not always in sequence, owing to the occasional earlier implementation of a higher performance system, but the overall trend has been toward higher performance as time evolves.

in military research and development in the post-Vietnam era. Of particular concern are the high concentration; the heavy (almost exclusive) emphasis on technology, from management through the labor force; the large amount of vertical integration (from parts through systems, and from R&D through production); the very high barriers to entry into the military business; and the distinctly "dual" economy, in which the prime contractors control the small subcontractors and the parts suppliers. Each of these factors influences the military R&D decision process, from requirements through contract awards and program results.

Defense R&D is highly concentrated. In fiscal 1977, eight companies received approximately 45 percent of all the dollars spent.[8] How does this concentration affect military R&D decisionmaking and the effectiveness of the work? Scherer pointed out that the more concentrated markets are, the more intensely R&D is encouraged by the firms involved.[9] However, more recent data show questionable correlation between concentration and amount of R&D spending. Anyway, most military R&D is government-funded, and since World War II the Department of Defense has been successful in its desire to increase the emphasis on R&D.[10] This desire appears to match the objectives of the defense firms. However, growth in R&D has often come at the expense of production. Since 1945, the ratio of defense R&D to production expenditures has gradually increased from around 5 percent to a peak of over 50 percent, with cyclical variations during periods of conflict (figure 4.2). There is certainly no other major U.S. industrial sector with such a high ratio.[11] (The typical civilian-product levels are 2–5 percent.)

The combination of this high level of defense R&D and the concentration of the work in a very small number of firms, particularly in any given product area, clearly encourages fierce oligopoly rivalry. The firms push R&D extensively in order to win the next big contract and to keep out new entrants. (The same eight firms that had a significant share of the R&D dollars in 1977 received 25 percent of the defense production dollars spent that year.) Additionally, the Department of Defense permits firms to charge an "independent research and development" account, which is based on a percentage of the firm's defense sales;[12] this amplifies the concentration.

This concentration of defense R&D has very distinct impacts on the R&D decision process, and therefore on military R&D effectiveness. These large firms emphasize risk minimization, and thus tend not to push new ideas or applications. Research is more likely to be done on increasing the performance of a device, rather than on developing some totally new device. This "evolutionary" R&D tends to match the forms and objectives of the firms and the DoD, and even to address the questions these organizations are willing to ask.[13] (More far-reaching questions pose a threat to existing organizations—an airplane manufacturer would not want the usefulness of airplanes questioned, nor would a military pilot.) There is ample corroboration of the "application orientation," or the innovative (versus inventive) role, of the large firms.[14] Basically this comes from the institutional inertia in these firms—which is due partly to their cumbersome internal management decision process.

Consider next the extreme emphasis, within the defense industry, on

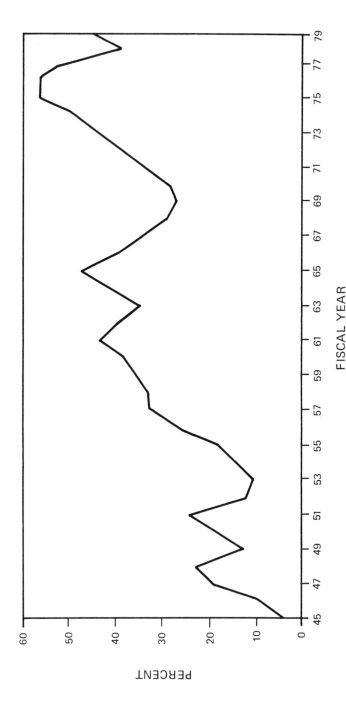

Figure 4.2
Ratio of R&D outlays to procurement outlays for defense (in terms of constant 1976 dollars).

technology. Part of this comes from the military wanting the best possible equipment, with the implication that cost is less important than performance. But part comes from the fact that the management of the defense firms is largely in the hands of engineers who have moved up through the organization, from designer to program manager to corporate officer. (By contrast, the executives in civilian firms often come from finance, marketing, legal, or production departments.) In the aerospace industry it is common for 30–50 percent of a factory's workforce to be made up of engineers and scientists. The presence of so many engineers in a plant not only results in very significant expenditures for "routine" engineering work on full-scale developments, but also results in a considerable amount of R&D money being spent on products already in production.[15] Many of the changes that result from this kind of R&D improve capability only marginally but increase cost significantly. Some have referred to this as the technological imperative—"because we can do it, we must do it." In essence, these engineers are establishing military "needs" based on promised technological advances. The promises are well received by the government's engineers (both civilian and military), largely irrespective of the likely cost impacts of the changes.

As discussed previously, vertical integration has been increasing in the defense industry as large firms have been acquiring their suppliers. The effect of this has been to place even greater R&D emphasis on the engineering work done by the dominant prime contractors and to eliminate the drive for technological innovation and invention at the subcontractor and parts supplier levels—which are the historically critical levels for advances in military hardware.

The second kind of "vertical integration" that exists in most sectors of the defense industry arises when one firm takes a product from research through development and production. This tie between R&D and production is the key structural link in the defense industry, and influences the R&D decisionmaking process greatly. Because of this kind of integration there is an R&D emphasis on items that have significant production potential in the near term, since the firm always has in mind the need to keep its factories full. Government-funded R&D is not a business unto itself, but only an entrée into the production business. The result is a significant pressure to put all developments into production, even those originally intended as competing alternatives to each other.[16] (In the Soviet Union, where R&D and production are separate, there are typically more alternatives developed, relative to the number of designs that go into production, than in the United States.)

This tie of R&D to production means that each plant, or at least each firm, must have its own R&D capability and its own production capability. In view of the normally very small number of items in a defense production program, this tends to result in inefficient production, yet interestingly this does not cause the R&D programs to emphasize production costs.

The barriers to entry into defense work discourage new R&D ideas—particularly the kind that lead to significant qualitative changes—by maintaining the status of the large defense firms and keeping out small, inventor-led firms.[17] Other barriers keep out even the large civilian-oriented firms,[18] which would tend to bring in the lower-cost philosophy of the commercial world. Thus, the overall effect of these barriers to entry is to reduce both the likelihood of new inventions and the potential for emphasis on cost-reducing R&D efforts in the defense industry.

While the prime defense contractors tend to have the highest ratios of R&D to capital expenditures of all sectors in the U.S. economy (the aerospace industry has six to ten times the ratio of R&D to capital expenditures of the auto industry),[19] the smaller defense firms (lower-tier subcontractors and parts suppliers) are unable to afford large R&D expenditures, are required to make relatively more significant capital investments, and have lower profits. The availability of government plant space, production equipment, and financing and the large IR&D allowances of the prime contractors also operate against the smaller firms. This "dual economy" is rarely recognized in establishing DoD policies—in terms of either profit, source selection, or R&D policy—but it has a distinct impact on overall R&D decisionmaking; for example, when the preponderance of R&D money goes to the large prime contractors for full-scale development and production changes, critical work on component technology (often done by smaller firms) does not get proper emphasis.

These structural characteristics on the supply side are matched and reinforced by the structure of the demand side. For example, institutional inertia—one of the most significant negative characteristics of a monopsony buyer—is particularly evident in such a large institution as the

Department of Defense, which is fully committed to maintaining things as they are. Thus, the "requirements" for defense equipment tend to perpetuate themselves because of parochial interests, both within the buying community (for example, pilots do not want airplanes replaced by unmanned, remotely piloted vehicles) and in the defense industry (tank makers don't want tanks to be considered obsolete). Before becoming Secretary of Defense, James Schlesinger, in commenting about the DoD said, "Large hierarchical organizations tend to be remarkably efficient mechanisms for the suppression of new ideas and alternatives."[20]

4.2 The Impact of the Acquisition Process

The way in which the government does its business with the defense industry amplifies the effects of the industry's structure on military R&D decisionmaking. For example, the high public visibility and accountability of the R&D decisionmakers places them in a position in which they feel they must minimize the risk associated with a particular R&D program. Thus, there is a tendency to give the business to large, well-established firms, and to select very conventional ideas for development. Such results need not follow from the desirable requirements of visibility and accountability. High risks should be taken on promising R&D projects. It is this high-risk approach that has traditionally resulted in the qualitative breakthroughs necessary to maintain technological superiority over the long run. However, the decisionmakers should state explicitly that contracts to relatively unproven firms or fundings for relatively unconventional ideas are high-risk approaches for which it may be necessary to develop "backup" alternatives.

A second impact of the Department of Defense's acquisition process on R&D is that it encourages low initial cost estimates in order to get R&D programs through the kickoff approval rounds (including the budget cycle). This requirement of "buying in" not only limits the competition to the large firms—who are making enough on their current production programs to afford it, and who are looking for a sole-source position in the production follow-on to the new R&D program—but also encourages these firms to make significant design changes during the R&D program. These changes increase the cost and stretch out the development schedule, and thereby enable the contractor to modify his contract and recover the initial "buy-in" costs. Such cost and schedule changes create for the outside world the appearance of program overrun and slippage that has given military R&D the reputation for mismanagement it has had for many years.

Since the initial R&D program on which the competition is held is usually for a relatively small amount of money, and since the bids are made extremely attractive by the bidders, the primary criterion for selection is the application of new technology for improved performance. Thus, each bidder is encouraged to make high performance the stated objective of its designs. This is in contrast to the design objectives of the civilian world, which include unit production cost as well as performance.

The combination of competition early in the R&D program and sole-source contracting through the remainder of the program provides no incentives for cost reductions either in the R&D program or for the production program. In fact, the contractor is encouraged to increase the development and production costs as much as possible to maximize profits. In a sole-source environment, there is no risk attached to doing so. This lack of incentive for cost reduction should be compared with the case in the civilian sector, where competition is maintained into production and therefore technology is used to drive down the cost of systems rather than solely to increase performance, as in the defense area.

These acquisition practices of the Department of Defense mutually reinforce the requirement for each large firm to have the capacity for both R&D and production. Thus, both the industry's structure and the DoD's acquisition process greatly diminish the possibility that production will be done by a different firm than the one that did the R&D. This prevents natural competition at the beginning of production.

There is a belief, held particularly within the procurement community, that by mandating competition during the initial R&D phase, Department of Defense officials are satisfying the legislative requirements to have competition on government procurements. Thus, there is a tendency to take new ideas submitted by "outsiders" or small firms and have those put out for competition. Through the Request for Proposal (RFP) process the new idea becomes widely disseminated, and the ensuing competition is usually won by a large firm that spends a considerable amount of money on the proposal effort and cross-subsidizes to lower its bid for the proposed R&D activity. In this way new ideas from outside the existing defense industrial community are greatly discouraged by government procedures.

Other factors that discourage the smaller firms from defense R&D are the long development times (seven to ten years), which prevent the smaller firms from staying in until the time for the big production dollars, and the fact that by the mid-1970s venture capital for the small firms had completely dried up.[21]

The last of the major influences of the defense acquisition process on R&D decisionmaking is the Department of Defense's lack of an industrywide perspective in major R&D decisions. Essentially, each major program is treated independently, without regard for the long-term maintenance of a viable R&D establishment. This contrasts with the industrywide perspective taken by almost every other country in the world. The result of this program-by-program perspective is that individual firms go through booms and busts whose uncertainties are amplified by the vagaries of the annual budget process. This causes a very short-term perspective on R&D work in most firms, and also discourages many creative scientists from even going into defense research.

4.3 Summary

The importance of research and development to the Department of Defense make it critical that R&D dollars be spent efficiently and effectively, yet there are problems in this area and the trends are in the wrong direction. The lengthening development time for new equipment has been raising the cost of development and often resulting in the deployment of obsolete equipment. Also, because of the increased costs of developing new equipment and of completing equipment already in production, fewer and fewer different types of systems are being developed and produced and thus flexibility is decreasing.

Because the intense rivalry for the few new programs is based on technological competition rather than real price competition, little if any cost reduction results. In fact, the wrong costs are usually considered in the competition for the development program—the evaluation is based on the bids for development rather than on the larger production and support costs inherent in the different designs. In addition, the government spends most of its R&D money with the large companies, and the small "venture" R&D firms have had increasing difficulty in obtaining support. Together these two factors reduce the opportunity for obtaining the more innovative and less inexpensive designs the smaller firms have often been able to come up with. Similarly, the decreasing amount of R&D being done at the parts-supplier levels discourages both the development of lower-cost parts and the exploitation of new parts technology. Finally, an increasing share of government R&D is being done in government laboratories, where a significant portion of the money goes to "management" of R&D. Greater efficiency could be achieved by spending these dollars in the private sector, where the profit motive is present.

The cumulative effect of these factors of inefficiency and improper incentives is that less R&D money is going for new inventions and innovations (either for economic or strategic advancements), and more for routine product engineering, data gathering, and so on, and for supporting the large teams of engineers and support people at each of the major defense-industry establishments.

The Department of Defense's excellent past record in the R&D area is demonstrated by America's proven military technological superiority. However, the DoD will have to change its way of doing business and the structure of its supporting industry in order to keep pace with rapid geopolitical and technological changes and in order to maintain its technological superiority into the twenty-first century.

5 Industrial Mobilization Capability

The most common rationale for the economically inefficient structure of the defense industry (for example, the excess of plant space and equipment) is that it is needed for industrial mobilization in time of war. This argument, and the current ability of the U.S. defense industry to respond rapidly to increased demand for production outputs in times of national emergency, must be examined.

America's planning for industrial mobilization has always been inadequate (and often nonexistent), and timely surge in production of military goods has also been deficient.[1] In the early months (or even years) of conflicts, the United States has always been able to mobilize troops far faster and more effectively than it has been able to arm them.[2] The current era is no exception, but the consequences today may be far more significant for three reasons: A future war may be far shorter than previous ones; the development and production times for the sophisticated equipment of today are far longer; and the potential adversary, the Soviet Union, appears to be far more prepared both in quantities of available military equipment and in industrial preparedness (including higher current production rates of military equipment). Clearly, in the long run, the industrial might of the United States could be fully brought to bear and would be overwhelming in any "traditional" conflict. However, the difference between America's potential long-run industrial mobilization strength and that which is currently either planned for or readily available is quite great.

Our most recent experience, the Vietnam War, was perhaps not typical of future conflicts. We were fighting a greatly underequipped force in a war that built up very slowly, allowing ample time for industrial response. With the Congress authorizing greater funds than could be utilized, it still took the U.S. defense industry four years to increase production to the levels demanded by the military requirements. Although this response was not made under conditions of all-out mobilization (full impact on the civilian economy), it still is indicative of the slow responsiveness of the U.S. defense industry today.

The many people who still think the United States could quickly resume the rate of industrial military production that was present at the end of World War II neglect the increased complexity of today's military equipment. The production process is more difficult, the skill levels required are higher, the material lead times longer, the part tolerances much tighter, and the designs far more complex. They also neglect the long buildup time allowed by America's physical isolation from that war's beginnings in Europe. A comparable interval may not be available in the future. Thus, a critical question in the area of strategic industrial responsiveness is the likely intensity and duration of a future military conflict.

The opinions regarding likely military scenarios vary widely. Some analysts go so far as to suggest that the next war is likely to be so short that industrial mobilization planning would have no value and the only thing that would matter is the instantly available forces.[3] Others go even farther and suggest that all-out nuclear destruction is the likely consequence of any war that is started. They base this on the fact that the United States, having significantly lower quantities of fighting equipment than the Soviet Union, would be forced into nuclear conflict, with its consequent destruction of both the American and the Soviet industrial societies. These people too argue there is no value in industrial planning for mobilization or for postwar recovery. However, others argue that these are U.S. perspectives, not matched by the Soviet concepts of war in the nuclear era.[4] These thinkers point to Soviet policy statements viewing nuclear war as simply an extension of political actions and of conventional warfare, and note that the Soviets discuss, at length, both extended military conflicts and post-nuclear-war recovery. It has been amply demonstrated that the Soviets are taking significant actions in this direction.[5] This is seen in the fact that they have enough equipment for postwar occupation, in the dispersion of their defense plants and the hardening of their equipment, and even in their actions with regard to civil preparedness.[6]

The United States and the NATO allies must be prepared for the short war by having sufficient equipment for the reserves and for sustained operation under brief high-intensity conditions. However, we must also plan and spend some money to improve our industrial surge and mobilization capability to respond in crisis periods. The costs are small, but the potential effectiveness is high. It is the incremental return on investment (relative to the current defense posture) that must be emphasized. The increase in overall force effectiveness will be far greater for the few dollars spent on industrial preparedness for an extended conflict than if the same money were to be spent on adding a small number of pieces of equipment to the current forces.

In its 1975 annual report the Joint Committee on Defense Production asked the ten questions in table 5.1, which adequately summarize the

Table 5.1
The Joint Committee on Defense Production's Ten Questions on Industrial Preparedness

---

Does the United States have or can it rapidly develop adequate productive capacity for wartime needs?

Are the vital materials necessary to support military operations under various assumptions and for varying lengths of time now available to the government, or can they be made available to the government in sufficient time?

Does there exist an adequate mechanism for ensuring that standby or preparatory financial support is available to meet emergency needs?

Have measures been taken to ensure that there is an adequate manpower pool possessed of the requisite skills to carry out a conversion to a wartime economy?

Are contingency plans for converting from peacetime to wartime production adequate?

Has sufficient attention been paid in contingency planning to maintaining essential civilian production?

Do contingency plans make allowance for conversion to peacetime production upon the cessation of hostilities or termination of mobilization?

Has consideration been given to least-cost approaches to the problems of industrial mobilization?

Do ongoing readiness programs meet the test of minimum interference with the civilian economy consistent with ensuring industrial preparedness?

Are current readiness plans and programs keyed to realistic threat estimates and scenarios, or do they merely reflect the lessons learned from World War II and the Korean War?

---

uncertainties about industrial preparedness that still exist today. Another important consideration is whether a surge in industrial output is to be achieved under peacetime conditions or under all-out, wartime mobilization conditions. Until very recently, all Department of Defense planning was done under the assumption of wartime conditions, with total industrial mobilization (complete impact on the civilian sector). However, since World War II (through the Korea, Vietnam, and Middle East conflicts) the United States has decided to have both guns and butter—to achieve defense production surge capability without explicit impact to the civilian economy. No plans existed for this combination, and as a result it was not effectively achieved.

5.1 Evaluation of Current Programs

There are essentially four major efforts being made by the United States in the area of industrial-mobilization planning: the stockpiling of strategic raw materials, the planning done by the government and industry (characterized by the "1519" forms[7]), the machine-tool reserves (both in storage and in identified lines), and the war reserve materiel (WRM) inventory of finished military goods. In general, each of these four actions is desirable; what is not clear is whether they are sufficient, effective, or the most important things to be done.

In 1976 a study for the National Security Council (chaired by the Federal Preparedness Agency) showed that the current stockpiles of raw materials include many items not required for the likely scenarios and are missing many critical items.[8] The cost of the materials which the study said was needed was in the billions of dollars. The study recommended a major revision to the stockpiles and an annual update of the planning process so that the correct materials would be available for the future. However, the concern of special-interest lobbies with the raw-materials stockpiles makes such legislation difficult to obtain. In addition, implementation of this program would take a significant number of years, since the law requires that it must be done "without disruption of the market." Thus, for the present, there is a significant deficiency in this area. Of equal importance is the fact that, with current lead times for the manufacturing of complex military equipment, the time between release of material from the stockpiles and a piece of hardware coming off the production line for wartime use (even under wartime, priority conditions) is three to four years. In order to improve significantly the rate of delivery of military equipment to the troops, stockpiling at a later stage (castings, electronic parts, or even subassemblies) should be considered.

In 1976 a Defense Science Board task force was chartered to assess the effectiveness of industrial-mobilization planning. This group concluded that the current method is largely worthless and should be drastically revised.[9] The surge capability information the large contractors supply annually to the government in the "1519" forms is for individual programs only, and does not reflect the impacts of two programs in the same plant, or two programs using the same supplier. Also, these forms do not consider the "bottlenecks" at the subtier levels. And since the preparation of these forms is charged to company overhead, very little effort is expended on them. Thus, if required, this information is likely to be of almost no value. As previously noted, this was proved in 1974 when the Army tried to rapidly increase the production of tanks. Ample capacity existed at the prime-contractor level, but the only casting contractor did not come close to meeting the demand. The current planning process makes little attempt to determine the availability of critical subsystems or the existence of bottlenecks. Rather, the planning is done on a "universal" basis by the prime contractors only.

Additionally, the current planning system does not provide for emergency waiving of the "normal" defense procurement practices, such as competitive bidding, equal employment opportunities, and compliance with environmental and health requirements. Without special advance provisions, these practices would significantly constrain mobilization.

Next consider the machine tool program, the major elements of which are the Plant Equipment Packages (PEPs). These packages comprised active and idle production equipment identified as necessary to support specific weapon systems or components. Table 5.2 shows the percentage of plant equipment packages in each sector of the defense industry. In total, there are almost 35,000 pieces of industrial plant equipment assigned to approved PEPs. While an idle PEP provides additional potential production support, a PEP supporting active equipment is nothing more than an administrative tool to prevent the phaseout or disposition of underutilized equipment below a predetermined surge or mobilization production output level.

A 1976 Department of Defense investigation concerning the metal-cutting tools (a critical portion of the machine-tool reserve) owned and planned for industrial mobilization showed that the average age of such tools owned by the government is over twenty years and that those owned by the industry and "planned" for this function average over fifteen years. In view of the very rapid technological advances in the area of computer-controlled machine tools, it must be concluded that the vast majority of this machine-tool reserve equipment is obsolete. (A reassessment by the Army of its munitions mobilization line has confirmed this

Table 5.2
Percentage of Plant Equipment Packages in the Defense Industry, by Sector

Aircraft and helicopters	18%
Ammunition	50
Weapons (tactical missiles, bombs, and rockets)	12
Combat vehicles	9
Classified and other	11

finding, and the Army has a multi-billion-dollar modernization program underway.) The significant deficiency of some critical labor skills that would arise if some of these old machines were to be taken out of storage and reactivated has not been planned for at all.

A detailed 1976 Army study of the war reserve materiel—the finished goods that would be needed in the early days of a high-intensity conflict—showed that the stockpiles of finished goods and the spare parts to support them are grossly inadequate. Partly because of such studies, the Congress, in the second half of the 1970s, significantly increased the defense production account (25 percent yearly in 1976 and 1977). Even with these increases, and their effects three to four years later, there is still a gross mismatch between the stated requirements and the available stockpiles of WRM; and even if the current plans to purchase more equipment were to be carried out (which is not likely) there would still be in many minds a lot of uncertainty as to the adequacy of the stockpiles. There are two principal areas of concern: the vulnerability of the equipment stored in Europe (largely out in the open) and of the logistics routes (harbors, docks, and sea lanes), and the degradation in equipment performance under battle conditions (for example, the reduction in a weapon's probability of kill, and the very high attrition that is likely with modern equipment such as antitank, antiaircraft, and antiship missile systems). Both of these problem areas seem to indicate the need for greater quantities of equipment. The fact that defensive missile systems are so effective, and that therefore the losses of ships, planes, and tanks would be very high, was indicated by the 1973 Mideast War. The attrition would be even worse with the most recent missile systems, and many claim that current U.S. equipment budgeting and force-structure planning do not realistically consider this. Some say that the difference between the American and Soviet assumptions on these points partly accounts for the large differences in force size and rate of modernization between the two countries.

The criterion for any industrial-mobilization planning must be its effectiveness in a relative test, for example with the Soviet Union. Here the American and Soviet emphases differ considerably, in terms of both force size and industrial planning. Ultimately it comes down to the fact that the United States emphasizes quality and the Soviet Union emphasizes quantity (with the gap in quality narrowing rapidly). To generalize grossly, one could say that the U.S. posture today is based upon the assumption that "the Soviets have more equipment, but ours is better so we will win," whereas the Soviet planners take the position that "the United States has better equipment, but we will outlast them with our greater quantities." This asymmetry in basic planning partly accounts for the difference in industrial-mobilization planning on the two sides, but there is also the historical difference between America's isolated position in prior wars and the Soviet Union's "Stalingrad experiences." Thus, the Soviets place heavy emphasis on large stocks of finished goods and on continued high production of equipment. In addition, their planned economy provides high visibility, and perhaps more credibility, to their short-term industrial responsiveness. This demonstration of concern for industrial mobilization is achieved through such actions as planning to build both civilian products and military products (such as railroad cars and fighter aircraft) in the same plants so that conversion could take place rapidly, and dispersing and hardening production equipment so that it could continue to operate after an attack. Not only do these actions have considerable actual value for industrial mobilization; they also provide a stabilizing strategic factor by increasing the credibility of the Soviet Union's deterrent posture. (Similar U.S. measures would therefore likely have a stabilizing effect as well.)

Where does this leave the United States, on a net basis? Clearly, if deterrents fail and high-intensity conventional or tactical nuclear warfare begins, the Soviet Union is in a much better position in the short run with regard to current stocks of equipment, current rates of production, plans for industrial mobilization, and so on. However, in the long run the United States would be in the stronger position because of its far greater industrial might and its advanced technology. The Soviet Union recognizes this long-run U.S. advantage, and thus would attempt to move as rapidly as possible. The United States must strengthen its position for potential short and medium-length conflicts.

5.2 Theoretical Analysis

Figure 5.1 illustrates the prime analytical tool used in the past to address the wartime mobilization situation, the D-to-P model. Mobilization day (M-day) is assumed to coincide with the day on which the planned military deployment commences (D-day). In other words, there is assumed to be no industrial "warning time." Thus, the variables for the production planning process are the wartime materiel consumption rate $c(t)$; the initial production rate; and $P(t)$, the speed of response of production lines in increasing output to the maximum rate. At some future time (shown on Figure 5.1 as P-day) the production rate catches up with the attrition rate, and from that point on the defense industry is producing at a satisfactory rate to maintain at least a constant force level in the presence of attrition. (The excess allows for additional force increases.) Because the attrition rate is usually considerably higher than the initial production rate, a considerable amount of war reserve materiel (WRM) must be maintained as stock for the initial period of the conflict. This includes tanks, munitions, and the like as well as spare parts and supplies. Clearly, if t_1 (the time after which the production rate increases appreciably from its peacetime levels) is significantly longer than the expected duration of the war, there is little value in any industrial-preparedness planning.

This model provides a systematic approach for conducting cost-tradeoff analyses between investing in an increased production response and increasing inventories of war reserve materiel.[10] Of course, there is some minimum-cost combination of these two variables, with everything else held constant, at point P_3 shown in figure 5.2. However, the fact that

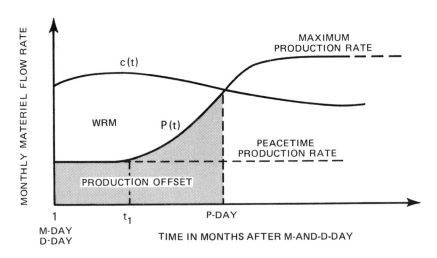

Figure 5.1
The D-to-P model. $P(t)$ is production rate; $c(t)$ is consumption rate; WRM (war reserve materiel) $= \int_D^P [c(t) - P(t)]$.

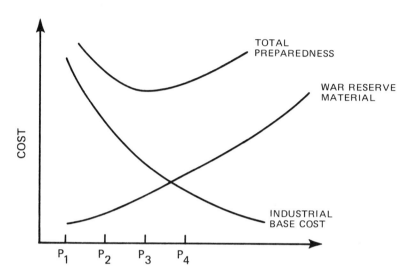

Figure 5.2
Preparedness cost-effectiveness analysis.

such variables as attrition rate and vulnerability of the stocked WRM must be considered, along with the wide variety of potential war scenarios (and their probability of occurrence), greatly complicates the analysis and introduces significant variations based on judgmental factors. Then, too, there are numerous industrial-preparedness measures that can be taken, many of which have different impacts. Table 5.3 presents some of these possible measures, and indicates what their initial impact would be relative to the D-to-P model. Clearly, many of these items would have significant impacts not only on industrial preparedness, but also on peacetime economic efficiency and even the structure of the industrial base. Thus, once again we see the strong interrelationship between strategic planning and economic efficiency in the defense industry.

To give some idea of the relative effectiveness of the industrial-preparedness measures listed in table 5.3 the information in figure 5.3 has been drawn for a hypothetical piece of tactical-warfare equipment. Conditions 1–3 assume a "warm base" (production already in effect), while cases 4–6 assume that the production line is initially "cold." Inventories of long-lead-time materiels and special tooling have significant impacts in both cases.

Another significant variable would be the degree of industrial-base

Table 5.3
Types and Impacts of Industrial-Preparedness Measures

	Impact			
	Decrease Lead Time	Increase Prod., Accel. Rate	Increase Max. Capacity	Reduce Requirements
Provide gov't facilities	×	×	×	–
Retain gov't facilities (PEP)	×	×	×	–
Additional special tooling	×	×	×	
Prestock mfg. mat'l and components	×	×	–	–
Develop multiple sources	–	×	×	–
Maintain warm base	×	×	–	–
Increase reliability of equipment	×	×	–	×
Identify substitute items	×	×	–	×
Develop wartime spec. changes	×	×	–	×
Use commercial items	×	×	–	×
Use standard electronic components	×	×	–	×

warning time relative to the force-mobilization date. The effect of this is shown in figure 5.4 for the same piece of equipment, starting from a cold base, with industrial warning times of up to six months. This concept of "turning on" the defense industry in anticipation of possible conflict, particularly in the case of long-lead-time parts and (possibly) selected labor, is very realistic—often there is at least six months' worth of "warning time" as international tensions increase. Under such conditions it is considered highly undesirable to begin force mobilization, because of its destabilizing characteristic; but this is far less the case for industrial activities. Yet current planning does not consider this distinct option of industrial mobilization in critical areas. In fact, the predominance of mobilization planning, throughout the history of the United States, has emphasized rapid increases in fighting troops—not in equipment.

A major problem in dealing with industrial-base planning for surge or mobilization is deciding which systems to plan for. The traditional answer has been "all of those currently in the force structure." This has two very significant defects: First, it means that in the panic of the initial period of mobilization there is a conflict for resources between those systems that

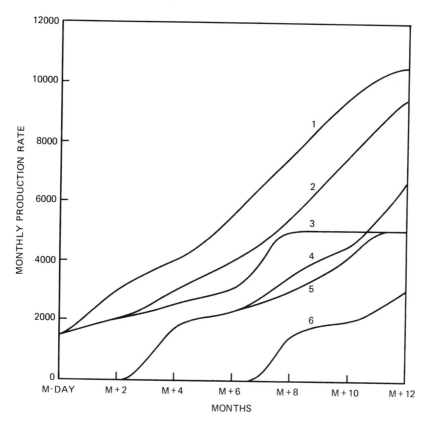

Figure 5.3
Comparison of some industrial-preparedness measures listed in table 5.3. (For these examples, "warm base" means current production on the order of 1,500 units per month.) (1) Warm base, prestocked manufacturing materials, additional special tooling; (2) warm base with only special tooling; (3) warm base alone; (4) cold base, prestocked materials, special tooling; (5) cold base with only prestocked materials; (6) cold base alone.

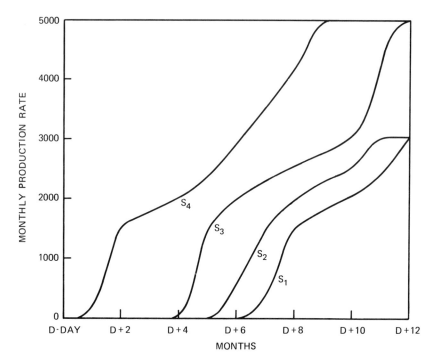

Figure 5.4
Impact of "warning time" on production rate (cold-base posture). S_1: D day = M day. S_2: D day = M + 30 days. S_3: D day = M + 60 days. S_4: D day = M + 180 days.

could be built in a relatively short time and those that will take years. In these cases, the systems that can be built quickly should get priority; work on the longer-term ones should wait a few months to eliminate any conflict. This would also result in far fewer systems having to be planned for in advance; thus, a far better job could be done on those few systems that are planned to have surge capability. Second, the present requirement that planning be done only for those systems currently in the inventory eliminates planning on many systems that could provide very useful wartime capability but for which there is no current force plan. A very clear example of this is the F-5 aircraft, which is in production in relatively large quantities but almost exclusively for foreign sales. Pilots could be trained to fly the F-5 in a much shorter period than it would take to set up and provide skilled labor to some other "cold" aircraft production line to produce the aircraft required for the current force mix.

Which specific systems are amenable to relatively fast response? The small, tactical systems are a good starting point. It may not make sense to do a lot of planning for surge capability on strategic systems, although Herman Kahn argues that, with enough industrial warning time and in the event of a "mobilization war" (due to the disregard of SALT limits or some other cause of increased international tension), it would be desirable to rapidly build strategic as well as tactical systems.[11] Kahn's scenario, in which the "winner" is the country that mobilizes most rapidly, may not be a particularly credible one. Instead, the United States might be better off putting its limited preparedness resources into those tactical and/or tactical-nuclear systems that could have significant war-fighting impact. This is an area requiring further, quantitative analysis.

Perhaps aircraft and ships, like strategic systems, need not be considered in detail for industrial mobilization. Here the issues are the long time it takes for such production lines to get up to a high rate and the fact that they would drain significant material, labor, and equipment from the tactical systems, which could be deployed more rapidly. Currently, to reach a production level of any significant military value, the aircraft industry would take approximately three years; the shipbuilding industry's response is estimated to be at least that long. There are industrial-preparedness measures (such as introducing "industrial warning" or ordering long-lead parts in advance) that would reduce this time period, but in any event it would take years for the aircraft and shipbuilding industries to respond. Thus, instead of planning for mobilization activities in these sectors, we should plan for rapid production of spare parts for these weapons systems.

This brings up another area in which the Department of Defense's mobilization planning is currently ambiguous: planning for maintenance of military equipment in an emergency. The traditional plans assume that maintenance will be done in government depots. However, a General Accounting Office report on Air Force maintenance depots has pointed out that the current planning for maintenance-depot surge capability is poor, and that perhaps more reliance should be placed on the industry's ability to assist in maintenance during crises.[12] It was the experience of many industrial suppliers during the Vietnam War that the contractors were frequently in a better position to maintain the equipment than the Department of Defense, because of such factors as their knowledge of the equipment and their access to skilled technicians and test equipment. The GAO also pointed out that current mobilization planning for maintenance has the same deficiencies as equipment planning: little, if any, planning for the skilled labor, or the repair parts and production equipment.

The importance of planning at the subcontractor and parts-supplier levels is an additional production-responsiveness consideration. What little production-surge or mobilization planning is currently done is usually limited to the prime contractors (because they can absorb the costs in overhead, and because the government deals directly with the industry only at this level), yet the problems in production responsiveness seem to occur primarily at the lower levels.

Multinational planning is another area of mobilization planning that warrants far more attention in today's environment. Here a number of considerations are raised. First, while we plan to fight together with our NATO allies, they do essentially no industrial-preparedness planning (since they assume the likelihood of a short war on their territory).[13] Second, for reasons of "self-sufficiency," even in peacetime emergency conditions the United States has traditionally placed no production orders with its allies. For example, in 1974 we could have ordered tank castings from Krauss-Maffi in Germany to satisfy the shortage described above, and when there was a problem with Minuteman missile shock mounts they could have been bought from Belgian sources; but in both these cases the option was not taken. In fact, even third-world sources could be used for surge capability during tranquil periods or when a world crisis was not in their area. Thus, Israel could also be used as a source of tank castings today. Interestingly, with all of the talk since the late 1970s about the United States and the European nations standardizing on equipment, little or no attention has been paid to multinational surge or mobilization planning. A third consideration in the multinational arena is whether U.S. mobilization planning should include supplying military equipment to the NATO allies. Current planning does not include this, but history has shown that it is a very likely future requirement, and it may be an "insurance policy" worth buying. Finally, there is the question of the specific relationship between current foreign military sales programs (in both directions) and the U.S. potential for surge. One could assume that equipment could be diverted from foreign buyers to the United States, but under many conditions this would be unlikely—for political reasons—unless it had been prearranged. Similarly, when the United States depends upon foreign sources for critical parts or materials, the conditions of delivery and the penalties for nondelivery should be very clearly spelled out beforehand, not after a crisis has arisen.

There is today virtually no industrial-preparedness planning for skilled labor.[14] Such planning should be done in areas of potential conflicting demands for personnel, such as between industry and the armed forces, between different factories in the same area, and between the defense factories and critical civilian needs.

Additionally, it is worth a small amount of effort to consider the impact of sabotage, or selected bomb damage, to critical U.S. industrial facilities. There are a number of plants—perhaps a larger number than is necessary—that are sole sources of very critical military parts, chemicals, etc., and that are highly vulnerable. Perhaps this is an area where some money should be spent for dispersion or security.

Last, the issue of industrial planning for postattack recovery must be raised. In the initial years of the nuclear era, the United States had a position of total superiority and simultaneously was able to maintain its traditional geographic isolation from war, which made postattack planning unnecessary. In more recent years, as the Soviet Union developed a credible nuclear strike capability against the United States, the concept of mutual assured destruction led the United States to take the basic position that nuclear war was unthinkable and therefore postattack planning was still not required. However, this does not appear to have been the case in the Soviet Union, where such obvious manifestations as plant dispersal and hardening of facilities and production equipment indicate the presence of postattack considerations. The Soviet Union's long history of political and strategic experience and doctrine (as revealed in both open and closed literature) indicates that the Soviet leaders think not only in terms of survival, but also in terms of an industrial society capable of successful operation in a postattack environment. Some believe that this apparent superiority of the Soviets in being able to recover from a nuclear exchange represents the reason why they believe they would win a war.

It would be desirable for the United States to undertake some preliminary planning and analysis in the area of postattack industrial recovery. The initial considerations should include identification of the industries required for rapid recovery of the defense and the critical civilian industries and indication of the current capabilities for recovery in these industries (for example, in terms of dispersal relative to likely targeted areas). To support a set of likely recovery scenarios based upon a variety of assumed nuclear exchanges, from "limited" to "all-out," a preliminary analysis should include much of the current input/output and demand data available from the Commerce Department and the Federal Preparedness Agency. The analysis would also have to consider such variables as lead times, labor skills, manufacturing equipment, parts, energy, and number of plants. Analysis and planning of this kind, which would not be expensive, would indicate areas of high sensitivity in which a small amount of money, spent properly, could have a very significant impact, not only on the realization of postwar recovery—should it be required—but also on the Soviet Union's perception of the credibility of the American deterrent.

5.3 Organizational and Institutional Considerations

The Department of Defense is legally (by the Defense Production Act of 1950 and the Defense Industrial Reserve Act of 1973) and administratively (by Presidential Executive Order 11490 and Defense Mobilization Order VII) required to ensure the existence of a viable industrial base to supply military needs in time of national emergency or anticipation thereof, and a basic defense-policy document (DoD Directive 4005.1) contains guidance in this area. However, the reality of the matter is that overall responsibility for industrial preparedness is considerably dispersed around the executive branch. Some of the reasons for this are understandable; there are civilian industrial concerns that overlap with those of defense. Thus, partial responsibility was delegated to the General Services Administration (through the Federal Preparedness Agency), the Commerce Department, the Transportation Department, the Labor Department, and others.

Even within the Department of Defense there were multiple organizations (such as the Defense Civil Preparedness Agency, the Office of the Secretary of Defense, and the Service Activities) involved with industrial-preparedness planning. For a long time, this whole organizational question was ignored because the general issue of industrial preparedness planning did not receive significant attention. However, the Carter administration raised it as a question for review, and the result was the establishment of the Federal Emergency Management Agency. It is hoped that this agency will achieve the needed overall coordination and planning; additionally, its charter allows much of this industrial planning to be better integrated into other national crisis and natural-disaster planning (defense civil preparedness and industrial postattack recovery have many problems and solutions in common with earthquakes, fires, and floods).

A closer tie between the peacetime weapons-system procurement activities and industrial-preparedness planning efforts on these same systems should be encouraged; today they are totally separated. The program manager for acquisition of a given weapon system is responsible solely for satisfying the quantity demands within his budget. Some other organization then does the planning for surge or mobilization requirements on that program. Thus, if a program manager is asked "Suppose we double your demand; will you be capable of meeting it?" he is unable to indicate either the problems or the remedies. At the very least, the program manager should be given the responsibility for surge planning; and possibly that for mobilization as well. One immediate peacetime benefit of such action would be for the program manager to become far more familiar with the actions necessary to speed delivery of his equipment should Congress authorize an increased budget. The experiences of World War II give ample demonstration of the great improvement in speed of response that is possible from U.S. industry when its inventiveness is fully applied to this task.[15]

5.4 Summary

The defense industry's ability to rapidly expand production is an essential part of the overall defense posture. There are many reasons for believeing that this capability has been eroding badly in the U.S. over the last few decades, owing to the nature of the equipment as well as the problems within the defense industrial base. For example, the lead times for equipment and parts are now far longer than they used to be, because of the increased complexity and sophistication of the equipment, the low production rates, and limited number of parts suppliers. Also, the manufacturing equipment that would be needed for the higher production rates is far more complex to operate and the labor skills required are thus considerably greater. Finally, this manufacturing equipment is much more expensive and therefore far less likely to be sitting around unavailable (much of it is in three-shift use in peacetime). However, much of the reserve production equipment is well over 20 years old, difficult to operate, unreliable, inefficient, and not likely to have skilled laborers familiar with its operation. The low levels of defense procurements means that there are far fewer production lines and skilled laborers available for rapid surges in production. These same deficiencies appear to be even worse at the subcontractor and supplier levels, where the shrinkage in the number of firms doing defense business has been even greater and where there is now a growing dependency on foreign sources. Even at the raw materials level—where steps have historically been taken to provide strategic stockpiles of materials—most of the stockpiled materials appear to be either the wrong ones or of the wrong quantities for current wartime needs, and the dependency on foreign sources here has been known for some time. Yet the ability to make rapid increases to high production levels is even more critical today, because of the higher attrition rates expected in wartime.

Surprisingly, the U.S. government has taken no steps to address this problem. Brief studies that have been done have shown that current programs are largely ineffective and expensive. Policymakers have not even been able to decide on what possible wars they are preparing for, and thus have been unable to take any effective planning actions. There is not a sufficient stockpile of completed military equipment and spare parts to last until the production lines get up to full speed to produce new equipment; nor are any efforts being made to reduce the long and increasing lead times to achieve these production rates. In fact, there are not even any institutions within the government effectively addressing these problems. What seems sad is that hundreds of millions of dollars are being spent annually to cover the costs of ineffective planning devices, such as the filling out of forms, and to support excess labor, plants, and manufacturing equipment in the hope that these will be useful for future defense industry surge requirements (although the data demonstrate that they will not be of significant value).

This chapter has noted a number of steps that could be taken to enhance the overall responsiveness of the defense industry—few of which are even being planned, let alone implemented. Chapter 12 will discuss these actions in much more detail, but it should be noted here that the costs of these actions would be very small if they were to be implemented in a highly selective and effective fashion and that the usefulness to even peacetime production could be highly valuable if the planning for surge were combined with the planning for current production programs. To be effective these selective plans must be done in detail and must be properly funded and implemented. The most important point, however, is that all of these preparedness actions and plans must be accomplished now—in peacetime—in order to have any significant effect on our future deterrent or fighting posture. The preparedness deficiencies of the United States and NATO must be corrected by appropriate planning, done well in advance, and fully implemented. The response time is too great to do it later, and the potential cost too high to not do it at all.

6 Subcontractors and Parts Suppliers

As noted in the preceding chapter, the lower tiers of the defense industry—the parts suppliers and the subcontractors—represent the bottlenecks in the production surge capability. This chapter will show that a major cause of economic inefficiency in the defense industry is the rapid decline in the number of suppliers at these lower levels, which reduces competition and causes extraordinary price increases. The history of American military technology indicates that it has often been the small, inventor-led firms that have made the qualitative breakthroughs so critical to military superiority of the U.S. forces; thus, their disappearance affects our long-range future as well.

If these small, lower-tier firms are so critical, why do the Congress and the Department of Defense think only in terms of the "giants" of the defense industry, such as Lockheed, Boeing, and McDonnell-Douglas, and assume that there is uniformity across the overall defense industry? Further, why do they assume that legislation, regulations, policies, and procedures should be applied equally to the large and the small contractors, to those that deal directly with the government and those that deal through the prime contractors; and to those that supply weapons systems and those who supply parts?

Because of the gross differences between the upper and lower tiers of the defense industry, the application of uniform practices serves to amplify the existing problems and differences. There is basically a "dual economy," comprising the upper level (the large contractors) and the lower levels (the subcontractors and suppliers). The latter group, which includes a wide diversity of firms, will be dealt with in this chapter. For purposes of this presentation, the case of subcontracting between large firms, where they are simply sharing the prime-contractor business, has been excluded. (This was discussed in chapter 2.) However, there are still at least three broad categories to be covered by this chapter: the medium-sized subcontractors and parts suppliers that are actually divisions of large firms (often as a result of conglomerate acquisitions), the medium-sized independently owned firms, and the small businesses operating as subcontractors or selling directly to the government. Among these categories there are significant differences; however, the similarities among these firms in comparison with the large prime contractors warrant their inclusion under one general set of structural characteristics.

Averitt, Galbraith, and others have described the dual nature of the overall U.S. economy.[1] Galbraith calls the two distinct economies the "planned" economy and the "market" economy. This is a particularly interesting naming, because it represents the direction that should actually be taken in correcting the problems in the two areas. At the prime-contractor level it appears impossible to disengage the government, and therefore there should be far more sectoral planning introduced through coordination of government policies; at the lower levels the government could create much more of a market economy. However, at present neither of the two levels is either an adequately planned economy or a sufficiently free market. Rather, each level combines (differently) some of the worst features of both possibilities. The differences between the two levels of the defense industry are not simply matters of degree. Rather, the levels are totally different in almost all respects, for example the way in which business is done, the basic structures, and the problems (which are almost exactly opposite). Therefore, the actions to correct these problems must be different.

Rather than recognizing the differences between the two levels, the Department of Defense has not only treated them uniformly, but, since 1963, has not even collected data at the subcontractor level and below.[2] This is the opposite direction from that in which the government should have moved, and for both strategic and economic reasons the action has gotten the government into considerable and worsening trouble. Between 50 and 60 percent of a weapons system is normally subcontracted by the prime contractor.[3] For the DoD to ignore over half of the costs of its weapons systems is a very questionable practice. If corrective actions are not taken, the problems of the lower tiers of the defense industry could very well become the most significant problem facing the defense industry.

6.1 The Increasing Problems

From 1968 through 1975 the number of active aerospace-industry subcontractors decreased from over 6,000 to under 4,000 (over 35 percent).[4] In this same period the foundry industry experienced a net of 240 closings. Between 1970 and 1975, the Air Force reported that the number of subcontractors leaving defense per year more than doubled.[5] This reduction was not limited to the very small companies, but also included medium-sized suppliers (usually subcontractors). For example, the number of $100-million-to-$1-billion-per-year companies listed as significant contractors with the Department of Defense went from 42 in 1958 to 14 in 1974.[6] One Navy program manager reported that in a six-month period 9 critical suppliers went bankrupt; many of these were sole-source suppliers.[7]

The fact that many of these lost lower-tier contractors were the only suppliers of a particular product is undoubtedly the most critical of the growing problems. In 1973, McMillan Radiation Laboratories, the only producer of the C5A aircraft radome, went bankrupt. That same year the Solar Division of International Harvester, the sole producers of the slotted leading wing edge for the F4 aircraft, discontinued the operation because it was not profitable (it took over a year to qualify another source). In some cases the situation has gotten so bad that prime contractors have been unable to find any suppliers, and have had to resort to building the parts themselves. Westinghouse Electric Corporation was unable to get a subcontractor to make a special traveling-wave tube for only twenty radars (over half the suppliers in this field had left the business), and had to start handcrafting the parts in its own laboratory—with increased costs and production delays.[8] A representative of Hughes Aircraft Company commented that it was so difficult to obtain "space-qualified" parts for their communications satellite business that this company too was forced to build these small-quantity, highly specialized items "in house."[9] The problems appear not to be limited to electronic and mechanical parts, but to extend across the board. For example, Dupont, one of only two U.S. suppliers of nitrocellulose, stopped production in 1977, leaving Hercules as the sole supplier.[10]

Table 6.1 lists a number of critical subcontractor areas in which current

Table 6.1
Some Critical Areas with Small Numbers
of Subcontractors

	No.
Airborne radar systems	2
Aircraft engines	2
Aircraft landing gears	3
Aircraft navigation systems	2
Infrared systems	2
Tank hull castings	1
RPV/drone engines	2

quantity production is limited to a very few suppliers. Because of the unusual nature of oligopoly rivalry, two subcontractors is often a sufficient number for real competition. Take the case of large jet engines, in which two sources—General Electric and Pratt & Whitney—appear to compete strongly domestically and worldwide and have also been able to keep improving the technology. However, other than *ad hoc* "rescue" actions by concerned government officials, there is nothing preventing one or the other of such companies from losing two competitions in a row and going out of the business, or from simply choosing to leave it for more attractive markets.[11]

The problem of diminishing sources is seen not only among large high-technology subcontractors but also among the suppliers of more conventional parts. This can be seen in the numbers of bidders when competitions are held and in the prices being paid. Because the Department of Defense has little information about what the prime contractors and their subcontractors are paying for parts, some data were obtained from the Defense Logistics Agency.[12] These data generally reflect the problems. The first set of data concerns the number of responses to bid requests. In a comparison between 1969 (a high-demand year in defense and across the whole economy) and 1975 (a poor economic year), one would expect (everything else being held constant) the 1975 data to indicate more interest in defense business because the rest of the economy was quite slack. Instead, the number of responses was down by about 25–30 percent. Table 6.2 shows some typical data. It shows a very big dropoff in 1974, when all suppliers were very short and commercial demands were so high as to be drawing away many of the defense suppliers to the civilian sectors. However, in 1975 the suppliers did not come back to the defense business, even though the civilian sector was weak.

When consolidation eventually reduces the number of suppliers to one, the prices rise rapidly. The data in table 6.3 represent a sampling, again from Defense Logistics Agency data, of the price increases of typical products from one year to the next and the reasons given by the agency for these price increases. This table clearly shows that the price increases are far greater than those caused by either inflation or quantity reductions. In many cases the increases from one year to the next are between 200 and 500 percent. In almost all cases, the "explanation" is one form or another of monopoly pricing. With such large price increases, one would ex-

Table 6.2
Ratios of Responses to Bid Solicitations for Selected Items in
Three Contrasting Years

	Fiscal Year		
	1969[a]	1974[b]	1975[c]
Belts (drive, fan, and miscellaneous)	41%	14%	12%
Valves	63	9	47
Lubrication equipment	67	15	17
Wire and cable	18	14	10
Instruments and test equipment	47	41	34

a. High-demand year.
b. Short-supply year.
c. Recession year.
Source: Defense Logistics Agency.

pect—according to traditional free-market economic theory—that a large number of other suppliers would immediately jump into the field. The products themselves are not particularly complex, and the profit margin is high. However, the data clearly indicate that this is not the case, and that in fact companies are not coming into the defense business. Thus, the only explanation must be associated with either the very low volume or the barriers to entry. Such huge price increases, when multiplied by the large number of parts being bought for all of the defense systems and then combined with the associated markups applied to them through the subcontractors and prime contractors, must result in the Department of Defense paying far more for its finished weapons systems than would be the case if there were more competitive pricing at the parts level.

6.2 The Prime Contractor's "Make or Buy" Decision

The prime contractor's decision between making an item in his own factory or buying it from a supplier is a key element of any industrial-organization analysis. It indicates such things as the percent of value added by the prime contractor and the degree of monopoly control. Usually, the more competitive the situation, the larger the tendency towards subcontracting for the price advantages (in terms of specialization). In looking at the defense prime contractors' "make or buy" decision one sees two distinguishing characteristics relative to the rest of U.S. industry: the different criteria used and the far wider variations from year to year in the percentage of subcontracting.

The almost total absence of price sensitivity in the defense industry (in contrast to many commercial areas) creates different reasons for subcontracting. The most unique characteristic is that in defense work profit is directly related to cost, and thus in the defense "make or buy" decision one is faced with the desirability of maximizing cost.[13] This criterion clearly favors keeping work in house. There are complementary motivations for a "make" decision, such as the desire to increase market power and workforce flexibility, the ability to absorb more overhead (through increased direct labor), the desirability of keeping a large engineering force in house, and the ability to have greater control and flexibility over engineering design changes.

The other unique characteristic of these "make or buy" decisions is directly related to the wide oscillations in the defense industry's sales due to the ups and downs of crisis periods (including wars) and the all-or-nothing competition among the firms. The great cyclicity of sales in an individual firm is amplified at the subcontractor and supplier levels. A report of the Commission on Government Procurement stated that

When federal procurement expenditures decline, large contractors become concerned about maintaining their work force, and operating their facilities to capacity. As a result, the large prime contractors tend to "make" rather than "buy"; and, then when they do buy, first consideration often goes to firms that can offer subcontracts in return.[14]

Johnson and Hall collected data on typical aerospace firms and found that in fifteen years one firm went from 30 percent to over 60 percent to under 40 percent subcontracting and another firm went in five years from almost 70 percent to under 40 percent and back to over 60 percent.[15] A large number of commercial firms over the same fifteen-year period showed great consistency from year to year as to the ratio of subcontracting.

Clearly, this wide annual variation in the percentage of work subcontracted is a way for the prime contractor to shift the risk of doing defense business onto the subcontractors.[16] From the viewpoint of the subcontractors or suppliers, the sales volume available to them is the product of the large annual variation in the total defense budget times the variation that they see in the percentage of subcontracting being done by the prime

Table 6.3
Price-Increase Trends and Official Explanations for Selected Items

	Prior Cost ($)	Current Cost ($)	Defense Logistics Agency's Explanation
Static discharger	6.23 (FY 74)	7.70 (FY 75)	Previous supplier no longer certified; new source.
Relay arm	22.84 (Aug. 74)	50.51 (Oct. 74)	Original supplier bought out.
Crystal	6.53 (Jan. 72)	14.75 (Dec. 74)	Revision of specification. Item no longer commercially made.
Intersleeve connector	134.00 (FY 72)	382.15 (FY 74)	Increase in royalties.
Plug connector	2.50 (FY 73)	4.21 (FY 74)	Company absorbed. Also now only one approved distributor.
Circuit module assembly	235.46 (Apr. 73)	336.00 (Dec. 73)	Contractor claimed smaller production.
Rotary switch	132.52 (FY 73)	160.14 (Sep. 73)	Company readjusted pricing structure.
Armature	7.77 (Apr. 73)	14.73 (FY 74)	Company readjusted pricing structure.
Electron tube	135.00 (Jan. 72)	240.00 (Dec. 74)	Company became sole source.
Variable resistor	106.75 (FY 72)	158.85 (Dec. 74)	Company stopped absorbing setup costs.
Variable resistor	88.65 (May 73)	114.25 (Dec. 74)	Company no longer produces except on job-shop special basis; no satisfactory substitute available.
Loudspeaker	19.25 (FY 73)	38.80 (FY 74)	Increase due in part to cost of special metal casting. Only two firms in Midwest can do this casting, because of environmental controls.
Electron tube	3.18 (FY 73)	4.61 (Dec. 74)	Supplier recalculated cost on all items.

Table 6.3 (continued)

	Prior Cost ($)	Current Cost ($)	Defense Logistics Agency's Explanation
Wear ring	32.00 (FY 73)	161.57 (FY 74)	Loss of competition resulted in sole source.
Aerial refueling hose	1,456.00 (FY 73)	1,694.25 (FY 74)	Original source went out of business.

Source: Defense Logistics Agency study, January 10, 1975.

contractors. Since the "primes" tend to bring more work in house when the defense volume decreases, the subcontractors see a far wider swing in their potential sales volume.

Even an initial decision (for example, to "buy" parts in order to make a proposal attractive) can be reversed, more or less at the discretion of the prime contractor, once the award is made or even after development has begun. Sometimes these shifts must be justified; however, the government normally takes the position that the prime contractor is responsible for the total program, which makes justification easy. Frequently, such a reversal (from a "buy" to a "make" decision) is made well before the subcontractor is able to "qualify" a system, thus eliminating future competition between the in-house producer and the subcontractor because there are no other qualified sources at a later date.

The prime defense contractors' unique "make or buy" situation is further complicated by the trend toward vertical integration (which accelerated in the 1970s). In terms of price or efficiency, there is not enough business to justify the desire of many prime contractors to establish in-house capabilities in many of their supplier's traditional business area.[17] The justification is usually based on either the difficulty of obtaining outside suppliers or the prime contractor's need to achieve a more "competitive" proposal position by demonstrating a "make" capability within the firm. The other distinct form of vertical integration in the post-Vietnam era is the tendency of the large prime contractors to acquire subcontractors. McDonnell-Douglas acquired Conductron as a subcontractor for some electronics work, Rockwell acquired Collins for avionics subsystems, and ITT acquired Cannon Connectors for electronics parts. The reasons for this kind of vertical integration, too, are multiple. Often it is based on the prime contractors' desire to keep a certain share of a declining market. Other times it is done in order for the firm to have the capability to respond to all of a weapons-system request for proposal from in house. This tendency is greatly influenced by the government's criteria for selection and contract award. If the government asked for more use of specialty houses, because of their lower cost, then the prime contractors might be less tempted to develop the in-house capability, either through investment or acquisition. Monopsony on the demand side "tends to lead to vertical integration on the supply side of the market."[18]

Such vertical integration clearly changes the competitive environment at the subcontractor and supplier levels, although the prime contractor normally claims that his subcontracting divisions still operate autonomously in a competitive market. The corporate management has a strong motivation to ensure that the prime contractor's "sister division" receives full consideration, and often goes so far as to "cross-subsidize" the sister division in order to get it into a program.[19]

To improve the overall efficiency of the defense industry the DoD should require more "buy" decisions rather than encouraging "make" decisions. This would have the added advantage of broadening the base for strategic responsiveness. There are various techniques that the government could employ to encourage greater use of subcontractors and suppliers, but the major effort has to come through the government's recognition of its responsibilities in this area:

The government cannot [continue to] abdicate its responsibility of assuring by direct action that subcontracts are diffused as widely as possible, and that a broad industrial base is maintained and fostered. After all, can the fox, however amiable and gentle his disposition, be entrusted with stewardship over the henhouse?[20]

6.3 Other Problems for Subcontractors and Suppliers

The president of a large subcontracting firm listed the following five reasons why firms such as his are no longer doing defense business: excessive documentation requirements, interrupted and delayed procurement, government regulations that ignore allowances for real costs (such as interest), imposition of government requirements on the conduct of business, and delays in payments after delivery of parts.[21] A Conference Board study of the views of the financial community with respect to defense contractors in general states:

Subcontractors to the major contractors involved in the survey were considered to be in even worse circumstances than the prime contractors. Problems cited here include single product and single prime contractor characteristics of many subs; their inability to get needed non-bank financing; the lack of continuity that often characterizes their participation in programs, making them especially vulnerable to stretchouts and cancellations; their vulnerability to prime contractor decisions to pull back subcontracted work in-house during slack periods; and overall lack of management talent, especially in such areas as cost and quality control and meeting delivery schedules.[22]

This section will pursue a number of specific causes of problems at the subcontractor level; however, two specific areas—barriers to entry and R&D problems—will be delayed until later in the chapter.

First consider profit, the most important business criterion to the typical smaller firm (in contrast to the larger firms, which tend to emphasize sales volume). In general, the small defense contractors (subcontractors and suppliers) have lower profits and far higher risks than the larger ones. Table 6.4 takes the average-profit information from chapter 3 and gives some visibility to the spread. The "top" row essentially represents the larger firms, and the "bottom" row the realm of the subcontractors and suppliers. Comparing the commercial firms in comparable industries with the defense firms, one sees that the larger firms make essentially similar returns on investment in the two sectors. However, there is a significant difference in the return on sales—because the DoD controls this directly. The difference between the two types of businesses, which allows the return on investment to be the same, is that the large investment by the government at the prime-contractor level in the defense industry enables the large firms to realize big sales dollars with little investment of their own, whereas there is essentially no government investment in the smaller contractors. So, since the sales per unit of capital are similar for the defense and the civilian contractors, and the profit per unit sales is made very low for the small defense contractors, the return on investment is prohibitively low. Although the typical return on investment for a small commercial firm is low (relative to the large firms), it is still acceptable in comparison with the "going out of business" level. This is not the case for the small defense firms, who end up with a return on investment that is essentially less than one would get by putting the money into the bank.

Table 6.4
Comparative Profit Performance of Selected Defense and
Commercial Durable-Goods Firms, 1965–1967

	35 Defense Firms			208 Commercial Durable-Goods Firms		
	Percent Profit/ Sales	Ratio Sales/ Capital	Percent Profit/ Capital	Percent Profit/ Sales	Ratio Sales/ Capital	Percent Profit/ Capital
Top quarter	6.1%	5.2	31.4%	20.7%	1.8	37.1%
Bottom quarter	2.7	2.2	6.1	5.5	1.9	10.4
Average	4.9	3.2	15.5	11.6	2.0	22.9

a. Profit before taxes.
Source: Industry Advisor Council Report to Secretary of Defense, June 11, 1971.

The "Profit '76" study cited in chapter 3 provided much more insight into the defense profit structure. However, the final report tended to take the same position previously taken by most analysts of the defense industry: It dealt with the defense industry at the aggregate level and did not look at the differences between the prime contractors and the subcontractors or the differences due to firm size. Plotting the Profit '76 data versus firm size (figures 6.1 and 6.2) yields very interesting results.[23]

Figure 6.1 shows that profit, as a function of sales (the criterion the Department of Defense uses for negotiation and measurement), is more or less constant for both the medium-size units (those with sales of over $30 million) and the larger ones. For the smaller units (those of the size typical of subcontractors and parts suppliers) profit drops significantly, and for the very small ones (those normally legally defined as "small business") the average profit is actually negative. One can conclude from this curve that the larger firms clearly have more negotiating power with the government, probably start from a higher initial negotiated profit, and actually realize a larger profit at the end of the program. One can also see that the medium-sized firms appear to do about as well as the large

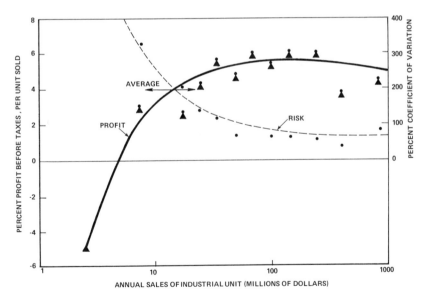

Figure 6.1
Return on sales by size of defense industrial unit (division or firm).

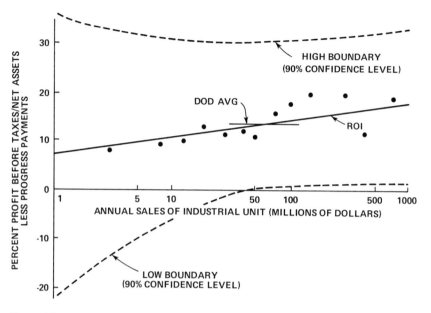

Figure 6.2
Return on investment (ROI) by size of defense industrial unit.

ones in terms of return on sales. This point is often overlooked by defense analysts—both the Comptroller General's report[24] and Fox's analysis[25] took the data for "major defense subcontractors" as representative of the lower tiers (when in fact many of these are actually prime contractors doing subcontract work) and showed that their returns on sales were slightly higher than those of "large defense contractors." This confirms the data in figure 6.1 but ignores the significantly lower returns on sales for the small firms (figure 6.1 and table 6.4).

Figure 6.1 also shows an estimate of risk versus size of the firm, based upon the variation in return on sales (a number of prior studies have shown that this measure of uncertainty is a reasonable risk criterion). These data indicate that the small firms have far higher risk than the larger ones. This would be expected in the commercial world; however, so great a difference might not have been expected to be "typical."

Figure 6.2 shows return on investment versus size of profit center. The average profit for the small industrial unit is an unacceptably low 7–8 percent, which is comparable to the 6.1 percent of table 6.4, while for the larger operations it goes up to 18–20 percent. The confidence boundaries (risk measures) show that, on the low profit side, the large companies have almost no chance of losing money whereas the small operations have a very high probability of doing so. Yet on the high profit side, where one would expect that the small companies could have a large swing (both negative and positive), it turns out that the variation at the upper end of the profit level is essentially the same for both the small companies and the larger companies. My explanation for this distortion is that the small companies were constrained by the Renegotiation Board from making the exceptionally high profits that one would expect them to have a potential for (in order to balance their equally high probability of a large loss). This board applied its rulings "mostly to the small firms,"[26] and reduced the profits significantly, after a contract was complete. Thus, the subcontractors and suppliers are constrained on the high side of their profit, but have a high probability of loss on the low side, whereas the prime contractors appear to have a high average return on investment with a very likely positive profit. Specifically, the data show that a larger firm is likely to make two or three times as much profit as a smaller firm, and with one-third to one-half the risk—the opposite of economic theory, which says that higher profits are the reward for assuming higher risks.

Figure 6.3 represents a cross-check on my assumption regarding the data in table 6.4 that the bottom portion of the spread in defense contractors profit is related to the size of the firm. Here the variation in sales per

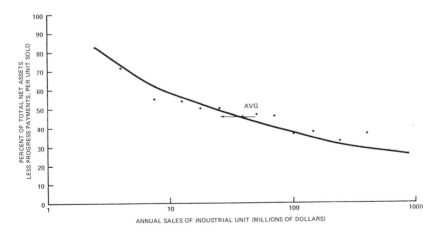

Figure 6.3
Ratio of net assets to sales by size of defense industrial unit. Source: "Profit '76" data.

unit assets for the defense industry, as shown in table 6.4 (with the large spread that does not exist in the commercial sector) is related to the size of the firm. There appears to be no question that the profit for the subcontractors and suppliers (the smaller defense contractors) is significantly less on either a return-on-sales or a return-on-investment basis, and that one reason for this is the difference in amount of capital (both equipment and money) supplied by the federal government to the large contractors but not to the small ones.

Another very interesting difference between the prime-contractor business and the subcontractor and supplier business is the type and amount of competition. The data in chapter 3 show far more competition for the smaller programs and the subcontract-and-parts-level business than for the large, prime-contractor level. In terms of type, at the prime-contractor level the government uses performance almost exclusively as the criterion for evaluation, while at the subcontractor level the "primes" will often use cost as an important criterion, and will play the subcontractors against each other for the lowest prices because here there may well be similar technologies competing. Additionally, once the "prime" has been awarded the development contract, he is almost always assured of continuing with the program and being the sole source on through the production phase if the program goes on at all. By contrast, the subcontractor, even after having won the initial competition for the development phase, is in continuous evaluation against other contractors, who want to come in and replace him, and the prime contractor, who frequently would like to replace him and switch from a "buy" to a "make" decision.

These options are kept open as long as possible by the prime contractor, as a continuous threat to the subcontractor, and they are very often exercised. Thus, a subcontractor may be replaced during the production phase. During one defense electronics program the initial supplier of a power supply was replaced by a second supplier after he went bankrupt, and the second supplier was then replaced by the prime contractor's in-house organization after the second firm ran into technical problems. Such experiences are relatively common at the subcontractor and supplier level. Had this happened at the prime-contractor level, the government would probably have come in and kept the first contractor going with increased dollars and time to get well.

"Second sourcing" is another frequent experience of the subcontractor rarely found at the prime-contractor level (except in the cases of some relatively simple weapons). Here, after the product has been developed and initial production begun, the drawings of the first contractor (owned by the government) are provided to industry to elicit competition for a second source. The bidders for these production programs are often small contractors who have no research-and-development overhead to carry and therefore offer relatively low cost. (Many refer to them as "garage shops.") The original subcontractor cannot compete on a cost basis, and is frequently replaced, even though he was forced to make a significant investment during the early phases. Additionally, he is not in a position to compete on commercial work because of the heavy overhead due to defense R&D, paperwork, specifications, and so forth.

One aspect of the subcontracting business that tends to balance out this high level of competition and provide an opportunity for some monopoly pricing is the ability of a subcontractor or supplier to become the only qualified source. This happens on a high-technology product when the development supplier has his product fully qualified (through exhaustive testing, both separately and with the weapons system) and where the development and/or the testing is so expensive that it is not worth trying to repeat in order to generate competition. In such a case, both the prime contractor and the government are "locked in" to the supplier, who is then frequently in a position to recover many of his initial investment costs and to charge future production quantities on an essentially "cost plus fee" basis. It is actually a fixed-price contract, but the price is based upon previous costs. If the contractor can achieve any significant amount of "learning," he should make a very handsome profit. To minimize this problem, the obvious answer is to qualify two sources and to have them compete during the production phase. However, for most defense programs there always is a desire to minimize the "initial costs" in order to get the program started, without the proper concern for the fact that a slightly increased initial cost might yield significant downstream savings.

The data clearly indicate that the number of suppliers at the subcontractor and parts level is significantly diminishing, and yet there appears to be no government planning to do anything about it. The tank casting situation is a typical example of the problem. As table 6.5 shows, between 1959 and 1974 the number of suppliers of castings went from competitive multiple sources down to a single facility supplying both turret and hull castings. Table 6.6 shows the wide variations in quantities ordered by the DoD from the final remaining source over the ten years from 1964 to

Table 6.5
Numbers of Sources of Tank Castings, 1959–1974

	1959–62	1963–71	1972	1973	1974
Turret sources	3	2	1	1	} 1
Hull sources	2	2	2	1	

Table 6.6
Blaw-Know Hull and Turret Production,
1964–1974

	Hulls	Turrets
1964	240	120
1965	237	204
1966	216	363
1967	180	165
1968	239	194
1969	195	59
1970	177	213
1971	370	323
1972	129	118
1973	475	188
1974	512	512
1974 add-on	518	518

1974. Notice that in 1974, when Congress authorized an "add-on," doubling the quantity required for that year above what was already an all-time high for the ten-year period, the one available source was not able to handle the increased demand. The solution to this problem need not have been to have two facilities continuously supplying these castings; alternative plans for backup sources would have eliminated the major problem. This case demonstrates a total lack of government planning which also appears to be typical of much of the activity at the subcontractor and supplier levels.

The history of the TACAN aircraft navigation system is another example. In 1970, when the Air Force decided to have a competition for the next-generation system, a number of companies that had previously been in the TACAN business needed this new program in order to stay in the business. The Air Force chose two contractors for the development phase.

One of them was a new contractor that had never been in the TACAN business before. Because there were no more programs coming along, all but one of the prior suppliers of TACAN equipment were now out of the business. That remaining firm won the subsequent competition and thus became the sole TACAN supplier. Treating this problem as an industrial-base consideration rather than as an opportunity for "open competition" would probably have kept some actual competition in the field.

There are other complementary reasons for the diminishing number of sources. Certainly the high complexity of the products being introduced in the newer generations of equipment requires far more specialization and frequently far more capital equipment, both of which tend to limit the number of firms capable of keeping up. However, even a bigger reason is the generally low annual volumes of parts procurement in the post-Vietnam era. As noted above, the effects of low volume are amplified by the vertical integration at the prime-contractor level.

To see the greater effect of low volume on the subcontractor, consider that when an aircraft is being built at the rate of one per month this low rate can still be handled in an aircraft plant; however, a production line for building parts at such a prohibitively low rate could not in any way be justified as even semiefficient. In fact, these very low annual quantities, in the teens rather than the thousands, are both undesirable (for a production plant) and inefficient (for any type of production). The addition of the fact that the Department of Defense is no longer the predominant user of high technology now that the civilian sector has gone into high-technology products makes it clear that, for those firms that have the choice, defense is considered an undesirable business area. For example, the DoD used to use the overwhelming majority of semiconductors and integrated circuits. Today these are used in commercial products that range from hand calculators through automobiles, and the volume for these commercial applications reduces the DoD to a very small minority user. For this reason the semiconductor firms no longer have any interest in doing the highly specialized, very low-volume defense work, and often the only way that the DoD can get semiconductor suppliers is to set up a very expensive "captive" line solely for its own use.

As if the above-noted problems were not enough for a small subcontractor or parts supplier, add the simple difficulty of doing business with the Department of Defense. All of the problems that affect any defense contractor, such as the statutory requirements, the complex procurement regulations, the special accounting systems, the single-year awards, the military specifications and standards, and the excessive data requirements are applied to the subcontractor by the prime contractor. In addition, the prime contractor frequently adds on his own set of additional "desirable" requirements. Even in the performance area, the prime contractor usually adds his own "safety factors" to the performance requirements that are given to him by the federal government. Thus, the technical risk and the delivery schedules are much more difficult for the subcontractor than for the prime contractor. However, the subcontractor must commit to these stringent requirements because they are part of the competitive bid.

In addition, contractual terms and conditions, which the government often adjusts according to the prime contractor's risk, are passed on to the subcontractor in much more difficult terms and conditions. One study found that in more than 85 percent of the cases where the prime contractor had a cost-plus-fee contract, the subcontractor had a "firm fixed-price" contract[27] (and, as noted above, usually the subcontractor has the higher technical risk). A recent check of four major programs in which the prime contractor had a cost-plus-fee contract showed that 92 percent of the 114 subcontracts were issued on a firm-fixed-price basis. In addition, the government often gives the prime contractor special clauses to cover "extraordinary inflation." While these provisions can be passed on to the subcontractors, the "primes" do not normally do this, and thus, again, the subcontractor does not have the same benefit. (In the mid-1970s, the subcontractors and suppliers suffered from the unexpected high inflation, for which the prime contractor was usually let off by the government.)

Naturally, the prime contractors are used to doing business in the DoD fashion, and have the very large overheads necessary for such practices. The subcontractors and suppliers, in order to achieve reasonable volume, should be able to combine commercial and military production. However, to be commercially competitive in the civilian market they must have very low overhead, which is all but impossible under the DoD's requirements. Consider, for example, the paperwork required of a small firm to satisfy just a few of the DoD's requirements on a relatively unsophisticated, small quantity item:

- DoD 250 special shipping documents on small-dollar orders,
- changes in accounting systems to satisfy the Cost Accounting Standards Act (P.L. 91-379),

- data to satisfy the Truth in Negotiations Act (P.L. 87-653),
- records reflecting compliance with various socioeconomic programs, such as Equal Opportunity, Walsh-Healy, Small Business, and Labor Surplus Utilization,
- records reflecting compliance with inspection and testing requirements, such as MIL-I-45208,
- technical manuals and provisioning requirements beyond normal commercial manuals, and
- a multitude of "boiler-plate" provisions which require the advice of a lawyer.[28]

A considerable staff is needed just to satisfy the large number of "standard" DoD data requirements. Most or all of these provisions are unnecessary for small firms and not cost-effective from the government's viewpoint. What they lead to is the creation of separate firms or separate divisions to work only with the DoD. These specialized operations lack the high-volume commercial business necessary to smooth the ups and down of defense business, to absorb overhead, or to provide low-cost design advantages. All of these would come through combined operations, but all of them are now prohibited through the way in which the government handles its subcontracting business.

A simple example of how firms leave the defense business, and how those who are left specialize in DoD business only, is shown by a brief history of military electric generators. Since 1963 there have been approximately twelve suppliers of generator sets to the Department of Defense; of these, five are no longer in business (42 percent).[29] On a request for proposal sent out in 1977 only five of the remaining seven firms responded with a bid, and of the five who responded only one was then an active supplier in the civilian marketplace. Thus, four of the remaining interested firms were working exclusively in the low-volume defense business. In order to get such business in a competitive environment they are forced to "buy in" and then to use the changes clause to try to raise the cost during the duration of the contract. Because such manipulations are much more difficult for a subcontractor than for a prime contractor, there are constant financial problems at these single-product, single-buyer small firms.

One danger of such problems is the possibility of firms resorting to illegal operations, which are most frequent at the parts-supplier levels. For example, the six firms making self-locking nuts for the aerospace firms were found guilty of price fixing.[30] (These six firms account for 93 percent of the almost $20 million of defense business in this area.) Such cases are still in the minority, but the increasing financial problems of the small contractors are leading to bankruptcy more and more often—and that alternative raises the temptation.

Chapter 2 discussed the difficulty the prime contractors face in obtaining money from the financial community. Each of the financial firms surveyed indicated even greater reluctance to supply money to subcontractors. In addition, there have been frequent complaints by subcontractors about arbitrary withholding of payments by prime contractors. The Government Procurement Commision stated:

Many prime contracts provide for advance and progress payments, but subcontracts seldom do. In addition, subcontractors sometimes are required to indemnify a prime contractor in areas where the prime contractor has no similar obligation to the government.[31]

It is not hard to see why the U.S. government put up money to rescue the Lockheed Corporation, which had 24,000 employees, $2.5 billion in outstanding contracts, and $240 million advanced by the airlines and banks.[32] However, similar assistance does not exist for the small subcontractor or parts supplier who has all of the above-noted problems and yet lacks power with the government. The job of the federal government should not be to bail firms out, but it is the government's responsibility to do business in such a way that it does not get so many of these subcontractors (who want to do business with the DoD) into bad financial situations.

6.4 Barriers to Entry

Chapter 2 emphasized that, for the large prime contractors, the barriers to exit from defense work appeared to be a major problem preventing reduction of excess capacity. However, at the subcontractor and parts supplier levels the problem appears to be the barriers that keep large numbers of firms from *entering* the defense business. We must look carefully at the barriers to entry in order to determine how to make the operation at the subcontractor and parts level more of a real market economy. In general, each of the barriers to entry noted in chapter 2 for the prime contractors appear to apply at the lower tiers, but in many cases the impact is far greater. Let us consider how each of these barriers relates specifically to the lower tiers and what other entry barriers may exist here that do not exist among the prime contractors.

- *Marketing problems* Contrast the marketing of commercial products with that of defense products, particularly at the subcontractor level. In the commercial area advertising is a major market activity, while in the defense sector it is not an allowable cost and the major share of the marketing is done through personal contacts with the prime contractors and the government. Rarely is commercial marketing experience transferable to the military.
- *Inelastic demand* Basically, the demand is fixed by the government's requirements and passed on through the prime contractors. Thus, a lower cost due to economies of scale or product redesign will not usually result in increased volume. Similarly, to enter the market one firm must replace another, which is far more difficult than simply increasing the total market by entering with a lower-cost product.
- *"Brand loyalty"* Here the situation is different than at the prime-contractor level. At the "prime" level laws require that all interested bidders be allowed to compete, while at the subcontractor level bidders who have not proved themselves can be disallowed. This can create a significant barrier for a firm that has not been doing defense work in the past because it is believed not to have the right experience.
- *Demand for higher performance* As at the "prime" level, technical characteristics are usually important selection criteria. With different products, bidders must promote higher performance as well as lower price. But how can a new supplier prove his product's qualifications if he cannot get in on the program?
- *Need for significant engineering and scientific capability* Because a subcontractor usually begins with the development phase and works with the "prime" right through the production phase, the subcontractor must have a significant engineering force in order to be able to handle the initial phases. Because of the very high ratio of R&D to production in defense work, the engineering and scientific staffs must be larger than in a commercial firm of comparable size.
- *Existence of expensive specialized equipment* For the small competing firms, technological advances exacerbate the problem of the government's placement of production equipment with present suppliers.

- *Need for capital*   As noted, it is even more difficult for the subcontractors and suppliers to obtain loans in the defense area because of the views of the investment community. The subcontractors must continue to spend money and work with the prime contractors throughout the full proposal effort if they expect to "make the team," and only a few firms can afford such investments.

- *Reporting and other overhead requirements*   This is a particularly difficult area for the subcontractors, whose own reporting systems, accounting systems, standards, welding practices, and so on are geared to the minimal needs of the civilian market and are totally imcompatible with the requirements of the defense community. The need to hire lawyers, military-oriented engineers, data people, and other experts in order to even be in a position to respond to government business discourages many potential suppliers from entering the defense business.

- *Market environment*   The shrinking market, the low volume, and the low profit make initial entry into the business extremely unattractive.

- *Political considerations*   The efforts of legislators to keep their home-state or home-district suppliers in the defense business make it difficult for a new supplier to replace one that has such high-level support. Congressmen will often argue that it is in the interest of national security to keep a particular supplier in business, even when he may not have been the low bidder. Such arguments, passed down to a prime contractor through the DoD from Congress, have considerable weight.

- *Federal regulations*   All of the general federal statutory requirements are passed on from the prime contractor to the subcontractors. Additionally, the "primes" pass down many specific defense business regulations to the subcontractors. Thus, while the prime contractor frequently has the size and capital to be able to accept such regulations, the big burden falls on the small subcontractors and suppliers. Many, in fact, refuse to do defense business because of these regulations, feeling that they are an undue burden that would jeopardize competitive operation in the civilian market.

- *Necessity of "buying in" at beginning of program*   A large firm can cross-subsidize a smaller division, but the small companies cannot afford to play this game. The alternative that used to exist for the small firms—going directly to the government for research-and-development money and then bidding their product to the prime contractors—has also been significantly reduced. Because the government has tried to reduce the number of unsolicited contracts awarded, when a small company takes a good R&D idea to the government the DoD is likely to hold a competition on this idea; a large company can buy in and take the award away from the small company that originated it.

- *Probability that a project will not remain sole-source throughout its life* This is a far greater problem for a subcontractor than for a prime contractor, because often the subcontractor is replaced. Thus, a subcontractor that makes a large investment during the development phase does not have much assurance of getting the contract for the high-volume, full production run.

6.5 Small-Business Legislation

Congress has required that "a fair portion of the total purchases in contracts or subcontracts for property and services for the government be placed with small business enterprises."[33] At the request of either the government or the contractor, specific contracts are set aside to be awarded to a small business that can show its prices to be "reasonable and competitive."[34] Additionally, small business firms that get into trouble on defense contracts often ask the government for "relief." The performance of small businesses on defense contracts is probably even worse than in the commercial area, because of the high technology and special nature of much of the defense business. Overruns, late deliveries, and even defaults on contracts are relatively common. In fact, the attrition rate among the higher-technology small businesses is around 50 percent.

The amount of business given by the Department of Defense to small businesses varies quite widely among the different sectors, primarily as a function of the technology involved. This is shown clearly by the data in table 6.7.[35] (For comparison, more than half of the awards by the General Services Administration are to small firms.)

In R&D business, which is an entry point into potential production activities, about 10 percent of the long-range research and advanced technology funds go to small business (often to universities). This is an area where the DoD can gain from additional expenditures—particularly in the area of advanced development, which is usually done by industry, not universities, and leads to marketable products. However, for the period 1970–1975, the percent of overall DoD dollar awards to the small

Table 6.7
Percentages of Military and Space-Program
Purchasing Dollars Awarded to Small
Businesses, Fiscal 1966

Construction	63.2%
Textiles, clothing, and equipage	58.7
Subsistence	52.2
Procurements of less than $10,000	51.1
Miscellaneous hard goods	37.4
Ordnance weapons	26.2
Fuels and lubricants	24.4
Services	23.0
Ammunition	16.8
Ships	16.1
Tanks and automotive vehicles	13.5
Electronics and communication equipment	12.7
Civilian space program	6.7
Aircraft	3.6
Missiles and military space systems	2.2

businesses in the advanced development category decreased from 10.7 percent to 8.3 percent.

Actually, the small business firms' share of subcontract work is larger than their share of direct business with the federal government (in spite of the set-asides and other legislative provisions)—a relatively consistent 35–40 percent of the overall defense subcontracts that have been reported.[36] (However, few data at the subcontract level are reported, so this information may be considerably in error.) The DoD could and should do more to stimulate small business awards in many areas.[37] However, in the past such awards were often made to firms that clearly did not have the technical or management expertise to satisfactorily complete the job; and often these awards were made at the expense of a proven supplier. When such an action drives a dependable supplier away from defense business or results in large increased costs and delays due to the supplier's failure to deliver, then it is not in the government's best interest to make such a "forced" award. Essentially, more awards should be made to small business firms, but some criteria of "qualification" and potential impact on total program costs and on the overall operation of the industrial base must be applied. The intent of the Congress can be satisfied without many of the current negative results.

6.6 The Small High-Technology Business

A special kind of small business is the high technology, inventor-led firm. Historically these firms have been very important in the evolution of American industry and technology. Because of the flexibility and innovative genius of their founders, they have often been able to capitalize on small inventions that advanced the frontiers of scientific knowledge. A large share of the research and development funding for such firms has come from the Department of Defense, since other sources were not willing to pay for this external research and since the founder-inventors often lacked the capital. Many of these inventions found their way into the defense components business, and then later into civilian areas.

In the post-Vietnam era a number of significant actions have worked against these small, inventor-led firms. It has been extremely difficult to get venture capital for such firms. University research, which once nourished such companies, has been cut back by the government, and much of the funding that is provided is now kept within the universities. The tendency of new technology to require significant capital investment further complicates their efforts. The Department of Defense's emphasis on competitive bidding for research and development contracts effectively wipes out the small company that cannot afford to compete against the "buying in" tactics of the large firms.[38] The effect of all this has been, as one inventor-president stated, "the 50 percent attrition of high-technology, inventor-led electronic instrument companies"—a "problem of grave national importance . . . [that] grows daily."[39] According to this same writer, "signs point to a 90 percent attrition rate within a very short time unless immediate priority is given to the situation." To back up his case he wrote to a number of similar firms and compiled the replies. The following are brief extracts from these responses and from others that I received while in the DoD.[40]

"Since 1970, I have put all my energies into placing my company in a position where we will never again have to do business with the Federal Government. This is paying off for me and I do not plan to waste any more of my time pleading with the Federal Government."

"[My company] has always offered the best development and engineering services in its area of expertise, but yet, as a result of unpredictable, unfair, or politically influenced government procurement practices, we have watched our government-based business all but vanish, and our highly skilled staff disperse because of sharply reduced sales. . . . we have turned our energies away from the low-yield, unprofitable, and difficult-to-acquire government work. . . ."

". . . it is much easier (for a government engineer) to place orders with large corporations rather than with small companies."

". . . it is difficult for us to deal with government contracts, so in most cases, we avoid them . . . we should not bid even though we have a better price and more performance. . . . As the [large] companies copy our designs so frequently, it is disheartening when we cannot compete, only because we cannot afford the imagery and the kind of marketing effort they are able to put on."

". . . our device exceeds the performance of the big corporation's by about 10 times, and it is less expensive [yet we were not allowed to compete for the government contract]."

"If such firms are to serve in today's economy, the government must assume a more preeminent role in fostering their development or such technology will simply cease to exist. . . . Firms such as these have had to finance research and development by the use of their own funds [whereas the large firms use DoD money]."

"I, too, am most concerned that large companies can "buy in" by offering extremely low prices for the initial units and then become automatically locked into ongoing procurements."

"After two years of utter frustration in trying to be a supplier to the U.S. Air Force, we are writing you this letter because we feel we have a responsibility to our government. After weeks of stalling and after a meeting at the site, we entered a protest with GAO, after we were told we would not get the order. Rather than go through the established protest procedure, the AF cancelled the bid. . . . Why could not simple parameters be established outlining results required rather than specifying nuts and bolts? . . . Why is the U.S.A.F. willing to spend nearly double (which is where the low bid this time will be) to get the same item they first wanted 2 years ago? Is this prudent use of the tax payers' money?"

"A root source of the problem is the tendency of government specifying engineers and contracting officers to ignore the capabilities of this vitally important segment of the American industry and increasingly to structure government procurements so as to favor the marketing activity oriented segment of the industry."

"You have undoubtedly seen the article from Electronic News reporting the details of the passing of Holt Instrument Laboratories. . . . I had not realized . . . that a government contract was the immediate cause of death. I assume you also have noticed there has been considerable disclosure in the news media recently about the apparently unethical and illegal, ostentatious sales promotion techniques the [large] companies have been using in order to secure business. When the big boys wheel and deal in high fashion, the [small entrepreneur] doesn't have a chance, no matter how good a product he has or even if he has the lowest price. Hopefully public opinion will apply the stimulus for corrective actions. . . ."

"(We are) doing magnificently with several overseas governments, having been standardized as the preferred product line in their military procurement program. It is funny that we are good enough for Sweden and Norway, but not good enough for the United States military. As a matter of fact, my feeling is that, considering the problems we get in trying to deal with the United States military bureaucracy, it is better to take our business elsewhere."

"We are directing our efforts to the commercial applications of our products. We feel somewhat unpatriotic as it leaves the government agencies at the mercy of the [large] companies. However, we do not have the resources to compete effectively and to try to do so is futility."

"Our company was basically founded to serve as a supplier of special products in support of our defense needs. I believe that we reflect the real issues in this matter when I report that we are directing our efforts along nongovernment areas of activity, not because we prefer commercial . . . work, rather that the classic relationship between customer and supplier no longer seem available when serving as a vendor to the Government."

Clearly, some of these responses indicate that many small high-technology firms are being driven from the defense supplier business, while others are bemoaning their problems in doing such business. All in all, they certainly present a bleak picture for the future of this critical segment of the defense industrial base.

The Department of Defense should be far more sensitive to this problem. "Bailout" solutions are not the answer. What the inventor-entrepreneurs justifiably want is for their worthwhile unsolicited R&D proposals to be supported (so that they can develop new, lower-cost and/or higher-performance systems, usually at a small R&D expense), and for the large-quantity production procurement practices to be revised so that awards will be made on the basis of which design performs a certain function at the lowest cost rather than on the basis of detailed technical (design) specifications. In this way, the small inventor-led firm will be favored on the R&D award but a "real" market will be created for the production award. In such an environment the small firm will be able to prove itself technically before the government takes a big risk with the production award, and yet will be given a fair chance to demonstrate its lower costs in the production bid. Such steps (and possibly others) should allow the preservation of this important part of the defense industry.

Schumpeter was correct in describing the small entrepreneur-led company as the source of the qualitative breakthroughs in new technology that can break the monopoly of the large existing suppliers.[41] This is the basic essence of the capitalistic system. However, in the unequal competition between the giants and the small high-technology firms it is necessary for the government (the sole buyer) to help balance the scales in order to preserve and stimulate this competition by going out of its way to assist the small R&D firms.

6.7 International Trends

The defense subcontracting and parts supply business, like all commercial and defense businesses, is going international. However, at the subcontractor and supplier level the tendency seems to be to hasten the decline in numbers of U.S. suppliers at the lower levels. For example, consider the case of metal fasteners (nuts, bolts, screws, and the like), which are critical to defense production. Imports of nuts have increased by 138 percent since 1968, bolts by 85 percent, and cap screws by 380 percent. In 1968 there were approximately fourteen domestic companies with substantial nut-manufacturing operations. Today there are about nine left, and the reduction is attributed to the foreign imports. In 1968, approximately 66 percent of the common nuts consumed in the United States were domestically produced, as were 84 percent of the common bolts and cap screws. By 1974 this had decreased to approximately 48 percent and 56 percent, respectively, and indications are that this trend is continuing.

Perhaps the most significant point about this change is the fact that the foreign producers are producing the standard components in high volume, and therefore at low cost. (Some allege that the Japanese nut, bolt, and screw manufacturers, who account for most of the above-mentioned production, are being subsidized by the Japanese government). As a result, the U.S. suppliers are being underpriced on the standard items and forced to sell only specialty items, which are required in much smaller numbers and which in the past were kept reasonable in price by the large dollar volume associated with the standard items. Today the overhead costs associated with these specialty items are spread over a smaller production quantity, raising the costs significantly. Unfortunately for the Department of Defense, these specialty items are purchased almost exclusively for defense hardware (because of the special nature of defense requirements), and thus the significant increase in imports of standard items drives up the price of defense specialty items by a very high factor.

This situation is not unique to the metal fastener industry. For example, the same thing is happening in the capacitor industry. In 1966 less than 6 percent of the capacitors sold in the United States were supplied by imports; by 1974 approximately 22 percent came from imports. Again, the U.S. capacitor firms are being driven toward specialty items. Many, to escape this problem, have set up overseas capacitor production houses to take advantage of the low labor costs. Beside having the obvious strategic disadvantages, such overseas production lacks the advantage of overhead absorption associated with domestic production of special military items. Thus, it helps the firm and the commercial buyer, but it raises defense costs and increases the strategic dependence on overseas sources.

This is not an argument against the use of foreign suppliers for the defense industry or against free trade for products that are both used in the civilian and defense industries, but an attempt to highlight the fact that their impacts are not currently part of the overall defense picture. One solution would be to allow foreign sources to compete with U.S. firms for the overall market, but with sensitivity to the costs of defense products as a major consideration in determining when exceptions to these free-trade rules will be allowed. Also, when the number of domestic suppliers of an item is reduced to only one or two it would appear undesirable to allow foreign competition to eliminate the last domestic source. The ideal situation in these cases is to allow foreign competition (to keep prices low), but to require sharing of the total market with the remaining domestic supplier(s).

This is not a hypothetical problem—such cases arise often in normal defense procurements (especially since the early 1970s). For example, in 1975 the United States decided to buy a Belgian-designed machine gun for vehicles, rather than any of the proposed domestic alternatives. This choice was made partly because of the design superiority and greater reliability of the Belgian gun, but also partly to "offset" the Belgian procurement of the F-16 fighter aircraft from the United States. There is only one U.S. manufacturer currently building vehicle-based machine guns, so it was decided (properly) that this company would produce the Belgian design in the U.S.—for national security reasons. Thus, the domestic manufacturing capability is maintained. But it would appear to be desirable for the United States to consider sponsoring a "next generation" research and development project to maintain the technology base as well.

This example raises the point of the "offset" agreements (discussed in more detail in a later chapter), whereby the United States sells a prime weapons system to a foreign country and in turn agrees to buy some subsystems or components from that country. Again, such agreements have the undesirable impact of considerably weakening the domestic subcontracting and parts-supply base, unless it is made explicit that only subsystems and parts that are price-competitive and will not significantly increase America's strategic dependence (either at the time or in the future) will be purchased abroad.

In many cases, U.S. dependence on foreign military producers has already become total. For example, one leading aerospace company cannot get any U.S. suppliers for some special forgings; Germany and Japan are the only sources. (The contractor claimed that the small quantity required high capital investment, and that environmental restrictions had caused the U.S. firms to stop doing the work.) Table 6.8 lists some other critical defense subsystems and parts which are only produced today in foreign countries.

Table 6.8
Examples of Foreign Sole Sources

TR-41 engine for A-7 aircraft	United Kingdom
Precision optical glass	West Germany
Hexachlorethane for smoke bombs	France/Spain
Self-luminous light sources	Switzerland
Hollow electro-slag refined billets	Japan

All data indicate that the trend towards foreign production is accelerating, and because of the low DoD visibility of the subsystem and parts levels there is little awareness of the potential problems or of the possible corrective actions.[42]

6.8 "Specialty Houses"

It is impossible and unnecessary for the Department of Defense, or even for the government in general, to keep track of all types of parts and subsystems and all sources. Items in commercial use by a wide number of users, or for which there are significant number of suppliers, clearly do not warrant such considerations; in fact, these are the desired market conditions that should result in both economic and strategic considerations being well covered. Rather, it is those few items for which the military is the major user, and for which a limited numbers of suppliers exist, for which it is desirable for the DoD to keep track of suppliers, prices, and possible future demands. Thus, the problem here is primarily that of the two types of "specialty houses": those that have a significant share of their business with defense and are limited in terms of the number of their products and the number of suppliers in the industry, and those whose product has very special technical requirements and very few suppliers. For either of these two special cases, the DoD should keep track of the situation and take action as required.

The heavy metal forging industry is an example. This industry uses large, expensive capital equipment (mechanical and hydraulic presses and hammers), has complex production process, requires skilled operators, and is a basic element in the defense industry. Components that are forged include landing-gear struts, large wing spars and bulkheads, helicopter rotors, missile nose cones, jet-engine turbine blades, nuclear-ship valve bodies, and ship propeller blades. Table 6.9 shows the DoD's large share of the forging industries in the 1969–1973 time period.

A current problem with large forgings is that the hammers used for making them violate the federal noise and vibration standards. This, compounded by the federal insistence on environmental protection and occupational safety and health requirements, is making many of the basic material suppliers uncompetitive with foreign producers, who have both lower-cost labor and freedom from the EPA and OSHA regulations. Thus, a very serious problem could occur in this area.[43] Additionally, the

Table 6.9
The Department of Defense's Share of Forging Industries, 1969–1973

Size Class of Forgings	Aluminum	Titanium	Steel
I (small)	58%	74%	25%
II	54%	62%	13%
III	57%	68%	35%
IV (large)	73%	83%	31%

Source: U.S. Air Force forging-industry study, 1974.

serious reduction in the supply of skilled laborers for this industry, especially die makers (because of the very undesirable working conditions) is a major concern of the industry. The DoD should monitor this critical specialty industry for both economic and strategic reasons.

In the cases of many specialized industries the situation is one of dual dependency: The specialty houses are dependent upon the DoD for their survival and the DoD is also dependent upon them for its future products.

6.9 Summary

In spite of the fact that over half of the dollars for defense materiel acquisition are expended at the lower tiers of the industry, there is almost no recognition by the government policymakers of the significant qualitative differences in structure, conduct, and performance between the business done with the subcontractors and parts suppliers and that done with the large prime contractors. Rather, the government continues to treat this dual economy as though it were uniform, and to apply all of the same rules. Even worse, the government assumes that the prime contractors are "taking care of" these lower tiers (in the government's interest) and that it can thus afford to completely ignore them.

The problems of the lower tiers of the defense industry may be significantly worse and far more critical to the U.S. defense posture than even those at the prime-contractor level. The industrial base at the lower tiers is shrinking rapidly as a result of bankruptcy, corporate mergers, prime contractors' decisions to "make" rather than "buy," and the voluntary departure of many suppliers. With this rapid departure of suppliers from the lower tiers, monopoly conditions are appearing more and more. In some cases, it has been impossible even to get part suppliers to bid on defense business. Those firms that are "forced" into the market do so at very high prices.

The result of all of the problems at the lower tier of the defense industry has been far more sole-source business, fewer suppliers, rising prices, lengthening lead times, and a lack of production surge responsiveness. Yet, in spite of the fact that over 50 percent of all the costs for defense hardware are at these lower tiers, there is essentially no government awareness of or high-level coordinated policies to address these problems.

Government must take positive steps to make defense business more attractive at the lower tiers. Barriers to entry—particularly those that affect firms that normally supply civilian equipment—must be removed. Steps that the government could take include larger-volume buying (achievable by combining multiservice and multisystem needs), multiyear procurements, requiring the prime contractors to "buy" instead of "make," and—perhaps most important—ensuring higher profits and lower risks for the smaller firms.

More research and development at the parts-supplier levels and especially among the small high-technology firms would encourage the development of lower-cost parts, the exploitation of new technology for military advantage, greater competition, and the building up of production surge sources at the lower tiers.

Additionally, it may be necessary for the Department of Defense to assume part of the risk of defense business—perhaps by assisting in raising the capital for the necessary investments through indemnification. Finally, requiring a domestic source whenever there is a dependency on foreign parts or systems would bring foreign technology into this country as well as encouraging U.S. competition with the foreign sources and eliminating critical strategic dependence.

7 Sectoral Differences

Perhaps the U.S. defense industry's most important single characteristic is that it is not a single industry but rather is made up of a number of different industries, each with its own characteristics and problems. Unfortunately, current federal legislation, regulations, policies, procedures, and practices fail to recognize these sectoral differences, and treat the overall defense industry in a totally uniform fashion. In fact, this uniform treatment is a basic tenet of government procurement actions. The similar treatment of totally different sectors results in the government often taking actions exactly opposite from those that would improve either the economic efficiency or the strategic responsiveness of a given sector. In economic terms, this apparently perverse result is perfectly understandable. Since all of the defense industry's sectors have such unique and non-free-market characteristics, the proper corrective actions are, by necessity, those associated with "second best" solutions tailored specifically to the special circumstances—and they often do not match the actions prescribed by traditional theory on the basis of the assumption of a free and uniform market in each sector.

Table 7.1 shows some of the sectoral differences. Note that, even from this summary overview, there are significant differences in number of firms (and, therefore, degree of concentration), mix of public and private ownership, and role of the government.

Over time the government's demands shift from one sector to another, both as a result of changing perceived or real threats and as a result of the cyclical nature of defense procurements. (Both these factors are strongly driven by new technological discoveries.) Figure 7.1 illustrates this shift and also shows the predominance of aircraft, ships, electronics, and vehicles. Other important lessons are learned by comparing the data in Figure 7.1, based on firms, with the data in Figure 7.2, based on products. Figure 7.1 assumes that the large firms typically made a single type of defense product. This was mostly true in the World War II era, and probably lasted through Korea and, in many cases, even through the early 1960s, but it is certainly not true today. For example, Lockheed is very active in both aircraft and missiles, and General Dynamics, which is considered an aircraft company (and therefore put into that category in figure 7.1), in some years does more business in shipbuilding.

Thus, in the post-Vietnam era it is improper to discuss an "industry" solely in terms of the list of companies making a particular product. To adequately describe an "industry," one has to define a general product

Table 7.1
Some Primary Sectors of the Defense Industry and a Few Distinguishing Characteristics

Sector	Some Subsectors	Plant and Equipment Ownership	GOGO or GOCO Facilities[a]	Approximate No. of Firms
Aircraft	Helicopters Fighters Cargo planes	Mixed	Repair depots	14 (with considerable specialization)
Ships	Nuclear ships Large conventional ships Noncombatant ships	Private	Repair yards	11 (3 large)
Tracked vehicles	Tanks Personnel carriers	Mixed	Tank factories Repair depots	3
Munitions	Guns Bullets	Government	Almost all production	Large no. at parts level (a few for each part)
Aircraft engines	Large engines Small engines	Mixed	Repair depots	4
Electronics	Radars Computers Navigation systems	Private	Repair depots	Large no. in total (only 2 or 3 of each type)
Satellites	Communications Reconnaissance	Mixed	None	6
Missiles	Strategic Tactical	Mixed	Repair depots	8

a. GOGO: government-owned and government-operated; GOCO: government-owned and contractor-operated.

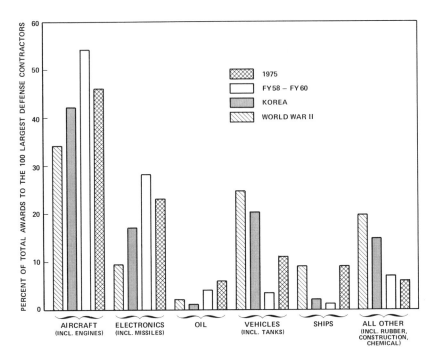

Figure 7.1
Distribution of defense dollars by industrial sector (based on top 100 firms).

type and then consider the plants that do work in that area. In fact, the characteristics of a particular "industry" are defined by the level of generalization of the product description. Certainly the specific industry cannot be characterized by the information provided at the cross-industry level of the conglomerates. Typical categories for industries might include aircraft, ships, vehicles, and such, but even among these there is considerable overlap in the production and engineering skills, equipment, and facilities. I favor the approach of trying to deal with the more general categories (for example, heavy equipment and high-technology manufacturing) and to apply fewer of the distinguishing characteristics that have historically been used. More emphasis should be placed on the manufacturing process or the basic technology as the distinguishing characteristics than on the specific nature of the military product.

The historical specialization in defense sectors is evidenced by the heavy concentration ratios[1] implied in table 7.2. However, the amount of con-

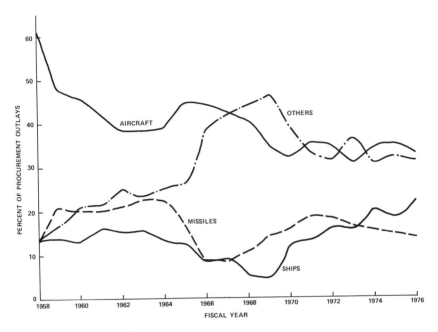

Figure 7.2
Trends in the distribution of defense dollars by industrial sector (based on products procured).

centration in each sector becomes far greater (approaching monopoly in some cases) when one goes to the next lower level (for example, from "aircraft" to "fighters," "bombers," and so on). The overall defense industry is clearly made up of a significant number of monopoly and oligopoly suppliers of specialized items that they design and manufacture. This characteristic is perhaps stronger in the defense industry than in any other part of the U.S. economy, primarily because of the emphasis by the Department of Defense on military performance and technological advancement as criteria for success. Thus, companies do not think of themselves as being in the "manufacturing business," but rather as being in (for example) the "laser-guided, short-range, anti-tank missile business."[2]

One reason for the gross differences between the defense industry's sectors is the different histories of these various sectors. For example, investments in the private shipyards were made totally by the shipbuilding owners, primarily because of the business potential in the commercial

Table 7.2
Concentration Ratios

	Contract Awards in Fiscal 1967 [a] (Millions of Dollars)	Percentage of Contracts		
		Top 4 Firms	Top 8 Firms	Top 20 Firms
Surveillance and detection satellites	$ 236	100	100	100
Nuclear submarines	211	99	99	100
Space boosters	262	97	100	100
Fighter aircraft	2,164	97	100	100
Attack aircraft	570	97	100	100
Missile inertial guidance systems	539	97	100	100
Inertial navigation systems	201	96	99	100
Missile reentry vehicles	278	95	99	100
Aircraft fire-control systems	414	95	98	99
Transport and tanker aircraft	1,003	94	99	100
Helicopters	1,208	93	99	100
Jet aircraft engines	1,892	93	99	100
Data processing systems	336	83	93	99
Missile solid-rocket propulsion systems	356	81	90	96
Combat vehicles	1,391	67	78	88
Surface-based sonar systems	278	63	82	97
Countermeasures systems	209	63	76	92
Surface radar systems	215	62	81	96
Missile systems	2,119	59	82	98
Drones	224	56	81	95
Communications systems	887	50	59	72
Navy power systems	887	50	59	72

a. 1967 was a peak demand year; thus the concentration ratios could be expected to be at their lowest levels. In many of the areas shown here concentration has increased significantly since that time.
Source: Computed by M.L. Weidenbaum from data supplied by Frost and Sullivan, Inc., *Defense Market Measures System,* fiscal year 1967.

shipbuilding. By contrast, in the missile area, significant government investments were requested and made. In some other sectors (such as the aircraft industry) private and government investments were mixed, and in yet others (such as the tank industry) there was total government ownership, based on the Arsenal Act. These different historical trends, combined with the government's failure to recognize the sectoral differences, resulted in very wide differences in profit, whether measured as return on investment or as return on sales (figures 7.3 and 7.4). (These data are from a study of actual division profits[3] rather than from the overall corporations' published profit data, and thus should be far more meaningful. However, even though these data were "cleansed" by CPA organizations, they may be less precise than desired.[4] Nonetheless, the relative information from sector to sector is believed to be approximately valid.)

Each of these different sectors is operating within the general character-

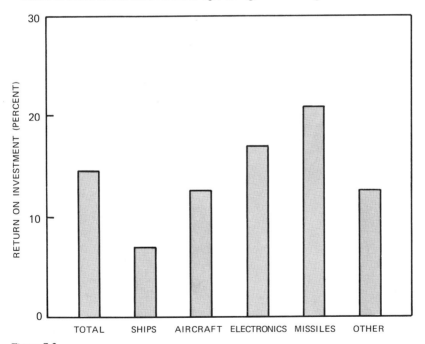

Figure 7.3
Return on investment in different sectors of the defense industry, based on government profit centers of major defense contractors. ("Other" includes chemicals, aircraft engines and parts, tank components and tanks, and general-purpose computers.)
Source: DoD "Profit '76" data.

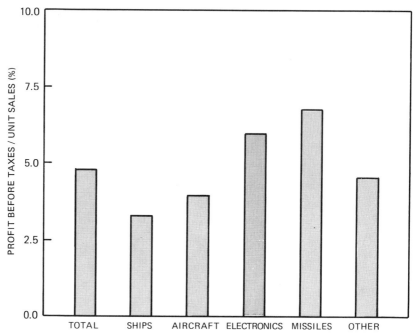

Figure 7.4
Profit before taxes as a function of sales for different sectors of the defense industry,
based on government profit centers of major defense contractors. ("Other" includes
chemicals, aircraft engines and parts, tanks and components, and general-purpose computers.)
Source: DoD "Profit '76" data.

istics and structures of the defense industrial base described in chapter 2,
and each has the dual-economy makeup described in chapter 6.
Nonetheless, if specific corrective actions are to be implemented, they
should be done on a sector-by-sector basis. For example, owing to the aircraft industry's redundant labor (especially engineering), old production
equipment, excess plant and equipment, and other factors, the proper
direction for this sector appears to be to reduce production plants and
research-and-development teams, to modernize the remaining facilities,
to improve production surge capability by planning second and third
shifts, and to stockpile long-lead-time parts. In the tracked-vehicle industry, one supplier (Chrysler) has been building tanks and one supplier
(F.M.C.) has been building armored personnel vehicles—both using
largely outdated government-owned equipment—for many years. The
Army recently built a new tank plant costing hundreds of millions of

dollars but as a complement to the old one; thus, the single source was maintained. Perhaps the desired direction for this sector would be to bring about competition through the introduction of more firms—including more at the supplier level.

As another example, consider the U.S. shipbuilding industry. Here there are now financial problems (low profits, large legal claims, big cost overruns) and significant labor problems (an annual worker turnover around 75 percent), but the future looks even bleaker. The yards are not competitive on the world market (partly because of the fact that foreign governments subsidize their shipbuilders, but also because of low productivity in the American shipyards), there is little U.S. commercial shipbuilding demand (even with U.S. government subsidies), and some DoD fiscal planning calls for a significant (perhaps 50 percent) reduction in new ship construction for the Navy. Thus, the question is whether to allow the majority of the shipyards to gradually shrink to below their minimum efficient labor force or to begin to allocate a reasonable level of relatively stable work to those yards that remain competitively efficient and allow others to close. The better direction maybe the latter; however, it will take conscious and thoughtful action on the part of the Navy and the Congress.

In munitions, another totally different defense-industry sector, the problem is getting very rapid wartime response from an industry that is hardly required at all in peacetime. The only option currently considered is huge stockpiles of munitions, which would be costly, potentially dangerous, and likely to become obsolete with advancing munitions and armor technology. The Army has traditionally built large munitions plants and, after an initial trial run, turned them off and placed them on standby. An idle plant cannot be instantly turned on at full production rates. The biggest problem is usually obtaining skilled labor—an area in which little if any planning is done. Since a new munitions assembly plant may cost around half a billion dollars, and since a number of plants are required for rapid production of different munitions, and since building plants does not ensure an available labor supply (especially for the three-shift operation desired in wartime), alternative options appear desirable. It is against the Army's tradition to have munitions plants in the private sector; however, serious efforts should be made to design and operate plants to produce munitions as well as some goods for the civilian market. In this way the very large investment in plants and equipment could be put to use in the national economy, and a skilled labor force would be available to be shifted to munitions production if required.

Finally, consider the strategic-missile industry. A few years ago this industry consisted of Boeing building Air Force missiles and Lockheed building Navy missiles. When the Air Force's Minuteman production came to an end, the Congress decided to keep the line open one year longer—at a cost of $300 million—for the reason that it was "the only strategic-missile production line." (The other one, down the coast, built only Navy missiles, for shorter ranges.) In recognition of this problem, some members of the DoD attempted to structure the cruise-missile program so that there would be honest competition, from two sources, during the program's production life.[5]

I have made some gross generalizations about each of the sectors of the defense industry discussed above. To really understand sectoral problems and discuss corrective actions, an in-depth look at individual sectors should be taken. The remainder of this chapter presents two specific examples: the aircraft industry and the shipbuilding industry. These are among the largest sectors within the defense industrial base, and each has both defense and civilian portions. The current problems in these two industries are sufficiently different that the corrective actions required, while both fitting into the general area of sectoral development planning, could not be implemented by a uniform action.

7.1 The U.S. Aircraft Industry

By the mid-1970s, the overall U.S. aircraft industry was operating at about 55 percent of its one-shift production capability. Such a high level of idle physical capacity, and the even larger burden of labor-related overhead structure, including engineering teams and marketing organizations, costs about $1 billion per year in inefficiency. The Department of Defense's share of this cost is over $400 million per year. It is estimated that better economic and market planning in the military-aircraft sector alone could save the DoD at least $250 million annually within just a few years. The reasons for this overcapacity, and other significant problems in this sector of the defense industry, are directly related to the unique market conditions that have characterized the aircraft industry in the post-Vietnam period.

Of major significance is the fact that, in constant 1977 dollars, the

DoD's aircraft procurement budget dropped from $17 billion in 1968 to $7 billion in 1975, while the major procurements of commercial aircraft in the United States were also shrinking.

Secondly, a dramatic shift in the sale of American military aircraft to foreign nations occurred during this post-Vietnam period. In 1968 foreign sales amounted to approximately 10 percent of U.S. military-aircraft procurements; by 1976 the figure was up to approximately 60 percent. These sales provided a short-term "stopgap," for the U.S. aircraft manufacturers, but the general international trend is towards "coproduction" or "host-country production" agreements. Future foreign sales are far less certain than domestic procurements.

Also of critical importance is the significant reduction in the total number of military aircraft being bought. During the Korean War period around 3,000 relatively inexpensive aircraft were produced per year in the United States. Through the mid-1960s the number was about 1,000 per year. Today, this country is producing annually about 300 extremely sophisticated military aircraft for our own use, and a slightly larger number for foreign military sales. Clearly, these trends toward reduced quantities and increased complexity have had an impact on the structure of the aircraft industry.

The lack of capital investment by the aircraft industry between 1968 and 1975 is the other area of wide concern. Unless investments are made, the resultant low productivity—combined with the low levels of demand —over the long term could lead to nationalization of the industry, as it did in Western Europe. A major impediment to the generation of new capital has been the heavy debts of the corporations (examples of which were discussed previously.)

With the defense mission so closely affected by the performance of the aircraft industry, there should be greater understanding of the changing economic conditions in this industry and the impacts of these changes.

7.1.1 Market Structure and Market Forecasts

There are a number of reasons for the unhealthy conditions in the aircraft industry, but foremost is the lack of awareness within government and industry of the gap between free-market economic theory and the reality of the aircraft industry. For reasons of historical "military necessity," the government owns a large part of the aircraft industry—approximately one-third of the current plant space, a significant share of the manufacturing equipment, and all of the repair depots. In addition, the financial position of the industry is very much dependent on the use of government financial resources (progress and advance payments, and loan guarantees such as those provided for Lockheed in the mid-1970s).

The aircraft industry exemplifies all of the non-free-market characteristics of the defense industrial base described in chapter 3. For example, on the military demand side, the Department of Defense, acting through the Armed Services Procurement Regulations, is essentially a monopsonistic buyer and, at the same time, the "regulator." Also, by selecting the contractors for the large aircraft programs, the government controls entry into and exit from this market, greatly affects the growth or decline of the firms manufacturing aircraft, and imposes its ways of doing business on the firms involved. This single-customer market also makes for an extremely keen type of "either-or" competition—that is, for a given type of aircraft, a firm frequently competes for all or none of the market instead of for a share.

Another general feature of the defense market seen in the aircraft industry is the manner in which contracts for major weapons systems are awarded. Once the original development contractor has been selected (usually on the basis of promised performance) from competitive designs, all the "follow-on" contracts, including the large-dollar production contracts, are negotiated with the same firm because of the government's prior investment in the program. The supplier is "locked in" and can charge monopoly prices with little or no incentive for cost reductions.

A detailed study of the specific economic efficiency and strategic responsiveness of the U.S. aircraft industry was undertaken in 1976 to determine its current status, recent trends, and likely future.[6] The seventeen major companies that make military and commercial aircraft (including helicopters and general-aviation aircraft) and the government-owned plants and equipment used by them were included in the study. These firms are listed in table 7.3.

To assess capacity, three utilization measures were chosen: a nominal one-shift capacity, the peak output capacity that had been demonstrated by each company during the last ten years (equivalent to about 1.4 shifts operating on a 40-hour week), and the mobilization output capacity that could be achieved by using current plant space on an all-out, three-shift basis. Results of the assessment show that the overall aircraft industry (excluding general aviation) was using about 55 percent of its nominal one-

Table 7.3
Manufacturers Included in Joint DoD-OMB Study of U.S. Aircraft Industry

Military and Commercial Airplanes	Helicopters
Boeing	Bell
Fairchild	Hughes
General Dynamics	Kaman
Grumman	Sikorsky
Lockheed	Vertol
McDonnell-Douglas	**General-Aviation Airplanes**
Northrop	Beech
Vought	Cessna
	Piper

shift capacity, about 45 percent of its aggregate prior peak experience, and about 20 percent of its mobilization capacity (table 7.4). Note that these approximate percentages are almost identical when one uses different measures of capacity, such as employment, sales volume (after adjusting for inflation), and physical output. It is normally considered good economic practice to operate at between 85 and 95 percent of capacity, on approximately a 1.3-shift basis, with critical machinery utilized on multiple shifts.

Figure 7.5 shows the overall market forecast that was made and the historical data for the last fifteen years for the industry. On the basis of internal DoD planning documents, the forecast for the military sector is for the fighter and attack-aircraft market to remain near the current level through the 1980s. Production of bombers and cargo planes was predicted to first decrease, then significantly increase by the mid-1980s.[7] These forecasts assume that the current foreign military-aircraft sales volume of approximately $3 billion per year will remain constant, and that the helicopter market of commercial and foreign sales will grow by about 70 percent. The forecast for fixed-wing civilian aircraft, based on contractor and Department of Transportation inputs, projects major replacement buys of commercial aircraft by the mid-1980s. Since the last assumption has by far the greatest impact on the study, it should be noted that the primary forecasting uncertainty in this area is the timing of replacement buys, and not the magnitude.[8]

A survey of industry and government officials indicated that these

Table 7.4
The U.S. Aircraft Industry's 1975–1976 Performance Versus Three Utilization Criteria

	Employment	Sales (Billions of Dollars)	AMPR Weight[a] (Million of Pounds)
1975–1976 performance	225,000	12	240
Mobilization capacity (3 shifts, 48-hr week)	1,040,000	56	240
"Peak" corporate experience (1.4 shifts, 40-hr week)[a]	490,000	26	135
Nominal one-shift capacity[b]	380,000	20	105

a. AMPR (Aeronautical Manufacturers Planning Report) weight is a measure of "value added" output. It would exclude, for example, the aircraft engine, which is produced elsewhere.
b. Adjusted for floor-space and productivity changes.

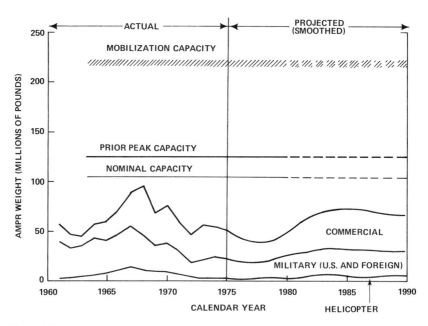

Figure 7.5
Historical and forecasted capacity utilization in U.S. aircraft industry.

overall market estimates are probably accurate to within 25 percent.[9] This level of uncertainty is more than covered by the likelihood that the current capacity of the aircraft industry will grow as a result of new productivity enhancements, such as the use of composite materials and computer-aided manufacturing. Figure 7.6 shows the sensitivity to these variations (a low level of productivity enhancement of 1.8 percent per year, based on the prior ten years' experience, is used). On the basis of this figure, it can be seen that this chapter presents a conservative forecast of future excess capacity, since it makes relatively optimistic market forecasts on the demand side and does not include the effects of computer-aided manufacturing and other productivity enhancements on the supply side.

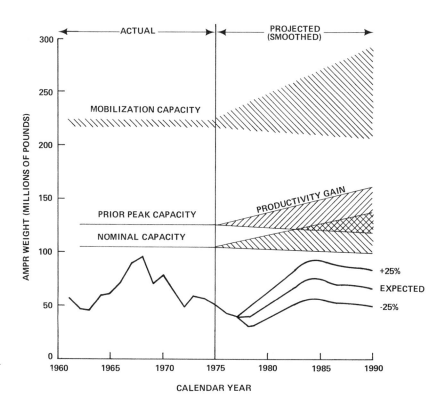

Figure 7.6
Sensitivity of aircraft industry to changes in capacity utilization.

7.1.2 Costs and Benefits of Excess Capacity

To facilitate quantification of the costs of the idle capacity shown by figure 7.5, a number of simplifying assumptions were made. First, it was assumed that the DoD share of the costs of the excess capacity should be equal to the defense share of the total industry sales: approximately 45 percent. This is believed to be a very conservative assumption, because it is estimated that defense actually pays a disproportionately large share of the industry costs of research and development. Secondly, the costs of excess capacity should be measured, not only in terms of idle floor space and equipment, but primarily in terms of the extra costs associated with redundant labor existing in these vertically integrated companies (for example, engineering, management and marketing people). In fact, these extra labor costs far exceed the idle plant and equipment carrying costs. This is particularly important, since the idle plants and production equipment are often cited as being an acceptable price to pay for maintaining production surge capacity in case of a crisis. However, the data indicate that the existence of these plants and this equipment makes it politically difficult to eliminate the redundant labor, and that in a crisis requiring a surge in production the required laborers are skilled factory workers, not the redundant engineers, marketing personnel, and managers. Thus, the costs are very high, but the benefits in terms of strategic responsiveness are very small.

Because of the uncertainties involved in calculating the DoD's share of the costs of excess capacity for the aircraft industry, it was decided to use multiple approaches. Thus, the analysis was conducted using the following independent techniques:[10]

- Comparisons were drawn between different levels of industry indirect costs beyond those required for designing and building aircraft on an efficient basis, and with changes in the level of capacity utilization. For this approach the annual cost to the DoD of the extra management, engineering and support teams was estimated to range from $300 million to $500 million per year.
- The historical level of sustaining costs that a firm must incur in order to remain viable was studied. The additional cost to the DoD of having too many vertically integrated facilities was estimated to be about $400 million per year.

- The historical cost of merely maintaining idle plant space and equipment was calculated and found to be approximately $80 million per year.
- The costs to the DoD of inefficiencies due to low production rates were approximated at $150 to $250 million per year.
- The cost to the DoD of extra competition beyond that required for the projected programs (for example, three or more firms when two would do) was estimated at between $150 million and $270 million per year.

All these approaches yielded reasonably consistent numbers, showing defense's share of the industry's excess-capacity costs to be $300 million to $500 million per year.[11]

The first four of the above approaches consider primarily economic efficiency, and exclude any desirable considerations of extra competition and production mobilization capability. Treating extra competition independently (and ignoring firm efficiency and other factors), the last method above and a separate analysis[12] both indicated that approximately $250 million per year of excess capacity costs could be eliminated while more than adequate competition could be maintained in each sector of the military aircraft industry. This competition, as noted above, is not primarily for price considerations in production (since the production contract is usually awarded on a sole-source basis), but it is essential in order to encourage technological advancement.

On the matter of quantifying the requirement for mobilization or surge production capability, the study had two significant and relevant findings. First, under current planning and mobilization policies it would take about two years before any increased outputs would be realized from existing, in-use production lines (figure 7.7), and three years before any significant effect on force structure would be felt[13]—even with the unrealistic assumptions of a one year of warning time prior to actual warfare and full availability of skilled labor. The longer response time relative to earlier mobilization periods, such as World War II, is due to the sophistication of modern aircraft systems as well as to the increased lead times for critical parts and subassemblies. Thus, for a "short-war" scenario, the existence of substantial excess production capacity has limited value. A significant surge in production could be achieved simply by going to multiple shifts on current production lines, and this should be considered in long-term mobilization planning. The second major finding

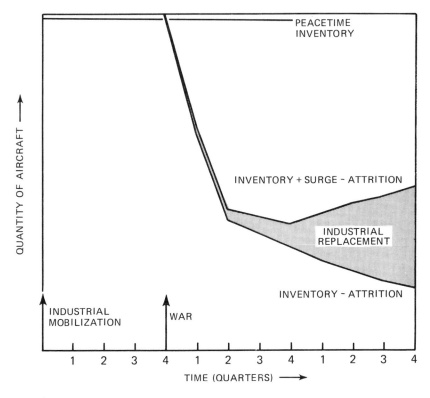

Figure 7.7
Potential response of existing, in-use aircraft production lines to mobilization (one year of
warning time assumed).

of the study is that the surge-production capability of the aircraft industry
is limited primarily by the availability of critical parts, subassemblies, and
manufacturing equipment rather than by lack of extra plant space or production capability at the prime aircraft companies. Accordingly, prime-
contractor aircraft production capacity could be reduced substantially
below current levels without becoming a constraint to surge capability.
However, corrective actions are clearly needed to improve the availability
of critical components and equipment. Studies should be done to investigate the cost versus the benefits of prestocking some of these long-
lead parts and of ordering a few additional pieces of critical assembly
equipment.

7.1.3 Policy Alternatives

There is a wide range of potential corrective policies. At one end of the spectrum is the establishment of policies to encourage the full operation of a free market in the aircraft sector. There appears to be no way for the government to disengage itself from the prime contractors to an extent sufficient for this to be a feasible solution, although a free market can and should be created at the subcontractor and parts-supplier level. Thus, even a policy to leave things as they are means a major governmental role. Therefore, we must accept a non-free-market solution—a "second best" solution.

At the other end of the spectrum of possible alternatives for the aircraft industry is nationalization—the route taken by many other countries, and frequently advocated for the United States by such eloquent spokesmen as John Kenneth Galbraith. However, it is neither the will of the Congress nor the desire of the American people to take this path; nor do I believe, on the basis of historical experience elsewhere and lack of a proper incentive system, that it represents the ideal second-best solution.

The actions that seem to have the highest probability for success for the aircraft industry fall somewhere in the middle of the policy spectrum. Instead of a free market, the more pragmatic approach is limited competition among two or three competing developers. In some areas, in spite of some historical consolidation (as shown in table 7.5), we now have more firms than are necessary for competition. (Notice that many of the consolidations shown simply represent integration at the corporate level, while the original, vertically integrated plants still remain; for example, McDonnell in St. Louis and Douglas in California). Contrary to the conventional wisdom, the proposed reduction in numbers should result in increased efficiency and responsiveness. Also, instead of indirect or direct subsidization, future policies should emphasize greater sectoral planning by the Department of Defense. For example, the DoD should encourage the mixing of commercial and defense product lines, the generation of investment capital (to be used for improving productivity instead of merely increasing plant space), the elimination of excess capacity, the control of allowable overhead expenses, and the maintenance of competition for as much of the industry as possible (preferably, including production).

To assess the effectiveness of various policy alternatives, a Delphi technique was used with knowledgeable participants from the Depart-

Table 7.5
Competing Firms in the Aircraft Industry, 1960–1976

	1960	1968	1976
Fighter and attack planes	Lockheed Convair Douglas McDonnell Vought Republic Northrop Grumman Rockwell (L.A.) Rockwell	Douglas McDonnell Vought Republic GD (Fort Worth) Northrop Grumman Rockwell (L.A.) Rockwell (Columbus)	McDonnell-Douglas Vought Fairchild GD (Fort Worth) Northrop Grumman
Bombers	Boeing GD (Fort Worth) Rockwell	Boeing GD (Fort Worth) Rockwell	Boeing Rockwell
Military transports	Boeing Lockheed Douglas Fairchild Grumman Convair	Boeing Lockheed Douglas	Boeing Lockheed McDonnell-Douglas
Commercial transports	Boeing Douglas Lockheed Fairchild Convair	Boeing Douglas Lockheed	Boeing McDonnell-Douglas Lockheed
Helicopters	Boeing Lockheed Bell Sikorsky Hughes Kaman Hiller Gyrodyne Cessna	Boeing Lockheed Bell Sikorsky Hughes Kaman Hiller	Boeing Bell Hughes Sikorsky

ment of Defense and the Office of Management and Budget.[14] The alternatives presented are shown in table 7.6 and the results in table 7.7.

Because a decision to make no change probably involves the DoD spending well over $240 million per year more than would be otherwise necessary, and because no clear path to the establishment of a free market is apparent in this environment, the government should be looking seriously at some of the other alternatives.

There are basically three areas in which the executive branch and/or the legislature can play a role in influencing future trends in the aircraft industry: short-term budget actions on specific programs and facilities, decisions on each individual aircraft program as it evolves, and longer-term procurement and planning actions which could influence the overall trends and directions of the industry.

Possible short-term budget actions include

• termination, or early completion and then termination, of low-rate production contracts (so that, for example, a small production or modification program is not supporting a large engineering overhead effort aimed at future proposal activities,

• prohibition of the building of new or add-on facilities unless rigorously justified for productivity reasons, and

• closing of selected government-owned facilities (such as depots and repair facilities), whose functions and programs could be transferred to industry.

Table 7.6
Policy Alternatives for Reduction of Extra Capacity

Continue current aircraft procurement practices with evolutionary improvements.

Allow more free-market operation.

Establish acquisition procedures that encourage consolidation and contraction of industry.

Mandate rigorous policy of procuring aircraft at efficient production rates; buy out or terminate low-rate production.

Phase military aircraft procurements to avoid large industry buildups and drawdowns.

Augment demand on private sector of industry by shifting activity from military depots to private industry.

Reduce active extra capacity of industry by closing several government-owned plants or product centers.

Achieve modernization and workforce stabilization at selected facilities.

Table 7.7
Estimated Future Annual Savings Due to Measures Listed in Table 7.6

Alternative	"Expected" Annual Savings (Millions of dollars)	Variation (Millions of dollars)	Ease[a]
Current practice—Evolution	10	0–20	1–2
More of a free market	50	10–80	2–6
Encourage consolidation	70	10–120	4–8
Efficient production rates	100	20–180	3–7
Deliberate phasing of programs	60	0–120	3–8
Shift depot activity	30	–20–80	5–9
Close government-owned plants	40	10–70	4–9
Modernize and stabilize selected facilities	130	50–210	6–10

Estimated overall savings:	$240 million per year
Range:	± $110 million per year
Most preferred alternatives:	efficient production, phasing, consolidation

a. On a scale of 1 to 10, where 1 is the easiest.

Decisions that should be made on each aircraft program as it approaches key points include

- timing of programs (so that, for example, three new helicopter programs do not all start at the same time, with none planned for the next five years),
- combining the competition for the developmental phase of programs with more explicit planning for the specific site to be utilized in the production of the aircraft,[15]
- reviewing the plans for a program, in terms of its production and major subcontract decisions, early enough in the development phase so that future labor capacity, manufacturing equipment, and plant space can be better utilized,
- reviewing production-rate plans to maintain a constant work load and efficient facilities and overhead utilization,
- reviewing individual program plans to ensure that major contracts and subcontracts are not awarded to firms that have exhibited only marginal performance,[16] and
- reviewing individual competitions and source selections to ensure that

major contracts and major subcontracts are not awarded (without extraordinary cause) to firms or plants that are essentially out of the aircraft business.

In the area of long-term policy initiatives, the first action is to develop an institutional approach to the aircraft industry's development. This involves not only making the decisions that will influence future trends in the industry, but also assembling data and assessing the impact of major acquisition decisions. To maintain democratic checks and balances, such data should be fully available to Congress, the industry, the executive branch, and the public.

Another possible long-range objective is the establishment of special suppliers for critical or high-technology work (such as titanium forming and composite fabrication) in order to realize efficient operation, through economies of scale, in these highly specialized and capital-intensive areas. Here again, competition can be fostered by maintaining a few firms with these capabilities, but it would be wrong for every aircraft firm to make the large investment and then have the equipment lay idle, as many are doing now.

Additionally, as the government encourages more use of modern (for example, computer-aided) manufacturing technologies, it may become efficient for only a few selected plants to build the small quantities of production aircraft planned. In some cases, production and R&D may have to be separated in order to achieve this efficiency.

It will be extremely desirable to modernize the remaining production facilities to further reduce the cost of building the aircraft. Orienting capital investment toward improving productivity, not just increasing physical capacity, is a key concern. Increasing productivity with the same or more physical capacity but with relatively low demand would only add to the present problems of overcapacity.

New planning guidelines for surge production capability need to be developed to address the full range of potential conflicts, and not just the high-intensity, long-duration World War II–type conflict. This new direction should emphasize the full integration of all the factors of production—labor, equipment, material, and parts. Successful implementation will depend on developing the institutional capability to identify significant industrial bottlenecks and quantify the cost-benefit tradeoffs. Two critical actions that should be considered are the prestocking of long-lead materials and parts and the development of multiple sources for critical parts.

In some cases the above actions may require modification, or special waivers, of normal procurement regulations. Such actions are within present DoD acquisition authority and should require no legislative changes. However, in the implementation of most of the above-described policy actions, the understanding, cooperation, and support of the Congress will be indispensable.

7.2 The U.S. Shipbuilding Industry

The three primary characteristics usually listed for an efficient free-enterprise industry—reasonable profits, stable growth, and sufficient competition—appear not to be present in the American shipbuilding firms. Profits have been far lower than in comparable industries, civilian or defense; there have been wide variations from year to year within the individual yards and complete unpredictability in each yard's projected annual workloads; there is high turnover of labor (about 75 percent per year); there is essentially no competition in the research-and-development area (the big-payoff area of defense work) at the preliminary design stage, and little for prototyping; and for most classes of ships there is no competition for most of the follow-on production money. On the civilian side, American shipbuilders are not competitive on the world market. Essentially all civilian ship construction is subsidized by the Maritime Administration, at up to 35 percent of total costs. The result has been that, in terms of design, manufacturing, and management techniques, the industry has demonstrated very little innovation in either technology advancement or cost reduction—the normal results of the desired forms of competition.

Current shipbuilding capacity is adequate to handle the expected future civilian and military demands, including potential increased military demands in periods of crisis. Thus, the primary problems to be addressed are the interrelated areas of instabilities and uncertainties in the future market and inefficient utilization of labor. If future demand for shipbuilding is reduced, then the above problems will be compounded by political pressure to keep yards open (even inefficient ones), which goes against the military need to get as many ships as possible for the money available.

While there are over 400 yards engaged in shipbuilding and repair in the United States, only 26 perform any new construction. Since more than 75 percent of the new ship construction in the United States is for the Navy, since much of the civilian work is done in the same yards, and since essentially all of the civilian work is subsidized by the government, I will concentrate on the 11 privately owned yards currently building new Navy ships.

Table 7.8 identifies these yards. Note that nine companies own these yards, and that many of the yards have recently been taken over by large conglomerates. These takeovers have had significant positive and negative impacts on the overall industry. Modern management techniques have been introduced, but the fact that the new owners are oriented primarily towards profits, whereas the earlier owners focused on shipbuilding, has contributed to the friction between the industry and the Navy in the 1970s.[17]

It is clear that the first three yards listed in table 7.8 control the majority of the Navy construction. In fact, these three yards employ over 72 percent of the current work force. Additionally, the majority of the 11 yards are operating at a level higher than they have been averaging for the past ten years, so one would expect to see "growing pains" in some of these yards. However, the current level clearly does not approach the maximum (mobilization) level. Thus, with proper balance among the yards, there is ample capacity for significant surges in shipbuilding.

The industry, by any measure, is very concentrated. The percentage of industry sales represented by the top four companies is 90 percent of all new construction on military ships; this contrasts with figures of 40 percent for nonmilitary ships, 65 percent for the aircraft industry, and 10 percent for fabricated steel products.[18] These figures are important in two respects: The high concentration in Navy construction can be interpreted as a measure of the lack of price competition, and it would make some form of allocation of Navy shipbuilding among the yards relatively easy.

In terms of the types of ships being built, this concentration is even greater. There are some ship classes where only one shipyard is active, and in some cases there is only one or a very few yards even certified to build a certain class of ships. Only Newport News and Electric Boat are currently building nuclear ships. However, both Quincy and Ingalls have previously built nuclear ships and certainly could be recertified in order to increase

Table 7.8
Yards Doing Navy Ship Construction

Yard	Owner	Employment			Current/ Maximum (%)	Current/ 10-Year Average (%)	Building Position	Largest Navy Ship Built	Location
		Maximum Mobilization	Current	10-Year Average					
Electric Boat	General Dynamics	35,000	27,590	15,204	79%	175%	7	SSBN	Groton, Conn.
Ingalls	Litton	32,000	24,715	15,565	77%	158%	12	LHA	Pascagoula, Miss.
Newport News	Tenneco	41,000	23,730	22,820	58%	104%	8	CVN	Newport News, Va.
Avondale	Ogden	18,000	6,554	7,853	36%	84%	2	AOE	New Orleans, La.
National Steel	Kaiser	10,000	6,508	3,812	65%	171%	4	AOE	San Diego, Calif.
Quincy	General Dynamics	24,000	4,335	6,206	18%	69%	5	LHA	Quincy, Mass.
Bath	Congoleum	12,000	3,440	3,008	29%	114%	3	AS/AD	Bath, Maine
Bethlehem Steel	Bethlehem	15,550	3,234	3,542	21%	94%	5	AOE	Baltimore, Md.
Lockheed	Lockheed	6,660	2,857	2,483	43%	116%	3	AS/AD	Seattle, Wash.
Todd, San Pedro	Todd	8,000	2,054	2,296	42%	89%	2	AS/AD	San Pedro, Calif.
Todd, Seattle	Todd	7,500	783	1,591	10%	49%	3	DD	Seattle, Wash.

Source: U.S. Navy (December 1976).

competition and/or to stabilize the workforce in these yards. (This would be particularly important if Title VIII legislation, which requires that all large ships be nuclear, is rigidly adhered to.)

Figure 7.8 compares the labor history of the past 25 years in the shipbuilding and ship repair industry with other comparable sectors of the U.S. economy. It shows that the aggregate shipbuilding industry has had a very desirable labor history of relative stability and growth. This is particularly significant in comparison with some of the other sectors, such as the aircraft industry, where fluctuations have been wide. Also, note that the shipbuilding industry is relatively small compared to other sectors of the economy using comparable, highly skilled labor. Thus, if the salaries, working conditions, and locations of the yards were proper, the industry should have access to the necessary labor force. Unfortunately, these characteristics do not hold, and thus there are significant problems in achieving the desired workforces in some of the yards.

Figure 7.9 projects the total labor requirements for the next six years for both naval and commercial shipbuilding.[19] As this figure shows,

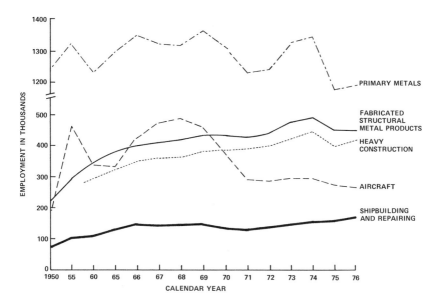

Figure 7.8
Total employment in selected industries. Source: U.S. Department of Labor, Bureau of Labor Statistics, bulletin 1312-10.

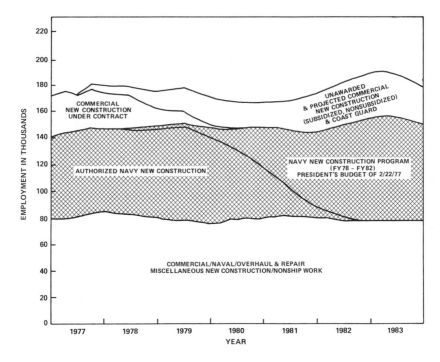

Figure 7.9
Workload forecasts for naval and commercial shipbuilding.

repair work is a relatively constant and reasonably large base that, if properly planned in terms of workforce utilization, can be used for "filling in." Secondly, new naval construction represents approximately 75 percent of all new U.S. shipbuilding, and will continue to be the predominant factor; thus, if properly planned, it would directly influence the overall industry. Also, as figure 7.9 indicates, the stability of the aggregate workforce observed over the past fifteen years (in all shipbuilding and in Navy construction alone) is likely to continue.

However, the data in figures 7.8 and 7.9, which show a stable aggregate workforce, are highly misleading in terms of individual yards. In fact, in the separate yards one finds just the opposite characteristic: very large variations from year to year. There also appears to be a lack of mobility in the shipbuilding labor force. Numerous examples have been cited of workers refusing to move from one shipyard to another (for example, from the Boston yard to the Philadelphia yard when the former was closed, or from Quincy, Massachusetts, where there was unemployment, to Groton, Connecticut, where there was a severe shortage)—even when jobs were guaranteed. Shipyard workers appear not to go from yard to yard with variations in the workload, but rather to leave the industry for other work in the same geographic area.

Consider two large yards doing only Navy construction.[20] Figure 7.10 shows that Yard A initially has a workforce that greatly exceeds its prior ten-year average and even its peak prior year, but still falls short of its required workforce for the very short term. Yet, as the figure shows, expected construction in Yard A will result in a workforce reduction from around 26,000 to below 7,000 workers over the next two years, then a further reduction to 4,000, and then an increase to about 14,000. It is not possible to conceive of this amount of instability over such a short period (in this case seven years) as representing efficient use of labor. Probably the initial level of demand for labor in this yard is too high for the relatively low-skilled labor force in the area. A projected workforce of between 15,000 and 20,000, which would stay relatively constant over the next ten years, would be likely to result in a far more efficient operation.

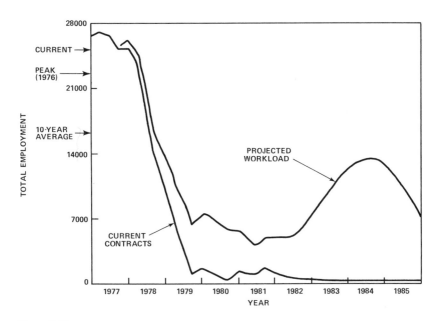

Figure 7.10
Workload forecast for Yard A.

By contrast, consider the situation at Yard B (figure 7.11). Here the initial workforce is about twice the average for the prior ten years, and the projection shows considerable growth even from the high initial level. In addition, the projection in this figure is based upon the planned delivery schedules of the ships under construction, which is likely to change as the scheduled delivery dates for these ships begin to slip. Also, the workforce probably cannot be built up as rapidly as shown. Thus, the shape of the curve will change; the buildup will be less rapid, but will likely continue to much higher levels in the future (as shown by the dashed line). This figure, and the Navy's planning, make the assumption that there will be an increasing labor force available in the Yard B region, but actually it has been extremely difficult to get more workers to come to this area, and it is extremely unlikely that a significant portion of the workforce being laid off at Yard A will move to the Yard B area. Thus, one can project that there will be a constant shortage of laborers at Yard B, and that the schedule for deliveries will be continuously slipping—even if there is a significant increase in salaries and in overtime being paid at this yard.[21]

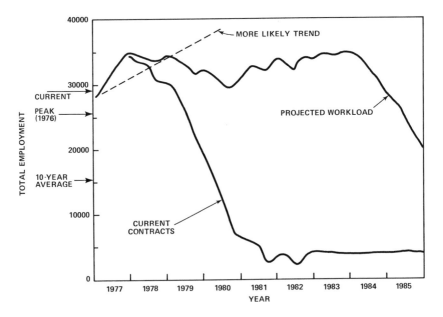

Figure 7.11
Workload forecast for Yard B.

The data in figures 7.10 and 7.11 represent a very poor case of labor utilization planning. Since the shipbuilding industry is very labor-intensive, this represents one significant source of economic inefficiency.

7.2.1 Labor Problems

The most striking labor characteristics of the private shipbuilding industry is the extremely high turnover rates at the yards—approximately 75 percent of the workforce per year. Table 7.9 compares turnover in the private shipyards with other comparable sectors, including the Navy-owned shipyards.[22] The turnover rate in the private yards (around 6.5 percent per month) is two or three times as high as in other comparable industries and more than five times that in the Navy's shipyards, where a stable planned workload exists. This high turnover, of course, represents a very significant inefficiency factor for the private shipyards. It has been estimated that a new worker in a yard is approximately 50 percent efficient in his first two years of work. Even more alarming is that turnover appears to be even worse (on a percentage basis) among the more skilled employees.[23] Again, from the viewpoint of efficiency, this is very undesirable in that highly skilled workers tend to be the most efficient and represent the highest value added.

In trying to understand the cause of this extremely high turnover rate, a look must be taken at the wage structure. For the 1950s and the first half of the 1960s, the shipbuilding industry's salaries were very competitive with those of comparable high-skilled industries, but after the mid-1960s, on a constant-dollar basis, the shipbuilding industry was paying essentially the same salaries while other competitive industries were raising their salaries significantly.[24] By the mid-1970s the shipbuilding industry paid considerably lower hourly rates than competitive labor

Table 7.9
Monthly Turnover Rates in Selected Industries (per 100 Employees)

	Accessions	Separations
Private shipyards	6.7	6.3
Primary metals	3.0	2.9
Fabricated structural metal products	3.9	4.2
Aircraft	1.4	1.7
Navy shipyards	1.1	1.0

markets—approximately 25 percent less than the heavy construction industry. This could account for many people leaving the shipbuilding industry as soon as they can get work elsewhere, often after they have been trained at the shipyards.

An additional reason for the very high turnovers among skilled shipyard workers is that after the initial years income in the shipbuilding industry does not rise much with the age of the worker.[25] Since this does not appear to be the case in other industries, it is an extra incentive for skilled workers to leave shipbuilding. Two other factors undoubtedly playing a role in this labor analysis are the fact that many of the shipyards are located in areas without large pools of highly skilled workers for the shipyards and their labor competitors (industries such as construction) to draw from, and the fact that the private shipbuilding industry's short and non-career-oriented training contrasts greatly in terms of efficiency gains with the two-year, intensive training and the on-the-job instruction program of the Navy yards.

Complicating the labor problems is the fact that, although the labor in the shipyards is almost all production workers, ship construction cannot be thought of as a production line. Each ship is different and individually constructed. As a result, automation does not have a great payoff, and the work continues to be done by mechanics and craftsmen. This labor-intensiveness is shown clearly by figure 7.12, where it is seen that the value added per worker in the shipbuilding industry is less than in other comparable industries. This is particularly significant when it is realized that approximately 80 percent of the workers in a given private shipyard are production workers (as contrasted to the aircraft industry, where in a typical plant about 48 percent of the employees are production workers and many of the others are engineers). The other thing clearly shown by figure 7.12 is that productivity in the shipyards has been going down over the last 15 years (the output value added per worker has not been keeping up with the wage increases)—it shows a total decrease of more than 25 percent over this period. The industry is inefficient and getting more so.

7.2.2 Design Problems
The separation of design work from production work is unique to the shipbuilding industry. Designing is done by independent design companies, with guidance from Navy personnel; then the designs are turned over to the private shipbuilding yards for planning and carrying out con-

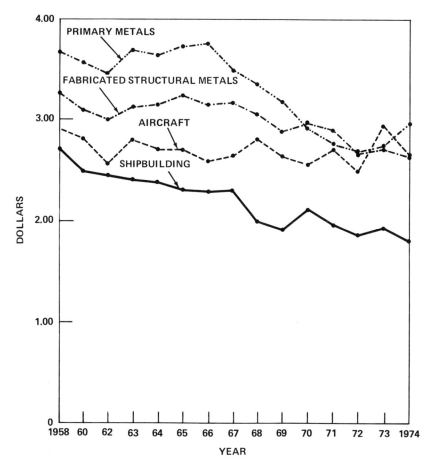

Figure 7.12
Value added per labor dollar, in constant fiscal 1977 dollars. Source: Annual Survey of Manufacturers, 1971 and 1974.

struction. (This explains the far smaller percentage of engineers in the shipyards than in the aircraft plants.) This total separation of design and production encourages design for performance without sufficient consideration of production methods and costs, and can lead to significant inefficiencies in manufacturing. The complexity of a very-high-performance design can make a component expensive to produce, thus reducing the overall cost-effectiveness of the ship and certainly lowering the economic efficiency of construction.

The policy of selecting a single firm to do the preliminary design of a ship together with the Navy has the added undesirable feature of eliminating competition. Instead, two competing firms might be asked to design for similar performance, and the Navy might then select the least expensive ship (or the emphasis might be placed on maximum performance for a predetermined "affordable" cost). The current approach almost ensures the design of the most expensive possible ship—one having maximum potential performance. This design is then put out for bids in order to get the least expensive cost estimate for the building of the basically expensive ship.

7.2.3 Investments and Profits
Though shipbuilding is heavily labor-intensive, there is still a relatively large private capital investment per unit sales dollar. The 1976 asset/sales ratio was 60 for private shipyards, around 27 for missiles and aircraft, and around 33 for defense electronics.[26] Two reasons for this are the extremely large and heavy materials and facilities required for shipbuilding (such as cranes, drydocks, and machine shops) and the fact that there is no government investment in capital equipment and facilities in the shipbuilding industry, as there is, for example, in the aircraft industry (where one-third of all of the plant space is government owned and so is much of the capital equipment).

As table 7.10 shows, there was considerable investment over the 1964–1975 period in the shipbuilding industry, and investment has increased in more recent years as a result of the combination of the projected demands for tankers (which were not realized), the Maritime Administration subsidies (which increased the commercial demand), and the increased Navy construction program (which in some cases required government indemnification of the capital investment). However, a closer look shows that only about one-third of this investment was made in yards

Table 7.10
Capital Investment in Shipbuilding Industry

	Investment[a]
1964–1966	$228 million
1967–1969	$372 million
1970–1972	$398 million
1973–1975	$627 million

a. Constant 1976 dollars.

building Navy ships[27]—despite the fact that 75 percent of all new construction is Navy work.

There are at least three significant reasons for the low level of capital investment in shipbuilding yards doing Navy work. First is the very high uncertainty of the future Navy market for an individual yard (discussed in detail below). Second, most contracts written by the Navy have been fixed-price, incentive-fee contracts, with unattractive industry-government fee sharing ratios. (This results in a significant lack of incentive for capital investment: Under a typical sharing arrangement, a company that invests and realizes savings gets to keep only 10 percent.) However, the most significant cause of the low investment is simply the poor profits in the industry.

As figures 7.3 and 7.4 demonstrated, in comparison with all other sectors of the defense industry the shipbuilding industry (both naval and commercial) is significantly lower in return on investment and return on sales. Since the data in those figures exclude two large shipbuilding yards that had large losses, the real differences are even greater.

7.2.4 Inadequacy of Planning
Figure 7.13 shows a superposition of actual annual Navy shipbuilding budgets and the amounts that had been forecast in preceding years (all adjusted to constant dollars). The shaded number at the beginning of each year's estimate is the realized budget, which has stayed approximately constant at around $4 billion–$5 billion per year. However, in the 1971 five-year forecast (top line) the budget was expected to drop by 1976 down to only $2.5 billion, whereas the projection in 1977 (bottom line) was for the budget to grow to over $8 billion in five years.[28] In fact, if one takes a vertical slice of the projected budget for, say, 1976, as it evolved over a six-year period (cross-hatched column), one sees that the estimates began

FIVE – YEAR PLAN	FISCAL YEAR										
	72	73	74	75	76	77	78	79	80	81	82
JAN 71 FYDP (72 - 76)	5209	3486	2830	2243	2646						
JAN 72 FYDP (73 - 77)	4707	5143	5434	3868	3518	2995					
JAN 73 FYDP (74 -78)		4181	5492	4686	4708	4295	4308				
JAN 74 FYDP (75 - 79)			4916	4142	4320	3923	3457	3277			
JAN 75 FYDP (76 - 80)				3691	5910	6135	5963	6072	5669		
JAN 76 FYDP (77 - 81)					4263	6290	5441	5726	6165	7367	
JAN 77 FYDP (78 -82)						5474	5408	6436	8427	8192	

Figure 7.13
Forecast and actual Navy shipbuilding budgets (see text for explanation). Based on annual presidential budget submissions, January 1971 through January 1977. (Constant fiscal-1977 dollars in millions.)

at about $2.6 billion and rose to almost $6 billion, and that the actual amount in the final budget was slightly over $4 billion. This uncertainty causes significant capital and manpower planning problems for a company in the shipbuilding business. In reality, there were no major external world changes of relevance during this six-year period to cause such large variations; rather, these large variations are generated actions on the part of the Navy, the Office of the Secretary of Defense, and Congress.

These aggregate variations are amplified significantly when individual ship classes are considered; thus, a shipbuilding yard specializing in selected classes of ships sees far larger variations—shown by figure 7.14 for nuclear ships and figure 7.15 for non-nuclear ships. Looking down the columns for calendar year 1976, and remembering that a single ship in or out of the budget can amount to a variation of $1 billion or more, one sees the impact of "planning" variations in the extreme ups and downs. In reality, these are not even plans; they are simply the result of an annual budgetary and force-structure exercise that largely ignores the considerations of economic efficiency in the shipbuilding industry.

7.2.5 Impacts of Inefficiencies on Navy Programs
The first place one would expect to see an impact of these factors is in cost growth and/or schedule slippage for authorized ship construction. Figure 7.16 shows the trends in both of these areas to be getting worse over the five-year period covered. Graph *a* shows that the annual cost growth (as

	FISCAL YEAR											
	71	72	73	74	75	76	77	78	79	80	81	82
SSN (SUBMARINE)												
JAN 71 FYDP (72-76)	4	5	5	5	5	5						
JAN 72 FYDP (73-77)		5	6	5	5	5	5					
JAN 73 FYDP (74-78)			6	5	5	5	5	5				
JAN 74 FYDP (75-79)				5	3	2	3	2	3			
JAN 75 FYDP (76-80)					3	2	3	2	3	2		
JAN 76 FYDP (77-81)						2	3	2	2	2	2	
JAN 77 FYDP (78-82)							3	1	2	2	2	2
SSBN (BALLISTIC MISSILE SUB)												
JAN 71 FYDP (72-76)						1						
JAN 72 FYDP (73-77)				1	3	3	3					
JAN 73 FYDP (74-78)				1	3	3	3					
JAN 74 FYDP (75-79)					1	2	2	2	1			
JAN 75 FYDP (76-80)					2	1	2	1	2	1		
JAN 76 FYDP (77-81)						1	1	2	1	2	1	
JAN 77 FYDP (78-82)							1	2	1	2	1	2
MAJOR SURFACE COMBATANTS (NUCLEAR)												
JAN 71 FYDP (72-76)	1	1	1	1	1							
JAN 72 FYDP (73-77)		1	1	1								
JAN 73 FYDP (74-78)			1	1								
JAN 74 FYDP (75-79)					1	1	1		1			
JAN 75 FYDP (76-80)					1	1	1	1	2	2		
JAN 76 FYDP (77-81)						0		1			1	
JAN 77 FYDP (78-82)							0					

Figure 7.14
Variations in DoD five-year nuclear ship program. Based on annual presidential budget submissions, January 1971 through January 1977. Source: Institute for Defense Analysis.

	FISCAL YEAR											
	71	72	73	74	75	76	77	78	79	80	81	82
MAJOR SURFACE COMBATANTS (NON-NUCLEAR)												
JAN 71 FYDP (72-76)	6	7	7	7	2	3						
JAN 72 FYDP (73-77)		7	8	7	7	11	10					
JAN 73 FYDP (74-78)			8	7	7	11	10	3				
JAN 74 FYDP (75-79)				7	14	11	10	11	11			
JAN 75 FYDP (76-80)					10	10	12	10	15	10		
JAN 76 FYDP (77-81)						6	9	8	11	11	11	
JAN 77 FYDP (78-82)							8	10	12	15	17	16
OTHER SURFACE SHIPS												
JAN 71 FYDP (72-76)	2											
JAN 72 FYDP (73-77)		0	2	9	13	7	7					
JAN 73 FYDP (74-78)			0		7	13	14	2				
JAN 74 FYDP (75-79)				0	7	15	14	2				
JAN 75 FYDP (76-80)					4	2	9	8				
JAN 76 FYDP (77-81)						0			1	4	7	
JAN 77 FYDP (78-82)							0		2	6	8	9
AUXILIARY/SUPPORT												
JAN 71 FYDP (72-76)	2	6	1		5	9						
JAN 72 FYDP (73-77)		3		8	9	9						
JAN 73 FYDP (74-78)			2		4	9	7	7				
JAN 74 FYDP (75-79)				0	3	8	9	9	4			
JAN 75 FYDP (76-80)					2	5	2	8	5	3		
JAN 76 FYDP (77-81)						4	2	6	3	5	6	
JAN 77 FYDP (78-82)							3	9	12	12	8	3

Figure 7.15
Variations in DoD five-year non-nuclear ship program. Based on annual presidential budget submissions, January 1971 through January 1977. Source: Institute for Defense Analysis.

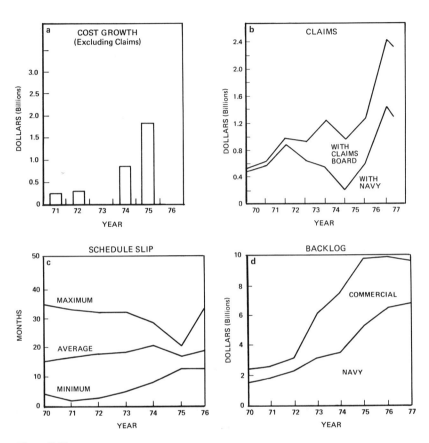

Figure 7.16
Levels of (*a*) cost growth (excluding claims), (*b*) claims, (*c*) schedule slippage, and (*d*) backlog for overall Navy shipbuilding programs.

agreed to by the Navy and authorized in those years; therefore, excluding possible future contractor recovery on outstanding claims) rose to almost $2 billion—a cost growth, for 1975 approved programs, of around 50 percent. Clearly, not all of this could have been due to inflation. Additionally, as graph *b* shows, legal claims outstanding against the Navy had also built up significantly over the same period, and exceed $2 billion. Whatever portions of these claims the Navy finally agrees to pay to the contractors will then be added back into the cost growth shown in graph *a*.

Graph *c* of figure 7.16 shows that, in the seven years covered, the average schedule slippage grew from 15 months to 18 months. (This is total program slippage, including production and budget-induced slippages.) Significant schedule slippage has persisted for the past ten years and is increasing. Rarely has a ship been delivered on time; some are more than three years late. Part of this problem must be attributed to unrealistic scheduling; however, this alone causes significant cost increases—the attempts at an early, expedited schedule require overtime and delivery premiums, and the later disruptions, as the schedule begins not to be realized, cause more inefficiencies. In some extreme cases the Navy has scheduled delivery of a ship 18 months earlier than the contractor said it was possible, and has attempted (unsuccessfully) to have this earlier date met. Even if the initial schedules had been realistic, other factors would have caused schedule slippages resulting in increased costs to the shipbuilding program—for example, the inability to hire and keep enough skilled laborers.

As ships fall behind schedule in the yards, and as cost increases affect subsequent budgets, there is bound to be an excessive unplanned buildup of uncompleted work. As shown by graph *d* in figure 7.16, this has been happening, and it has increased significantly by the additional orders that have been placed but on which work cannot begin immediately (especially in those yards that are already overloaded). Clearly, it will take a considerable period of time to "work off" the $7 billion Navy backlog—especially if there is no reallocation of this work from overloaded yards into yards that are projected to be underutilized in future years.

An additional important point illustrated by the combined data in figure 7.16 is that the $7 billion worth of backlogged Navy ships (including money for current construction and that which is congressionally committed for future construction) are likely to be an average of about 18 months late on delivery and to actually cost around $10 billion, on the basis of experiences with comparable ships over the last five years. This $3 billion projected cost increase, or at least a large share of it, will have to come from increased defense authorizations or from a reprogramming of other defense equipment needs. In either case, the amount is significant, it is not budgeted, and it will have a significant impact. Corrective actions, if implemented early enough, will help; but much more realism in schedule and cost estimating is required.

The following list summarizes fifteen factors of inefficiency that have been identified as causing increased costs to the Navy shipbuilding program:

- variations in workload,
- lack of skilled laborers,
- high labor turnover,
- attrition after training programs (due to higher pay elsewhere),
- low salaries for skilled workers,
- increased complexity of designs,
- lack of series production,
- frequent technical changes,
- market instability,
- emphasis on performance with underemphasis on cost,
- lack of automation and mechanization,
- schedule slips and associated disruptions,
- unrealistic scheduling,
- subcontractor problems,
- poor Navy-shipbuilder relationship.

About half of the items on this list are "supply side," and the other half are on the "demand side." Thus, corrective actions must address both. Also, only the last factor—the poor relationship between the Navy and the shipbuilders, which is complicated by contractual relations, the use of government-furnished shipboard equipment, military specifications, and other things—is unique to Navy shipbuilding; the others are, to varying degrees, also found in the civilian sector. Thus, corrective actions should also significantly improve the overall efficiency of the civilian sector of the American shipbuilding industry—a necessary action, since today it is not competitive on the world market.

Because of the current shortage of Navy ships, the listed inefficiencies should not be eliminated in order to save money on shipbuilding. Rather, more ships per year could be delivered for the money authorized to the Navy if the overall operation were managed more efficiently by the Navy, the Office of the Secretary of Defense, the Congress, and the industry. In order to identify the area in which corrective action would have the greatest payoff, future studies should attempt to quantify each of the inefficiency factors. Of course, they are not independent, and there is bound to be a very large amount of overlap. However, an order-of-magnitude measure should be possible. A preliminary estimate (checked with senior Navy officials) suggests that if the inefficiency of each of these factors could be greatly reduced, there should be a major gain—perhaps greater than 20 percent of the overall program (over $1 billion) per year. However, this is considered an unrealistic basis for analysis. A more appropriate measure would be to determine how much could be saved through modifications in the areas listed over, say, the next five years. Applying this more practical approach to each of these areas and their interrelated impacts, the DoD should be able to save (or avoid wasting) at least $300 million to $500 million per year on Navy shipbuilding after perhaps five years. Such a large potential yearly saving would mean more ships for the Navy. The amount is certainly significant enough to warrant action.

7.2.6 Competitive Allocation
In order to achieve these potential benefits the government must find a way of allocating some of the workload among the individual shipyards. The full use of open competition, as has been traditionally sought in defense acquisition, is obviously excluded. Since large defense procurements such as ships and aircraft do not readily lend themselves to classical open price competition, a "second best" solution should be accepted. Limited competition should be encouraged as an alternative to the status quo of excessive sole-source dependence with lip service to open competition. To be effective, this policy must involve sectoral planning.

This limited competition should, whenever possible, incorporate a process of "competitive allocation" wherein the work on individual or multiple classes of ships is divided.[29] This would bring about competition between yards while assuring each yard some percentage of the work, depending upon the relative bids.[30] The objective is to create more valid and credible competition, more comparable to that achieved in the commercial world.

This approach will allow for other relevant considerations to be brought into the award process when decisions on the most efficient competitive allocation are made—for example, likely "real cost" versus bidder's proposal price, ability of the bidder to hire the needed workers, and the total cost to the Navy not just for an individual program but for all of its shipbuilding. This would avoid the problem wherein one yard, which is currently heavily utilized and thus has a low overhead, makes a low bid under the assumption that it can hire all of the necessary skilled workers, while the losing, underutilized yard then passes on its increased overhead cost to the Navy on a different shipbuilding program. If all relevant economic considerations in the source selection (rather than just the individual yard's cost on the current bid) are utilized, the winner (or winners) of the competition will, in fact, be the "lowest cost" supplier(s), and the basis of the cost calculations will be the long-term costs to the Navy for its overall shipbuilding program.[31] Increased real competition should also lead to technological advancement, while, at the same time, through partial allocation, a more constant workforce will be achieved in the individual yards, thus achieving far greater labor efficiency. Such concepts have been implemented in the past by the DoD, but the details of the procurement methodology, in today's environment and for the shipbuilding industry, must be worked out—with the understanding and cooperation of the Congress.[32]

8 Multinational Considerations

In 1976 the Shah of Iran was quoted as saying that, because he did not want to bankrupt the Grumman Corporation (the sole producer of the U.S. Navy's premier fighter aircraft, the F-14), he would provide $28 million of "advanced payments" against a future military equipment purchase.[1] Until the mid-1970s such a strong link between the posture of the U.S. defense industry and foreign governments would have been unimaginable, but the situation has been changing rapidly.

For reasons of national security we traditionally think of the defense industry as self-sufficient, and even require that it be so. Thus, we tend to treat it as a closed economy, and largely ignore the implications of the growing multinational involvements. Similarly, the few economic analyses of defense policy that are done tend to address solely military issues rather than the interrelationships between defense economics and foreign policy. Today it is difficult to be blind to the international scope and dependence of the U.S. defense industry and to the effects of these factors on its economic efficiency and strategic responsiveness. Yet current national policy appears to be just that: blind.

Of particular concern is that over the past few years—with increasing intensity since 1973—the major U.S. defense contractors have been placing more and more emphasis on the sale of military hardware to foreign governments and, as a result, have been building up a dependency on these sales. This dependency could have significant long-range economic, strategic, political, and even moral implications.

It is not at all difficult to see how this situation has come about. After Vietnam, the U.S. defense procurement account was reduced drastically. In real buying power (constant dollars) it went from a high in 1968 of $44 billion for procurement of new arms to a low in 1975 of $17 billion. Simultaneously, there was a rapid rise in worldwide wealth and demand for arms—most notably in Europe, the Middle East, and the Far East, but increasingly even in South America, Africa, and other developing areas.

In the nondefense area, there was a significant shift by U.S. corporations toward the international commercial markets. In fact, most large U.S. corporations have become transnational in their operations and in their overall outlook. In the military area, this was aided by the "Nixon Doctrine" of encouraging military equipment sales rather than military aid or foreign placement of troops.

Another cause of concern in the area of foreign military sales has been our attempt in the era of "détente" to encourage trade with Communist countries. In fact, U.S. trade with Communist countries increased by a factor of 6 between 1970 and 1974. Furthermore, it has frequently been difficult to distinguish between military and commercial applications of the equipment and technology requested by the Communist countries. Because of this ambiguity, there has been a significant "bending" in the area of military equipment export controls. This has been combined with the international shift toward multipolar centers of world power, in contrast to the bipolar concept of world power upon which most of the arms-control regulations are based.

Also, there has been a drastic change in the quality, not just the quantity, of military equipment sold to other nations. Until the 1970s, most foreign arms sales involved prior-generation equipment and offered little in the way of advanced technology. Such sales had the advantage of keeping the production lines warm in the event that they would be needed for wartime mobilization, and technology transfers were relatively easy to control. Recently, however, there has been a shift in the demand to primarily "first-line" equipment,[2] and in many cases even for new weapons development beyond the requirements of the U.S. Department of Defense.[3] There also is an increasing demand by foreign buyers for engineering and manufacturing technology, coproduction, "turnkey" factories, training, and military construction. The technology transfer involved is similar to that occurring in the civilian area.[4] In a growing number of cases, the American company neither sells a product nor takes an equity position in the new plant but simply sells management and technical knowhow.[5]

Add to these trends the historical fact that foreign arms sales, like foreign commercial sales,[6] have always been far more profitable than domestic sales.[7] (The DoD even allows a higher profit in negotiations on foreign military sales.) Thus, it is easy to see why there has been such a drastic shift by U.S. arms suppliers toward the foreign market.

These same trends have been observed in other supplier countries, particularly the Soviet Union, France, and England. Many countries are now entering the market (for example, Sweden, Italy, Israel, the Federal Republic of Germany, the People's Republic of China, and Canada),[8] and it is expected that still more (such as Argentina, Brazil, and Indonesia) will soon be entering.[9] Partly to counter this foreign competition and partly for political and international-security reasons, there has been another major change taking place over the last few years: The U.S.

government now plays a more significant and direct role in assisting U.S. firms in the sale of their military goods and services to foreign countries. This began with the executive branch (particularly the Department of Defense) playing a major role in the foreign marketing activities of American companies, and reached a peak with such programs as the sale of the F-16 aircraft to a consortium of NATO countries.[10] Here the DoD became the major sales organization in combating the joint efforts of the foreign competitors and their governments.

The U.S. Government is under increased pressure (from both sides of the military-industrial complex) to "sweeten the pie" in order to make foreign military sales more and more attractive. For example, the Airborne Warning and Control System (AWACS) airplane was priced for the NATO countries at $69 million each, while the U.S. was paying $104 million each.[11] In this case, the U.S. was picking up its share—and more—in the purchase of these aircraft for the NATO alliance.

Part of the U.S. government's involvement in these sales to NATO countries has been motivated by a sincere belief that both military and economic benefits will result (for both our allies and ourselves) if the NATO forces use common equipment; that the larger market (both the United States and Europe) could result in volume savings, and common research and development could improve the effectiveness of the total NATO R&D expenditures. So far, these have been mostly political hopes. For example, the result of the F-16 sale to NATO was that the cost of the aircraft to the United States was significantly higher, because of the complexity of the multinational program and the high initial learning costs for the allies. It seems clear that if the DoD were primarily interested in improved NATO force effectiveness it would start with such areas as common munitions, common fuel, common logistics support, and common communication systems. None of these has been achieved. Thus, so far the executive branch's role in NATO standardization appears to be oriented more toward foreign sales of military equipment than toward real improvements in the total NATO force.

The Congress, too, decided to play a more significant role in foreign military sales. The first step was requiring essentially all foreign military sales to be done through the U.S. government, rather than by U.S. companies directly as had been the case in the past and as many American firms would prefer.[12] Therefore, the U.S. government becomes the selling party rather than simply the approver, and assumes all associated contractual and financial responsibility. Naturally, many of the foreign governments prefer this arrangement because it formally commits the U.S. government to stand behind and support the sales over the long haul.[13] This action makes U.S. military products more attractive to overseas buyers, and somewhat reduces the risks to U.S. suppliers (for example, in the event of a foreign government's abrupt cancellation[14] the U.S. government could cover the firm's termination liability costs).

The net effect of all of these trends is that U.S. foreign military sales increased by almost a factor of 10 in five years—to well over $10 billion worth of very sophisticated equipment and logistics support, as well as advanced technology, including engineering, training, and full factories. This has had two very significant impacts on U.S. defense policy. First, it has raised the issue of national self-sufficiency—a basic tenet of military planning and programming for conventional forces, logistics, and the industrial base. The present trend is toward corporate dependency by many prime defense contractors in the United States on their foreign sales of military commodities and toward U.S. dependency on foreign suppliers of critical military parts and materials. These two trends could well influence future industrial and governmental decisions. Secondly, another basic tenet of historical U.S. strategic planning—technological leadership—is being brought into question. Competition for the increasing foreign arms market and the greatly strengthened negotiating position of oil-rich foreign buyers have led to almost uncontrolled selling of military technology, factories, engineering, advanced manufacturing equipment, training, and facilities. Often it is the company that cannot compete effectively in the equipment market that wins a foreign sales award, because of its willingness to give away more technology in order to make the sale. For example, Rolls Royce was in a weak position in the international market for jet aircraft engines, so it agreed to sell engineering and manufacturing technology to Communist China, and Britain pressured the U.S. Department of State into allowing the sale over the DoD's strong objection.[15]

The basic question is whether short-term economic and political considerations are taking too great a priority over long-term economic and strategic considerations. Particularly bothersome is the fact that although the United States does not have a simple "yes or no" choice, most of the answers given are of this simplistic nature ("If we don't sell, someone else will," or "It's morally wrong to do this, so it should be stopped immediately"). This extremely difficult and sophisticated policy area, which has been inadequately addressed by the U.S. government, industry, and the public, must be addressed in the very near future before the cumulative effects become irreversible.

8.1 The Magnitude of the Problem

Consider the following points:

- Between 1965 and 1975 the United States transferred to foreign governments 866 F-4 jets, 2,375 helicopters, 185 destroyers and destroyer escorts, 1,500 Hawk antiaircraft missiles, 25,000 Sidewinder air-to-air missiles, 28,000 antitank missiles, 16,000 armored personnel carriers, 25,000 pieces of artillery and 28,000 tanks, plus enormous stocks of weapons, spare parts, and services.[16]
- Between 1970 and 1975, U.S. orders for foreign military sales went from $1.5 billion per year to about $12 billion (including direct sales by the companies).[17]
- New foreign orders for military equipment from the United States stayed in the $9 billion–$13 billion range in the second half of the 1970s, in spite of the government's stated objectives to reduce these sales.
- The current level of foreign military sales generates 840,000 jobs in the United States.
- Current U.S. foreign military sales include considerable support for the infrastructures of foreign governments, such as construction, training, engineering, and communications. Some examples: complete military and civilian communications systems for Iran and Saudi Arabia[18] (each worth well over $1 billion); over $15 billion worth of construction of transportation systems and facilities in Saudi Arabia supervised by the U.S. Army Corps of Engineers.[19]
- The United States is currently developing and supplying equipment for oil-rich foreign governments that is technically more sophisticated than that which the United States has or can afford. For example, Iran was buying a version of the DD963 destroyer more advanced than the American version.[20]
- The United States is sharing with foreign customers production lines for first-line equipment not yet fully deployed in the U.S. inventory, for example the Maverick and Harpoon missiles and the F16 aircraft.[21]
- Much of the volume of foreign military sales is going to the third-world

countries, and in many cases this represents "the principal way in which the U.S. relates to these countries."[22]

- In 1975 the United States procured for itself only $17 billion worth of military equipment, compared with the $12 billion worth it bought from the U.S. defense industry for foreign governments. Thus, in many areas, foreign military sales were the predominant demand factor; for example, the U.S. Army Missile Command bought 70 percent of its equipment for foreign sales.

- From 1970 to 1976 the top 25 defense contractors had a 45.5 percent increase in foreign military sales, but their U.S. defense business in this same period fell 23 percent (both figures in constant dollars).

- More military aircraft and more Army missiles were built in the United States in 1975 for foreign sales than for the American military.

- The U.S. Department of Defense is currently providing logistics support for 10,000 aircraft in foreign inventories and for only 9,000 in U.S. inventories.

- The sale and use of U.S. military equipment on both sides in foreign conflicts has become more commonplace—consider Greece and Turkey, the shifting alliances in Africa, and Boeings's $200 million deal with Iraq for wide-bodied jets[23] while that country was in conflict with Iran, which was also using U.S. equipment.

- In 1976, eight of the top 25 defense contractors had over 25 percent of their total defense business in foreign military sales: Northrop, Grumman, Litton, Raytheon, FMC, Textron, LTV, and Todd Shipyards. Another five of the top 25 had over 15 percent of their total defense business in foreign sales. In total, the percentage of foreign relative to domestic military business for these top 25 defense firms rose from 4 percent in 1970 to 20 percent in 1976.

- Foreign military sales do not reduce concentration in the defense industry. Rather, as in the civilian sector,[24] the large firms with the extensive R&D and marketing organizations are in a better position to capture this market, and thus to use the foreign sales volume to enhance their position in the U.S. market.

- Bribery appears to be a major factor in the international competition for arms sales.[25] In the United States, many of the major arms suppliers are or have been under investigation in connection with foreign bribery charges.[26] Lockheed has been accused of paying bribes in at least fifteen countries, and in at least six of them it has caused serious governmental crises.[27] It has been claimed that Lockheed and Northrop have paid off officials from Japan, Southeast Asia, the Middle East, West Germany, the Netherlands, and South America. Over a three-year period Northrop is alleged to have put out $30 million, which is about equal to Northrop's total net income during the same period.[28] The stakes in this competition are very high. Bribes are used for two purposes: most obviously, to get customers to buy from the company making the bribe, but also to encourage the country to buy weapons it might not otherwise even buy.

- The United States is currently selling the communist countries, under the guise of civilian needs, precision manufacturing machines that are indispensable for building advanced military equipment. For example, in 1972 we sold the U.S.S.R. 164 machines for building precision ball bearings required to achieve high accuracy with intercontinental ballistic missiles.[29]

- In 1976 the Department of Defense was pushing a U.S. loan (via the Export-Import Bank) to assist Poland in the purchase of $200 million worth of machine tools for a General Motors plant. The objective was to help the American machine tool industry,[30] but the plant would be capable of building military vehicles.

- Even embargoed products are finding their way into the foreign markets. An example of this is the illegal flow of electronics technology from the United States to the Soviet-bloc nations. The methods range from the diplomatic pouch to simple diversion after initial sales to third-country sales by divisions of multinational corporations operating from such locations as Singapore, Lebanon, Austria, Sweden, and Switzerland.[31] Controls over these third-country passthroughs are "virtually useless."[32]

- Recently the Soviet Union has been acquiring a wide range of technology (including computers) from Western European and Japanese subsidiaries of American firms.[33]

- U.S. arms have already found their way into thousands of terrorist and guerrilla actions spanning four continents, from Northern Ireland to the Philippines.[34] Gradually, more and more sophisticated equipment is starting to appear. A few years ago U.S. antiaircraft homing missiles were found in the possession of terrorists in Italy, near the end of the approach to the Rome airport.

- There are increasing numbers of requests (from both U.S. industry and foreign governments) for sales to Communist countries of semiconductor production facilities, computers for automation and data processing, and sophisticated manufacturing equipment. In the spirit of détente, more and more of these orders were being filled; the products have obvious military value.[35]

- A communist country requested production equipment for "supersonic aircraft brake linings." When it was discovered that the process could also produce sophisticated heat-retardant material for use on advanced ICBM reentry vehicles (a technology the Soviets lacked at that time), the sale was terminated.

- Since 1965 the U.S. government has been involved in extending credit for foreign military sales.[36] Since 1969, loans from U.S. commercial banks and the Export-Import Bank have become increasingly important to the foreign military buyers.[37]

- A good deal of the military equipment sold abroad has been built in U.S.-government-owned plants and with U.S.-government-owned manufacturing equipment, frequently contained within company plants. Until recently, these sales were made on a rent-free basis. Numerous other "hidden costs" have been absorbed by the U.S. government.

- Many of the countries buying U.S. equipment are now requiring "offset agreements," in which the United States agrees to buy from those countries a certain amount of equipment in exchange for their having bought U.S. equipment—with full waiver of the "Buy American" act. These offsets help the U.S. prime contractors to consummate sales at the expense of the U.S. subcontractors and parts suppliers.[38]

- In many cases, a "foreign" company involved in multinational coproduction or licensing is simply a U.S. multinational firm's overseas division selling the product and technology it received under license or direct transfer from its U.S. sister division. Such actions clearly profit the firm; the question is their effect on the overall U.S. defense position and whether the U.S. government gets its money's worth.

- There has been a significant increase in foreign investments in U.S. firms,[39] including critical defense suppliers. For example, one of the companies the Department of Defense is supporting in order to maintain the militarily critical domestic miniature-precision-bearing industry is foreign-owned.[40] Also, France's Aerospatiale has bought

Vought Helicopter Co. from LTV and operates it as a wholly owned subsidiary.[41]

- The heavy debt of many large U.S. defense contractors has been partially alleviated by large foreign military sales, which have frequently provided better cash payment arrangements than domestic sales. The potential for problems here is exemplified by the Lockheed case. When Lockheed had nearly $600 million in loans outstanding, almost $200 million of which was guaranteed by the U.S. government, the Secretary of the Treasury testified that the company was in stable condition. However, he emphasized that his projections did not reflect what might happen if Lockheed's contracts with other nations were canceled. Shortly after these remarks, the Lockheed bribe scandals broke out and Japan threatened to cancel $1.3 billion worth of business with that company.[42]
- Very little of traditional economic theory appears applicable to the overall field of international arms trade. Most of the decisions are politically driven, and little effort has been made to derive new theories that might be useful.

8.2 Concerns About Foreign Military Sales

Foreign military sales have been a major issue since the 1976 presidential campaign. In June 1976, the Comptroller General of the United States issued a report, entitled "Foreign Military Sales: A Growing Concern," that raised such issues as the need for methods to achieve international arms control, the economic impact of technology transfer to foreign manufacturers, the implications of providing logistical support for defense equipment sold to foreign countries, the problems of recovering full cost (including DoD costs) for military goods and services sold to foreign countries, and the need for greater congressional oversight of foreign military sales. In this last area, Congress passed legislation indicating its concern and its intent to play a more active role. On the executive side, there were presidentially directed studies of the subject; these produced expressions of concern, policy statements, and directives, but little substantive change. Finally (and this could have the most significant long-range impact), some people raised the concern that the defense industry's attention had been diverted from America's defense needs to the very attractive area of foreign military sales.

To these new economic and political concerns about foreign military sales must be added the traditional military ones: Will the equipment we sell be used against us? Against our allies? Will the sale of this equipment result in security leaks which weaken the U.S. defense posture? Today these military concerns have been considerably heightened. Certainly the worldwide instability in the less developed countries has shown that U.S. equipment could be used in fights against countries also using U.S. equipment for their defense. With the sophistication of modern technology, security leaks become far more significant. If the details of operation of a sensor on a U.S. antitank missile system become known to a potential enemy, the United States must develop a countermeasure for this sensor and employ it on all of its own tanks (since it is likely to appear in Soviet missile designs); then the United States must develop and deploy a new countercountermeasure device on its missiles, since the Soviets are likely to deploy a countermeasure to this missile sensor on all of their tanks; and so forth. When we were selling "old" equipment to known allies, these problems were not so severe, but today, with the most advanced equipment going to third-world countries, the issues becomes more significant.

From the industry side, it has been argued that foreign sales are necessary for the maintenance of a viable U.S. defense industry. Defense-industry executives argue that these sales allow them to stay competitive on a worldwide basis, reduce the cost of equipment to the United States through the increased volume of business, and allow the government to recover research-and-development expenses by selling equipment with R&D charges.[44] The firms also point out that reinvestment of the additional profit from these sales improves productivity for the U.S. military. They argue that it would be foolish to stop foreign sales unilaterally, since the international market would simply go to a foreign competitor's industry. (Experience has often shown this to be correct. When the United States didn't sell aircraft and tanks in South America, the French did; when the United States refused to sell advanced nuclear reactors to Brazil, the West Germans did.)[45] Many American defense contractors go so far as to admit that they are dependent for survival on the current level of foreign military sales.

One obvious alternative is to begin multinational negotiations toward controlling foreign arms transfers, including both sales and security assistance. The Nixon-Ford administrations claimed to have tried this with Middle East sales, but it appears that there was very little effort made, very little political leverage used, and very little success. These activities seemed to focus on the trading of oil for arms. The short-term political and economic exigencies of the time appeared to indicate that such trading was more desirable than the pursuit of international arms-control negotiations or even the negotiation of oil price reductions. The only course of action appeared to be to sell, make money, and stay friends. The Carter administration stated that it would reopen the possibility of multinational arms-control negotiations, but results were slow in coming.

The significant parties in arms-control talks should be France, England, and (in some areas) the Soviet Union. If sincerely and properly pursued (including full coverage in the foreign press), such negotiations would be extremely difficult but could be highly effective.[46] Interim agreements would be a positive first step, even if the United States had to give up a small share of its current market.[47] Time is very important, since more and more new suppliers are entering the field.[48]

A major unanswered question is whether or not making a foreign country dependent on American military equipment is consistent with U.S. strategic objectives in today's environment. The old theory was that by withholding training, logistics, and spare parts we could get a nation to do more or less what we wanted in the international arena. Such a "blackmailing" technique has certainly worked in the past, but today there are two factors operating against it. First, there are alternative sources. When the Soviet Union apparently told Egypt that it would no longer overhaul the engines of the Soviet-supplied Mig-21 jet fighters, China agreed to supply the parts to Egypt free of charge.[49] All signs point to a broadening of the arms supplier market, and often with similar (licensed) equipment. Second, most countries are now aware of the problems that withholding of logistics support can bring, and are asking for a "total package." For example, Iran asked that repair depots be set up for maintaining the Hawk missile system, that personnel and managers be trained, and that manufacturing facilities be established.

Now consider the complementary problem, pointed out in chapters 2 and 6, of the growing U.S. dependency on foreign parts and raw or semifinished materials. Here again, the old policy assumes U.S. total independence, but the reality of today's interdependent world may make this an impossible situation. Current U.S. policy is extremely ambiguous. On one hand, we state that we want to have more coproduction with our NATO allies, and in some cases this has led to our dependence on them for individual parts. If this is the intended policy, it should be clearly stated and not left uncertain as to whether this policy is to apply or whether we are simultaneously to have total self-sufficiency and therefore duplicate European products in the United States. Similarly, in the areas where we do not currently have substitutes for products coming from other countries, we should pursue research and development work on substitutes or else we should make our dependence explicit. We should evolve a policy based on the implications of our dependence and the consequences of possible actions by our suppliers. This has been somewhat thought out in the case of our dependence on overseas sources of raw materials (see the discussion of strategic stockpiles in chapters 2 and 6), but component and subsystem dependence is a relatively new phenomenon for the United States and has not at all been thought out in terms of explicit and unambiguous policy guidance. Perhaps it needs to be considered on a case-by-case basis.

There is a danger that the U.S. reaction may go too far and prohibit the buying of any foreign components for defense products. This would be wrong, since these foreign sources (particularly when there is only a single U.S. source) clearly represent viable competition, as well as surge capacity—under some conditions—which would not have otherwise existed. The problem, then, is to establish a clear policy that allows foreign sources to compete in the United States but prevents total dependence, or one that allows dependence but makes it explicit and therefore consciously provides for its consequences.

Another major concern about America's foreign arms trade (raised by a congressional study)[50] is the lack of foreign-policy flexibility these sales are creating for the United States in parts of the world where there are large commitments of U.S. manpower. One Senate staff study concluded that, prior to the 1979 revolution, Iran was so heavily dependent on U.S. personnel (to operate and support the sophisticated equipment we had sold them) that Iran could not have gone to war "without U.S. support on a day-to-day basis." This report estimated that there were almost 20,000 Americans in Iran in a military-related training capacity.[51]

However, dependency today is a two-way street. Stanley Hoffman, in a *New York Times* editorial entitled "Grouping Towards New World Order," made this point very clear:

There is a new uncertainty in world affairs which gets added to traditional physical insecurity: I don't know where my power ends and yours begins, since my power is partly your hostage and vice versa, and the more I try to force you to depend on me, the more I depend on you. World politics now becomes a test of vulnerability, and degrees of vulnerability are not identical with quantities of power. This explains why the United States, even though it is on top of almost every hierarchy of power (military, economic, monetary), remains a tied Gulliver.[52]

Our growing dependence upon foreign materials and parts suppliers is certainly a genuine basis for Hoffman's concern. The growing feelings of power (particularly among third-world countries) and the use of non-military measures such as boycotts make defense considerations in this area of interdependency more and more complex for the future.

Another important question concerns the long-term economic and military benefits of these arms procurements to the recipients. For example, Peru's purchase of tanks and jet fighters has brought demands from Chile, Argentina, and Brazil for similar equipment to be sold to them.[53] This raises the question of the social costs to less-developed countries who are spending their very limited resources on munitions procurements instead of internal development. Oil-rich countries pose an additional problem by introducing military instability into a volatile area of the world by importing billions of dollars' worth of arms. American military commanders raise an even more immediate concern about these foreign military sales by pointing out the large amount of DoD manpower devoted to training and logistics activities for these foreign governments.[54] (These resources must come directly out of the manpower ceilings established by Congress for the DoD.) This potentially weakens the U.S. defense position in order to support foreign sales. The counterargument states that foreign military sales are only allowed (by law) if they are in "the U.S. defense interest"; thus, the manpower being used in support of foreign military sales strengthens our allies' position and should, in the end, result in a reduced requirement for U.S. military manpower. In the case of many military sales today, the support for the latter argument is very hard to trace.

One of the more significant concerns about recent foreign military sales, and one raised by the GAO study, is the implication of logistical support for the orders that have been booked but not yet delivered, and those still to come (there is perhaps $30 billion in military equipment on order). The DoD is already having some problems supporting the large amount of equipment that was shipped in the past, but that is nothing compared with the equipment that will start to come from the over $10 billion per year of foreign military orders that began in 1975. Additionally, experience has shown that some of this equipment may remain in use in these foreign countries for thirty years—often longer than its life in the U.S. inventory and longer than the existence of the production facilities. During this time the foreign governments are likely to keep coming back to the U.S. government whenever support problems arise.

It is important to note that the sole legal justification for all military assistance—whether sales or grants, and whether through the federal government or directly from U.S. companies—is its value to the overall U.S. defense posture.[55] This is the criterion under which the export license reviews are made. Other rationales, such as improving the balance of trade and providing jobs, are clearly intended to be only secondary considerations. Yet in almost all foreign military sales efforts there are major interdepartmental conflicts—for example, the efforts of the Department of Commerce to encourage exports and the political needs of the State Department (including requests for arms from our friends and allies overseas) versus the security need of the Department of Defense to control equipment and technology. Even within the DoD there is conflict between the "marketing department" (the Defense Security Assistance Agency) and the various "control" groups. In this conflicting interdepartmental arena there is no "higher court" to resolve the issues, only the president. Consequently, arbitrary decisions get made at the lower levels for valid short-term objectives. Many of these decisions would be far less arbitrary if U.S. laws, policies, regulations, and institutions in the arms sale and control area were updated from the world of the 1960s to the economic and political realities of the late 1970s and the 1980s—from a world in which there were two major powers to one with multiple interdependencies, from foreign sales of equipment to technological enhancement, and from the sale of outdated systems to the export of the most modern equipment.[56]

Finally, the government needs to think out more fully the strategic implications of the effect of the multinational arms trade on the U.S. production surge capability. We could redirect equipment intended for foreign governments if we needed it, but would we redirect it? We could recall many of the trained U.S. personnel from overseas, but would they be released? Because of the standardization of equipment we could count on our allies to support or supplement our equipment, but would (for example) the threat of an oil embargo prevent this? The foreign plants producing U.S.-originated equipment for our allies could supplement our own supplies, but in a crisis would they allow this diversion? Our dependence on foreign materials and parts threatens our surge capability; do we have bigger "threats" with which to retaliate, and would we use them? Would foreign ownership of U.S. defense firms (primes or suppliers) affect our surge capability? If we nationalized a domestic defense plant, what would be the retaliatory actions against foreign branches of the American firm? While the considerations and questions can be easily listed, the answers are far more difficult. Particularly bothersome is that the questions are not being asked, and that even if they were the answers could not be derived from current legislation, policy, or governmental actions. The existing policies are outdated and not usable under today's conditions of worldwide interdependence.

9 Assessment of Problems and Future Trends

The prior chapters have given many examples of decreasing economic efficiency and reduced strategic responsiveness throughout all levels and sectors of the U.S. defense industry. The basic question, however, is whether these are merely symptoms of the normal postwar decline in defense procurements that will somehow be survived, as has always been the case, or whether there is evidence of a much more serious problem (or set of problems) that is building up and will become critical over the next decade.

A significant portion of today's problems are either unique to the current era or greatly exaggerated by current conditions, such as the existence of sophisticated and rapidly changing technology, global interdependence, and shortages of raw materials and energy. The weaknesses within the defense industry are much more serious today because of the worldwide military environment—the fact that the United States is significantly "outgunned" by the Soviet Union, the large standing armies on both sides, the continued threat of nuclear warfare, and the vulnerability of the homeland. The overriding fact is that the United States is spending more and more money on its defense posture and yet is building fewer and fewer systems and presenting less of a credible defense posture each year. The objective, then, should be to see whether there are actions which the United States can take in order to strengthen its overall defense posture without significantly increasing expenditures.

Such results can only come through increased efficiency and better utilization of resources. Suggestions in this direction will be the subject of chapters 10–12. However, it is appropriate at this point to estimate (in summary fashion) the approximate costs of the current inefficiencies—and, thus, the potential for improvement—and to forecast the likely future trends if these inefficiencies are not corrected.

The problems within the U.S. defense industrial base have not yet reached a critical level, but they must be highlighted at this time so that corrective actions can be taken before the critical point is reached. Public awareness of some of the problems was suppressed by three phenomena of the second half of the 1970s: the very high level of foreign military sales, the rapid increase in defense procurement budgets, and the big increase in commercial procurements for the replacement of old aircraft. Without these factors, many of the strains would have begun to appear earlier. However, because of them there is still time to take corrective actions to minimize the danger, if not to prevent the occurrence, of the problems that can be foreseen.

Because these problems have not yet reached critical magnitude, the actual dollar value of the inefficiencies is still (on a percentage basis) relatively small. On the basis of the data for the aircraft and shipbuilding industries given in chapter 6, the current inefficiencies account for about 6 percent of the dollars spent in the overall defense industrial base. This is a relatively small percentage, but still a large amount of money. It represents over $3 billion per year of potential improvements in the U.S. defense posture—that is, added military equipment for the dollars allocated. The amount of money to be wasted or saved will grow significantly in the future if corrective actions are not taken.

9.1 Summary of Cost Inefficiencies

In order to show the basis for the estimate of at least $3 billion annually in inefficiencies, the summary data in tables 9.1 and 9.2 were generated independently.

Table 9.1 lists a number of the major problem areas discussed in the earlier chapters and estimates the annual potential savings that might be realized out of an overall annual Department of Defense acquisition budget of around $50 billion (roughly that of fiscal 1980). In each case, the basis for the estimated cost savings is shown and can be traced through earlier discussions in the book. These areas are not independent, and thus it is inappropriate to sum up all of the estimated potential savings. Thus, for this table, the total of $4.5 billion has been arrived at through a root-sum-square combination of the numbers.[1] It is equally important to emphasize that the numbers shown in this table are quite conservative,[2] and are certainly realizable if the appropriate changes are made over, for example, the next five years. For each of the numbers shown, it is believed that significantly greater cost savings could be achieved were it not for such characteristics and problems as institutional inertia to change and special-interest lobbying; however, the realism of these constraints is recognized and the numbers in the table have been reduced accordingly.

Because the list in table 9.1 is by no means complete, the total of $4.5 billion is probably lower than one might estimate with a more extensive list. A comparison between the limited functional-area estimates of table 9.1 and the estimates by *product* areas shown in table 9.2 (which yield a

Table 9.1
Estimates of Cost Inefficiencies (By Functional Problem)

Problem	Basis for Suggested Saving	Estimated Annual Potential Saving (Billions)
Lack of production competition	Data from prior defense programs (net savings $\approx 25\%$ of applicable prime and sub contracts—at least 20% of production).	$1.75
Lack of multiyear funding	Multiyear funding would allow and encourage capital investment and more efficient production (minimum saving: 2% of production).	0.70
Very low production rates	Learning-curve theory (minimum saving: 2% of production).	0.70
Redundant prime-contractor facilities and labor	Current amount is more than required for competition or surge ($\approx 5\%$ of prime-contractor production).	1.00
Design for maximum performance	Lower-cost and more producible products would save a minimum of 5% of production.	1.75
Lack of budget stability	Reducing program stretchouts would save 1% of production; reducing congressional add-ons would save $\approx$ $200M/year	0.55
Long and unrealistic development schedules	Better scheduling could reduce cost of full-scale developments by at least 5%.	0.50
Large design teams and excessive data requirements	Following example of similar European developments could save $\approx$ 10% of development costs.	1.00
High overhead	Following example of civilian business could save at least 3%.	1.50

(continued on following page)

Table 9.1 (continued)

Problem	Basis for Suggested Saving	Estimated Annual Potential Saving (Billions)
Lack of automation	Computer-aided manufacturing and design could save ≈ 3% of production and development.	$1.35
Poor labor stability at plant level	More stability on programs and in firms could save at least 3% of production.	1.05
Lack of standardization of systems and subsystems across services	Higher volume should have a net production saving of 25% (applicable to at least 5% of production products) and a net R&D saving of 5%.	0.95
Specialization of military plants, parts, and specifications	Commercial parts (where applicable) would reduce costs by at least 50%; use of commercial specs should save at least 5% (where applicable); integrated plants would reduce overhead.	0.75
Excessive design specifications	Current requirement that all systems perform perfectly under extreme conditions raises unit cost of production equipment by 5% and increases development program costs by at least 5%.	1.85
Total (root-sum-square)		$4.5

Table 9.2
Estimates of Cost Inefficiencies (by Product Area)

Area	Approximate Annual Expenditure (Billions)	Potential Improvements (Basis for Inefficiency Estimate)	Estimated Annual Saving (Billions)
Aircraft production	$13	Higher production rates: $300M Less excess capacity: $400M Automation: $450M Other: $500M	$1.0 (8%)
Missile production	5	More competition: $500M Multiyear procurements: $300M Lower-cost designs: $400M Other: $300M	0.8 (16%)
Ship production	6	Improved labor stability: $500M Lower-cost designs: $800M Improved subsystem mgmt.: $400M	1.0 (16%)
Tracked vehicles production	2	More competition: $400M Improved subsystem mgmt.: $250M	0.3 (15%)
Other production (includes munitions, space systems, electronic systems, etc.)	10	Improved electronics mgmt.: $1,000M Other: $500M	1.0 (10%)
Research and development	10	Reduced full-scale development times: $500M Other: $400M	0.5 (5%)
Support equipment	4	Integration with programs: $300M Multiyear procurements: $200M Other: $200M	0.4 (10%)
Total	$50		$5 (10%)

total of $5 billion of estimated annual potential improvements) yields consistent results—for the rough estimates being made. Table 9.2 is based on the same set of assumptions as table 9.1,[3] and here too the estimated potential improvements are extremely conservative. In no area do the estimated savings exceed 16 percent of the dollar expenditures, and the total of $5 billion corresponds to a potential improvement, after five years of implemented changes, of only 10 percent of the total expenditures. This corresponds closely to a much earlier estimate by Frederick Scherer,[4] and is considerably less than the 20 percent many others have estimated as being potentially realizable. The 20 percent figure could be supported by a less conservative use of the data in tables 9.1 and 9.2, or by considering the cost impacts these changes could have on the other half of the total defense budget (the manpower costs, civilian and military)—for example, through the reduction in maintenance costs that could be achieved by producing more maintainable equipment.

In spite of the fact that the data in tables 9.1 and 9.2 indicate savings of around $5 billion per year, and that this estimate is confirmed by prior independent studies, it is necessary in such an analysis to make as conservative an estimate as possible in view of the extremely powerful vested interests that will resist any change in such a large and visible institution as the defense industrial base. A $3 billion annual improvement in the U.S. defense posture—through the changes to be described—appears to be a realistic minimal objective.

9.2 Near-Term Trends

In terms of the defense budget itself, the reluctance of Congress and the military to significantly cut back on military personnel means that an increasing percentage of the total budget will continue to pay for manpower costs (because of such factors as legislated salary increases, inflation, comparability pay, and increased retirement costs), and thus a smaller and smaller amount will be available for developing and procuring defense equipment unless there are very large budget increases.

On the research-and-development side, the data indicate that development of major weapons systems is taking longer and is becoming more expensive. Thus, fewer and fewer programs will be put into full-scale development. The industrial impact of this will be much more severe oligopoly competition. This means much more effort to win the initial R&D program—and, therefore, increased "buying in." It also means more waste on multimillion-dollar proposal efforts to win these few available programs. More and more of the R&D work will go to the large firms. Therefore, with less available business and more difficulty in getting venture capital, it is likely that a large number of the innovative smaller R&D firms will be driven out of the defense market. This will be particularly critical at the lower tiers.

The response by the defense industry to this shrinking business will likely take a variety of paths. First, a significant increase may be expected in the sharing of the business among the various large defense contractors. These "teaming" arrangements begin in R&D and carry on through production. They include joint arrangements between prime contractors (such as that between Northrop and McDonnell-Douglas on the F-18 aircraft and that between Hughes and Boeing on the Roland missile system), between prime contractors and subcontractors, and even between subcontractors (Westinghouse and ITT each have divisions working in the electronic warfare field, and have recently teamed up for the development of an electronic countermeasure system[5]). Joint development and coproduction are also increasing between U.S. and European firms (and even firms in the third world); again, the likely effect is to reduce the total market, since the European and third-world defense markets have been dominated by U.S. contractors. Second, the prime contractors are increasing their share of "make" versus "buy." This will be complemented by increased efforts at vertical integration—through acquisition—by the prime contractors (again, to keep their shares of the market, and simply to get parts). Such actions will reduce competition, raise prices, and result in less business being available to the independent subcontractors and parts suppliers.

The fact that an increasing share of available defense dollars is going to the prime contractors means that more and more subcontractors will be leaving the defense business—either through bankruptcy or because of the desire to get into a more attractive business. This diminishment of suppliers at the lower tiers will continue to result in rising prices (because there will be more sole-source situations), more dependence on foreign suppliers, and considerably reduced surge capability. Eventually, it will get to the point where the government will start to get concerned about these lower tiers and begin to do some selective planning. This may result in more "captive lines" (wherein the government assumes responsibility for setting up and maintaining parts production lines solely for military purposes). This is an expensive solution, but it may be the only way, within the current structure, for the defense suppliers to get their parts.

In parallel with this inevitable consolidation in the private sector, the government is bringing a larger share of the work into its arsenals and depots in order to keep them occupied. These facilities are manned by Civil Service employees, and it is far more difficult to either fire these people or close these facilities than it is to get rid of firms in the private sector. Thus, as has previously been the case in postwar periods, the share of the business being done in the government arsenals and depots will increase significantly. Naturally, the defense industry will attempt to have a lot of the work being done in the depots awarded to plants with large excess capacity. However, the Department of Defense and the Congress tend to resist this, and the net effect is likely to be an increased percentage of work being done in government facilities.

The effects of this consolidation will be felt strongly in at least two areas. First, the large U.S. manufacturing firms will (both intentionally and because of the market trends) become less and less dependent upon defense business. Some may lose their interest in doing any DoD work—even some that are among the few remaining suppliers of given items. Second, there is likely to be much more political influence on source selection than in the past, because of the pressures labor and management will bring to bear on their representatives as a result of the shrinking total business and fewer individual programs.

On the industrial side, with the above trends a continued lack of investment for modernization is anticipated as well as a growing excess of capacity. Both of these are bound to lead to a continued reduction in productivity. The shrinking volume is more likely to be matched by a cutback in direct labor personnel than by a reduction in the "overhead" personnel, so the already high overhead rates will go up significantly. This will be amplified by the increased Social Security costs and other government social requirements placed on the defense firms. Also, attention will begin to be paid to the labor market. The average age of the defense workers in many sectors is approaching retirement age, and there will be a need to hire and train new employees. With such undesirable trends in the defense industry, it is going to be difficult to get young employees to enter and remain without significantly higher wages. However, with the increased competition for the few weapons programs available and the closer attention that the government is expected to pay to costs, we can expect to see much more bitter labor battles than in the past. This disruption will further reduce the overall economic efficiency of the industry.

All of the above factors lead to an anticipation of continued rising costs for both development and production of defense systems. Also, the fact that increased performance will continue to be required from these systems in order to match the improving Soviet systems will lead to significant reductions in the quantity of systems that can be bought (in view of the low total dollars available and the higher unit costs). The consequent lowering of production efficiency due to the inability to have large, efficient production runs will raise costs further. The defense firms are already heavily in debt and cannot stand a shrinkage in business. Therefore, far more government involvement in financing, guaranteeing of loans, indemnification of capital equipment, and even bailouts is anticipated. Still, it can be expected that a number of the firms will eventually be forced out of business.

In the international arena, there is likely to also be far more government involvement in the defense industry. The push for common NATO equipment and the associated coproduction and offset agreements will frequently require the U.S. government to be involved in industrial teaming arrangements. Additionally, as foreign military sales remain high, the defense industry will become increasingly dependent upon these sales for its survival and increasingly vulnerable to political changes. Also, as the United States becomes more and more dependent upon foreign raw materials, energy, and military parts, it is expected that their prices will rise rapidly and that the government will begin to play a more significant role because of the strategic vulnerability that this represents. Whether the U.S. government's involvement will take the form of speeches or actions remains uncertain. The initial U.S. response to the recognition of the energy shortage and energy dependency mostly took the form of speeches, and little solid action followed for some time.

In the area of strategic responsiveness, the U.S. defense posture will likely continue to stress high-intensity, short-duration NATO wars. Therefore, in spite of the clearly decreasing strategic responsiveness of the defense industrial base, it would not be a surprise if there was less attention paid to such areas as production surge responsiveness and mobilization. Resources will be limited, and preparedness planning will simply have lower priority. Similarly, limited resources will continue to restrain the needed equipping of American forces for potential wars (growing in probability of occurrence) in the Middle East, the Persian Gulf, or even Central America.

Thus, there will be great pressures for a significant increase in the defense budget—from the industry (which is threatened with a loss of business) and from the military (which is threatened by the rising costs of military personnel, the greatly diminishing quantities of military equipment, and the rising quantities of Soviet military equipment). These pressures, combined with the increasing world tensions likely to be brought on by energy problems in the Soviet Union and the West and by political changes in the developing nations, can be expected to bring pushes from the Congress for large increases in the defense budget. (This tendency began in the late 1970s, and was certainly accelerated by the Iranian revolution and the Soviet move into Afghanistan.)

The Congress is likely to respond to these pressures by approving higher defense spending,[6] but this spending will not lead to either a significantly improved defense posture or a strengthening of the defense industry unless major structural changes take place in the defense industry. Rather (as discussed in chapter 1), these increased expenditures will simply raise equipment costs (because of the bottlenecks in labor, material, and production equipment with the present selected suppliers, who are likely to get the new orders). Therefore, the increased expenditures will simply be inflationary, and will thus have a negative effect on the overall U.S. economy.

It is not the intent of this book to project the ultimate impact of a greatly weakened defense industrial base for the long-term defense posture of the United States. The industry has historically been an important part of the overall U.S. defense capability, and the problems listed above clearly indicate not only that its potential contribution is decreasing, but also that the rising costs and resultant lower quantities of equipment are significantly reducing the deterrent and fighting capability of the existing forces. Thus, corrective actions are clearly warranted in order to get the best defense posture for a limited number of dollars. Additionally, maximum efforts at both arms control and stable disarmament are desirable. However, the defense industrial base is unprepared for major progress in this area, and without assistance and planning such cutbacks would have further undesirable impacts.

This overall forecast is not a bright one; but, given current conditions and trends, and without corrective action in the very near future, it almost certainly will hold true.

9.3 Future Uncertainties

The near-term projections made above are based on the assumption that the trends will continue more or less as they have been going. Certainly the corrective actions proposed would take a considerable period of time to dramatically reverse the current trends. However, there could be external and internal changes that would rapidly alter the defense industry's overall posture. The most obvious is the onset of war—either limited, large-scale, or "proxy." Considerations of warfare should not be limited to traditional scenarios. In the not-too-distant future one might expect to be confronted with nuclear terrorism. If the energy, food, or raw materials crises become much more severe, there may be wars between the "haves" and the "have nots." Other forms of geopolitical realignment could take place; for example, the breakup of NATO if some of the countries go communist, or the United States and some communist countries combining for mutual interest. As mentioned, significant success in arms control or disarmament (in either strategic, tactical, R&D, or foreign-military-sales areas) could accelerate many of the trends discussed above. In the technology area, there could be an unexpected foreign action such as the launching of Sputnik, which kicked off a great American technological drive. Or there could be a domestic reaction to a gradual loss of technological preeminence.

Finally, there is the possibility of a revolution in weapons technology.[7] In 1878 Friedrich Engels wrote that "the weapons used in the Franco-Prussian War have reached such a stage of perfection that further progress which would have any revolutionizing influence is no longer possible"; within thirty years aircraft, tanks, chemical warfare, submarines, and radio communication were introduced. A 1937 study entitled "Technological Trends and National Policy" failed to foresee that within twenty years the following systems would become operational: helicopters, jet engines, radar, electronic computers, nuclear weapons, rocket-powered missiles, recoilless rifles, nuclear submarines, and satellites. New technology can be developed and introduced into modern warfare, with an all-out push, in only a few years. It is almost impossible to predict from which direction such inventions will come. However, major breakthroughs in certain areas would demand redirection of the U.S. defense industry. Some examples would be a Soviet breakthrough in antisubmarine warfare, the acceptance by the United States of the vulnerability of aircraft carriers, the deployment of an effective anti-ballistic-missile system, or even the successful demonstration by the Soviet Union of an effective civil and industrial preparedness program.

In view of the 200-year history of the United States and the 2,000-year history of the Western World, war is a very real possibility. This is acknowledged by the United States, its allies, and its potential adversaries through their large defense expenditures. Certainly it is in the interest of the United States to make maximum use of the industrial resources being paid for by these dollars—to present the strongest possible deterrent posture for the money available.

10 Criteria and Alternatives for Improvement

I begin these remaining chapters with considerable humility and almost with fear. For over 200 years people have been trying to improve the U.S. defense industry, and I acknowledge the magnitude of the task. One must recognize the extreme difficulty of making any change in government. As Machiavelli said,

. . . it ought to be remembered that there is nothing more difficult to take in hand, more perilous to conduct, or more uncertain in its success, than to take the lead in the introduction of a new order of things. Because the innovator has for enemies all those who have done well under the old conditions, and lukewarm defenders in those who may do well under the new. This coolness arises partly from fear of the opponents, who have the laws on their side, and partly from the incredulity of men, who do not readily believe in new things until they have had a long experience of them. . . . Thus it happens that whenever those who are hostile have the opportunity to attack they do it like partisans, whilst the others defend lukewarmly . . . .[1]

Nonetheless, the information in the previous chapters presents an overwhelming case for the need to change the structure of the U.S. defense industry and the government's way of doing business.

Basically, the problem can be stated as follows:

The Department of Defense is a monopsonistic buyer, with shrinking buying power in peacetime. What form of supporting industrial structure would give the maximum defense capability for the approved dollars with the least adverse impact on the public, and what actions (if any) should the Department of Defense be taking towards achieving this form of industrial base?

This question will be dealt with in three steps. This chapter is devoted to defining the criteria, and to presenting broad alternatives—including those represented by a variety of other existing models. Chapter 11 considers the approach taken to this basic question by a number of other countries, both capitalistic and communistic. Finally, chapter 12 presents specific recommendations that can be implemented within the broad social, economic, and political structure that exists in the United States today—a democratic, private-enterprise system.

One last cautionary note: It must be continuously kept in mind that we are not dealing with solely economic considerations. The industrial structure has "serious social and political consequences, as well as implications for economic performance."[2] Of particular importance is the need, when considering potential corrective actions, to weigh the impact on each of the various groups with vested interests and to consider their likely reactions in resisting any proposed changes.

10.1 Criteria

Since we are discussing broad economic policy, in considering specific defense-industry criteria we should stay within acceptable definitions. In the general sense, we are looking for "the achievement of economic growth and stability within a democratic, private enterprise system."[3] In applying such a definition to the defense sector, one would have to interpret "growth" as being represented by such areas as research-and-development improvements and productivity gains for cost reductions —improvements in both quality and quantity that will yield military advantage.[4]

If we are to make more effective use of the defense industry, we must consider that industry's specific objectives. Historically, there have been five:

- To provide the maximum deterrent and battle capability for the dollars allocated. (This involves both the performance and the quantity of the weapons systems produced, and might be called allocative efficiency.)
- To achieve maximum production efficiency, for the long and the short term, with the given resources (dollars, facilities, and equipment)—that is, to avoid waste.
- To provide sufficient surge capability (the ability to increase production rates rapidly) for likely emergencies ranging from proxy wars such as the 1973 Mideast War to various levels of wartime mobilization. (This is an economic as well as a strategic consideration, since surge capability must be provided out of peacetime allocations.)
- To achieve maximum technological advancement for future military advantage with the resources available. (The danger of not maintaining research-and-development leadership in the military area is particularly critical, but R&D is always an investment for future needs, and must be balanced against current requirements.)
- To minimize adverse effects on society and the political process. (This includes balancing defense priorities and civilian demands, accepting the role of the Congress in the procurement process, and weighing carefully the political impact of changes in the existing industry-government structural relationship.)

Many of the current problems of the defense industry result from policymakers' trying to optimize these five goals either simultaneously or (even worse) independently. A better solution lies in defining a single objective—producing defense equipment during peacetime with economic efficiency (the second goal listed above)—while recognizing the other four. Thus, the provision of additional surge capability, the requirement for small numbers of different systems, and the requirement for pursuing different technological approaches through the maintenance of a large R&D establishment would each be considered as constraints in optimizing the single objective of developing and producing, at minimum peacetime cost, the equipment necessary to maintain a strong defense posture.

Since the money available is limited by the Congress, this production-efficiency criterion means producing the maximum number of units of an economically designed product for the dollars available. This definition has the particular advantage, for dealing with the military, of putting the issue in terms of quantity of equipment, which has more direct military meaning than quantity of money. This is particularly important today, because of the Soviet Union's overwhelming numerical superiority.

This selection of production efficiency as the optimization criterion is likely to meet with objection from two directions: from the special-interest groups representing any of the other four criteria, and from those who beleive that the defense posture of the United States is weakened by considering it in terms of a peacetime economic or political-economic problem. These arguments must be considered, since they represent strong interest-group positions. However, there is a more fundamental criticism that is bound to be raised: the current—and false—belief that the U.S. defense industry is operating in a free-market economy, and that therefore the proper balance among the five objectives will be achieved automatically through the interaction of market forces and the government should "keep its hands off." There clearly is no free market at work in the defense industry. The desired efficient allocation of resources has not been achieved (and the trends indicate things are getting worse). There is no way in which the government can become uninvolved, since it is the sole buyer, the banker, the regulator, the specifier of equipment, and the user. Ignoring this reality often gets the DoD into trouble. The real question is "What is the *best form* of coordinated government policy—economic and strategic—to correct the growing problems?"

Anyone setting out to propose a desired structure for the U.S. defense industry would be wrong to assume a clean slate; not only the present conditions, but also the history that has led to these conditions and the ongoing trends must be considered. Also, it is absolutely essential to accept the facts, as presented in the earlier chapters, rather than to continue to believe the myths that underlie many of the decisions made in recent years (for example, all production surge planning for the U.S. defense industry is based upon the assumptions of all-out mobilization, which has not taken place in any of the wars over the past thirty years; and U.S. controls on international arms shipments are based upon the assumption of a bipolar world, whereas in reality power is now multicentered). In addition, it must be recognized that if the market is not working, then the "theory of the second best" must apply, and using traditional free-market theory will not always achieve the best overall impact. The many small corrective actions that have been taken by the Department of Defense have often had effects exactly opposite to the effects that were intended and would have followed if a free market were in operation. A simple example of this is that it would appear, on the surface, highly desirable to have a uniform profit policy and other uniform procurement policies, in order to give equal treatment to all defense contractors. However, the data clearly show that this uniform policy has resulted in very nonuniform results across the various sectors, as well as the various tiers, of the defense industry. The "second best" answer, nonuniform procurement policies, could yield more uniform results.

Furthermore, in view of the fact that stability is such a desirable characteristic of overall economic policy, it should be an objective of future defense-industry policy. At the micro level, a great deal of planning could be done to introduce stability into the industry (for example, individual programs could be coordinated in timing, particularly as they relate to each other but also as they relate to the civilian economy). At the aggregate level, the fact that trends in overall defense expenditures are cyclic (owing to periods of worldwide crisis and relative calm) should be recognized, and the structure of the overall defense industry should be made flexible enough to respond to such ups and downs in aggregate demand. Specifically, if arms control and disarmament agreements suit the mutual interest of the United States and its potential adversaries by reducing international tension and the likelihood of war, the industry should be capable of adjusting to the reduced demand whether the agreements cover strategic arms, tactical arms, or foreign sales.[5] With such flexibility, the industry would also be capable of responding to the normal postwar reductions. To be capable of making these downward adjustments the defense industry must remove the current barriers to exit, which put considerable pressure on the policymakers to not reduce arms expenditures. Clearly, an industrial structure without the current large excess capacity, and integrated with the civilian sector rather than specializing in military equipment, would be in a far better position to accept reductions. Of equal significance is the fact that it would also be in a better position to respond rapidly to increased demands in periods of crisis.

Any proposed solutions for the problems of the defense industry must recognize the absolute necessity for a clearly defined system of checks and balances. For example, if a group were to be established to obtain and analyze data on various sectors of the defense industry, it would be highly desirable to separate this data group from the policymakers. Similarly, if more data on the industry were available to outside parties, many decisions might be based less on political influence and more on rational judgment. Related to this point is the need for a firm commitment by Congress and the executive branch to efficiency and effective management in the overall defense industrial base. This means, essentially, recognizing that this industry is a vital national resource and that its economic efficiency matters both to our economy and to our strategic posture. An easy way to see this is to think not in terms of minimizing cost, but in terms of maximizing the military equipment produced for the dollars available. In reality, what is needed is a firm commitment to making the cost of equipment a primary design and management criterion, along with performance.

The U.S. government frequently makes the mistake of holding endless debates on the wording of new, broad national policies and devoting far too little attention to the details of implementation. Broad initiatives taken in connection with the defense industry must be accompanied by legislation, regulations, policies, practices, and organizations dedicated to achievement of the recommended changes. This is the only way in which an institution as large and publicly visible as the Department of Defense can respond to change. However, in working out the details of the implementation plan, maximum advantage should be taken of natural incentives (such as profit, competition, the will to survive in business, and workers' employment continuity), in contrast with the use of directives. Directives are much more difficult to implement successfully, and require continuous followup, whereas natural incentives are reinforced as the desired changes occur.

It is equally important to recognize that the cost of any proposed change must be considered even more carefully than the potential benefits. Here, I recommend the normal investment criterion applied throughout industry: that the expected benefit from a change be on the order of ten times the cost if there is any risk involved, or three times the cost if the risk is minimal. This method ensures a reasonable probability of achieving at least some of the desired impact. Not all "costs" of making changes can be measured solely in economic terms, and other negative impacts must be carefully considered. For example, anyone who recommends any form of sectoral development planning must address the potential dangers of overcentralization (for example, the elimination of real competition) and must show specifically that these dangers will not arise.

There will be no difficulty in identifying many of the potential problems associated with implementation of structural and procedural changes in the defense industrial base—representatives of all of the special-interest groups involved will immediately point them out. These groups, both inside and outside the government, are not to be taken lightly. Their constituencies are powerful and important, so their views must be addressed explicitly. Wherever possible, their help must be sought. In some cases compromises will be required in order to achieve improvements that are acceptable to these groups—the ideal solution may be unachievable. Sometimes, proposed solutions will receive enough support from certain special-interest groups or the general public so that the arguments of other special-interest groups can be overcome. All recommendations for change must be carefully considered in terms of these special-interest groups; to ignore their existence would be foolish.

10.2 Broad Alternatives

Rather than looking at the criteria listed above and attempting to come up with a large number of small actions that could move the defense industry in the direction of these criteria, it is better to first take a far broader perspective and configure a number of possible models that might be considered as the long-term objectives; then specific corrective changes to achieve the desired model can be proposed.

The nine alternative models about to be presented are neither mutually exclusive nor applicable to the entire defense industry. The best solution would be a combination of some of these models, with different solutions for different sectors of the defense industry (such as aircraft, ships, and tanks) and for different tiers (prime contractors, subcontractors, and parts suppliers). With this warning in mind, consider the following nine basic models:

- nationalization
- treating the defense industry as a public utility
- designating sources for each product (while maintaining maximum competition
- encouraging open competition
- separating R&D from production
- combining civilian and defense business
- having an interdependent, multinational defense industry
- structuring the industry for medium- to long-duration wars
- oligopoly, with little or no explicit government involvement at the industry-structure level.

For a number of reasons, the option often though of first is nationalization—the direction many nations (both capitalistic and communistic) have chosen and the one that many of the European nations have taken. John Stuart Mill long ago proposed this solution (or else regulation) because he felt that the economies of scale would predominate in the defense sector and would lead to monopoly. Nationalization of the American defense industry has been proposed often and for a very wide variety of reasons. In 1914 Congressman Clyde Tavenner said it would prevent "profiteering, fraud, and false patriotism."[6] The call was repeated again two years later out of the fear that the arms manufacturers were leading the country into war.[7] The concept of nationalization again received wide support in the United States during the early 1930s; again the reason was the fear that the "merchants of death" would lead the country into war in order to make profits.[8] More recently, John Kenneth Galbraith has argued that nationalization would be a recognition of reality, that by getting the manufacturers to concentrate on efficiency rather than sales it would be a step forward, and that it would end lobbying and other political activity on behalf of weapons expenditures.[9] Galbraith also argues that nationalization would bring these firms under public control. The question, however, is whether it would achieve public control or just provide political shelter (in that companies directly under the control of the Pentagon would be less visible to the public and less susceptible to effective criticism of such actions as bailout).

Nationalization is neither the "second best" solution nor the will of the Congress and the people. The basic issue is not really ownership but the overall structure of the industry, and simply changing from monopoly capitalism to state capitalism is not likely to make that great a difference in overall efficiency. (Most likely, without the profit motive it would decline.) Nonetheless, this idea continues to come up frequently.[10] Unless many of the corrective actions to be described are actually taken, the United States is very likely to end up nationalizing its defense industry in some way, simply to save the industry from severe financial problems. This is a far less desirable alternative than taking corrective actions to improve the structure of the defense industry within the private sector.

A second broad alternative that has been proposed is treating the defense contractors as a public utility.[11] In spite of the fact that all actions of the defense contractors are controlled by the Armed Services Procurement Regulations, the defense industry is almost never listed as a "regulated industry." This is primarily because there is no external regulatory commission (the DoD is its own regulator). The concept behind making defense production a regulated industry would involve establishing a defense regulatory commission as an outside monitor with checks and balances on the defense industry. One apparent advantage to such a suggestion is that the profits of utilities are currently higher than those of the defense firms, so that if the defense firms were similarly regulated they would be likely to receive higher profits. However, regulation would bring with it even greater inertia than currently exists in the industry. With the changes in world conditions and technology moving so rapidly, regulation would only be a block to progress. This can clearly be seen in the case of the utilities (in terms of modernization and research and development), and certainly the utilities have not been known for cost consciousness—they can simply pass on their costs to the customers.

A third general approach is the designation of sources for the development and production of selected military equipment. This approach takes into account the fact that, with a shrinking total defense market, fewer and fewer contractors are likely to be left. To ensure adequate research, development, and production capabilities, certain contractors would be designated as the sources of particular items—at both prime-contractor and subcontractor levels. This model is very similar to the practices of most other countries. It tends to make sense when the market is relatively small and yet there is a need to ensure work being done in each of the critical areas.

Under this model, the government is responsible for channeling sufficient funds to the designated sources so that they can do research and development as well as production at all times. Whenever a new product comes up for development, one or more of the designated sources is selected for R&D on that particular product. Later, one or two firms are selected for production of the product. (They need not be the same firms that did the development.) This allocation of work to selected firms achieves long-term stability, ensures sufficient funds so that labor can count on future work, and encourages investment. A major decision required with this model is whether to designate only one supplier or an oligopoly of suppliers for a given item. This is primarily dependent upon the size of the market. With a small enough market, a monopoly is far more efficient as long as the government can control costs. However, if a given market is fairly large (as is the case with most U.S. defense products), the advantages of competition outweigh the advantages of economies of scale, and it is desirable to designate at least two sources so that competition will spur technological advances as well as cost savings. This may well be a suitable model for some sectors of the U.S. defense economy. In fact, it is already in effect in a few areas because of the very high barriers to entry and the fact that there are only one or two firms already present. The manufacturing of large jet engines by General Electric and Pratt & Whitney probably fits this model, although certainly not officially, and with little or no explicit or positive government actions to ensure stability.

This "designated sources" model would treat each sector of the defense industry separately and would probably create many different structures. It does not require detailed input-output planning (as is done with the Soviet model, discussed in chapter 11, which is not useful for the United States and will not be considered here). Rather, the government would look at the broad structure of each industry sector (in areas such as competition, capital investment, labor stability, and research and development) and would guide the industry toward the desired structure through actions taken on individual programs or through tax policies. Thus, many of the current detailed forms of regulation would be removed.

The opposite model would be the "free market," in which there would be open competition for all defense business. At the prime-contractor level this situation would be extremely difficult to create, because of the monopsony buyer's ability to play the "oligopoly game"—to pit against each other contractors who, because of the small volume of business available, are likely to be underutilized and financially weak. Also, a free market at this level is likely to lead rapidly to a monopoly in each sector. The company that started with the most business and the greatest financial resources would easily eliminate the few remaining competitors after only one or two rounds of competition. One suggestion, made by James Kurth, is to constrict the size of the prime defense contractors (for example, to under $1 billion each), and thus create more competition by having them each sufficiently small so that no one contractor could do the complete job on any large program.[12] This would ensure multiple sources of innovation and, if done properly, would also institute the desirable effects of competition. (Naturally, a "sharing" of the program, where one contractor builds a part and the other one builds a different part, would not involve any real competition.)

This "free market" model would be an excellent one for the lower levels of the defense industry. Here there are multiple customers and multiple suppliers in most areas, and breaking down the current barriers to entry would create far more of a free market than now exists. However, at the prime-contractor level this model might prove very inefficient, in that it would negate some of the economies of scale associated with the development of large, high-technology military equipment (for example, it would require extra, redundant laboratories, design teams, and test facilities).

Consider now an alternative model, recommended by a number of students of the defense industry,[13] that is intended to address directly the fact that most defense business is awarded as sole-source "follow-on" (that is, production business that comes from having won the research-and-development competition). Here, the R&D work must be separated from the production programs in order to foster production competition and efficient utilization of production plants. In this model, R&D becomes a separate "business" unto itself, and is not done for the sake of getting production programs. Also, there would be far less reason to "buy in" on the R&D program, and yet there would still be ample R&D competition.[14] This separation of R&D and production is essentially the model originally followed by the U.S. Atomic Energy Commission. It is also followed by the Soviet Union. Ownership is not the issue, because this model could be applied either in the private or the public sector.

In order to ensure smooth transition from R&D to production with this model—wherein the contract may actually transfer from one firm to another—some incentives are needed to tie the two activities together. In the Soviet Union this is done through withholding part of the development group's bonus and awarding it to them after the system has gone through its first year of production. Similarly, in the United States the two programs could be tied together through the profit on the development contract (the developer would get his full profit only if the product were successfully put into production) or through the use of royalties on the production contract. (The latter is similar to what is done when a U.S. firm transfers production to a European firm.) A variation on this approach is to have two firms compete for the R&D and then split the production between them, with the winner getting the larger share but with both companies building the same system[15] (perhaps with the loser under a license or royalty arrangement).

The next model simultaneously addresses the cyclic nature and the low volume of the defense industry, by combining defense business with civilian business in the same firm, and, more importantly, within the same plant. Here, the low-cost design priority of civilian work would influence the military work, and the intermixing of production lines would mitigate the large ups and downs of the defense demand cycles. Similarly, this model would provide for military production surge capability by making it easy to shift production lines and workers from civilian to military work. Soviet production plants are sometimes set up this way, but the U.S. defense industry is almost totally separated. The reasons often given for this separation are the barriers to entry and exit noted in chapter 2; however, these could be broken down through conscious effort. Defense producers would view themselves more as in the "manufacturing business" rather than just in the "defense business."

A seventh model directly addresses America's growing dependence on foreign sources and the importance of U.S. foreign military sales both to the U.S. defense industry and to the foreign governments. It also acknowledges explicitly the increasing pressure for standardization of NATO military equipment and the fact that U.S. allies are becoming economically equal to the United States in defense production capabilities as well as in new product developments. This is essentially a model of multinational interdependence. It could be limited to just a few countries (for example, the United States and Europe), or it could incorporate, on individual programs, a number of different countries on a one-to-one or multiple-country basis (as in the F-16 program). The major difference between this model and the current system is that with this model the United States would consciously decide not to be self-sufficient in certain products, parts, or technologies. Clearly this leads in the direction of more specialization and higher volume, both of which improve economic efficiency. However, it directly confronts the strategic question of dependence, which to date has not been faced by the policymakers.

The eighth model raises the issue of the likely duration of military conflict. At present, the U.S. defense industry is basically unprepared for any extended conflict. If a war were to go on for three years or more U.S. industry would be able to build up and respond, but for a war of more than a few days but less than a few years it is unready. Thus, the question posed by this model is whether or not the assumption of a short war (for which the defense industry is essentially not required, and therefore not asked to take any specific actions) is the only realistic scenario, or whether there should also be preparations made for a longer conflict (in which case there may be some added resources required to adequately prepare the defense industry and there certainly will be a need for effective planning).

The last of the nine models reflects the prevalent situation in the defense industry and in many sectors of the civilian economy, such as steel, autos, and oil: oligopoly, with little or no explicit government involvement at the industry-structure level. Certainly there are applicable broad national policies (such as antitrust laws) and detailed laws (such as occupational safety and health regulations, minimum-wage laws, equal-employment laws, and, in the case of the defense industry, the detailed regulations of the Armed Services Procurement Regulations). But the large oligopoly firms otherwise operate in an environment in which the public believes that the market is achieving efficient and effective distribution of resources. This book has shown such a belief to be inaccurate in the case of the defense industry, and events in many other critical sectors of the civilian economy (such as steel, autos, and oil) have raised doubts about this model—especially relative to its behavior for the public good. This model must be given serious consideration, since it is the current situation in much of the defense industry. However, the structure, conduct, and performance under this model must be realistically appraised, not simply "lived with."

As noted, these nine general models are not independent; a considerable amount of overlap is possible and probably desirable. However, the "correct" model is probably a different one for different sectors and tiers of the industry. The proper approach is not to simply step back and say which of these nine models, or which combinations thereof, are most attractive. Rather, it is to look at the current structure and problems of each industrial sector and to determine how best to get to a desirable "second best" solution for that particular sector—perhaps ten years hence.

11 The Approaches of Other Nations

Using the criteria shown in the last chapter, and noting the problems detailed in the preceding chapters, it is appropriate to look to the experiences of other countries for possible models, or at least for areas of potential improvement to the U.S. system. This chapter looks at three different cases: that of the Western European countries (especially France, the United Kingdom, Germany, and Sweden), that of some other capitalistic countries (Japan, Israel, and prerevolution Iran), and that of the Soviet Union. In general, the defense industry is much more "planned" in all of the other countries of the world—capitalistic or socialistic—than in the United States. In fact, the United States is the only country to advocate total *laissez faire* in the defense industry, and even there it is not practiced.

Although they employ different degrees of government ownership and direct government involvement in the management of defense manufacturers, all countries except the United States appear to recognize the dominant role of the central government in the defense area, and each attempts to optimize this characteristic rather than to ignore its impact (as the United States traditionally has done). In some countries, internal competition is greatly encouraged; in other cases the competition is between manufacturers in different countries. However, all the other nations seem to recognize the non-free-market nature of the defense economy, and appear to work within this constraint by developing selected sources (often competitive ones) and having the government explicitly concerned with support of research and development, production capacity, and financing. The overall impression is that these countries all treat their defense industry as a national resource, and are officially concerned about it at the highest government levels. Again, it is not a question of the form of the overall economy, but rather a question of attitude towards the defense industry. The major lesson to be learned from looking at these countries is that the United States could easily adopt such an attitude of concern for its own defense industry, and, without major structural changes, could achieve significant improvements in both economic efficiency and strategic responsiveness.

11.1 Western European Countries

Because of the NATO alliance, the U.S. defense industry and the Department of Defense have been closely tied to America's European allies, yet doing defense business in Europe is very different from doing defense business in the United States. The primary difference is in the role of the government in choosing its industrial suppliers. Whereas the United States claims to leave that selection to "the market," the European approach is to select one or more preferred sources.

In Germany, two companies are designated as the military computer companies; any R&D or production to be done (including any work to be done under a license on a foreign product) will be done by one of these firms. The two are still in competition, and thus have the necessary incentive for pushing new technology and lower costs. In fact, there appears to be far more cost sensitivity in European defense business—perhaps because of the smaller budgets, but most likely because of the importance of the export market—than in the United States. Even in those countries where the domestic market for a particular product is too small to support multiple preferred sources, the single supplier still is extremely cost-sensitive because of his recognition of the export market. Dassault is France's only aircraft firm, yet it produces a low-cost, high-performance military aircraft that is one of the world's most successful (from both military and economic viewpoints).[1] Many of Dassault's desirable characteristics are not found in the U.S. aircraft companies (for example, very small design teams, a continuous emphasis on incremental improvement of existing designs, minimal paperwork, a maximal amount of subcontracting,[2] a continuous emphasis on low-cost designs for both domestic and international reasons, and a very close working relationship with the government). Again, it must be emphasized that all of these characteristics exist within a sole-source, private-sector defense supplier—but with conscious government involvement, largely limited to the macro level and a hands-off policy at the micro level.

Sweden has a limited domestic market and a policy that discourages arms exports (there is a small amount of exporting to Switzerland and one or two other small countries, but it must be made absolutely clear that such exports are to countries that would use the weapons only for self-defense). Yet, while accepting its small defense market, Sweden insists upon self-sufficiency and has developed one of the best defense industries in the world. The Viggen is one of the world's most sophisticated and best-performing aircraft. This demonstrates that the United States, with its far larger domestic market, could quite easily develop an efficient defense industry that would require essentially no foreign military sales and yet would be economically efficient and strategically responsive. (Sweden spends under 4 percent of its gross national product on defense, versus about 6 percent for the United States.)[3]

Much of the Swedish defense industry's success is due to its stability, which derives from two main factors. First, the defense budget covers five years (it is updated annually, and there is a reevaluation of the current year's budget at that time). This five-year plan allows the defense industry (which operates in the private sector) to make long-term capital-equipment and manpower commitments, and thus achieve far greater economic efficiency.[4] It also helps to achieve some political isolation of the defense budget, without removing much of the flexibility that an annual congressional review provides in a democratic system. The second factor introducing great stability into the Swedish defense industry is the planned phasing in and phasing out of major weapons systems. In the Saab aircraft plant, production is essentially continuous, with the smooth transition from production of one generation of aircraft to another.

Sweden's defense industry is well integrated with the civilian industry, because of a law that no Swedish company may have more than 25 percent of its business in defense. Thus, while Saab is a major defense producer, it is also one of the two major automobile manufacturers. This combination has a number of distinct advantages. It allows for absorption of defense manpower during slack defense-expenditure periods; it makes the companies much more price-sensitive, and even "business-sensitive," as a result of their commercial experiences; it makes the companies much less dependent on either domestic military sales or foreign military sales (such dependence is a significant problem in many U.S. defense companies); and it facilitates the transfer of technological gains derived from defense R&D to the civilian sector. It does have the potential disadvantage of discouraging small firms from entering the defense sector, but this could easily be overcome by a special provision that not only would allow such an event, but, through taxes and other incentives, would encourage those firms which are first successful in the defense arena to diversify into the civilian area with their defense technology.

Sweden (perhaps alone among the European countries) plans for industrial survival of a war. Most other European countries simply assume the likelihood of a short high-intensity war on their territory, and thus believe it impractical to provide for industrial survival. Sweden goes to the expense of building some plants and depots underground, and has an extensive civil-defense planning program involving shelters and population evacuation. Proximity to the Soviet Union make such planning realistic for Sweden. However, this is indicative of an overall attitude reflected in the other points noted: that Sweden treats its defense industry as a national resource that must be protected.

There are perhaps two distinct trends in the overall European defense market: consolidation (in some cases, nationalization) of defense industries, and increased multinational ventures. The United Kingdom first nationalized the shipbuilding industry,[5] then amalgamated the two main aircraft groups (Hawker Siddely and British Aircraft Corporation)[6] and then nationalized them. These nationalization trends were brought about because of the diminishing defense market and the overall international collapse of the economy in the mid-1970s. Essentially, the firms were headed for bankruptcy and the government had to step in. (Critical subcontractors, such as the Rolls-Royce aircraft engine division, were also nationalized by the U.K.)

A full assessment of the effects of nationalization on European defense industries is not yet available. However, in some countries nationalization has begun to be questioned, and it is clear that this step would be a wrong one for the United States to take in an effort to improve efficiency and responsiveness. The incentives are all in the opposite direction—bureaucracy is neither efficient nor responsive.

The European trend toward joint ventures has been growing significantly over the last fifteen years.[7] It began with a large amount of cross-licensing and multinational corporate activity[8] (there was a heavy involvement of the U.S. multinationals in transferring defense technology to the European countries whose defense industries were just evolving). More recently, however, the tendency has been toward multinational joint ventures between firms in different European countries who want to stay self-sufficient but recognize that their separate markets are not large enough, nor their resources great enough, for them to be able to do it alone. Thus, the multirole combat aircraft (MRCA) program was planned jointly by Britain, Germany, and Italy, and provided for production lines to build essentially similar airplanes in each of the three countries. This trend is continuing and expanding to include American participation in these joint ventures in the future.

11.2 Other Capitalistic Countries

Among the more recent entrants into the defense-industry community, Japan, Israel, and prerevolution Iran are three specific cases of capitalistic countries that chose to set up defense industries in the private sector and yet to include significant government involvement and planning.

Japan—a highly industrialized country—has not in the years since World War II established a significant defense industry. Less than 1 percent of the Japanese gross national product has been devoted to defense. Recently, the Japanese have started to address the issue at the urging of the United States, which is concerned with its high cost of providing defense for Japan. They have chosen the "Japanese model" that has been so successful in civilian industry. Using government-based, informal, "indicative" planning, they develop estimates of likely demand, and then allocate (among a few of the large, private-sector companies)[9] the task of achieving these objectives. The firms tend to stay within these "targets," and the banks appear quite willing to lend money in support. To get the initial R&D (including training), the Japanese play the "oligopoly game" by using companies within the United States to compete against each other and against firms from other nations. But there is never any question about ownership—the firms will be Japanese-owned. Within a short period, the Japanese will be doing their own research, development and production in the plants of their "preferred" private-sector sources. In fact, one can probably expect that, in the not-too-distant future, the Japanese defense industry will become export-oriented, as have the majority of their civilian sectors.

Israel is defense-oriented; while Japan spends less than 1 percent of its GNP on defense, Israel spends over 35 percent. Most of the leaders of Israel's industry and government are former military leaders, and the whole nation is defense-conscious. Originally, Israel was totally dependent upon the French for defense equipment, but after the 1967 war the French stopped all arms shipments. The Israelis learned a bitter lesson about dependency, and vowed that from that point on their defense sector would be self-sufficient. In the short period since that time they have built up an impressive capability for equipment development and production. They have a new tank plant producing a tank of their own design and an aircraft plant producing planes of their own design, and they are designing and producing missiles, ships, and guns that are equal to any in the world. With such a small market, there is essentially one supplier of each type of critical equipment. These firms are kept price-sensitive by continuous competition with alternative, worldwide sources. In many cases the firms are jointly owned by the government and the private sector, and there is a very strong tie between the Ministry of Defense, the Ministry of Commerce, and the private sector, including government responsibility for the maintenance of the defense industry.

Israel represents an extreme case of a country absolutely requiring a very strong defense for periods of crisis and yet not having the resources to pay for this capability. The United States, in its efforts to help Israel in the mid-1970s, compounded this problem by supplying over $2 billion per year of U.S.-made military equipment. (Congress actually allocated the money to Israel, but required that it be used to purchase the military equipment from the United States.) From the viewpoint of helping the Israeli defense industry, the United States would have done better to allocate some of this money to be used in purchasing equipment in Israel, thus providing support for their industry. Otherwise, Israel is forced to look to arms export as the only way to maintain a viable defense industry.

The Israeli experience demonstrates that a viable and advanced defense R&D and production industry can be maintained with a very small market if it is properly scaled, properly managed, and properly planned.

Finally, consider the case of prerevolution Iran, a "developing" nation, with very large, oil-based resources, directly on the border of the Soviet Union, that chose to spend a considerable amount of its new-found wealth (about 12 percent of its GNP) on buying arms and building up its defense industry. Iran, though a capitalistic country, was essentially following the "Soviet model" by focusing a major portion of its industry in the defense area (partly for political reasons, but also partly because it is the easiest area to plan).

Most of the large efforts were joint ventures with western firms—the aircraft plant was jointly owned by Northrop and Iran, the helicopter company by Bell and Iran, and so on. The Iranians required that not only products be transferred, but also manufacturing plants, management capability, engineering capability, and total training for factory workers. Thus, they expected that within five to ten years they would have their own defense industry, equal to any in the world. A representative of one of the U.S. electronics companies said: "We are building an electronics plant in Iran that will be far superior to any defense electronics company in the United States; we are putting all of the most modern capability in because they can afford it and want the best."[10] The question this raised was whether or not there would be a sufficient long-term market in this small country to support such a defense industry. The revolution answered the question much earlier than most American firms expected.

In industrial terms, it would have been wiser for Iran to have built integrated civilian and military plants so that the initially defense-oriented techonology, management, and facilities could have been shifted into the civilian sector once defense "needs" had been satisfied.

11.3 The Soviet Union

The Soviet Union spends approximately 12 percent of its GNP on defense—a dollar-equivalent amount somewhat larger than that which the United States spends.[11] However, because the Soviets have a draft, they are able to pay much lower salaries, and thus they have significantly larger amounts of money available for research and development and weapons procurement. During the late 1960s and the first half of the 1970s, while U.S. defense procurements were dropping rapidly, the Soviet Union was continuing to increase military expenditures (in the late 1960s by about 8 percent and in the early 1970s by about 4 percent per year).[12] Many of the structural problems that have appeared in the U.S. defense industry as a result of the shrinking defense budget may have not been visible in the Soviet Union because of their increasing defense budget. However, from the quantity and quality of the products the Soviets are turning out, it is clear that they have a well-developed defense industry. Therefore, it is appropriate for us to study it and to highlight those features that are unique, not because of public ownership, but because of the approach taken.[13]

Perhaps one of the most distinguishing characteristics of the Soviet defense industry is the separation between research and development and production. Weapon systems are developed in the "development centers," under team leaders who have long periods of continuity. These development centers are technically controlled by the "research establishments," which publish "rules" defining what designs and equipment can be used. The new developments are then tested by the research centers, and a decision is made by the senior military and political figures as to which of the various competitive developments should be put into production, and where. This system has a number of desirable characteristics. The development laboratories produce a significant number of different systems (often far more than in the United States) relative to those that go into production, and thus there is more competition for the production designs. Controlling the designs and products allowed in the development centers achieves far more standardization than is achieved in the United States. Separating development and production makes it possible for a number of development projects (by different R&D "firms") to be carried on in the same production plant, which increases the overall efficiency of the production plants. Also, development can be a "business" unto itself, rather than just something done for the short-term objective of getting a follow-on production program. All of these factors improve the overall efficiency of the defense industry.

The Soviets do tend to develop some ties between the development community and the production community, which considerably aids in the transition between phases. They have also developed other techniques, such as personnel transfers, for smoothing this transition, which the U.S. industry often argues is a very difficult transition to achieve (even though frequently the U.S. companies will do development in one part of the country and production in another part of the country).

In spite of the separation of development and production, the Soviet system tends to develop systems oriented towards ease of production. Part of this is achieved by the Soviet incentive system, which awards the developer half of his total bonus the first year after the system is in production, thus encouraging him to both win the competition for production and to design a system that is readily producible. Also, because of the lower levels of technology in Soviet production plants, designs are made less demanding in terms of tolerances and materials. The net effect of all of this is that a Soviet design intended to achieve performance similar to that of a U.S. system might cost considerably less to build than the comparable American system, even in a U.S. plant.[14] A clear example of a very high-performance, low-cost system design is the Soviet Mig-25 aircraft:

It does not require advanced electronics, exotic materials, precise manufacturing techniques, or complex structures. Similarly, it used stainless steel and aluminum as the primary airframe materials, instead of synthetic materials, as used by the U.S. Rivets were left unground (except in aerodynamically critical areas), and welding was said to be crude, but adequate. Larger engines were used to overcome the drag penalties. The radar, though based on technology that is out of date by American standards, is one of the most powerful ever seen in an aircraft, and therefore less vulnerable to jamming. The overall Mig-25 has been described by American aerospace analysts as "unsurpassed in the ease of maintenance and servicing," "a masterpiece of standardization," and "one of the most cost-effective combat investments in history."[15]

Naturally, the Soviets' approach to defense production is conditioned by their political system and their history. Many of the senior government leaders came from the military, and the country has a history of defense orientation. Thus, the defense industry receives priority in manpower and materials,[16] and is the high-status area for scientists, engineers, and managers (in contrast with the U.S. case). Because of the longevity of these leaders, military planning has far greater stability, which is an asset from the viewpoint of economic efficiency.

This stability of planning in the Soviet weapons-acquisition program extends into the research and development area. Here stable budgets and constant manpower levels for the research institutes and design bureaus result in a regular progression of design and prototypes, and allow the Soviet research and design bureaus to maintain and develop a core of expertise (as compared with the constant manpower shifting in the U.S. defense industry).[17]

Because of their historical experiences, as well as the planned nature of their economy, the Soviets place considerable emphasis on industrial-preparedness planning (in contrast with the U.S. efforts described in chapter 5). One particularly relevant aspect of this planning is the fact that the Soviet Union often combines, in one plant, the manufacture of civilian and military products; for example, railroad cars and aircraft. This allows greater surge capability (in terms of available skilled workers), whenever such an increase is required, and it also provides for absorption of defense workers during slack periods of defense production. Combining civilian and defense capability in the same factory is a positive step towards simultaneously addressing the issues of economic efficiency and surge capability.

An excellent summary of the Soviet defense industry is the following:

By Western standards, Soviet defense industry is virtually on a war footing. But this "war footing" essentially reflects both "the Soviet way" in defense preparation and the bureaucratic rigidities of a centrally planned economy. The Soviets, like their Czarist predecessors, do not subject their armed forces to feast and famine cycles, depending upon the pendulum swings of political mood between pessimism and optimism over the prospects for war in the near term. It is the Russian/Soviet heritage *always* to expect conflict, crisis, and war.[18]

It has not been my intention here to discuss the advantages and disadvantages of the structures of various foreign defense industries, nor the way in which various countries procure weapons. Rather, I have tried to select features that might be of value in evolving a set of solutions for improving the operation of the U.S. defense industry. However, it is appropriate to point out some of the problems with the Soviet system, lest it be viewed by the reader as an ideal model for the United States.

Studies of the Soviet system have shown that, while their defense industry is undoubtedly more effective than their civilian industry (because of the greater ease of planning and because of the far higher priority that it has for both manpower and materials), "the Soviet defense industries are less efficient than formerly believed, and . . . the ruble cost of equipment is higher than previously estimated."[19] The cause of this inefficiency must be attributed to both the industrial and political structures. The centrally administered Soviet economy tends to greatly discourage technological innovation. In comparison with U.S. standards, it is rigid and constrained. The Soviets emphasize design continuity, they continue to use the same designers, they require that all designs conform to detailed plans and regulations, they have high barriers to entry for new organizations in established fields, they have large penalties for failure, and they tend to manage R&D conservatively. Additionally, because the overall economy is planned on a detailed input-output basis (part by part, product by product, factory by factory, and so on), any small change (for example, a new part or a new material) causes a significant revision to the overall plan, and thus is greatly discouraged. Similarly, simple changes in the budget are greatly resisted, because of their impact throughout the plan. Also, the unreliability of the suppliers greatly discourages the introduction of new parts or new suppliers once a reliable source has been found.

Additionally, in the Soviet Union there is an obsession with secrecy in connection with anything to do with the defense industry. This has many negative effects, among them the lack of technology transfer (even within the defense area, and certainly between defense and civilian industry) and the low level of accountability to management, government, and the public.

One other factor that contributes greatly to the ineffectiveness of the Soviet system is the fact that decisionmaking and planning are combined. This makes it extremely difficult for a decisionmaker to recommend a change when he knows that he will then have to redo all of his plans. This institutional structure is a major retardant to technological advancement, and in a military environment where technology is rapidly advancing this is a very significant disadvantage.

In summary, examination of the Soviet defense industry suggests six changes for the United States:[20]

- Make research and development profitable on its own terms.
- Separate production from research and development, so they can be independently optimized.
- View "manufacturing" as the function of the plant—not, for example, "the building of military aircraft."
- Combine civilian and military production in the same plant.
- Aim for greater workforce stability in both R&D and production.
- Separate planning and decisionmaking.

11.4 Future Trends

Two significant developments now taking place will certainly affect the U.S. defense industry.

The first of these is the increasing tendency toward joint development and coproduction. Joint development has already been increasing within the European countries. In 1976 eleven European nations (including all European NATO members except Portugal and Iceland) formed a group to work together in the arms area, recognizing that none of them separately had a sufficiently large market or sufficient resources to compete against the United States, but that collectively they certainly could compete.[21] The joint-effort trend that best reflects the growing economic power of Europe is the tendency towards joint European-American development and production projects. Here the effort is an attempt to achieve NATO standardization, for both economic and military reasons.

The overall form for all of these joint efforts is for two or more countries to agree to collectively produce a product in one of a number of different ways. Each will produce half (or some percent) of the identical product; or one will produce some parts and the other will produce different parts. In the former case, the idea is to take advantage of common, nonrecurring costs, such as research and development, tooling, design, and testing; in the latter case, it is to take advantage of the relative advantage (in "terms of trade") of the two countries. Both cases allow for joint sales efforts with third countries, common maintenance, and common logistical support. These activities have been particularly attractive to the Europeans, not only because of the scale advantages offered by such combined programs but also because of the attendant transfer of advances in such areas as engineering and marketing.

Examples of coproduction programs between the United States and Europe are the F-16 fighter aircraft (developed in the United States and being produced jointly in the United States and in Europe) and the Roland missile (developed in France and Germany and now being produced jointly in the United States and in Europe). Whereas these systems were developed by one country and then produced jointly, the trend is toward joint development. For example, two international teams were formed to do preliminary design work on a future fighter aircraft (one team of British Aerospace and Grumman and another of McDonnell-Douglas and Messerschmitt-Boelkow-Blohm). (As is typical of the long lead times in the defense industry, these two preliminary design efforts are aimed for the late 1980s and the mid-1990s, respectively.)[22]

This tendency towards joint development and production programs will probably extend to the major subcontractors. In the 1960s and 1970s most joint activities in this area were based upon U.S. licenses to European producers. However, the tendency in the 1980s will probably be in the direction of joint developments, and, again, preliminary indications of teaming arrangements are being seen. (For example, Westinghouse (U.S.) and Plessey Aerospace (U.K.) initiated joint development work on power-generation and management systems for the next generation of air-superiority fighter.)[23]

The second general trend that has been seen in the Western European countries is toward a far greater government role.[24] To a certain extent, this is a reaction to the joint programs noted above, because many of these countries feel it is essential to have an independent and self-sufficient defense industry (in both production and engineering). However, they also recognize that the size of the market is too small to do this without significant government involvement. Thus, in Italy, many of the "private" defense firms are owned by one of the government-owned holding companies. The French government, in order to keep a national computer industry, absorbed Machine Bull—for "national security" reasons. In the United Kingdom the government first nationalized the Rolls Royce Aircraft Engine Division in order to "prevent high unemployment," then nationalized the shipbuilding industry and the aircraft industry in order to maintain these important defense sectors. The effect of these "nationalization" actions is to keep out foreign competition, because these industries, which are now in the public sector, are usually well protected.

Thus, these two trends—joint efforts and nationalization of defense industries—are being combined more at the political level than at the industrial level. Because of America's political involvement in the defense industries of the Western European countries, these trends are bound to have a significant impact on the U.S. situation, especially since the United States has been promoting NATO standardization in order to make its own industry and military forces more efficient and effective. Thus, it is likely that there will be more government-to-government negotiations on joint programs, with the American and European defense firms playing supporting roles. The overall trend resulting from the development and production of defense equipment having gone multinational appears to be toward even greater U.S. government involvement in the U.S. defense industry.

12 Proposed Solutions

Having now reached the point where it is possible to make specific recommendations for future of the U.S. defense industrial base, I must say that I do not propose to solve all of the problems previously described, or even to indicate all of their likely solutions, in a few pages.[1] However, what I hope is to give sufficient indication of worthwhile directions to be pursued by industry executives, by scholars, and particularly by government policymakers such that initiatives can be taken toward reversing the trend of diminishing American military-industrial strength.[2] The approach to be taken, and the general assumptions on which it is based, are outlined in the following paragraphs.

The defense industrial base is a national resource that makes up a significant portion of the overall American deterrent and defense posture, and therefore we cannot afford to ignore it or to allow it to deteriorate.

The U.S. market is large enough to support a viable defense industrial base without requiring foreign military sales.

Government and industry are wrong not to expect cyclical ups and downs in the defense budget due to changes in the world environment. The structure of the defense industry, and its relation to the government, must be flexible enough to accept these variations. A significant problem exists in this area. Theories, policies, practices, and organizations are all based on the assumption of an essentially static situation. However, in reality the world in which the defense industry operates is clearly dynamic and has undergone a complete structural transformation[3] in the post-Vietnam era, while the Department of Defense's basic policies and structures have remained essentially the same. Not only must these policies and structures be revised, but also the new policies and structures should be designed to accept and take advantage of the likelihood of future changes, such as arms-control and disarmament agreements in the tactical, strategic, foreign-military-sales, and space fields.

The policymakers fail to recognize that an effective market does not exist at every level of the industry. The assumption that market forces are operating is a valid argument against government action—market forces are the most effective way of achieving optimum resource utilization and adjustment to changing demands and new technologies. However, the data presented in this book demonstrate that, in fact, an effective market does not exist in every sector. Under these conditions (to quote Scherer), "there is almost universal agreement that when markets go astray the government must intervene."[4] The question is: How? In the case of the defense industrial base, the government is already intimately involved. Thus, the issue is: What should the government properly do? The answer is that, wherever possible, a viable free market should be created (for example, by requiring the use of multiple sources). This done, the government should then disengage itself and only keep track to ensure that the market is maintained. In those few areas where a viable free market cannot be created (for example, in some of the sectors of prime contracting), it must be recognized that this will be the case, and that "second best" solutions—each tailored to the individual sector—are required.

To improve the defense industrial base economically and strategically, it is necessary to ask questions from the perspective of the overall industry—to think in terms of "engineering" and "manufacturing," not just in terms of "weapons systems." In essence, it is necessary to recognize the tie between the industrial base's structure and the results of its operation—in terms of being able to deliver the maximum amount of military equipment for the dollars allocated—and to recognize the tie between the way in which defense business is done and the resulting industrial-base structure. In this way the relevance of the structure of the industrial base, and its resources, to the long-range national security can be fully appreciated.

The government has taken a very large number of actions—at the micro level—intended to correct for some acknowledged market imperfections. The result is that, essentially, the defense industry is totally regulated. Too often these actions become counterproductive, or work at cross purposes. A significant part of the overall problem is that the government tries to prevent *all* mistakes, and thus overregulates. Trying to prevent *almost all* mistakes would be more efficient.[5]

Far less government involvement at the micro level, and a far more coordinated government policy at the macro level, are needed. The major weaknesses of the current set of legislation, policies, and structures are their basic incoherence and logical inconsistency and the lack of recognition of their broader impacts.[6] In the 1930s Keynes found that without government involvement at the macro level (in the U.S. economy) there was underutilization, inefficiency, and lack of attention to public interests. He observed that automatic adjustments would not come about, and he then went on to lay the theoretical basis for the role of the government, through macroeconomic actions, in the post–World War II period. Keynes's basic objective was to make capitalism work. Thus, his was an optimistic view of the future—if the proper corrective policies and actions were to be implemented. Because of relatively large post-Korean War defense expenditures, the U.S. defense industry was able to get along without conscious government involvement at the macro level. However, in the post-Vietnam era, with significantly reduced expenditures and the evolution of the many structural problems described in this book, unless the government begins to take some action, inefficiency, underutilization, and lack of responsiveness will increase in the defense industry.[7]

The answer to the problem is that the Department of Defense should be planning to make the best use of its suppliers. Effective planning is the essence of management. Large firms, defense and civilian, plan the current and future use of their resources carefully. The DoD performs extensive planning for force structure, annual budgets, and the five-year fiscal outlook, and some for industrial-mobilization preparedness. However, still missing is a consistent and rational set of coordinated policies for utilizing each of the defense industry's sectors and for optimizing the overall defense industrial base.

Such planning must be done in a manner consistent with democratic principles, and must leave the industrial resources in private hands. This is perhaps the most difficult and important goal. All such planning would be indicative only, and as broad as possible (in contrast with the present detailed government interference in the operation of industry through vast numbers of regulations and through design and manufacturing standards). There can be no unilateral direction by any one government group. Checks and balances must be established between the involved government bodies, and the planners must be accountable to the people.

Credible forms of competition must be either maintained or, where they currently fail to exist, created in order for the private enterprise system to operate effectively. Here, the competition must be carefully analyzed to ensure that the proper incentives are being applied, so that cost reductions are in fact achieved and so that profits are used for reinvestment and for future economic and military improvements.

The great difficulty of making even small structural changes in the defense industry must be recognized. Some changes will be perceived as threatening by the powerful vested interests involved (the industrial giants, the labor unions, the military services, or the Congress). To "sell" such changes, each of these groups must be made aware of the broader advantages to them and to the nation.

The desire for maintaining an open, democratic system brings with it certain inefficiencies; for example, the annual political actions on the defense budget as it passes through Congress. However, these small penalties in economic inefficiency are more than worth the costs of safeguarding the social, economic, and political system.

All of the general goals of a democratic system with checks and balances and a competitive, private-enterprise economy are easy to state, but are difficult to achieve, especially in the presence of the strong vested interests which exist in the defense area. What I most fear is that these objectives will be pushed aside in an attempt to make corrective actions that give the appearance of maintaining a democratic, private-enterprise system, but in fact give it up in order to achieve the easier path of unilateral government direction and government ownership.

The proper approach to arriving at the desired overall government policy is to start from the current laws, regulations, structures, and organizations and to modify them only as required. Thus, more of a cultural change than a total restructuring of the defense industry and its relation to the Department of Defense is recommended. Essentially, the government-industry interface must be reassessed in light of the current conditions and their historical evolution.

The remainder of the book explores seven specific steps toward bringing the U.S. defense industrial base into the desired form for the last decades of the century and beyond. The combined effect of these steps could reverse the current undesirable economic and strategic trends in the U.S. defense industry. Because of the many ties between the defense industry and the civilian sector, these changes would have a significant positive impact on the civilian economy as well.

Implementation of these recommendations would strengthen the free-enterprise system and prevent the otherwise likely drastic "solutions": nationalization of major portions of the defense industry, deeper government involvement in the details of operation of the firms, attempts to break up the large firms in order to introduce artificial competition into prime defense contracting,[8] significantly higher defense budgets (without any increase in real military effectiveness), bailouts of weak companies, or increased support of the industry through foreign military sales. Following these recommendations, the Department of Defense will be able to procure, within a few years, well over $3 billion annually in additional military equipment from the same overall budget. Also, it will have a far more strategically responsive industrial base to handle future production surge demands.

12.1 Coordination of Government Policies—Sector by Sector

The primary overall recommendation is to recognize the defense industry as a critical national resource that should—like every other resource—be optimized for the national good and protected, where required, to ensure its availability for the future. The data of earlier chapters show that currently the market is ineffective in shaping a desirable structure for the industry. Therefore, the government must determine what the best form for the industry should be. And, because the government controls this overall structure—through its policies, practices and regulations—it should take action to direct the defense industry towards the desired form as rapidly as possible, rather than following its current *ad hoc* patterns. The criterion for the desired evolution should be economic efficiency, within the other constraints. What is badly needed is coordinated policy and actions. For example, the government currently encourages greater capital investment on the part of the defense industry while simultaneously discouraging firms from leaving the business (at least at the prime-contractor level). The net effect of these investments will be increased excess capacity, rather than the desired productivity enhancements. A coordinated policy would address these two actions together, reducing the amount of excess capacity while increasing the productivity of that which remains.

As indicated by the discussions of sectoral differences in earlier chapters, such planning must be done sector by sector. To quote Roger Noel, who discussed such a policy in terms of technological innovation, "No universal policy covering firms in differing markets and technological environments is likely to lead to an efficient rate and direction of technological innovation . . . for each industry, policy interventions [must] be tailored to the specific aspects of its economic and scientific environment."[9] However, as George Eads correctly pointed out, considerable attention must also be given to interindustry influences and to the effects of firm diversification.[10] To this, add the significant attention that must be paid to the multinational operations within the firms and sectors.

Specific sectoral data needed for coordinated government policy action include the number of firms and the number of plants; the percent capacity utilization; whether there is sufficient research and development being done; whether surge capability exists and is properly planned for; the labor turnover rates; the labor distribution by region and skill category; the degree of competition; the amount of diversification; the opportunity for diversification; whether the projected future supply and demand match; whether productivity is improving or getting worse, and what actions could be taken to improve it; whether there is sufficient investment in modernization; whether there are problems in getting financing; whether there is a heavy debt structure; the impact of government policies on prices and on profits; the effect of the sector's overall structure on its economic efficiency; the number of firms in production; the relationship between the subcontractor and prime contractor; and whether there is sufficient competition at the subcontractor level.

Notice that these questions are far broader than those required by the normal Armed Services Procurement Regulations. Also notice that these can be considered "macro" questions. The government's emphasis clearly should be less on detailed government management within the firms and more on broader planning at the aggregate sectoral level. One can draw an analogy between this activity and the macro planning already being done by the government to address aggregate economic problems in other areas, such as unemployment. However, the best example that the Department of Defense can follow is the planning done by the large corporations, which are clearly the world's most effective planning bodies (they have whole staffs doing nothing but planning and coordinating company policies and actions). Many businessmen have said that they cannot run their companies without a long-range plan, and that the government will continue to make bad, *ad hoc* decisions unless it also has one. As Barnet and Müller state, "The managerial revolution in private industry has not been duplicated in government. The public sector had its managerial revolution under the banner of Keynesianism almost forty years ago. That revolution established a new body of official truth: artful government regulation of the economy is necessary to keep unemployment down, to prevent inflationary price rises, and to stimulate economic growth, [but since then] the breakthroughs in the art of planning in this generation have been in private industry rather than public administration."[11] This is a somewhat pessimistic assessment, because the DoD does some of the best planning in the world in its force planning and its budget planning. However, what it needs to do is to complement these forms of planning with resource planning for the defense industry. This element will complete the DoD's overall planning by complementing the current "demand side" planning with the necessary "supply side" planning.

A set of recommendations very similar to those being advocated here were made in January 1976 by the National Commission on Supplies and Shortages.[12] This commission was made up of members of the Ford administration, the Democrat-controlled Congress, and representatives of industry, labor, and universities. They were looking at the narrower area of raw materials, but their recommendations are applicable to many other sectors of the U.S. economy, including the defense industry. They called for "major improvements in governmental collection and analysis of information regarding supply and demand, including 'better warning of impending problems' and more long-range policy planning, including budgeting for more than one year at a time."[13] They also suggested "creation of an economic and industrial monitoring unit," and felt that a "more sophisticated, more responsible role for government in interpreting and supplementing market signals" was required. In their opinion, "it is essential that government policies be consistent and exert a stabilizing influence on the economy. This cannot happen unless the government understands the effects of its actions, not only on the economy as a whole, but on important segments of it." In discussing the data-collection requirements, Executive Secretary George Eads stated: "The government [currently] lacks the capability to take the required detailed looks [at an industrial sector] despite the fact that decisions implying such knowledge are being made daily."[14] The commission emphasized the importance of separating the data collection and analysis from the government's programmatic and promotional responsibilities —in the words of commission chairman Don Rice, "to assure their objectivity and credibility."[15] The commission further went on to state that policy analysis must also be separated from the other two functions of data collection and analysis and programmatic and promotional responsibilities, and that it is important to make all data public so that the policymakers, the industry, and the public could all work from comparable and consistent information.[16] In summarizing his views Chairman Rice stated: "Quite apart from monitoring, and the institutional reforms needed to make it a useful tool of policy, the government must be forced to consider the longer term and broader implications of its actions.

This requires comprehensive policy planning, designed not to set detailed economic and social goals for the nation, but to broaden understanding of how government policies affect one another, and also affect important sectors of the economy."[17]

If the need for such a coordinated government policy is presented properly it should be accepted by all parties involved. The defense industry certainly requires the greater stability and predictability that would come with such a policy. Thomas Jones, president of Northrop, stated: "In recognition of the need for sound and interrelated economic, social, and defense planning, the U.S. is moving towards more predictable and less cyclical defense operations. This allows a perceptive company to make its own long-range plans and investments in the future."[18] The Conference Board report on the U.S. investment community's views on the defense industry (cited in chapter 2) suggested a far greater willingness to lend money to defense contractors if there were greater stability and predictability in the industry.[19] Overall, one would expect that with greater stability would come less labor turnover, more investment, higher profits, and lower risk.

The increased coordination of government policy, on the basis of adequate data, could be far more effective in achieving long-term stability in the defense industry if complemented by the adoption of multiyear defense budgeting by the Congress. The Congress has begun, in recent years, to address its responsibility for improving the coordination of government policy. Specific actions in this direction were the establishment of the Joint Budget Committees and the deliberations on the Humphrey-Hawkins full-employment bill and the Humphrey-Javits Balanced Growth and Economic Planning Act. Multiyear budgeting would be another major positive step.

Any planning should be indicative, not mandatory. It should not be expected that the plans will be precisely realized; they are intended to show desired directions, and to provide a basis for individual policy decisions. In this way, individual actions can be properly related to a common objective, and the impact of an act in one direction can be seen in other areas. Such planning must produce different policies for sectors whose characteristics are clearly different. For example, the shipbuilding industry has a low profit, employs mostly production workers, and may need more nuclear shipbuilding yards; by contrast, the aircraft industry has decent profit, employs mostly white-collar workers, and probably has an excess of plants and equipment. Surely corrective actions for these two industries should be different; however, they are not likely to be unless policymakers are aware of differing characteristics and problems.

The change will not be rapid. Rather, an anticipated evolutionary change will take place through a combination of structural, legislative, organizational, and policy actions. Consider the following examples of areas in which coordinated government policy can have a significant positive impact and therefore should be initiated soon.

First, effort must be made toward separating R&D and production into business areas that would stand on their own.[20] This change would give far more flexibility to the operation and structure of the defense industry. Making R&D a "business" unto itself would tend to make it profitable—which it is not today, even at a sales level over $10 billion per year. It would also encourage optimal use of production facilities (which no longer would necessarily be tied to the same firm that did the development work) and would allow production facilities to become more efficient by encouraging automation (for higher volume) and by lowering the engineering overhead. Furthermore, it would introduce competition at the production point, where the big dollars are, rather than encouraging "buying into" a sole-source position at the development phase. In addition, this would be a very major step towards breaking down the "barriers to exit" for major prime contractors.

Plant and equipment ownership is the second major area for coordinated government policy in the near future. There is a great deal of ambiguity, in congressional legislation and executive-branch interpretation, over the "desired mix" and even the criteria for it. It is the responsibility of the Congress to address this issue directly, and to establish a clear criterion based upon economic considerations, which are not the basis of current criteria. It must be recognized that we have mixed ownership, and that this is likely to continue—because of the very large current government investment in plants and equipment and because it will continue to be necessary for the government to supply some special-purpose equipment and to make some high-risk investments. On the other hand, the maximum amount of ownership should be in the private sector, where the profit motive can be used to achieve higher utilization.[21] In some cases this may require government action to help industry in these investments through indemnification or other forms of risk sharing. Even those plants required to be government-owned should be made contractor-operated, to at least get more flexibility into decisions about their later being closed and to better utilize the profit motive and competition to drive down costs.

12.2 Integration of Civilian and Military Operations

The majority of firms in the defense industry have diversified through external acquisition, but many firms and almost all individual plants have continued to specialize in either military or civilian products. More integration of civilian and military business is required, within firms and especially within plants. Some of the advantages of such actions would be the following:

- The ability to respond rapidly to demands for increased production during crises, with available skilled labor, would be enhanced.
- The civilian business could absorb the cyclical ups and downs of the defense business (especially contraction in peacetime and as the result of arms-control negotiation).
- The dependence of defense firms on continued high domestic and foreign military expenditures would be reduced.
- Overall U.S. industrial productivity would go up, since the large government investments being made in plant and equipment could be utilized by the private sector more easily.
- The transfer of technology from military-sponsored research and development to the civilian sector would be much faster.
- There would be more emphasis on applying low-cost commercial design approaches to defense projects.
- The civilian part of the combined civilian-military operation would provide an overall growth environment for the defense industry.
- The improved stability and growth of the labor market would raise productivity and encourage young workers, managers, and engineers to go into defense work.
- Higher production rates would be conducive to more "labor learning" and would encourage investment. Essentially the firm would be in the "manufacturing" business, rather than in the defense business. (With modern computer-controlled machinery this is much more practical today.)
- The DoD would not have to award a contract to a firm in order to keep

it alive for future defense work.[22] Rather, a firm not engaged in defense work at a given time would operate solely in the civilian area.

- The combined civilian-military business would force the firms to be far more competitive in order to stay alive in the commercial world.
- Efficient civilian firms would enter the defense business. Many of the suppliers on which the Department of Defense now depends have specialized in defense business because they were unable to survive in the commercial world. Combining civilian and military business—particularly at the subcontractor level—would encourage many of the larger firms currently not interested in the small volume of military business to again take an interest—partly because of the advanced R&D that is characteristic of defense business and partly to be involved in any future large defense production (in crisis periods).
- Long-range balancing of military and civilian demands would be possible. When civilian business was down in a certain part of the overall industry, defense programs could be used to maintain the basic core; and when civilian business is up some non-time-critical defense programs could be delayed.
- There would be better utilization of both government-owned and private plants and equipment, because of the common use.
- The surge capacity for second and third shifts could be maintained, while at the same time single-shift operation would be efficient.

Such advantages clearly seem to favor the combination of defense and civilian business, yet the reality is that more and more firms have been separating their military and civilian business.[23] The government needs to create incentives for combining civilian and military business, rather than to encourage the current exit and entry barriers, which actually work in the opposite direction. One way to encourage such integration would be for the government to adopt commercial technical standards and business practices, which in most cases are as good as the current government requirements. The government also has other significant incentives available. These include tax credits (in areas where defense sources are needed) and encouraging R&D charges against defense work for civilian diversification (in plants that are solely military producers). Each action should be aimed at achieving diversification within existing plants and divisions. Today the DoD allows conversion planning as an acceptable cost against defense contracts.[24] However, little is done in this direction because the other ''barriers'' are far too high.

We might even go so far as to pass laws similar to the Swedish law that requires less than 25 percent of a firm's business to be in the defense area. Of course, any new legislation must consider overall coordinated government policy. In the case of this possibility, the firm and plant levels should be distinguished, because integrated diversification is of primary interest. Such a law should not apply to small research and development firms, because this would bar their way to getting started (with government R&D money); only better-established R&D firms should be required to diversify into the civilian area.

Melman and others have often warned that a danger of combining the military and civilian businesses would be to make the civilian more like the military.[25] There is the possibility that the smaller amount of military business will make the larger civilian sector less price-sensitive. However, if the combination is done properly, with this danger kept in mind, this is not likely to happen, because defense is clearly the smaller of the two sectors.

Other cautions should be mentioned. One is that, in trying to come up with new regulations and legislation to encourage the combination of military and civilian business, the policymakers must not expect to eliminate all improper charges. Rather, catching most of the abuses, particularly all of the large ones, should be the goal. In this way, much of the current regulation and overinvolvement of the government in defense business can be eliminated. There is also the danger that firms currently doing defense business may tend to lose interest once they are able to do the more desirable commercial work. Here, the proper answer lies in making defense work equally attractive, with profits and stability comparable to the civilian area and far less paperwork than at present. These changes are desirable in any case, and would make defense business sufficiently "competitive" with civilian business that the good commercial firms would become interested in doing defense business—which many currently avoid.

12.3 Recognition of the "Dual Economy"

Averitt, Galbraith, and others have suggested that in the civilian area there is a clear distinction between the large contractors and the smaller subcontractors and parts suppliers. As chapter 6 highlighted, this distinction is even more marked in the defense industry. The differences between the "two economies" are not just quantitative, but also reach into their basic structures, institutions, and even business environments. It would be expected that there should also be differences in the way in which the government does business with the two economies, and in the regulations and policies that apply. However, this is not the case.

With 50 to 60 percent of the dollar value of defense acquisitions going to the lower tiers, the government certainly should be concerned with ensuring an efficient operation at this level as well as at the prime-contractor level. Additionally, the government has a responsibility for maintaining an adequate subcontractor and supplier base for other needs, such as surge capability and research and development. The prime contractors often have little if any real interest in this, and in fact frequently have the contrasting desire to bring the lower-level work "in house."

The government has taken the opposite direction from this recommendation. Since 1963 it has chosen not to gather data on the subcontractors and suppliers and has assumed that the free market is operating satisfactorily. As the data in chapter 6 show, this is not the case, and corrective action must be taken to create an efficient and effective market at these lower levels.

The first step is to watch these lower levels, in a way that will not require large amounts of data to be accumulated but indicate in what areas the market is not operating satisfactorily and will provide sufficient warning to allow corrective actions. This observation can probably be confined to selective areas in which critical components or subsystems will be monitored in a fashion similar to that proposed at the prime-contractor level. The questions to be addressed are: Is there sufficient research and development? Are there enough firms for competiton? Is the market large enough to match the supply and demand? Any such monitoring and planning at the lower levels would have to address not just peacetime economics, but also crisis preparation.

In some areas the government may have to force the creation of a market by requiring the prime contractors to have multiple sources for critical elements—thus also eliminating the sole-source "lock-ins" of subcontractors and the monopoly prices associated with them. Additionally, the government should require far more "buy" than "make" decisions by the prime contractors, thus breaking up much of the vertical integration that has occurred in the post-Vietnam period. A similar trend away from vertical integration has been taking place voluntarily, in many civilian sectors, in favor of the economic advantages associated with specialization. In some civilian areas the government has even made efforts to achieve this goal through enforcement of antitrust regulations.[26] Another suitable government action would be to require that, when there is only one source for a given critical component, a second firm should be awarded a research and development contract in order to create competition. This would be a particularly attractive alternative if the new contact could be awarded to a small R&D firm, which would more likely be oriented toward low-cost designs. However, if only one or two experienced suppliers are left in a certain field, then perhaps they should be the ones maintained, so that their experience would not be lost.

Combining civilian and military business and breaking up vertical integration should produce a considerable amount of improvement in overall economic efficiency by increasing volume and specialization in the lower tiers.

Increasing the use of commercial parts and subsystems, as well as commercial specifications, is another positive action the government can take. This would greatly expand the number of available suppliers, and would create much more of a free market at the lower tiers of the defense industry. Because commercial equipment has, over the last few years, evolved rapidly toward the high technological level of the defense sector, this move should result in little, if any, deterioration of military performance. It would certainly provide far more readily available production surge capability at the lower levels. However, it requires two significant changes in the way the DoD does its business. First, the most easily adjusted, would be the logistical implications. The contractors would have to be made responsible for maintaining a spare parts and logistics support system. The DoD would have to go in a direction more like that of the commercial world, even including the use of commercial warranties. Secondly, the defense procurement organizations would have to adjust to buying "off-the-shelf" equipment instead of equipment made to detailed DoD design specifications. Such actions can be implemented, and numerous studies have shown what steps are required.[27] However, to date the defense procurement community has resisted taking such necessary steps.

The specifications, reporting procedures, procurement practices, and other requirements passed on from the prime contractors to the subcontractors constitute another area at which the DoD must look carefully.

Clearly, these should be "tailored," and not just arbitrarily passed on (or added to, as has frequently been the case) by the prime contractors. In general, the goal of such tailoring should be to make the cost of the system as close as possible to that of commercial equipment while still achieving the necessary military performance. Meeting this goal and still minimizing the government's involvement in the detailed operation of the defense industry will require the prime contractors to do this cost-sensitive tailoring of subcontractor and supplier requirements—using general guidelines established by the government, and with the government sharing the potential risks with the prime contractors. Occasionally, the loosening of specifications will result in a problem requiring funds for correction, but these cases will be few and the amounts of money required will be very small in comparison with the large amounts now spent to have the lower-tier suppliers always design to the most demanding specifications.

One serious warning with regard to the subcontractor and parts levels (noted in chapter 5) is that the DoD should avoid gathering too much data, and should instead practice "management by exception" in order to avoid being inundated with excessive reports and having to maintain an organizational infrastructure producing little additional useful management information. Another warning concerns the need to recognize that many subcontractors and suppliers are not independent companies, but rather are divisions of larger firms. This need not be eliminated, but it does raise concerns that must be addressed as part of any investigation into these lower tiers: Those firms that are not independent have the advantage of potential cross-subsidization by the parent firm, or the disadvantage of being held "captive" by the parent companies. This is an area in which the trends toward vertical integration should probably be reversed, to increase competition and capitalize on the advantages of specialization.

12.4 Policies to Address International Interdependence

The U.S. government has not recognized the effects of changes in the international environment on all levels of the American defense industry—from raw materials through parts and subcontracting to prime contracting. New policies to consider not only the short-term economic and strategic concerns but also the longer-term concerns in these areas are now required. These new policies must reflect the new forms of transfer mechanisms (such as the multinational corporations, the international banks, the sale of production plants, the sale of management training, and the education of foreign science and engineering graduate students in the United States) and the fact that the defense industry is clearly a multinational business today.

These policies must also recognize the interdependence of countries in both civilian and military spheres—for example, the interdependence between oil-producing and arms-exporting countries. Corrective actions in this area must recognize that international negotiations at the governmental level have largely replaced market operations in foreign military sales. By law the U.S. government has a role in all U.S.-foreign military sales, so aside from the political realities it is unquestionable that the government plays the dominant role in this area. In many cases the long-term economic impact of foreign military sales (especially the impact of the technology and knowledge transfers) is unknown. It should be the job of the federal government to investigate in far more detail such areas as the long-term impacts on competition and international trade.

The government must recognize and directly address the growing dependence of the U.S. defense industry on foreign military sales. It should not be the policy of the government to encourage foreign military sales—and yet that is effectively what it does by offering additional profit (from 1 to 4 percent) on foreign military sales, by allowing its thousands of military attachés around the world to assist in foreign sales activities and by using military personnel to manage foreign sales.[28] Contractors should manage all foreign military sales, and should be fully reimbursed by the foreign governments. The U.S. government's role should be broad (but unambiguous) policymaking and specific sales approval.

The U.S. government needs to recognize the growing dependence on foreign sources of parts, raw materials, and processed materials, and to plan accordingly by stockpiling parts or taking other actions to minimize the effects of such dependence. For example, perhaps the overseas processing of raw materials should be discouraged through legislative measures and taxes. In the areas where dependence cannot be reduced, or is considered politically desirable, its negative effects could be counteracted by explicit policies establishing mutual dependence.

New U.S. policies on the transfer of manufacturing and engineering technology are needed. These policies probably will differ for different countries and different regions; for example, it is likely that we will have a different policy toward our NATO allies than we might have toward other countries. Even the current policy toward NATO is extremely ambiguous. Policymakers have been discussing the desirability of interdependence, but have been unclear as to whether the United States should freely give all of its engineering and manufacturing technology to the allies. If that is the desired objective, then it should be made explicit. However, if it is not, this should also be stated clearly so that technology-transfer decisions made at the "working level," on a day-to-day basis, can be consistent with broad yet unambiguous policy. If the development of a strong interdependence is intended, then this must be made very clear, since it will eventually lead to the United States being heavily dependent upon the NATO allies for some critical parts and possibly even for future research and development in some critical areas. As noted in chapter 8, this is already the case in certain fields—and it may be desirable, but if so the policy should be made very clear, and all parties should be fully aware of its implications and plan accordingly.

Strategic dependence is a major issue of concern. The United States should take the position of allowing and encouraging competition from foreign suppliers as a force to drive down U.S. prices for comparable equipment. NATO interoperability, common logistics, and common equipment are also highly desirable, for the sake of cost savings as well as military improvements. However, it does not follow that we need to become dependent for these reasons. Rather, when the United States gets to a position of having a single domestic source competing with foreign sources, then it behooves us to directly address this issue and to take some corrective action. Here I do not recommend such things as tariffs and quotas, but rather advocate licensing the American firm to build European-designed products and encouraging the American firm to do research and development in the area in order to come up with a lower-cost next-generation system.

Finally, in the area of surge responsiveness, the United States needs a clear policy to determine, case by case, if military items intended for foreign sale could be diverted to U.S. forces. Again, this is a difficult political issue; however, if the U.S. position were to be stated beforehand, there would be far less political repercussion than if diversion were done without prior notice. In any case, whether a firm decision can be made or

not, the issue should be clearly brought out beforehand and policy alternatives should be developed.

12.5 Improved Planning for Production Surge

A strengthened production-surge plan, selectively implemented but credible, would greatly improve the U.S. deterrent and defense posture, as well
as strengthening the U.S. negotiating position in future crises or arms-
control discussions. Such planning could be done very inexpen-
sively—perhaps for the amount of money already being spent on largely
worthless industrial preparedness planning.[29]

Perhaps the most important single step in improving planning and actual responsiveness to surge and mobilization requirements would be to
integrate the program into the normal planning for peacetime production.
This would not only make preparedness planning a "mainstream" activity, but would also be far more cost-effective, and, in fact, would tie
preparedness planning directly into the overall goal of defense-industry
planning: cost-effective peacetime production with provisions for surge
capability, and continuing R&D.

The following points pertain to policy revision in this area.[30]

- The policy should state that planning is to be highly selective. Which
  military products would be required—and could be supplied—in a
  short-term surge response should be specified, and planning should include only these. (This would eliminate planning for ships, planes, and
  other large pieces of equipment which cannot be supplied rapidly.) The
  planning should begin by looking at the "bottlenecks" in any given
  surge response. Any form of universal planning, like the present
  method, would be expensive, undesirable, and probably ineffective.
- Current planning is done only for the case of full mobilization, assuming total impact on the civilian sector. A more likely scenario is that of
  surge requirements with little if any impact to the civilian sector—con-
  tinuance of the "guns and butter" mixture, with an increase in the
  guns. Thus, surge planning should be done assuming a peacetime environment.
- Critical parts and essential production machinery must be effectively
  planned for, whereas current planning is done only at the end-item,
  prime-contractor level. Such detailed planning must only be done for

the long-lead items, the parts for which there are only a few suppliers, or the particular machinery that is already in use on three shifts.

- There is a need to look at critical labor categories. Current planning largely ignores labor, and preliminary checks have shown this to be a large potential problem. Improved planning here must be done very selectively—only in critical areas where problems are indicated—and must include other demands on this labor, including military reserve requirements. (Organized labor could be of considerable assistance in this planning.)

- Industrial-preparedness planning must be funded—particularly at the lower supplier levels, where inadequate staffs exist for such functions. (Almost all current industrial-preparedness planning is done on an unfunded basis.)

- The planning—particularly at the lower supplier tiers—must not be done on each program in isolation, but must consider the combined demand on an individual plant (the opposite is now done).

- Foreign sources to satisfy surge requirements should be considered—particularly in peacetime. There are problems associated with the use of foreign sources, but to simply refuse to consider these sources, as the United States has, is a ridiculous policy.

- The stockpiling of critical materials must be removed from the political arena by basing the buying and selling of these materials on automatic requirements that come out of a detailed annual analysis (by the relevant government agencies) of specific needs for realistic scenarios. The funds for any new acquisitions could come from a revolving account that would receive money from selloffs of stockpiled items.[31] Additionally, to reduce the dependence on foreign-based raw materials, the United States needs to sponsor far more research and development work to find substitute materials.

- The integrated peacetime and surge planning program should fund purchases of all items which would significantly affect surge capability yet not significantly reduce peacetime defense production. For example, buying long-lead parts one or two years in advance might improve the surge capability significantly. Such advance procurement would have negligible cost impact on peacetime production, since the potential obsolescence costs would be balanced against the reduced equipment costs for the higher volume and reduced inflation impact. Additionally, the DoD might choose to buy (or, preferably, encourage the contractor to buy) an extra unit of a production machine currently in use on a peacetime program on a three-shift basis. If the peacetime program ran into any problems, this would provide backup capability and additional training for machine operators.

- The policy should state that the majority of the surge needs should be satisfied by going to multiple shifts, and that therefore the primary requirement is to ensure that the critical labor, machinery, and parts are available.

- If this means that much of the excess plant space currently provided at the prime-contractor level is unnecessary, then such facilities should be allowed to be closed. This would reduce the costs of potential "mobilization needs" and encourage the reduction of redundant labor forces. It should be made explicit that any excess plant space and equipment maintained will be charged directly against the contract, to discourage firms from maintaining excess capacity unless it is potentially useful. (Currently this is an "overhead" cost.)

- At least two sources should be required for all critical long-lead parts. This would introduce price competition as well as avoiding the sort of surge problems that arose in the case of the sole source for tank castings mentioned above.

- The United States must develop a concept of "industrial warning," which would not be destabilizing if done properly and would be extremely beneficial for short and medium-duration conflicts. Currently we only have a single point of warning for both forces and industry, and the time is too short to allow any useful short-term industrial response. Total national mobilization in response to a perceived long-range threat might be considered a destabilizing action, but release of selected long-lead parts at much higher rates, or perhaps the hiring and training of workers with critical skills, would be appropriate.

- There must be a plan for emergency waiver of many of the regulations that would constrain rapid buildup (such as competitive bidding, equal employment opportunity, occupational safety and health, and small business rules).

- There should be plans for the civilian sector to turn out many types of relatively simple military equipment (even including some guided missiles) in high volume and with quality comparable to that of the defense sector's products. As the fighting force should be a mix of a few very-high-performance systems and large number of lower-performance systems, the United States could be in a position to correct its quantity deficiencies in a relatively short time by using its commercial industrial might.

- Currently all mobilization planning assumes that the force structure would remain essentially the same as quantities increased; that is, the same equipment would be used in essentially the same ratios. Thus, many current production lines (even some producing military equipment) would not be utilized. The policy should be changed to allow the introduction of some different equipment in periods of national emergency. This could include such major steps as the introduction of F-5 fighter aircraft into the U.S. inventory, and could range all the way down to the use of civilian two-way radios in the military. Again, the primary objective would be to rapidly increase the quantity of equipment.

- There is a need to establish a list of critical plants and to briefly analyze their vulnerability to sabotage, to "likely" limited warhead exchanges, and to the economic and strategic impacts of such actions. Also, consideration must be given to the effectiveness and the cost of preventive steps such as security, dispersal, and limited hardening.

- Plans for postwar recovery (including recovery from limited nuclear war) must be prepared. The Soviets clearly do such planning, and the need for it grows more and more realistic as the scenarios are considered. Highly visible recovery planning would improve the credibility of the U.S. deterrent. It is essential to determine what U.S. actions would be worthwhile (for example, dispersal or multiple sources). Such planning must be done not just for critical military products but also for critical civilian sectors.

This is only a partial list of actions that could be taken by the United States and its allies, at minimal cost, to more fully realize the existing potential of the defense and civilian industries to assist in mobilizing all available resources in the national interest. It must be emphasized that, to be successful and cost-effective, such plans and actions must be highly selective, done in sufficient depth, and properly funded and implemented. The most important point, however, is that all of these actions and plans must be undertaken now—in peacetime—in order to have any significant effect on our future deterrent or fighting posture.

12.6 Cost as a Major Design and Acquisition Criterion

That cost should be a major design and acquisition criterion for defense equipment seems óbvious. However, it should be clear from the earlier chapters that this is not the case. Rather, performance is still the overriding criterion for design decisions and source selections. If the Department of Defense is ever going to reverse the downward trend in amounts of equipment procured without enormous budget increases, the only way to do it is to make cost a major criterion. This would be truly a cultural change for the Department of Defense, but it would bring the DoD closer to the commercial way of doing business and it would actually improve the U.S. military posture by increasing the number of systems procured.

For each individual product the most important cost figure is the cost of the total program, including research and development, production, operation, and support. On most programs the production and support costs are by far the largest. Thus, the design selected should have low inherent production and support costs—awards should not be based solely upon the lowest cost for product development, as is normally the case today. Similarly, the important characteristic for the Department of Defense, and therefore the criterion that should be used for each acquisition decision, is the total cost to the government for the military equipment produced by a specific sector of the defense industry (for example, all ships being produced). Turning production factories on and off in an effort to lower the cost of an individual weapons system (as is now done) often actually raises the total cost to the DoD for the equipment produced in that sector, since the DoD absorbs the overhead as well. This view requires an industrial-base perspective and relevant sectoral data. It also means that production must be planned much earlier for most weapons systems, in order to ensure that the production costs get major consideration.

Production cost must be made a major engineering design criterion. Since the mid-1970s the Department of Defense has been trying to institutionalize such an approach, called "design-to-cost."[32] It requires performance and contract flexibility, use of commercial specifications and standards, and other cost-reducing actions, and, most importantly, giving cost equal priority to performance. This is still a difficult process to implement in the DoD, because the significant advantages of quantity, versus the small increase in quality that is given up, have not yet been widely appreciated. (Some estimate that the last 5 percent of performance often results in a 50 percent cost increase, and therefore a very significant reduction in the quantity of equipment that could be procured for the same money.)

In the past, competition and new technology have been used by the DoD to advance military performance of weapons systems. The use of competition and new technology is required to continue increasing performance and yet to simultaneously reduce inherent production and support costs.

Other efforts can be taken to reduce costs, such as placing greater emphasis on return on investment as a profit policy, rather than on costs spent.[33] The intent here would be to figure out incentives to reduce total costs and give the contractors increased profit if they are successful in reducing costs. Another step in this same direction would be to have the government contract negotiators emphasize total cost—not just reduced profit, which is their current objective. Also, perhaps the government could give a tax break for research and development on lower-cost approaches. Finally, by keeping competition going into the production phase—not just in the early phases of development—the DoD could place greater emphasis on production cost reductions.[34]

Many of the other recommended changes are similarly oriented towards cost savings—for example, more specialization at the lower level, "buying" rather than "making," separation of R&D and production, combined buying for a variety of programs (in order to get the cost benefit of higher volume), and buying commercial equipment (which is usually much cheaper, as table 12.1 shows).[35] However, the major change is associated with convincing the military services that increases in quantities of defense equipment can result from making cost a major design and planning characteristic—a principle that requires the support of the Office of the Secretary of Defense and the Congress.

12.7 Institutionalization of Industrial-Base Considerations

A major fallacy in the operation of the U.S. government is its overemphasis on policy formulation at the expense of (or almost instead of) policy execution and evaluation. For an institution as large as the Department of Defense, the only way that changes can be implemented and kept up to date is through actions that involve policy issuances,

Table 12.1
Examples of Savings Anticipated from Use of Commercial Items

	Estimated Unit Cost		Cost Ratio
	Military	Commercial	
Army aircraft radio receiving set	$ 6,000	$ 1,300	4.6:1
Army aircraft distance-measuring set	15,000	4,000	3.7:1
Shipboard tape recorder	8,000	167	47.9:1
Shipboard telephone	70	42	1.7:1
Aircraft video tape recorder	7,000	2,500	2.8:1
Diesel generator set to replace turbine sets	56,000	14,000	4.0:1
16mm motion-picture projector	1,200	600	2.0:1
Shipboard navigational system (Transit-Omega)	115,000	27,000	4.3:1

organizational changes, new procurement practices, and day-to-day procedural changes. Additionally, there must be periodic monitoring of all major equipment programs. In each of these areas, industrial-base considerations must be incorporated into the DoD's overall operations and budgets, and a followup system must be initiated to ensure proper and timely implementation.

Equally important is the need, when implementing changes in the DoD and the defense industry, to make full use of natural institutional and individual incentives. Directing changes is much more difficult than having the various special-interest groups see the changes as acting to their benefit and thus implemented with their support. Each proposed action must be assessed in terms of its likely impact on the special interest groups, the way to structure and present it so as to gain their support, and the incentives to be utilized in order to gain positive reaction to the change.

These institutional changes will take years, and should take this much time in order to avoid shock to the system. Clearly, the right changes will not follow automatically from the issuance of a government directive or an act of Congress. Rather, the detailed implementation must be carefully thought out and the proper organizations—with the necessary checks and balances—must be established. Currently there are no data on and no plans for the defense industrial base, no organization to specifically address its problems, and no procurement system amenable to shaping its characteristics.

The total actions needed go well beyond the scope of the DoD. Organizational and procurement impacts should be governmentwide, affecting the Departments of Commerce and the Treasury, the Office of Federal Procurement Policy, and other organizations doing business in a similar fashion, such as the Department of Energy.[36]

Additionally, public checks and balances are necessary throughout the government (including the executive branch), as well as checks between branches. One area that needs greater public visibility is that of congressional budgetary add-ons. Perhaps a non-politically-appointed ombudsman with access to the press could encourage Congress to make decisions less for political reasons and more for economic and national-security reasons.

From an organizational viewpoint, it is clear that one of the major needs is for an organization to collect and analyze information on the overall industrial base—both the supply and the demand developments—and provide early warnings of impending problems along with long-range policy plans. Essentially this group would be similar to the "economic and industrial monitoring unit" recommended by the Supplies and Shortages Commission.[37] This group should be concerned not with the operational details of individual firms but with the broader industrial structure (supply and demand, the number of competitors, and so on). It would be looking for "second best" solutions tailored to each sector, such as how to create competition if it doesn't exist and what would be the costs and benefits of such an action. It could be located within the Department of Defense, but it must consider both military and civilian requirements, and it must be separate from the decisionmakers so it can present planning alternatives to them, and independently evaluate their decisions for likely impacts. Again, the planning data must be available to the public; not only to those with the necessary security access, but also to firms desiring to enter the business. Where necessary, the new policy should consciously set up additional checks and balances, for example between the Office of the Secretary of Defense and the services and/or within both OSD and the services.

A group doing sectoral analysis at the prime-contractor level of the defense industry could also be responsible for doing the analysis at the lower tiers; however, it must be made explicit that the impact of decisions would have to be separately evaluated for the lower tiers, and that the small suppliers must be represented equally. The analysts for the lower tiers should not be buried within the organization responsible for the large contractors, but could be an equal division of that organization. Since this group would be monitoring potential problems at the critical subcontractor and supplier levels, where the overall number of firms is so much greater, priorities would have to be established. The considerations should include a firm's percentage of defense business, the number of suppliers available for the given product, and the difficulty of obtaining substitutes. Most of the selected products being monitored would be special high-technology items, but there would be exceptions.

Other important organizational considerations include separating the management of the government-owned facilities from the services and possibly from the DoD (both to eliminate the conflict of interest between awarding work to oneself rather than someone else and to encourage more use of private contractors) and separating defense-industry regulators from policymakers. There are advantages to this action, but there is also the danger of the regulators becoming unresponsive to needed changes as demand and technology change. A way to improve their responsiveness would be to require them to justify the macro impact of any recommended actions, in terms of costs or structure, on a "second best" basis (that is, on the individual change's projected impact within the industry as it exists) before any regulation is imposed and to reassess this analysis every five years. Thus, the regulators' primary responsibility would be the economic efficiency of the industry being regulated, and therefore they would represent the public interest.

In the procurement area, all of the data in the earlier chapters indicate clearly that the DoD needs different policies and practices for different sectors and levels within the defense industry. For example, a profit policy could be evolved to assess risk and investment, but also the number of suppliers needed. Where there is a shortage of suppliers, increased profit could be made possible to encourage new entrants; where there is an excess of suppliers, the very large profits going to some of the firms using government plants and equipment could be reduced. Also, a policy could be evolved to ensure that the return on investment in each sector is comparable to the higher of either a comparable category of civilian business or the average of U.S. industry's return on investment for comparable-risk business. Similarly, a procurement policy could be issued to require more use of competitive allocation and fewer sole-source awards (currently, sole-source business accounts for well over 60 percent of total dollars). The myth of a free-market operation continues to perpetuate the belief that defense procurements are normally based on price competition; however, the data show that only 8 percent of the business is done that way, and that open price competition is often not really a usable solution for defense prime contracting. Increasing competitive allocation would reduce the amount of sole-source business.

Finally, procedural aspects must be considered. Here we get down to the Department of Defense's day-to-day operations and its interface with the defense industry. In the latter category, the needed changes are significant. The DoD should move in the direction of far more commercial-like business relationships, with far more mutual respect and trust, and only with those firms whose performance warrants it. (By contrast, today there usually exists an adversary relationship between business and the DoD over major military procurements.)

Industrial-base considerations—such as timing, source selection, separation of research and development programs, budgeting, resource allocation, force-structure factors (such as quantity versus time), and whether product modifications are to be done in government or private shops—must be worked directly into the DoD's decisionmaking process. All the basic policies that cover these day-by-day decisions must be revised to incorporate and balance industrial-resource concerns. Much of this must be done within the services. However, interservice rivalry often results in the establishment of a single preferred supplier for each service, whereas the "bigger piece of pie" that the combination of procurements for all three services present would increase industrial competition. Combined-services buying would result in far more "competitive allocations, and would keep multiple sources going while splitting the total buy in competitive fashion.

The preferred overall procedural approach was summarized well by Major General James Stansberry, Air Force Deputy Chief of Staff for Procurement and Manufacturing:

Our studies lead us to conclude that the effort should focus on the macro level rather than the micro or procedural aspects of service operations. For example, rather than looking at negotiation techniques for reducing overhead, correct the structural situations that cause high overhead. Rather than looking at incentives on individual contracts, look at the fundamental, structural incentives or requirements provided to the defense industry to build the organizations and cost base they have. Rather than looking at procedural techniques for more or less engagement in contract management, investigate the fundamental philosophy of individual contracting officers and procurement offices attempting to regulate an industry or individual firm thereof, through the force of individual contracts and programs. . . . In summary, look at the total environment in which we make our perfectly reasonable micro decisions which seem to add up to unreasonable macro results.[38]

Notes

Introduction

1. M. J. Peck and F. M. Scherer, *The Weapons Acquisition Process: An Economic Analysis* (Cambridge, Mass.: Harvard University Press, 1962); Scherer, *The Weapons Acquisition Process: Economic Incentives* (Harvard University Press, 1964); J. Ronald Fox, *Arming America: How the U.S. Buys Weapons* (Harvard University Press, 1974).

2. This two-level analysis is similar to the "dual economy" (described by Averitt, Galbraith, and others) in the U.S. civilian economy.

3. Price increases of 300–500 percent in one year have been observed.

4. For example, Grumman and Northrop in the aircraft area.

Chapter 1

1. For a detailed discussion of the history of the U.S. defense industrial base, with numerous references, see J. S. Gansler, "The Diminishing Economic and Strategic Viability of the U.S. Defense Industrial Base," Ph.D. diss., American University, 1978 (Ann Arbor, Mich.: University Microfilm International, 1978).

2. During the Revolution, ship construction and artillery-piece manufacturing were performed in the private sector, while guns and munitions came mostly from government arsenals (beginning with the establishment of state arms factories in Massachusetts and Virginia in 1774 and 1775, respectively, and the first federal arsenal at Springfield, Mass. in 1778).

3. Defense expenditures have also had a major impact on civilian manufacturing processes—from the first production of interchangeable parts (Eli Whitney's contract for muskets in 1798) through the development of computer-aided machine tools.

4. During World War II, $26 billion was invested in new plants and equipment (about two-thirds provided by the government), usually near or at existing private facilities. The lion's share went to the large firms; thus, when the war ended and these facilities were sold at attractive prices, it was not surprising that 250 of the nation's largest firms acquired more than 70 percent of the plants sold. See J. M. Blair, *Economic Concentration: Structure, Behavior, and Public Policy* (New York: Harcourt Brace Jovanovich, 1972), p. 380.

5. For example, see R. C. Edwards, M. Reich, and T. E. Weisskoff, *The Capitalist System* (Englewood Cliffs, N.J.: Prentice-Hall, 1972), p. 372; P. M. Baran and P. A., Sweezy, *Monopoly Capital* (New York: Monthly Review Press, 1966), p. 176.

6. P. Lewis "Defense Costs and the Economy," *New York Times,* December 19, 1976, p. E6.

7. B. M. Blechman, E. M. Gramlich, and R. W. Hartman, "Setting National Priorities: The 1975 Budget," Brookings Institution report (Washington, D.C., 1974).

8. W. Leontief and M. Hoffenberg, "The Economic Impact of Disarmament," *Scientific American,* April 1961, p. 9.

9. One way to measure the economic impact of defense expenditures is to use the stock market as a barometer. Murray Weidenbaum (*The Economics of Peace-Time Defense* [New York: Basic Books, 1974]) found that, from the time of the Spanish-American War, after each period of military conflict there has been a sharp rise of the stock market. This, he concluded, means that peace is a bullish factor; however, one could counter that argument by noting the significant demand in the civilian area after a war (because of deferred expen-

ditures) and the overall economic expansion during a war. An analysis of stock market prices and defense procurement levels from the mid-1950s to the mid-1970s shows that the stock market, and hence the economic picture it allegedly forecasts, reacted very favorably to the "crises" that occurred during this period—including the Vietnam War. One could infer that, as the nation spends more in the defense industry, the investment community feels that overall employment and the gross national product are likely to increase. In the post-Vietnam period, with the reduction in defense expenditures, there was a significant fall in the stock market. There is a strong counterargument that the Vietnam War caused significant inflation in the United States (because of overstimulation due to simultaneous "guns and butter" demands), and therefore, over the long run, had a very detrimental effect. In the short run, however, the war may have been an economic stimulant—if one believes the stock market to be a meaningful indicator of this.

10. J. F. Lawrence, "Spending for Defense: Boon or Detriment?," *Los Angeles Times,* January 10, 1978, p. 1.

11. J. K. Galbraith, *The New Industrial State* (Boston: Houghton Mifflin, 1967).

12. At the time there was an estimated shortage, in the Los Angeles area alone, of 30,000 engineers who could have been hired against existing contracts. (Whether they would have been underutilized is a difficult question, but there was enough money to pay for them if they could be found and were willing to move.) What was actually happening was that the total supply of engineers was not growing much; mostly there was shifting from one firm to another as engineers were offered 20–30 percent raises. This is an inflationary and inefficient result of increased demand in a saturated market.

13. Lead times for parts for the few (often sole) suppliers were being measured in years, rather than weeks or months.

14. Defense Systems Acquisition Review Council Working Group, "Final Report, Weapon Systems Costs," December 19, 1972. This same phenomenon (big increases in unit cost of equipment, after correction for inflation) is being seen in the U.K. as well, but costs there are not growing as rapidly as in the U.S. For example, in comparing the costs of military systems in the 1950s and the later 1970s, and again adjusting for inflation, it was found that a destroyer costs three times as much, a tank two times as much, a ground-attack aircraft four times as much, and an antiaircraft weapon eight times as much. (Source: London *Financial Times,* August 3, 1979, p. 17).

15. Perhaps the extreme of this position is presented by Seymour Melman ("Twelve Propositions on Productivity and the War Economy," *Challenge,* March–April, 1975). In this view, because of the large expenditures for defense during the 1950s and 1960s, the "defense way of doing business" permeated the whole U.S. economy, and thus the large increases in prices for defense equipment were reflected in the other major sectors of the economy. This is an extreme position, because defense is not the dominant economic factor—even in the areas of its most significant impact, such as among scientists and engineers, skilled production workers, and capital investments. Nonetheless, the national impact of the rising costs of military equipment has clearly extended beyond the area of defense.

16. Defense Science Board, "Final Report on Defense Electronics Management," January, 1974.

17. This indicates the declining significance of defense in the overall U.S. economy. However, this ratio is also often used as a measure of a nation's ability to "afford" its defense expenditures. The assumption is that the lower the share of the GNP expended on

defense, the smaller the amount other goods and services the nation must forsake (on a relative basis).

18. Some argue that this reduction in tactical aircraft has been partially compensated for by the increased number of missiles procured over this period. However, a comparison with the greatly increasing number of Soviet tactical aircraft and missiles argues strongly against this case.

19. For example, between 1973 and 1976 Congress annually cut procurement budget requests by about 14 percent.

20. International Institute of Strategic Studies, "The Military Balance 1977–78" (London, 1977), p. 82.

21. Central Intelligence Agency, "A Comparison of U.S. Outlays with Estimated Dollar Costs of Soviet Activities if Duplicated in the U.S.," January 18, 1976.

22. *Washington Post,* November 2, 1979, p. 1. (Data based on estimate made by the CIA and released to Congress.)

23. The only area in which the U.S. appeared to have numerical superiority was in helicopters. By 1973–1975 the U.S.S.R. had started to outproduce the U.S. by 1,100 to 506. (Source: *Aviation Week and Space Technology,* January 26, 1976, p. 20.)

24. The Soviets apparently believe in Lanchester's law, which states that overall military-force effectiveness is proportional to unit equipment effectiveness times the square of the number of units. Thus, as equipment becomes more comparable, numbers become overwhelming significant. If the American equipment is twice as good as comparable equipment of the Soviets, but they have twice as much, then Lanchester's law says that the forces are not equivalent; rather, the Soviet forces are twice as effective. In this comparison of the relative value of quality (the U.S. emphasis) and quantity (the Soviet emphasis) it is not reassuring to note that in World War II the German emphasis was on qualitative superiority (for example, the development of the V-1 and V-2 rockets), while the U.S. won through its emphasis on quantity (see Alan Milward, *War, Economy and Society: 1939–1945* [Berkeley: University of California Press, 1977], especially p. 186).

25. M. L. Harvey and F. D. Kohler, *Soviet World Outlook,* vol. 1, no. 4 (Washington, D.C.: Current Affairs Press, Center for Advanced International Studies, 1976), p. 12; M. Kaplan, *Bulletin of the Atomic Scientists,* March 1978.

26. J. S. Gansler, "Let's Change the Way the Pentagon Does Business," *Harvard Business Review* 55 (May–June 1977): 109–118.

27. For example, in fiscal years 1977 and 1978 the procurement budget was increased 25 percent each year.

28. R. L. Heilbroner and L. C. Thurrow, *The Economic Problem,* 4th edition (Englewood Cliffs, N.J.: Prentice-Hall, 1975), p. 427.

29. A good reference in this area is J. R. Fox's *Arming America: How the U.S. Buys Weapons* (Cambridge, Mass.: Harvard University Press, 1974).

Chapter 2

1. G. C. Lodge, review of *The Ethical Basis of Economic Freedom* (edited by Ivan Hill), *New York Times,* October 24, 1976.

2. R. G. Lipsey and K. Lancaster, "The General Theory of the Second Best," *Review of*

Economic Studies XXIV (1956-1957): 11-32. For a simple mathematical treatment of this theory see J. M. Henderson and R. E. Quante, *Microeconomics Theory: A Mathematical Approach* (New York: McGraw-Hill, 1971), p. 286-288.

3. Senator George Mahan, speech to the National Securities Industries Association, Washington, D.C., January 1976.

4. This is the traditional approach of the industrial organization economist (see for example F. M. Scherer, *Industrial Market Structure and Economic Performance* (Chicago: Rand-McNally, 1970). However, I have perhaps placed more emphasis on the "factors of production" than is typical of the industrial organization theorists. This is because of their uniqueness and importance in the defense industry.

5. Although individual members of Congress certainly have some control of their own, they mostly sense whether the nation is for or against increased defense spending and respond relatively quickly. For example, when President Ford was putting together the 1977 fiscal budget, Congress was pushing for significant reductions and for government economies; thus the president went so far as to fire Secretary of Defense James Schlesinger, who was fighting strongly for an increase in defense expenditures to provide what was believed to be much-needed military equipment to correct significant post-Vietnam deteriorations. Within six months after this action, Congress sensed constituent support of a strong defense posture, and then-Secretary Rumsfeld was able to get a 25 percent increase in the procurement expenditures for fiscal 1977. It should be emphasized that the large increase in demand was brought about not by a reduction in price (in fact, prices in the mid-1970s were rising rapidly), but rather by the public's "demand" for increased defense expenditures.

6. R. Kurth, testimony before House-Senate Joint Production Committee, September 1977.

7. In some cases, this mix of public- and private-sector work is the only way to foster competition. For example, in 1906 Congress provided funds for the Army to build a small plant to make gunpowder, since DuPont had a monopoly on military powder (A. D. Chandler, *Strategy and Structure: Chapters in the History of Industrial Enterprise* [Cambridge, Mass.: MIT Press, 1962]). As Scherer notes in *Industrial Market Structure,* this competition between the public and private sector may be the "second best" solution under some circumstances, such as when a monopoly supplier has such a strong position that he can charge very high prices. An example of this in the defense industry may be the competition for aircraft maintenance business between the government repair depots and the aircraft manufacturers.

8. For example, the government owns most of the plant space and equipment in the munitions and strategic-missile industries, one-third in the aircraft industry, and none in the shipbuilding industry.

9. The Army, using the Army Arsenal Act of 1853 (which clearly has a public-sector bias), tends to do more of its work "in house"; the Air Force, using the Air Force Arsenal Act of 1951 (which leaves the choice up to the Secretary of the Air Force), tends to favor the private sector for manufacturing but still uses its own laboratories and repair depots extensively. The Defense Industrial Reserve Act of 1973 maintains the ambiguity over the guidance of Congress in this area.

10. R. J. Barnet and R. E. Müller, *Global Reach: The Power of the Multinational Corporations* (New York: Simon and Schuster, 1974), p. 230.

11. "Fortune 500" listing, *Fortune,* 1975.

12. The 1960s was one of the great merger periods in U.S. history. The other two were

1897–1905 and 1925–1929. (J. M. Blair, *Economic Concentration: Structure, Behavior, and Public Policy* [New York: Harcourt Brace Jovanovich, 1972]).

13. F. M. Scherer (*The Economics of Multi-Plant Operation* [Cambridge, Mass.: Harvard University Press, 1975], pp. 385, 389) makes this same point when he says "Concentration in effect provides a second-best solution to the plant-specific scale economies problem . . . particularly if there are significant market failures present." The latter, of course, applies to the defense market, and the increased concentration need not reduce the amount of competition for defense business—unless carried to an extreme.

14. The high consistency from year to year of the same firms at the top of the defense lists is traceable over even longer periods.

15. Two types of firms are listed among the defense giants: those we think of as being heavily oriented towards the defense industry, for example, General Dynamics, Boeing, Lockheed, etc., and those we normally would think of as commercial firms, for example, AT&T, Exxon, General Motors, etc.

16. For example, in 1965 North American, McDonnell, and Thiokol were all over 75 percent defense; by 1977 North American (even before losing the B-1) was only 17 percent, McDonnell-Douglas was down to under 45 percent, and Thiokol was down to 33 percent. The shift of other firms was even more extreme. Companies such as Raytheon, TRW, Aerojet, and United Technologies were almost entirely in defense in the 1950s and early 1960s; today each of these has less than half of its business in the defense sector, and is consciously attempting to reduce this further. United Technologies was almost 100 percent defense in 1971, was under 50 percent by 1978, and was aiming to get to 15 percent by the mid-1980s (*The Economist,* September 30, 1978, p. 113).

17. Examples of commercial acquisitions by the defense contractors include United Technologies' acquisition of Otis Elevator and Raytheon's acquisition of Amana. Acquisitions have also been going on in the opposite direction, with conglomerates choosing to get into the defense area: Singer bought General Precision, Marietta bought Martin, and Rockwell bought North American. The primary exception to this acquisition path has been where some of the defense companies have been successful in selling to other *government* agencies which are also technology-oriented, such as the Department of Transportation, the Department of Energy, and the National Aeronautics and Space Administration. All of these do business in a fashion essentially similar to that of the DoD, and will be doing it in an even more similar fashion in the future under the new Office of Management and Budget regulations requiring uniformity of overall government procurement practices.

18. This trend is particularly apparent when viewed in the light of data compiled in 1965 by the subcommittee on antitrust and monopoly of the Senate Committee on the Judiciary (S.R. 233, "Competition in Defense Procurement," 1968, p. 16). At that time, the largest share of DoD business was done by the "middle-sized" firms (those with assets between $250 million and $1 billion). In this class were a lot of specialized firms which had a heavy share of their business in defense. Today, many of these are now divisions of larger conglomerates or "parent" divisions of diversified firms.

19. Cross-subsidizing is defined as "the actual use by a conglomerate of monopoly profits gained in another industry to subsidize sales at a loss or at an abnormally low profit" (Blair, *Economic Concentration,* p. 42).

20. G. R. Hall and R. E. Johnson, "A Review of Air Force Procurement, 1962–1964," Rand Corp. report RM-4500-PR (Santa Monica, Calif., 1965).

21. For a good discussion of the difficulties in identifying the SIC numbers in the groupings within the defense industry, see J. W. McKie, "Concentration in Military Procurement Markets: A Classification and Analysis of Contract Data," Rand Corp. report RM-6307-PR (Santa Monica, Calif., 1970), Appendix.

22. M. L. Weidenbaum, "The Military/Space Market: The Intersection of the Public and Private Sectors," U.S. Senate Hearings, Subcommittee on Antitrust and Monopoly of the Committee on the Judiciary, 90th Congress, second session, pursuant to S.R. 233, June 17 and 21 and September 10, 1968 (Washington, D.C.: Government Printing Office, 1969).

23. Blair, *Economic Concentration,* pp. 11–12.

24. Scherer (*Industrial Market Structure,* p. 123) found that even at the broad sectoral level, e.g., aircraft, shipbuilding, jet engines, "the principle defense and space industries are more concentrated than the average civilian products industries."

25. C. Kaysen and D. F. Turner, *Antitrust Policy: An Economic and Legal Analysis* (Cambridge, Mass.: Harvard University Press, 1959), p. 30.

26. J. S. Bain, *Industrial Organization* (New York: Wiley, 1959), p. 424.

27. McKie, "Concentration in Military Procurement Markets," p. 12.

28. J. M. Clark refers to this as "workable competition" (see Scherer, *Industrial Market Structure,* p. 36).

29. Weidenbaum, "Military/Space Market ," p. 910.

30. Blair, *Economic Concentration,* p. 40.

31. In 1967 the "failing firm" argument was used to allow the merger between McDonnell Aircraft (sixth largest aerospace firm) and Douglas Aircraft (eighth largest aerospace firm); but the lack of real consolidation resulted in an "unrationalized merger" (one where costs were not minimized).

32. These states are Alaska, Arizona, California, Colorado, Connecticut, Hawaii, Maryland, Massachusetts, Utah, Virginia, and Washington. (Source for geographic distribution data is "Military Prime Contracts by Region and State," DoD Comptroller, 1977).

33. There are also strong congressional pressures for defense expenditures to be more equally divided by regions of the country. For example, the South and West tend to get almost five times as much employment from defense expenditures as the rest of the country. (CONEG Policy Research Center, Inc. and Northeast-Midwest Research Institute, "A Case of Inequity: Regional Patterns in Defense Expenditure 1965 to 1967," 1977, Table 4.)

34. J. S. Bain, *Barriers to New Competition: Their Character and Consequences in Manufacturing Industries* (Cambridge, Mass.: Harvard University Press, 1956), introduction.

35. One effect of these barriers to exit has been to prevent defense firms from diversifying out of defense through any route other than acquisition, and even then not at the plant or division level. As R. DuBoff noted, "Efforts by military-oriented firms [divisions or plants] to diversify have been almost total failures" ("Connecting Military Spending to Social Welfare: The Real Obstacles," *Quarterly Review of Economics and Business,* spring 1972, p. 17).

36. The economic purist will object to my use of money as a factor separate from equipment—since the term "capital" is usually used to cover both money and capital equipment. However, because the word "capital" can be ambiguous, I've chosen the separation for clarity—at the expense of academic purity.

37. Another example: In 1966 Boeing hired 37,000 persons, but 25,000 quit. Boeing representatives said they "had to hire three to get one" (*Aerospace Daily,* September 1, 1978, p. 5). However, this short-term instability is not characteristic of all sectors of the defense industry. In fact, the aerospace and munitions industries tend to have smaller annual turnover rates than the rest of the U.S. manufacturing sectors. This can be attributed to the fact that, in the short term, the defense industries find it much easier to absorb the overhead of carrying the workers for periods when business is slack by simply adding the cost to their government contracts, whereas the price-sensitive civilian-oriented sectors find it necessary to lay these people off and rehire them when business gets better. Also, the wages are higher in the defense sector, so the workers tend to stay in the job as long as programs exist. Finally, there is the congressional "smoothing" of the labor market in the defense sector, wherein significant dollars are often added to a program in order to maintain employment in a given district or state.

38. Some say that defense is second only to advertising in terms of the labor instability among executives. In fact, a 1976 study by The Conference Board ("Report on Investment in the Defense Industry") listed "excessive management changes" as a major reason for concern in the financial community over investing in the defense industry. This executive turnover is largely due to the "either/or" type of contracting done in the defense business. It is common for a company to fire the director of marketing when a big proposal is lost, and to fire the program manager or vice president of operations when the company gets into trouble with the DoD for being unable to live up to its initial "buy-in" on a program. Similarly, the vice president of engineering is blamed when technical problems develop that were not "expected" when the optimistic proposals were made. Finally, the president of the division is often fired to "correct" the financial or sales problems of a division—which often are simply a reflection of the cyclic nature of the business. Frequently these executive changes are "requested" by the government customer in order to "correct" the problems on a particular program. Thus, a typical defense industry executive will usually have worked for a large number of defense firms and will find that the "increased experience" is often considered an advantage rather than a disadvantage in his job searches.

39. "Labor learning" is used here, in the traditional production-theory sense, to mean the cost reduction realized as a worker performs the same job repetitively, becomes more skilled at the task, and is therefore capable of doing the task in less time. This is usually calculated as a percentage reduction in unit cost as a function of the quantity of items produced.

40. For example, in 1979 there was a shortage of 30,000 aerospace and electronics engineers in the Los Angeles area alone, so extensive raids were made on the engineering forces of rival defense firms. The likelihood of all these jobs being required at the time of the next downturn in defense expenditures seemed very low.

41. A number of writers (for example, Killingsworth and Weidenbaum, *The Modern Public Sector* [New York: Basic Books, 1969], p. 47) have noted the very low proportion of blue-collar workers and the very high proportion of engineers and scientists in the defense labor force, which makes it more difficult to apply many of the government requirements for equal employment opportunities, employment of the "hard-core" unemployed, and awards to high-unemployment areas.

42. This higher wage rate can also be found in the Bureau of Labor Statistics data that show aerospace wages to be about 25 percent higher than equivalent skills in other industries, and is confirmed by General Dynamics data (personal communication) which show a growing wage differential (since WWII) required to obtain aircraft employees, relative to the general labor market. By the mid-1970s this differential had reached a premium of over 20 percent.

43. *The New Engineer,* a magazine aimed at graduating engineers and scientists, frequently runs articles warning them against going into the defense industry. See, for example, the 1978 issue. This same problem appears to exist in the U.K.: At an American Institute of Aeronautics and Astronautics seminar in Amsterdam, June 19, 1978, Admiral Bryson of the Royal Navy said "the U.K. has been having significant difficulty getting young engineers to work in the defense area."

44. System Planning Corporation, findings from aircraft-industry study (personal communication, June 1, 1976).

45. Ibid. Note that these high average age figures are the result of many cutbacks in greatly underutilized facilities. The remaining workers were retained because of their seniority in the unions.

46. For example, there are only two large (50,000-pound) presses in the U.S., and the DoD owns both of them. All studies of U.S. industry have shown that one limiting factor for overall industrial production is forging capability, including the skilled laborers required. Thus, such facilities would be better for the national interest if placed fully in the private sector (with the DoD having priority over their use), where the profit motive would more likely ensure full, three-shift utilization in peacetime. This would ensure the availability of trained labor for an emergency.

47. Assistant Secretary of Defense Frank Shrontz, letter to Vice President Nelson Rockefeller containing DoD's annual report to the Congress on defense industrial reserve, April 3, 1976.

48. For example, the Air Force plant at Fort Worth, Texas, used by General Dynamics for aircraft production, cost $96 million to build.

49. *Aviation Week and Space Technology,* November 28, 1977, p. 16.

50. In an analysis done in 1967, R. F. Kaufman (general counsel to the House-Senate Joint Economic Committee) pointed out that 15 companies, including 9 of the largest defense contractors, were reported to hold 84 percent of the $2.6 billion of government-owned industrial plants and equipment then in use in the private sector (Kaufman, *The War Profiteers* [New York: Bobbs-Merrill, 1970]). In 1975 I found that this imbalance had essentially remained the same: 84.4 percent of the plant and equipment resources in the private sector was in the hands of large firms.

51. Recognizing both of these points, in 1970 the DoD initiated a "phaseout" program for these government-owned plants and equipment. A memo from the deputy secretary of defense (February 13, 1971) stated that the DoD's basic policy would be to rely on the contractor to the maximum extent possible to provide production facilities, and to minimize government ownership of facilities, with the following exceptions: government-owned contractor-operated plants that produce no commercial products, contractors with approved plant and equipment packages essential for the support of current or mobilization products, contractors for whom mobilization requirements are in the process of being developed, and contractors for whom the phaseout would work an economic hardship. Clearly, this policy gave some "escape clauses," but it was powerful enough, compared with the existing legislation, to have some impact—particularly in the case of the Air Force.

52. The trend has been toward less government ownership. In the 1950s it was about 70 percent, by 1963 it was 55 percent, and by 1976 it was 35 percent. The amount is still very significant.

53. J. Robinson, *Economic Heresies: Some Old Fashioned Questions in Economic Theory* (New York: Basic Books, 1971), p. 22.

54. An indication of the pervasiveness of this view of the need to keep production lines "ready" is the fact that when I gave the Air Force a list of six government-owned plants about which I was interested in obtaining the percent utilization, I received an answer which said essentially that all six were being utilized at almost full capacity. I had just recently toured one of them, and the lights had had to be turned on so that I could take my tour. After two more rounds of inquiry and explanation, I received data for these six plants showing that the 1976 sales, in inflation-adjusted comparison with the peak-year figures, ranged from 12 percent to 99 percent, with a weighted average of 47.7 percent, and that the 1976 direct labor forces ranged from 11 percent to 69 percent of the peak-year numbers, with a weighted average of 38.2 percent. I do not believe that the initial Air Force answers were intended to mislead me; rather, they were the sincere answers being given by people who believed that a facility was "being utilized" when it was being held in a ready condition for reinstitution of the production lines for the aircraft that were originally built there. It would take years to get these lines back up to speed, because of the limitations of parts, subsystems, labor, and machines.

55. W. D. Nordhaus, "The Falling Share of Profits," Brookings Papers on Economic Activity (1974).

56. For example, in September 1974 the aerospace industry was operating at a claimed level of 71.4 percent (which is believed to be overstated), while all other major industrial sectors of the U.S. economy were operating at between 86.6 percent and 96.8 percent (Rinfret Boston Associates, "Survey of Capacity Utilization," *Congressional Record,* 94th Congress, first session, May 9, 1975).

57. These costs are covered under a plant's "indirect costs," so they receive very little scrutiny. A good alternative might be to highlight these costs on a separate budget line. This was tried by the Air Force in 1976, when it funded about $12 million for the annual "maintenance of vital capacity" at Air Force Plant 4 (General Dynamics) and Plant 6 (Lockheed).

58. *American Machinist* data (1976) show U.S. machine tools to be significantly older than those in Canada, Japan, Italy, West Germany, United Kingdom, or the Soviet Union.

59. International Economic Report of the president, March, 1975.

60. A series of studies during the 1970s all showed low investment in the defense industry. For example, a study for 1971–1973 by Assistant Secretary of Defense A. Mendolia, based on 105 "defense" firms and 500 nondefense firms engaged in similar types of business, showed that the average defense firm reinvests about 50 percent of each dollar of cash generated (net profit plus depreciation), while comparable nondefense industries reinvest about 75 percent of each dollar generated. This same study showed that a typical aerospace company invests about the exact same amount as its depreciation and amortization each year, while the average nondefense firm invests, in new capital, about twice as much as its annual depreciation and amortization. A similar result was found in another independent study done in 1971 (Industry Advisory Council, report to the secretary of defense by the Subcommittee to Consider Defense Industry Contract Financing, June 11, 1971, p. 45), which compared the percent of a firm's business in the defense area (for 65 leading defense contractors) with the amount of capital investment in facilities for each dollar of sales. Firms with 25–50 percent defense business invested 85 cents per sales dollar, firms with 50–75 percent defense business invested 14.6 cents, and firms with 75–100 percent defense business invested 8.3

cents. The "Profit '76" study (see "Profit '76, Summary Report," Office of the Assistant Secretary of Defense for Installations and Logistics [Procurement], December 1976) found similar results for the first half of the 1970s: The level of total investment was 35 cents per sales dollar in defense firms versus 63 cents in commercial firms, and investment in facilities was 11 cents per sales dollar in defense firms versus 26 cents in commercial firms.

61. *New York Times,* April 14, 1975, p. 50.

62. "Contractor Weapon Investment at $95.5 million," *Aviation Week and Space Technology,* April 7, 1975.

63. W. Gregory, *Aviation Week and Space Technology,* April 19, 1976, p. 43.

64. I. N. Fisher and G. R. Hall, "Risk and the Aerospace Rate of Return," Rand Corp. memorandum RM-5440-PR, December 1967.

65. Brig. Genl. J. W. Stansberry, internal DoD memorandum to Assistant Secretary of Defense Frank Shrontz, March 10, 1976.

66. Conference Board, "Report on Investment in the Defense Industry," January 1976.

67. A. H. Raskin, "Some Big Companies Have Their Hands Out," *New York Times,* December 20, 1970, section 4, p. 3.

68. The increase was the same from 1972 to 1974 (National Commission on Materials Policy, Final Report [Washington, D.C.: Government Printing Office, 1975]).

69. Barnet and Müller, *Global Reach,* p. 265.

70. This problem became critical in the 1973–1975 period—covered extensively herein—and again in 1978–1979. Each time the problem was more severe, with little corrective action taken to prevent a further occurrence.

71. For example, by the end of 1979 the lead times seen by defense firms had reached 100 weeks for aluminum extrusions, 115 weeks for large aluminum and steel forgings, 115 weeks for large titanium forgings, and 80 weeks for titanium sheet and plate (source: Joint Logistic Commander's Subpanel on Lengthening Lead Times, letter 173, July 25, 1979).

72. The petroleum industry is now the fifth largest sector of suppliers to the Department of Defense—after aircraft, electronics, shipbuilding, and combat vehicles, and larger than munitions.

73. Hearings, House-Senate Joint Committee on Defense Production, 1975, p.26.

74. Federal Preparedness Agency, "Stockpile Report," 1976, p. 1.

75. It should be noted that cash proceeds from the sale of these materials go into the general treasury, not to the DoD, and that requests for increases in the stockpiles require separate congressional action.

76. J. W. Finney, *New York Times,* November 17, 1976.

77. A few of the problems highlighted by Walter Adams ("The Military-Industrial Complex and the New Industrial State," *American Economic Review* LVIII, no. 2 [May 1968]: 655–661): Much of the material purchased was not needed. A substantial part of the orders did not meet the specifications of the stockpile; nor was a mobilization base established domestically, because when the purchases stopped the production stopped as well. Most of the expenditures went to the largest mining companies, which would have been in business even without these purchases. The price support levels of some materials (such as tungsten) were set two or three times the world prices, which led to windfall profits. Premium prices were often paid to contractors under the assumption that they would incur substantial

capital expenditures, yet the government never checked to see whether such expenditures were made. When materials were considered excessive, it was extremely difficult to actually make the sale, since the industry claimed that it would disrupt the market. See also Jack Anderson, *Washington Post,* December 14, 1976, p. B13.

78. An example of this was when President Nixon chose to change the "likely scenario" from a three-year conflict to a one-year conflict, and thus provide $4.1 billion as a result of the proposed selloff of the stockpiles (*U.S. News and World Report,* April 18, 1977).

79. National Commission on Supplies and Shortages, "Government and the Nation's Resources" (Washington, D.C.: Government Printing Office, 1976). This final report was considerably "watered down" because of the political mixture of the Commission (four presidential appointees, four members of the administration, and four congressional appointees).

80. Because of the short-term personnel assignments (due to military rotation) and the usual emphasis by the political appointees on day-to-day problems ("management by crisis"), the DoD pays little attention to problems that will occur more than four years hence, and has little ability to hold anyone responsible for this neglect at a future time.

Chapter 3

1. W. Adams, "The Military-Industrial Complex and the New Industrial State," *American Economic Review* LVIII, no. 2 (May 1968): 655–661.

2. J. W. McKee, "Concentration in Military Procurement Markets: A Classification and Analysis of Contract Data," Rand Corporation report RM-6307-PR (Santa Monica, Calif.: Rand, 1970, p. 16.

3. M. J. Green, ed., *The Monopoly Makers: Ralph Nader's Study Report on Regulation and Competition* (New York: Grossman, 1973), p. 8.

4. E. Raymond Corey, *Procurement Management: Strategy, Organization, and Decision Making* (Boston: CBI, 1978).

5. For example, Adams, "Military-Industrial Complex," p. 10; M. J. Peck and F. M. Scherer, *The Weapons Acquisition Process: An Economic Analysis* (Cambridge, Mass.: Harvard University Press, 1962), p. 46.

6. According to Scherer (*Industrial Market Structure,* p. 266), price collusion is less likely when orders are received in large lumps, infrequently, and irregularly (as in the case of defense). Under these conditions, firms cannot easily conspire to divide up a market, and there is the incentive for a firm to break a conspiracy by lowering its price in order to win a big contract.

7. Over 9,000 military and civilian people audit and investigate the DoD (D. Ignatius, "Duping Uncle Sam," *Wall Street Journal,* December 18, 1978, p. 1).

8. The basis for this was the Armed Services Procurement Act of 1947, which established the Armed Services Procurement Regulations (ASPRs). In 1978 the ASPRs were changed to the Defense Acquisition Regulations (DARs) by DoD directive 5000.35.

9. The Office of Federal Procurement Policy, established in the mid-1970s, has revised the ASPRs with the intent of making them into Federal Acquisition Regulations to be used in all government business.

10. For examples of some specific clauses consider the following: The authority given to the customer includes power to view and veto decisions as to which activities to perform in house

(section 3-900) and which to subcontract (1-800 and 1-707), which firms to use as subcontractors (7-203.8), which products to buy domestically rather than to import (6-100), what internal financial reporting systems to establish (3-800), what type of industrial engineering and planning system to utilize (1-1700), what minimum and average wage rates to pay (12-601), and how much overtime work to authorize (12-102-3). An example of the detailed matters covered in the voluminous military procurement regulations is the prescription that the safety rules followed in the offices and factories of the contractors must be consistent with the latest edition of the Corps of Engineers safety manual (section 7-600). The whole philosophy of close government review of the internal operations of its contractors is so deeply embedded that insertion of statements such as the following in the Armed Services Procurement Regulation evoke little public or industry reaction: "Although the Government does not expect to participate in every management decision, it may reserve the right to review the contractor's management efforts, including the proposed make-or-buy program" (section 3-901.1). See Weidenbaum, "Military/Space Market"; also see M. L. Weidenbaum, *The Modern Public Sector: New Ways of Doing the Government's Business* (New York: Basic Books, 1969), p. 48.

11. In Green, *Monopoly Makers,* p. 8.

12. Adams, "Military-Industrial Complex," p. 10.

13. An excellent description of this full process is given in Fox's *Arming America.* I won't repeat this material; rather, I will briefly summarize the critical elements of the process in order to show their relevance to the overall structure of the defense industry.

14. For a sophisticated presentation of this argument see J. Kurth, hearings, Joint Committee on Defense Production, 95th Congress, September 29 and 30, 1977.

15. On a typical proposal (by LTV Corp. to the Navy for a new airplane), each copy of the final document consisted of 194 bound books, having 82,000 pages, stacking 25 feet high, and weighing 7,500 pounds (LTV newsletter *Profile,* February 6, 1975). This particular proposal did not win a contract.

16. The total cost of the industry's proposal efforts on the TFX aircraft (later the F-111) was estimated to be $45 million.

17. Scherer, *Industrial Market Structure,* p. 9. For the defense case, since there are few sellers, each with differentiated products, this actually becomes "differentiated oligopoly rivalry."

18. For details on two examples see G. C. Wilson, "The Condor Missile and its Friends," *Washington Post,* November 9, 1976, p. A10, and R. J. Art, *The TFX Decision: McNamara and the Military* (Boston: Little, Brown, 1968).

19. The DoD has historically accepted the optimistically low development-cost estimates submitted by the hungry contractors, because they provide the DoD with an initially low-cost program to get through Congress; they give the appearance of a low-profit program, because the formal profit is often paid only on the initial dollars bid, not on the overrun dollars (but the "cost" base on the changes is often inflated to cover the buy-in losses); and they provide a method for keeping the "competitive base" for the DoD, because it is the contractors without business to whom the DoD is normally awarding the new contracts (the contractors who have business and are losing money on their current programs are not tempted to buy in on a new proposal).

20. This figure is based on an analysis of profit rates on completed prime contracts for fiscal years 1959–1974 (source: Office of the Assistant Secretary of Defense [Comptroller]. A typical cost-plus-fee contract grew by around 75 percent.

21. This cost growth normally results either from technical "improvements" suggested by the contractor and approved by the government, or from the government's exercising its unilateral legal "right" under the "changes clause" in the regulations to direct technical changes (for which the contractor is then entitled to request compensation), or from changes in delivery schedules or budgets, which require mutual agreement.

22. As an extreme example of the significance of these changes consider that claims for hundreds of millions of dollars due General Dynamics by the Navy on a single class of submarines included over 35,000 technical changes made in the first seven years after contract award (*Fortune,* April 14, 1978, p. 15).

23. In order to cut down on the industry's tendency to buy in on the award of the development program with the expectation of recovering on the price for the sole-source production equipment, the government first went to the concept of "total package procurement" (under Secretary Robert McNamara, in the 1960s), which required a bid (in a competitive environment) for the total program (R&D plus production). But the uncertainty of the program was too great and the financial risk too high for the firms (Fox, *Arming America,* pp. 243–247), so this approach was dropped. However, in the 1970s the services began to include the early production buys (for example, the first 100 systems) along with the R&D bid in an effort to keep the bidders honest. However, since the firms expected a large number of changes to the contract during the development phase, they felt confident that the contracts containing the prices for these initial production units could be broken, so they simply bid low to make their competitive R&D offer look more attractive.

24. Hall and Johnson, "Review," p. 43.

25. An important distinction often overlooked in government procurement practices is the difference between competition for an award and continuing competition during the execution of a contract. In the former case an initial award is made, often after severe competition, and then there is only one source of the product from that time on. This is the case for most military equipment. Thus, even though a competition was held for the design of a new military airplane, its production has almost always (except in World War II) been done on a sole-source basis. This distinction is often not considered when proponents of the current procedure state what percentage of military systems are procured competitively, and it contrasts with the normal civilian practice of maintaining competition during a product's entire acquisition cycle.

26. For example, an analysis of the awards for fiscal 1972 showed that contracts in the $100,000 range had 57.9–59.6 percent of the dollars awarded noncompetitively, while those in the $1 million–$10 million range had 60.6–68.1 percent awarded noncompetitively and those over $10 million (39.2 percent of the total dollars) had 76.8 percent awarded noncompetitively. Source: "Military Prime Contract Awards—Size Distribution," report, Office of the Assistant Secretary of Defense (Comptroller).

27. F. M. Scherer, *The Weapons Acquisition Process: Economic Incentives* (Cambridge, Mass.: Harvard University Press, 1964), pp. 46–49.

28. The traditional theoretical basis for desiring a large number of competitors is not at all relevant to this case, as traditional economics assumes that equal technology is offered by all the competitors. In defense development programs the technology being offered is quite different between competitors, and is the underlying basis for source selection.

29. Scherer, *Weapons Acquisition Process,* p. 48. A similar finding was presented in "Report of the Commission on Government Procurement" (Washington, D.C.: Government Printing Office, December 1972).

30. Scherer, *Weapons Acquisition Process,* p. 48.

31. The typical arguments that explain economies of scale—for example, Bain's list of greater specialization of the factors of production, lower prices for purchasers, and specialization of management—do not seem to apply in these large, highly vertically integrated defense corporations. In fact, Bain concludes that the primary benefit of economies of scale, in a case such as defense, appear to be in sales promotion activities (which are not necessarily in the government's interest). He finds that the data call into question the very large economic efficiencies claimed for economies of large scale. Similarly, the arguments that many use in favor of large defense firms, such as economies of scale for R&D, have not been quantitatively demonstrated. See J. S. Bain, *Barriers to New Competition: Their Character and Consequences in Manufacturing Industries* (Cambridge, Mass.: Harvard University Press, 1956), pp. 57 and 211.

32. This argument has been used in many sectors of the defense industry, for example, tank production and munitions production, where a single factory (often government-owned and contractor-operated) is the sole supplier. However, I do not favor this approach; at least not without far more justification than it has received in the past.

33. In general, competition appears to favorably affect prices and quality in the defense sector. The price effect was demonstrated by Hall and Johnson ("Review of Air Force Procurement, 1962-1964"), who showed that when competition was present the mean bid was 50 percent or more above the low acceptable bid. A more recent study of the use of competition during defense production programs (J. W. Drinnon and J. S. Gansler, "Predicting the Costs and Benefits of Competitive Production Sources," DoD Acquisition Research Symposium, Annapolis, Md., June 9, 1980) found the savings on 45 actual programs in which competition had been introduced to be 33 percent of what would have been the cost without competition. As for quality, a primary value of competition is the stimulation it provides to technological innovation. It is absolutely essential that competition be maintained, at least in the R&D phase, in order to continue to advance military technology. Perhaps by separating R&D from production it might be possible to have the best of both of these alternatives—technological competition in R&D and price competition in production.

34. An example was the joint proposal by McDonnell-Douglas and Northrop on the F-18 program and the teaming by General Dynamics and LTV in the competition against them.

35. The Navy's ASPJ electronic countermeasures program is an example of such a procurement strategy in which a team of two suppliers is selected in a competition for the development, and then the team members are split apart and forced to compete against each other in the production phase.

36. My 1976 survey of a large number of the aircraft firms found that each of them had plans which assumed that its own business would be increasing over the next five years, but that the total market would be shrinking considerably. Thus, each firm assumed that it would capture a larger and larger market share. Most of their plans obviously had to be wrong.

37. An extreme example of this was the case of McDonnell-Douglas, which in 1975–1976 asked the government for a $2 billion increase on its F-15 contract due to "overhead adjustments" resulting from a corporate decision to pool various divisions' overheads at the corporation level and then allocate the total back to its divisions on the basis of divisional sales. The case is a clear example of cross-subsidization (McDonnell's defense division in St. Louis supporting the old Douglas Aircraft division in California). The increase was to yield no more aircraft for the DoD. In such a case the government is largely powerless, because of its dependency on the contractor. (In this particular situation the DoD tried to get the con-

tractor to adjust its prices by cutting back on the number of aircraft bought, but Congress reinstated the lost planes.)

38. S. Lens, *The Military Industrial Complex* (Princeton, N.J.: Pilgrim, 1970), p. 99.

39. In the long run, these committees should have a very positive impact of forcing people to recognize the long-run commitments that are made both in defense and (particularly) in the nondefense sector of the federal expenditures. They will, if properly implemented, highlight when a new piece of legislation will have a big future dollar impact or when a new program that appears to be only a low-level effort will incur large future costs if it is carried through to deployment. Also, the existence of these new groups has publicized the defense budget as the most "flexible" of the various departments, since most of the others have built-in legislation which prohibits significant adjustment of projected expenditures.

40. For example, title VIII to the Navy's Shipbuilding Authorization (beginning in 1975) requires that all large surface vessels be nuclear-powered. A conventional destroyer costs on the order of $400 million; a nuclear one will likely cost over $1 billion. Additionally, the nuclear one will take approximately twice as many people to man and operate, therefore the annual cost will also be very much higher. An additional example of this type of congressional involvement is the legislation that requires any new munitions plant to be built at the site of an old one (sector 752 of the fiscal year 1976 Defense Appropriations Act said that funds could not be used for design, construction or procurement of equipment for munitions plants except at existing plants which are being closed, laid away, or experiencing curtailment of production). Most congressmen do not have munitions plants in their districts, yet such a bill could get through because the potential opponents knew that a similar bill that would involve their districts might someday be proposed.

41. Some examples of small additions: $18 million to the Army Advance Attack Helicopter in fiscal 1976, for which the DoD had requested $112 million (perhaps an example of "micro management" ["Defense Authorization," *Aerospace Daily,* May 13, 1976, p. 67]); the Senate Appropriations Committee's addition of $5.6 million in fiscal 1975 to require the DoD to start a new aircraft program called the Enforcer, which the DoD did not feel would be an effective weapons system (*Washington Post,* "Unwanted Plane Gets Funding," November 11, 1975, p. A4). Other additions are quite large: for example, the House Armed Services Committee's 1975 addition of $1.1 billion to build up the Navy's nuclear fleet; or the addition of $300 million a year for F-111 and A-7 aircraft to be built in Texas at very low production rates in two plants that would otherwise probably have gone out of aircraft production ("Spending More, Getting Less," *Forbes,* April 15, 1975, p. 28); or insisting upon a $500 million submarine instead of a $350 million alternative design that the DoD had proposed (ibid., p. 30); or adding $300 million to the fiscal 1977 budget to keep the Minuteman missile production line open for one more year.

42. This often occurs when there is a divided opinion on a program within the DoD—either between the service and the Office of the Secretary of Defense (OSD) or between different sections of the OSD. Word of this disagreement usually leaks (or is leaked) to Congress, and the argument of the dissenters is used by Congress to kill the program—often for a very valid reason. (For example, if the military and the OSD engineers want a system because it promises excellent performance, but the OSD financial staff feels the equipment is far too expensive or too risky, Congress may kill it.)

43. In the first half of the 1970s the congressional cuts were around 14 percent for procurement, 8 percent for R&D, 4 percent for operations and maintenance, and 1 percent for military personnel and retirement.

44. Lobbying is a way for labor, by acting through Congress, to play a major role in determining its own "market." Of course, the voters affected by a defense procurement decision are not limited to those directly employed in the defense industry, but extend also to those in the local community who depend upon the income of the defense workers for their own livelihood. Estimates of this multiplier effect range in the vicinity of 1.7 times the number of direct employees: The Bureau of Labor Statistics estimates that for each billion dollars of defense purchases from the private sector there are approximately 50,000 jobs generated (including the 30,000 employed directly). The B-1 bomber was estimated to employ approximately 25,000 aerospace workers directly and to result in a total employment of over 40,000 people, including the spinoffs from the increased spending in the California economy. Lobbying by labor tends to have two significant effects: It keeps workers on the job long after a downward shift in business would have normally required them to be laid off, and, correspondingly, it often increases the defense budget significantly in order to pay for programs that supports these workers.

The congressional "defense labor lobby" includes not only the usual conservatives, but usually even includes liberals who will attack overall defense spending but will strongly defend any defense program that has a significant impact on their own district or state. The number of jobs at issue need not be in the tens of thousands; simply a few hundred employees will cause a congressman to spend most of his time lobbying for a particular program or facility.

45. As my repeated references will demonstrate, I consider Scherer's *Industrial Market Structure* an excellent book on industrial organization—the theory of market operation under conditions other than those of a free market. For an earlier book in this same area see R. E. Caves, *American Industry: Structure, Conduct, Performance* (Englewood Cliffs, N.J.: Prentice-Hall, 1964).

46. Fox, *Arming America,* p. 449.

47. Internal DoD memorandum, "Unclassified Summary of a Classified Study on Aircraft Engine Costs and Design," enclosure to S-5463-DE-4, released January 14, 1977.

48. In the absence of competition there is no incentive to reduce the direct costs (such as material and labor) and the "overhead" costs (such as marketing, supervision, and engineering support). In fact, the incentives are just the opposite.

49. For an analysis of the historical ineffectiveness of incentive contracting in defense business see J. R. Hiller and R. D. Tollison, "Incentive vs. Cost-Plus Contracts in Defense Procurement," *Journal of Industrial Economics* XXVI (1978): 239–248.

50. W. D. Nordhaus, "The Falling Share of Profits," Brookings Papers on Economic Activity, 1974, p. 193. The quoted statistic is based on a survey of businessmen.

51. Scherer, *Industrial Market Structure,* p. 199.

52. I fully recognize that profit on sales is not the "business" measure to use. However, there are three reasons I have chosen to include it here: It is the measure used by the government, it provides useful insights into structural problems, and it provides useful relative measures between defense sectors and comparable civilian sectors.

53. Office of the Assistant Secretary of Defense (Comptroller), Directorate of Information Operations, "100 Companies Receiving the Largest Dollar Volume of Prime Contract Awards, Fiscal Year 1970." Such reports were compiled for the years 1964–1970, and the data are presented in Fox, *Arming America,* p. 308.

54. Based on an average of 35 defense contractors sampled in 1965–1967, and published in "Industry Advisory Council Report to Secretary of Defense," June 11, 1971.

55. Based on DoD "Profit '76" data obtained by Coopers and Lybrand (CPAs) from 61 companies having annual DoD sales of approximately $15 billion.

56. Fox, *Arming America,* p. 331. Based on a 1966–1969 DoD study (see note 53) of 61 large defense-oriented contractors and 13 large commercially oriented contractors.

57. W. J. Baumol, *Economic Theory and Operations Analysis* (Englewood Cliffs, N.J.: Prentice-Hall, 1972), p. 347.

58. J. S. Bain, *Industrial Organization* (New York: Wiley, 1959), p. 423.

59. This survey was undertaken by the Office of the Secretary of Defense (Procurement Directorate) as a part of the "Profit '76" study. See "Profit '76, Summary Report," Office of the Assistant Secretary of Defense for Installations and Logistics [Procurement], December 1976.

60. U.S. Government Accounting Office, "Defense Industry Profit Study," March 17, 1971; based on total capital invested by 74 large DoD contractors in 1965–1969.

61. U.S. Congress Joint Economics Committee, "The Economics of Military Procurement," 91st Congress, 1st Session, 1969, p. 15ff.

62. *Forbes,* January 9, 1978, p. 61; based on five-year averages.

63. This study found that for business with other government agencies (such as NASA, AEC, USCG), the firms' return on total capital invested was comparable to that realized through their civilian business (15.3 percent vs. 15.4 percent).

64. D. R. Bohi, "Profit Performance in the Defense Industry," *Journal of Political Economy* (1972): 721–728.

65. It is hard to get an exact comparison because of the product differences as well as the data base used. The "Profit '76" data were excellent for the defense divisions of the firms sampled, but the commercial-division data were weaker. Also, these data showed defense Return on Investment (ROI) higher in some cases and lower in others. A comparison with Federal Trade Commission durable-goods data showed defense ROI higher, but the product comparison is poor.

66. L. H. Goodhue, "Fair Profits from Defense Business," *Harvard Business Review,* March–April 1972.

67. I. N. Fisher and G. R. Hall, "Defense Profit Policy in the United States and the United Kingdom," Rand Corp. report RM-6510-PR (Santa Monica, Calif., October 1968), p. 601.

68. Scherer, *Industrial Market Structure,* p. 205.

69. *New York Times,* April 14, 1975, p. 50.

70. "Inaccuracy of Department of Defense Weapons Acquisition Cost Estimates," House Committee on Government Operations, November 16, 1979 (Washington, D.C.: Government Printing Office).

71. E. Pyatt, "Systems Acquisition Performance of U.S. Government Agencies," DoD memo, April 14, 1976 (based on SARS reports submitted by each agency to Congress).

72. To quote Jerome Stolarow, director of the Procurement and Systems Acquisition Division of GAO, "The planning estimates (sent through the DoD and on to Congress) are not

honest. I think they are highly optimistic for a specified purpose and that is to get the program started." (Source: House Committee on Government Operations, "Inaccuracy . . ." [note 70].)

73. Perhaps the most hypocritical attitude is that of the representatives who continue to give speeches about the need for more of a free market in the defense area and then vote to force the DoD to keep open inefficient plants in their home districts—at the expense of using the same dollars to buy more military equipment more efficiently.

Chapter 4

1. A. Crittenden, "Guns over Butter Equals Inflation," *New York Times,* November 19, 1978, p. 6F.

2. R. S. Morse, "A Government Takeover of R&D?," *New York Times,* December 19, 1976.

3. In 1975 the total amount spent in the United States on R&D was estimated to be $34 billion. Of these dollars, approximately 70% went to industry, 15% to government laboratories, 10% to universities and colleges, and 5% to other nonprofit institutions. (National Science Foundation report 95-334, 1976, p. 5.) Most of the nongovernment money comes from industry (*Business Week,* March 8, 1976, p. 90). Of the federal funding for R&D in 1976, national defense accounted for 52.5%. The second largest activity was space R&D (dominated primarily by the National Aeronautics and Space Administration), at 13.4%. This was followed by health at 8.8%, energy (likely to be the most rapidly growing area in the future) at 5.9%, and then a collection of other areas, including transportation, communication, environment, natural resources, and basic science and technology, which together account for 19.9% (National Science Foundation report 75-330, p. 2).

4. As Walter Adams notes, this is "tantamount to socializing the financial support for research while permitting private monopolization of its benefits" ("The Military-Industrial Complex and the New Industrial State," *American Economic Review* LVIII [1968]: 659).

5. Source: DoD study of "in-house" laboratories, done in 1976 by the Deputy Director of Defense Research and Engineering (Research and Advanced Technology) but never released as an official report. See also D. A. Charvonia, "Recent Policies Pertaining to the DoD Technological Base and In-House Laboratories," DoD Public Affairs Dept., March 18, 1976.

6. The defenders of government research argue that the government's laboratories share in the long-range objectives of the DoD, are free from profit motivation, have wide access to and intimate familiarity with the problems of the services, represent the DoD's technological "corporate memory," and provide the services with the technological knowhow to be "smart buyers." However, issues are raised by these arguments, including whether these claimed attributes exist and whether some of them are actually shortcomings. Since the long-term future of U.S. defense equipment is dependent upon this approximately $1.8 billion worth of "technology base," this is a particularly critical issue. In 1976 the DoD concluded that giving more and more technology work to government labs was undesirable and issued a policy directive to the services to reduce the government's share of the technology effort to 30%. It also directed that the size of the government labs be reduced while the total funding for technology work would be increased on an annual basis, thus funneling more of the work to industry and the universities.

7. These data come from the "Defense Science Board Summer Study of 1977." This same

combination of increased development time and increased development costs has been seen in other fields as the government has become more involved. For example, in 1960 it took about 2½ years and $1.5 million to bring a new drug to the marketplace. In 1978 it took up to 10 years and around $15 million, including the effort to get the approval of the Food and Drug Administration (*Fortune,* January 30, 1978, p. 121).

8. Lockheed, Boeing, McDonnell-Douglas, General Electric, General Dynamics, Hughes, Rockwell, and Raytheon (*Aviation Week and Space Technology,* January 26, 1976, pp. 22–27).

9. Scherer, *Industrial Market Structure,* p. 373. Scherer also notes (p. 364) that in the civilian world R&D expenditures follow profit, rather than the other way around.

10. C. H. Danhof, "Government Contracting and Technological Change," Brookings Institution report (Washington, D.C., 1968). Prior to 1940, total U.S. R&D (industry- and government-sponsored) was only around $1 billion per year.

11. As the ratio of R&D to procurement began to reach into the range of 50–60 percent in the mid-1970s it caused considerable concern about whether the DoD was balancing its resources properly. Representative Samuel Stratton of New York, a member of the House Armed Services Committee, stated "It's a weird logic that you should abandon weapons sytems which are finally made to work, and sink all of your billions into dream weapons of the future." (J. W. Canan, *The Superwarriors: The Fantastic World of Pentagon Superweapons* [New York: Weybright and Talley, 1975], p. 14). British defense expenditures appear to have followed the same pattern: In 1975–1978 the Royal Air Force spent 16% of its budget on R&D and 17% on procurement of production hardware (from a talk by J. E. Harrison, U.K. Ministry of Defense, at an American Institute of Aeronautics and Astronautics seminar in Amsterdam, June 19, 1978).

12. Recognizing the possible limitations on R&D due to institutional constraints, historical biases, and reluctance to try new ideas, the government wisely decided to allow a certain amount of company expenditures on research and development to be charged against government contracts and to be independently selected and managed by the company. This is the IR&D (independent research and development) area. It has been a matter of considerable controversy within the Congress, because it is an allowable government expense and yet not directly controlled by the government. Most industry executives feel that this small number of dollars (about 5% of the total amount for defense R&D, or $500 million per year) has been managed well by the companies. It is the one category of "allowable expense" that encourages a firm to do longer-term R&D work in order to establish a competitive advantage for capturing new business. Thus, management pays close attention to these funds, and they are managed far better than the lowest 5% of the overall "direct" DoD R&D expenditures would be. There are two areas of potential problems with these funds. First is the possibility of abuse. Companies in a poor business condition often use these funds for proposal activities rather than for research. Secondly, there have been cases where these funds have been used to support what would otherwise be overruns, or to even support R&D on civilian products. These problems can be addressed directly, without eliminating this source of valuable and normally well-managed research.

13. T. S. Kuhn, *The Structure of Scientific Revolution* (University of Chicago Press, 1970).

14. J. M. Blair, *Economic Concentration: Structure, Behavior, and Public Policy* (New York: Harcourt Brace Jovanovich, 1975), p. 204; Scherer, *Industrial Market Structure,* p. 356. Also see J. Jewkes et al., *The Sources of Invention,* second edition (New York: Norton,

1971), pp. 71–85; Hamberg, *Inventions in the Industrial Research Laboratory,* p. 96; Mueller, in *The Rate and Direction of Inventive Activity* (Princeton, N.J.: Princeton University Press, 1962), pp. 323–346. However, there are still many who will argue this point on the basis of the need for large capital investments in today's high-technology world.

15. In 1975, 56 percent of the aerospace industry's R&D dollars were spent on improving existing products.

16. Many criticize the DoD for "wasteful" R&D on systems that do not go into production. What they fail to recognize is that often the competition generated by the alternative design was the cause of the success of the other system. Also, they often fail to appreciate that R&D is an extremely uncertain business, and that often multiple approaches are needed to guarantee at least one success. The government, particularly, often fails to recognize these points—both in budgeting and in contracting. For a discussion of the latter point see H. B. Drake, "Major DoD Procurements at War With Reality," *Harvard Business Review,* January–February 1970, pp. 119–141.

17. The specific barriers that keep small firms out of defense R&D include the following:

- The government counts heavily, in its source selection, on prior technological experience to lend credibility to the claimed potential performance of the proposed design—a firm has to have had business in order to get business.
- There is an extremely high cost to bidding—often, millions of dollars. Thus, only the large corporations can afford to compete.
- The government often issues invitations to bid only to "qualified sources" (those that have the existing plant space and equipment to handle both the development and production programs).
- The DoD prohibits foreign competition on R&D contracts, for security reasons and because of legislation requiring domestic sources for R&D.
- The government feels that the large companies are more able to weather the possible financial storm of cost overruns and other such problems, and thus is more confident in going to them with high-risk programs. (In reality, however the financial risk of these programs is relatively small, since they are normally awarded on a cost-plus-fee basis.)
- Only the large corporations are in a position to support the overhead required by the government in such areas as auditing, reporting, security, and data gathering.
- The DoD prefers, for reduced administrative load, to contract in big chunks rather than to dispense a large number of smaller contracts. This frequently rules out the small companies that might compete only on the smaller programs.
- The large companies are usually the only ones that can afford the initial "buy-in" which often takes place during the early phases of R&D competition.
- Since the contractual cycle is often very uncertain, with ups and downs due to the "will" of Congress and the annual budget cycle, the large companies are the only ones that can afford to carry their engineering personnel during the low periods in the cycle.
- The DoD has usually emphasized promised technical performance as its primary criterion for selection of R&D products (and therefore suppliers). By contrast, the smaller firms (and the more commercially oriented firms) have traditionally been better at designing low-cost products, which have not been particularly sought by the DoD.

18. The barriers that keep civilian-oriented firms out of defense R&D include the low volume of production work, the strictness of the specifications, the special reporting requirements, the cyclical and inelastic demand, and the security clearances required. The relative inelasticity of the demand is a particularly interesting factor in defense R&D; it implies that if

you come up with a new idea for, say, a better airplane, you will simply be replacing the old design (which may well have been your own), with very little likelihood of being able to create increased demand, since the number of airplanes to be procured is a function of the force structure, not of cost or performance. Thus, technological advances that originate in the civilian sector are likely to be immediately applied in that sector, with very little thought given by the firm to military application. Only much later is it likely that a defense-oriented firm might pick up the idea and perhaps begin to apply it. By contrast, the Soviet Union tends to give first priority (in terms of resources and skilled manpower) to its military, so Soviet inventions tend to originate there.

19. H. R. Clauser, *Perspectives* magazine, 1977, p. 1.

20. Canan, *Superwarriors,* p. 106.

21. In 1976 the Department of Commerce, in "The Role of New Technical Enterprises in the U.S. Economy" (a report of the Commerce Technical Advisory Board to the Secretary of Commerce), found that, whereas in the mid-1960s an entrepreneur could come up with a good idea, build it up into a small business, and then be assured of a chance to go public to get further financing, that source of funds had completely dried up by the mid-1970s. Since the study attributed a very significant share of U.S. innovativeness to these small firms, it found that "the pace of technological innovation has faltered and is threatening the nation's chances to maintain a high standard of living, to develop new jobs, and to retain a world-wide economic advantage."

Chapter 5

1. J. S. Gansler, "The Diminishing Economic and Strategic Viability of the U.S. Defense Industrial Base," Ph.D. diss., American University, 1978.

2. For example, consider the war with Spain in 1898. By August of that year, a force of 274,000 men had been mobilized from the peacetime level of 25,000. There had been no planning for war reserves, so there was no materiel with which to equip this expanded force. Because industrial mobilization inherently lags behind manpower mobilization (and the more complex the equipment, the longer the lag), fewer than one-fifth of these men saw action. Transportation, clothing, guns, and food were all in short supply. Money from Congress was readily available, but it could not be spent because industry could not react rapidly enough. J. Huston, *The Sinews of War: Army Logistics 1775–1953* (Washington, D.C.: Government Printing Office, 1960, pp. 275–277.) This same pattern has been repeated in each U.S. conflict for 200 years.

3. The most common scenario for U.S. military forces is an all-out, initially non-nuclear war in central Europe, lasting only a few months but fought with high intensity and heavy losses on both sides.

4. See for example R. Pipes, "Why the Soviet Union Thinks it Could Fight and Win a Nuclear War," *Air Force Magazine,* September 1977, p. 55–56.

5. See for example L. Gouré, *War Survival in Soviet Strategy: USSR Civil Defense* (Washington, D.C.: Center for Advanced International Studies, 1976). The statements regarding Soviet actions in this area are not universally accepted. There is ample scholarly work taking the opposite position (for example, Kaplan, *Bulletin of the Atomic Scientists,* March 1978).

6. T. K. Jones of Boeing, testimony before Joint Committee on Defense Production regarding Soviet civil preparedness, May 23, 1975.

7. Form DD1519 is a three-page form filled in by a prime contractor and signed by a government representative. It concerns estimated mobilization rate needs and plant capabilities.

8. Leslie W. Bray, testimony before Joint Committee on Defense Production, November 24, 1976.

9. Defense Science Board, "Industrial Readiness Plan and Programs" (study done in August 1976; report published in April 1977).

10. A suggestion made by William Baumol (personal communication, 1975) was to treat industrial mobilization as a traditional inventory problem. This is a useful conceptual framework.

11. Herman Kahn, telegram to Andrew Marshall, Office of the Secretary of Defense (Telex no. 137343), 1976.

12. "GAO Concerned About Air Force Maintenance 'Surge' Capability," *Aerospace Daily*, November 3, 1977, p. 22.

13. In 1974 the Federal Republic of Germany passed a law on national emergency planning which requires some critical defense contractors to do some preparedness planning. More recently there has been some low-level logistics planning, such as for diversion of trucks for military use. However, there has been frequent criticism in West Germany of the lack of, and the poor quality of, industrial-preparedness planning.

14. The centralized labor unions might be a source of assistance in the planning of selected labor skills for periods of surge or mobilization.

15. For example, in World War II construction of a merchant vessel was reduced from 35 weeks to a little over 7 weeks and the time to make an Oerlikon gun went from 132 hours to 35 hours. Besides these time savings there were also considerable reductions in the man-hours (and therefore the dollars) required for the tasks; a 152-mm howitzer went from 4,500 man-hours to 2,400 and a large-caliber machine gun from 642 to 329. (Alan S. Milward, *War, Economy and Society 1939–1945* [Berkeley: University of California Press, 1977]).

Chapter 6

1. R. T. Averitt, *The Dual Economy: The Dynamics of American Industry Structure* (New York: Norton, 1968); J. K. Galbraith, *The New Industrial State* (Boston: Houghton Mifflin, 1967).

2. Senate hearings on competitive defense procurements, 1968, p. 18. The assumption behind this action was that the prime contractors would create a viable, competitive, efficient, and sufficient supplier base, in the same fashion as the large civilian firms.

3. Hall and Johnson, "Review," p. 551.

4. In the first half of 1970, in Southern California alone, nearly 1,200 defense subcontractors declared bankruptcy (*Los Angeles Times*, March 12, 1971).

5. Col. A. R. Dupont, U.S.A.F., memorandum, September 25, 1975. (Based on Air Force computer data.)

6. Lt. Col. R. A. Luther, U.S. Army, personal communication, December 3, 1975.

7. Cmndr. R. Hullander, U.S. Navy Electronic Warfare Program Manager, personal communication, September 1975.

8. *U.S. News and World Report*, September 13, 1975.

9. A. Whellon, vice-president, Hughes Corp., personal communication, September 1976.

10. Internal DoD memo to D. Church, July 29, 1977.

11. An example of such voluntary action took place on April 24, 1979, when Sears, Roebuck decided to stop doing business with the DoD. They gave up over $20 million per year worth of business because it was "very unattractive" business. More and more, large firms with only a small share of their business with the DoD are evaluating such moves.

12. The Defense Logistics Agency buys as spares the same parts that are originally bought by the prime contractors and subcontractors.

13. Hall and Johnson, "Review," p. 559.

14. *Report of the Commission on Government Procurement* (Washington, D.C.: Government Printing Office, 1972), vol. 1, pp. 131–132.

15. Hall and Johnson, "Review," p. 559.

16. Judith Reppy has pointed out an interesting parallel to this in Japan, where subcontractors similarly absorb the cyclic fluctuations.

17. A variation of this category is the increased use of "tapered integration" (Scherer, *Industrial Market Structure,* p. 247). Here the prime contractor chooses to build a small number of the parts and subcontract the rest. In this way he can keep maximum pressure on the subcontractor and retain flexibility to absorb the ups and downs of defense business.

18. Aerospace Industries Assoc. of America, Inc., "Monopsony: A Fundamental Problem in Government Procurement" (Washington, D.C., 1973).

19. The prime contractors' division managers tend to prefer outside subcontractors if they cannot do the work within their own division; they find it difficult to control sister divisions which have access to the corporate management.

20. W. Adams and H. Gray, *Monopoly in America* (New York: Macmillan, 1955).

21. Personal communication, 1976 (the source preferred not to be identified).

22. Conference Board report, quoted in Bureau of National Affairs, *News,* February 13, 1976, p. A-5.

23. Subcontracting versus prime contracting was not defined in the study, but prior data indicate that size is a good measure of the type of business, since the government normally does its prime contracting with large firms at large dollar values.

24. Comptroller General of the United States, "Defense Industry Profit Study," report B-159896 (Washington, D.C.: General Accounting Office, 1971), p. 31.

25. Fox, *Arming America,* p. 316.

26. Specifically, this board found "excess profits determination against 526 contractors . . . most of which had annual sales of under $10 million" (W. H. Jones, *Washington Post,* January 7, 1976, p. D13). In 1978 the Renegotiation Board was not renewed by Congress.

27. Brig. Gen. J. Stansberry, Air Force study of subcontractor management, spring 1972. An example of this was the AWACS aircraft. The prime contractor (Boeing) was supplying a modified commercial aircraft on a cost-plus basis, while Westinghouse and its suppliers were developing a new state-of-the-art radar system on a fixed-price basis as subcontractors.

28. Defense Supply Agency, "A Study of Increased Procurement Cost and the Industrial Production Base," June 1975.

29. Mr. O'Leary of Onan Corp., personal communication, November 1, 1977.

30. *Aviation Week and Space Technology,* September 23, 1963, p. 40.

31. Report of the Commission on Government Procurement, vol. 1. p. 88.

32. Barnett and Müller, *Global Reach,* p. 243.

33. The Small Business Administration implements this legislation. For this purpose, a small business is defined as one that, including its affiliates, is independently owned and operated, is not dominant in the field of operations in which it is bidding on government contracts, and is below a certain size. Usually the request for proposal specifies the definition to apply. In general, a "small business" has 500–1,000 employees (500 in the case of R&D firms, 750 for instruments, and 1,000 for computers). Or, occasionally, the criterion will be based on gross receipts, which might have to be under $5 million (again, this depends upon the type of industry). Refer to the Small Business Act of 1958 for further details.

34. In the case of "minority firms" the law goes even farther. Here the Small Busines Administration will actually be the "contractor," will take the job at the "market price," and will underwrite the difference (up to 40%, per a 1975 ruling) between this price and the cost to the firm.

35. Weidenbaum, "Military/Space Market," p. 896.

36. Ibid., p. 898.

37. In October 1978 the Small Business Act was amended (P. L. 95-507) in a specific attempt to award more government business to small and minority-owned subcontractors. The prime contractor is required to submit a precontract plan and to monitor compliance during the contract period.

38. R. A. Shaffer, *Wall Street Journal,* November 17, 1977, p. 1.

39. Julie Loebe, *Electronic Engineering Times,* July 28, 1975.

40. One would expect a relatively high attrition rate for new high-technology companies—in either the civilian or the defense area—simply because of the high risk of the business. But these responses are from firms that have gotten over the hurdle, and are now being driven out of business altogether, or out of defense and into civilian work, by actions of the DoD.

41. See, for example, Wesley C. Mitchell, *Types of Economic Theory* (New York: Kelley, 1967), vol. 2, p. 406.

42. For example, during a 1975 program review of a new U.S. missile system being released for large-quantity production, it was discovered that the only sources for two critical parts of the system were West Germany for one part and South Africa for the other.

43. D. C. Tennison, *National Defense,* May–June 1976.

Chapter 7

1. M. L. Weidenbaum, *The Modern Public Sector: New Ways of Doing the Government's Business* (New York: Basic Books, 1969).

2. With time, the firms will attempt to broaden their product lines, getting into other (but still narrowly defined) product areas.

3. "Profit '76" Summary Report.

4. The fact that cross-subsidation is a significant factor in the conglomerate firms undoubtedly has distorted the data also.

5. At the time of publication there was still strong opposition to this approach from industry, parts of the DoD, and some members of Congress.

6. J. S. Gansler (chairman), "Joint DoD/OMB Study of the U.S. Aircraft Industry," report issued January 1977; summarized by J. S. Gansler, "The U.S. Aircraft Industry: A Case for Sectoral Planning," *Challenge* July–August 1977, pp. 13–20.

7. This study was done before the B-1 cancellation, so the actual demand is likely to be less.

8. Since this study was completed it appears as though the civilian replacement buys may actually occur earlier, but this in no way changes the results of this analysis. Rather, it may serve to initially mask the underlying problems.

9. During this study I asked representatives of each of the 17 firms to review the data and assess their validity; this estimate is based on their review. The meeting took place at the Pentagon on October 17, 1976.

10. The last three methods are subsidiary to the first two.

11. The discussions cited in note 9 further enhanced the credibility of this estimate.

12. Mathematica Corp., unpublished report on long-term trends in the aircraft industry, December 1976.

13. "Joint DoD/OMB Study of the Aircraft Industry."

14. The Delphi technique involves interrogating knowledgeable people for their estimates and then iterating these results back through the group for further refinement. Both the average estimates and the spreads around these averages are important; these are presented in table 7.7.

15. Making plant location and workforce capacity utilization more important factors in source selection is one technique in this direction.

16. Currently there is little effective consideration of prior performance in source selection.

17. These conglomerate owners do not greet with enthusiasm a statement such as that of Admiral Hyman Rickover (one of the most powerful DoD officials, who literally runs a one-man show in the procurement of nuclear ships) that "it is [the U.S. shipbuilders'] patriotic duty to build Navy ships and submarines, and to build them perfectly, profit or not" (refer to Canan, *The Superwarriors,* p. 192). Evidence that this view is not shared by the contractors is that all of the firms building nuclear ships for Admiral Rickover were in court with claims against the DoD, and obtaining an injunction against the Newport News shipbuilding operation was the only way the Navy could get them even to bid or to work on shipbuilding programs.

18. Institute of Defense Analysis, unpublished study of the U.S. Navy shipbuilding industry conducted from February to July 1977.

19. Reduced plans for naval shipbuilding, which were generated after this study was completed, will only serve to make the problems described much worse and the need for corrective actions much more urgent. This is also true of the congressional rejection of the administration proposal of a "MARAD Cargo Preference Program" in 1977 and the questionable status of future MARAD subsidy programs.

20. These two examples are reasonable approximations to real cases, but have been generalized to protect the details of the data.

21. Since this prediction was made, the Navy has found that the schedules for these ships have indeed slipped, their costs have risen, and it has continued to be difficult to get the skilled labor force.

22. Institute of Defense Analysis study (note 18).

23. This is based on 1970 Social Security Administration data, and assumes that skill is relatively well correlated with age. These data show that the more skilled workers—those in the 35–55 age bracket—have a much higher turnover rate in the shipbuilding industry than in the other sectors.

24. U.S. Department of Labor, Bureau of Labor Statistics bulletin 1312-10.

25. Data from the Social Security Administration, presented in the Institute of Defense Analysis study (note 18).

26. From "Profit '76" study.

27. Institute of Defense Analysis study.

28. After this plan was submitted, the Carter Administration again reversed it—reducing the "outyear" shipbuilding budget significantly. In 1980 it was drastically revised upward.

29. Prior to 1966, it was common Navy practice to split the ship procurements among yards on a competitive basis.

30. The maintenance of a single yard to do quantity production—and thus to achieve economies of scale through "learning"—is less of a consideration with shipbuilding, which is more of a construction process than a production process (refer to Franz Frisch, "Production Industries," paper presented at Fifth Annual DoD Procurement Research Conference, November 1976).

31. One significant structural consideration for the shipbuilding industry (not discussed herein solely for reasons of space) is the debate (which has gone on since Revolutionary times) as to whether Navy shipbuilding should be done in the public or the private sector. The law states that every other ship must be built in government-owned yards unless the president requests otherwise in the national interest. Currently all Navy ships are built in private yards, with Congress' approval of the president's requests. With the extra capacity projected for these yards, they are likely to continue to get the work. (The longer the public yards go on doing only overhaul and repair work, the less likely they are to retain the new construction skills; thus, the future is relatively predictable.) Yet in the mid-1970s the DoD made a major effort to shift some of the new construction to the public yards—partly to create competition for the sole-source private yards building certain classes of ships. There is much to be said for this, but the anticipated higher costs for the public yards (in spite of their far lower labor turnover rate) and the existing extra capacity in the private yards will probably result in the debate continuing, but with little structural change in this area in the near future.

32. In 1979 the Navy was implementing the concept of competitive allocation on the FFG7 frigate program. They had three yards (Bath, Maine; Todd, San Pedro, Calif.; and Todd, Seattle, Wash.) building these ships competitively. They then wanted to reduce the number of yards to two through further competition (keeping only the two most efficient yards). However, a senator from the state of Washington (a member of the Senate Appropriations Committee) tried to block this reduction (the yard in his state was to be the loser). He argued not on the basis of savings to the Navy, but on political grounds, although the likely cost would be in the hundreds of millions of dollars (or fewer ships for the Navy). The senator's action is understandable, but letting him get away with it is not. Obviously, for competitive allocation to work will require consideration of the greater good above local interest. (For more on the FFG7 case see George Wilson, "Defense Funds Held Hostage," *Washington Post*, November 1, 1979, p. 1).

Chapter 8

1. L. M., Simons, "Grumman Set to Refund Iran $28 Million," *Washington Post*, February 10, 1976, p. A1.

2. R. E. Harkavy, *The Arms Trends and International Systems* (Cambridge, Mass.: Ballinger, 1974), p. xiv.

3. Simons, "Grumman . . . ."

4. Constantine Vaitsos, *Intercountry Income Distribution and Transnational Enterprises* (London: Oxford University Press, 1974), p. 157.

5. Jack Barenson, presentation to selected government officials, based on his study of cases of technology transfer for the Department of Labor, Marriott Hotel, Rosslyn, Va., December 1975.

6. Barnet and Müller, *Global Reach,* p. 1.

7. The "Profit '76" study found that foreign military sales were 2.5 times as profitable. Higher profits on foreign arms sales are also indicated for the British (U.S. Army procurement appropriations data January 2, 1976 [unpublished]).

8. Richard D. Lyons, "U.S. Arms-Sale Rise Stirs Capitol Concern," *New York Times,* October 19, 1975, p. 41.

9. By the end of the 1970s China and Brazil were already selling heavily to the Middle East (*Business Week,* December 3, 1979, p. 52).

10. "The F-16 and How it Won Europe's Orders," *New York Times,* July 27, 1975, p. F1. It should be noted that in 1977 the sales role for the estimated 2,000–3,000 U.S. Military Assistance Advisory Groups overseas was considerably reduced, partly as a result of the Government Accounting Agency's attack on this $70 million "sales force" of U.S. government employees ("GAO Urges Arms-Panel Cut," *Washington Post,* February 8, 1976).

11. John W. Finney, "Pentagon Accused of Selling a Plane at Too Low a Price," *New York Times,* March 3, 1976, p. 1.

12. Don Oberdorfer, "Senate Panel Approves Controls on U.S. Arms Sales," *Washington Post,* January 25, 1976, p. A4.

13. This has been a controversial point. The government actually writes a contract with the foreign government and an identical or very similar one with the U.S. supplier. Thus, the U.S. government is both the buyer and the subsequent seller. The intent is that since the terms and conditions are the same in the two contracts, there is no risk for the U.S. government. But clearly the "bargaining power" of the parties in the two contracts are different, and the U.S. government can be left holding the bag.

14. Such an abrupt cancellation occurred in February 1979 when the revolutionary government of Iran canceled U.S. foreign military sales worth between $8 billion and $10 billion (*Washington Post,* February 4, 1979, p. 1).

15. Robert Aliber, *The International Money Game* (New York: Basic Books, 1973), p. 8. Another example is General Electric's sales of communication satellite capability to Japan after GE had been largely eliminated from the U.S. market. Here again, they offered more technology transfer, along with the product, in order to win the competition.

16. Lyons, "U.S. Arms-Sale Rise. . . ."

17. Ann Crittenden, "Closing In On Corporate Payoffs Overseas," *New York Times,* February 15, 1976, section 3, p. 7.

18. "Litton, Saudis Agree on a System Valued above $1.5 Billion," *Wall Street Journal,* October 9, 1978, p. 6.

19. Some examples for an individual firm: Lockheed Aircraft Service (which in 1978 did

90% of its business overseas, whereas in 1973 it did almost all of its business for the U.S. military) had a $627 million air-traffic-control contract from Saudi Arabia and a $138 million contract to provide logistics services to Iran's air force (*Wall Street Journal,* December 26, 1978, p. 24).

20. *Washington Post,* February 12, 1976, p. A3.

21. The United States is not unique in sharing production of first-line equipment with foreign buyers: The French were helping the Egyptians build the Mirage 2000 in 1978, when the first planes had not yet come off of the production line in France (*The Economist,* September 23, 1978, p. 80).

22. Thomas Griffin, *Fortune,* August 1975, pp. 122 ff. See also *Congressional Record,* September 23, 1975, Vol. 121, No. 140, Sen. Culver, 516510.

23. Ray Vicker, "U.S. Concerns Outsell Foreign Competitors in the Mideast Market," *Wall Street Journal,* January 2, 1976. p. 1.

24. Charles E. Staley, *International Economics: Analysis and Issues* (Englewood Cliffs, N.J.: Prentice-Hall, 1969), p. 89.

25. S. Sansweet and W. Blundell, "On the Give: For U.S. Firms Abroad Bribery Can Often Be Routine Business Cost," *Wall Street Journal,* May 9, 1975, p. 1.

26. "Budgeting Cost Savings to the DoD Resulting from F.M.S.," Congressional Budget Office staff report, May 24, 1976.

27. Anthony Sampson, "Lockheed's Foreign Policy: Who, in the End, Corrupted Whom?," *New York,* March 15, 1976, p. 53. Also, for an excellent overall presentation of the foreign-military-sales story (including the area of bribery) see Sampson, *The Arms Bazaar* (New York: Viking, 1977).

28. Thomas Griffin, "Payoff is Not Accepted Practice," *Fortune,* August 1975, p. 202.

29. Dan Morgan, "U.S. Reportedly Sold Soviets Missile Bearing Machine," *Washington Post,* February 26, 1976, p. A3.

30. Evans and Novak, *Washington Post,* September 24, 1976.

31. "U.S. Frustrated by Embargoed Electronics Technology Finding Way to Soviet Bloc," *American Machinist Metalworking Trends Newsletter,* March 10, 1976, p. 1.

32. Jack Robertson, "GAO Criticizes U.S. Controls of Exports to Communist Bloc," *American Metal Market/Metalworking News,* February 19, 1976, p. 40.

33. David K. Shipler, "Soviet Buying Technology Despite U.S. Trade Curb," *New York Times,* January 25, 1976, p. 68.

34. "U.S. Military Sales to Iran," staff report to Senate Committee on Foreign Relations, July 1976.

35. Some examples: The truck factory built by the U.S. in the Soviet Union is also building vehicles and engines for the military; computers sold for commercial applications are being used for antiaircraft systems (see Walter Pincus, "Soviet Misuse of U.S. Machinery Seen," *Washington Post,* November 9, 1979, p. A18). According to "U.S. and U.S.S.R. Mobilization Policies," vol. 1: "Net Assessment" (Hudson Institute, Croton-on-Hudson, N.Y., 1969), "the Soviet defense industry can build almost anything that the U.S. can build—in close to a laboratory setting. What it cannot do, as yet, is to mass produce the microelectronic circuitry which is critical to nearly all high technology military end items". Yet the U.S. Commerce Department continues to push for U.S. electronics firms to build such factories in the U.S.S.R. or Warsaw Pact countries.

36. D. L. Morse, "Foreign Arms Sales: Two Sides to the Coin," published by the Association of the U.S. Army, vol. 26, no. 1, January 1976, p. 21.

37. Westinghouse officials noted that, for a proposed semiconductor plant in Poland, 45% of the money would come from the Export-Import Bank, 45% from U.S. banks, and 10% from Poland (personal communication, September 30, 1975).

38. J. S. Gansler, "Hearings on Civil Preparedness and Limited Nuclear War," Joint Congressional Committee on Defense Production, April 28, 1976, p. 53.

39. In the five years between 1972 and 1977, foreign investors purchased interests in 1,114 American companies—often a controlling share (*Wall Street Journal,* October 10, 1978, p. 1). This trend seems to be continuing.

40. In this case it is a Japanese firm (American Koyo Bearing Mfg. Co.). See "Bearing Plant Begins Operation," *Metalworking Trends,* March 10, 1976, p. 6.

41. Harkavy, *The Arms Trade and International Systems,* p. 173.

42. Crittenden, "Closing In. . . ."

43. Comptroller General of the United States, "Foreign Military Sales . . . a Growing Concern," June 1976.

44. A Congressional Budget Office staff study estimated the potential savings to the U.S. from $8 billion per year of arms sales abroad to be up to $560 million per year (Harkavy, *The Arms Trade and International Systems,* p. 238).

45. Bowen Northrup, "Unchained Atom?" *Wall Street Journal,* July 2, 1975, p. 1.

46. A good discussion of the potential for arms-trade agreements (and one that reaches somewhat different conclusions than I do) is A. H. Cahn, J. J. Kruzel, P. M. Dawkins, and J. Huntzinger, *Controlling Future Arms Trade,* (New York: McGraw-Hill, 1977).

47. Since the U.S. supplies almost half of the world market (and the U.S.S.R. is by far the second-largest supplier), the impact of a relatively small reduction by the U.S. would not be felt significantly here, but the increased market potential would be very important to the U.K. and France since it would represent a large percentage impact to them.

48. This expansion includes new entrants from the developed nations (such as Japan and West Germany) as well as from the developing world (such as Brazil, Egypt, and Israel).

49. "Soviets Reportedly Refuse to Repair Egypt's Mig-21's," *Washington Post,* February 20, 1976, p. A1; "Around the World," *Washington Post,* April 26, 1976, p. C24.

50. "U.S. Military Sales to Iran," staff report to Senate Committee on Foreign Relations, July 1976.

51. Leslie H. Gelb, "Arms Sales," *Foreign Policy* No. 25, Winter 1976–77, p. 8.

52. Stanley Hoffman, "Grouping Towards a New World Order," *New York Times,* January 18, 1977, section 3, p. 1.

53. Crittenden, "Closing In. . . ."

54. Adm. M. Michaelis "Aerospace Daily," February 18, 1976, p. 266.

55. J. S. Gansler, testimony before Joint Congressional Committee on Defense Production, May 23, 1975.

56. Even technology transfer has changed. Earlier, it took place primarily through products; today the multinational corporation acts in many cases as the transfer agent, and the transfer is mediated by engineering, training, and manufacturing, as well as by "civilian" products which have wide application in producing or utilizing military equipment.

Chapter 9

1. This statistical combination method recognizes the overlap between items, and gives a lower total. For this case, the arithmetic sum is $13.65 billion; the r.s.s. total is $4.5 billion.

2. To see the conservative nature of these estimates, consider the first two items in table 9.1. Many analyses have shown the advantages in net cost savings that could be realized through competition on defense production programs. An analysis of over fifteen other studies in this area (covering the period 1940–1980), which took into account over fifty different programs (for which second-source competition had been obtained during the production life of a defense product), found that the average saving due to competition on these programs was 33 percent (J. W. Drinnon and J. S. Gansler, "Predicting the Costs and Benefits of Competitive Production Sources," paper presented at Ninth Annual DoD Acquisition Research Symposium, Annapolis, Md., June 1980). It was estimated that such production competition could be applied to a very large number of current and future defense production programs. However, for the analysis shown in table 9.1 it was assumed that only about 20 percent of production programs would be amenable to competition, and that the net savings would be only 25 percent. Similarly, the second item on the list, the use of multiyear funding, is shown here to realize a total savings of only about $700 million a year, while the director of overall Air Force Acquisitions (General Alton Slay, head of Air Force Systems Command) has stated that multiyear buying could save "billions annually in unnecessary expenses" (*Government Executive,* October 1979, p. 18).

3. The production dollar distribution shown here is based on the Posture Statement to Congress of Dr. William Perry, Undersecretary of Defense for Research and Acquisition, February 1, 1979.

4. Scherer, *Industrial Market Structure,* p. 405.

5. *Aviation Week and Space Technology,* January 16, 1978, p. 4.

6. An example of Congress' response to the building pressures for increased expenditures is the fiscal 1981 budget: President Carter requested a significant increase (over 3% real growth, excluding inflation) in the budget for weapons research and production (a level of $46.8 billion); however, the House Armed Services Committee voted to add $5.6 billion worth of ships, planes, missiles and tanks (Terrence Hunt, "Panel Adds $2.2 billion for Navy Shipbuilding," *Washington Post,* March 27, 1980, p. A6).

7. These thoughts come mostly from a 1976 talk by Robert O'Donahue (then in the Office of the Secretary of Defense) on the subject of "Future DoD Needs."

Chapter 10

1. Niccolo Machiavelli, "On Introducing Change in Government," in *The Prince.*

2. Nancy Barrett, *The Theory of Microeconomic Policy* (Lexington, Mass.: Heath, 1974), p. 245.

3. Ronald Müller, "Global Corporations and National Stabilization Policy," *Journal of Economic Issues,* June 1975.

4. Bain (*Industrial Organization* [New York: Wiley, 1959], p. 459) uses a slightly broader definition of the objectives of U.S. government economic policy wherein he lists four criteria: full employment of productive resources, efficient use of employed resources in order to maximize output, reasonable stability of employment and economic activity, and a reasonably high rate of progressiveness. Here, for the defense sector we would have to con-

sider that allowance for production surge might be an acceptable characteristic under the requirement for full employment of resources. However, the definition of efficiency is left somewhat ambiguous, since there are three levels of economic efficiency that might be considered: allocative efficiency (production of the most desirable combination of goods and services from among those that are technologically possible), managerial or engineering efficiency (minimization of the cost of producing a particular quantity of a particular product, which might also be referred to as production efficiency), and dynamic or innovative efficiency (which determines the rate at which an industry is generating useful technological or service innovations and introducing them as market alternatives). These three are directly applicable to measures of efficiency in the defense industry, and are excellent criteria for establishing corrective actions for U.S. government economic policy. For a more extensive discussion of these three factors of efficiency see Lee Preston, "Hearings on the Industrial Reorganization Act," Part I, 1973, p. 296, discussed by W. Adams and J. B. Dirlam ("Private Planning and Social Efficiency," in *Markets, Corporate Behavior and the State,* edited by A. P. Jacquemin and H. W. de Jong [The Hague: Martinus Nijhoff, 1976], p. 214).

5. This point was emphasized in a personal communication from Judith Reppy of Cornell University on January 17, 1978.

6. Earl A. Molander, "Historical Antecedents of Military-Industrial Criticism," *Military Affairs,* April 1976, p. 60.

7. Ibid., p. 61. Expressed by Shailer Matthews in *Journal of Political Economy,* 1916.

8. Ibid., p. 61. Expressed in 1931 by Congress and by Bernard Baruch (*Taking the Profits out of War*).

9. J. K. Galbraith, "The Big Defense Firms are Really Public Firms and Should be Nationalized," *New York Times Magazine,* November 16, 1979. (I have found that the government-owned installations, such as arsenals and depots, were as strong if not stronger in their lobbying activities on behalf of getting programs for their operation, and in terms of not allowing cutbacks or closures to their operation; although they admittedly were not as motivated by growth as their private-industry equivalents.)

10. It was raised again by Admiral Rickover in the mid-1970s when the shipbuilders got into disputes over outstanding claims and refused to take on Navy business until the litigation was settled.

11. For a discussion of this approach see George R. Hall, "Defense Procurement and Public Utility Regulation," Rand Corp. report (Santa Monica, Calif., 1968).

12. James Kurth, testimony before the Joint Committee on Defense Production, September 30, 1977.

13. Herbert P. Spiro, "Optimal Organization of the Military Hardware Industry," Ph.D. diss., UCLA, 1972. This approach is also recomended by a number of members of the staff of the Rand Corporation.

14. In many parts of the defense industry such a model is actually used by single firms that have separate production and R&D facilities. However, vertical integration means that the same firm will still keep the program once it has gotten started in the R&D phase, and will carry it into production as a sole source.

15. Ludwig Boelkow, president of Messerschmidt, Boelkow, Blohm Corp., quoted in an *Aviation Week and Space Technology* editorial (April 30, 1973, p. 9).

Chapter 11

1. Edgar E. Ulsamer, "The Designers of Dassault: Men Who Take One Step at a Time," *Air Force Magazine* (August 1970): 32.

2. This achieves flexibility and minimizes overhead during slack periods. Matra, the French missile and space firm, subcontracts almost all of its manual work (*The Economist,* October 6, 1979, p. 83).

3. "The Military Balance (1977–78)" (London: International Institute of Strategic Studies, 1978). This is also the source of the other percent-of-gross-national-product figures quoted in this chapter.

4. In 1977 Denmark went from a one-year to a four-year defense budget (*The Economist,* January 28, 1978, p. 19). The U.S. may end up being the only country with one-year budgets.

5. Bernard D. Nossiter, "Britain's Investment in Private Investment," *Washington Post,* December 14, 1975, p. F7.

6. "British Industry Faces Radical Reorganization," *Aerospace Daily,* December 11, 1975, p. 219.

7. The European Economic Community Treaty encourages merging in order to "compete with foreign competition" (Scherer, *Industrial Market Structure,* p. 492).

8. C. J. E. Harlow, "The European Armaments Base: A Survey (London: Institute for Strategic Studies, 1967).

9. Mitsubishi Heavy Industry is the largest manufacturer of Japanese military aircraft, ships, armored cars, and other vehicles, yet less than 5 percent of the firm's overall business is in the defense area.

10. Personal communication, 1976.

11. "Soviet Forces: The Strain on Men and Money," *The Economist,* April 14, 1973, p. 31.

12. "Soviet Defense Cost Higher, CIA Says," *New York Times,* May 19, 1976, p. 4.

13. Much of the information in this section comes from the investigations of Arthur J. Alexander of the Rand Corporation, who has spent a number of years studying the Soviet defense industry. See the following examples of his work: "The Process of Soviet Weapons Acquisition," paper presented to the European Study Commission, Paris, April 1977; "Weapons Acquisition in the Soviet Union, U.S. and France," Rand Corp. report R-4989 (Santa Monica, Calif.: Rand, 1973); "R&D in Soviet Aviation," Rand Corp. report R-589-PR (Rand, 1970).

14. Recall the comparison of comparably performing U.S. and Soviet jet engines, where it was shown that the Soviet system, if built in the United States, would cost between one-third and one-half as much.

15. Alexander, "The Process of Soviet Weapons Acquisition," p. 4.

16. Amann, Cooper and Davies, *The Technological Level of Soviet Industry* (New Haven, Conn.: Yale University Press, 1977), p. 407.

17. To overcome the institutional inertia that often comes with stability—which is detrimental to R&D—the Soviets encourage invention through monetary awards (often as much as $10,000 per year, for three years) based on savings realized. This encourages invention for the sake of cost reductions (Scherer, *Industrial Market Structure,* p. 398).

18. N. Friedman and C. Gray, "U.S. and U.S.S.R. Mobilization Policies," vol. 1: "Net Assessment" (Croton-on-Hudson, N.Y.: Hudson Institutue, 1979), p. 142.

19. Alexander, "The Process of Soviet Weapons Acquisition," p. 6.

20. Based on a September 1976 personal discussion with Arthur Alexander of Rand Corp. after his return from a one-year stay in Europe, where he was studying the Soviet Union's military acquisition process.

21. Kenneth H. Bacon, "European Members of NATO Strive to Build Weapons Industry to Compete with U.S. Firms," *Wall Street Journal,* November 3, 1976, p. 36.

22. "Western Fighter Development Pressed," *Aviation Week and Space Technology,* November 21, 1977, p. 17.

23. *Aviation Week and Space Technology,* November 28, 1977, p. 11.

24. R. Aliber, *The International Money Game* (New York: Basic Books, 1973), p. 116.

Chapter 12

1. There is a 45-page list of specific step-by-step actions that can be taken to implement the broad policy initiatives described herein in chapter 15.3 of Gansler, "The Diminishing Economic and Strategic Viability of the U.S. Defense Industrial Base."

2. As a model for my approach in this book, as well as in my other work, I have used Leijonhufund's comment on Keynes: "In presenting his results, his sole objective was not to communicate these innovations to the academic community; rather the more important objective was to press for the adaptation of the policy proposals he had arrived at." (A. Leijonhufund, *On Keynesian Economics and The Economics of Keynes* [Oxford University Press, 1968], p. 19.)

3. R. Müller, "Globalization and the Failure of Economic Policy," *Challenge,* May-June 1975, p. 57.

4. Scherer, *Industrial Market Structure,* p. 412.

5. This same view was expressed by Herman Kahn of the Hudson Institute in a talk to the Federal Preparedness Agency in Washington, D.C. on January 18, 1978.

6. There are other sectors of the U.S. economy that will be gradually developing problems similar to those the defense industrial base is currently experiencing, and for which coordinated government policies will be required. These include energy, finance, food, transportation, and communications. Additionally, there have been frequent references to the need for such coordinated government policy in some of the basic-materials industries, such as steel. (For further discussion of the five general sectors noted above see Ronald Müller, "Macroeconomic Stabilization Policy and Global Corporations," in Apter and Goodman, *The Multinational Corporation and Social Change* [New York: Praeger, 1976]; for more on the steel industry see David Ignatius, "Government and the Steel Industry," *Wall Street Journal,* September 26, 1977.) Contradictory government policies exist not only in the defense industry but across the board, and recommendations for such policy coordination have begun to appear more and more frequently. For example, Ignatius (ibid.) points out that the various government agencies with control over the steel industry (Commerce, Justice, Environmental Protection, Treasury, Council on Wage and Price Stability, International Trade Commission, Occupational Health and Safety Administration, Equal Employment Opportunities Administration, and Mine Enforcement Safety Administration) all have conflicting requirements, and that the effect is that the government often acts to the detriment of both the consumer and the industry producing the goods.

7. Deliberations about changing the structure of the defense industrial base must consider what would happen without the proposed actions. Here, as I have indicated, the problems are getting much worse, and I would expect increasing cries for nationalization.

8. This is not desirable in terms of economies of scale—for a confirmation of this view see Oskar Lange and F. M. Taylor, *On the Economic Theory of Socialism* (Minneapolis: University of Minnesota Press. 1948), p. 27.

9. R. G. Noll et al., "Government Policies and Technological Innovation," vol. I, "Project Summary," Division of the Humanities and Social Sciences, California Institute of Technology, 1976, p. 28.

10. G. C. Eads, "Achieving 'Appropriate' Levels of Investment in Technological Change: What Have We Learned?," Rand Corp. report P5998 (Santa Monica, Calif.: Rand, 1977), p. 7; see also "A Plan for the U.S. Economy?," *Dun's Review,* March 1976, p. 36.

11. Barnett and Müller, *Global Reach,* p. 255.

12. National Commission on Supplies and Shortages, "Government and the Nation's Resources" (Washington, D.C.: Government Printing Office, 1976).

13. H. Dewar, "Measures to Guarantee Resources Urged," *Washington Post,* January 10, 1977, p. A3.

14. Eads, "Achieving 'Appropriate' Levels. . . ."

15. D. Rice, "Shortages and Economic Planning," *Wall Street Journal,* March 14, 1977, p. 15.

16. National Commission on Supplies and Shortages, "Government and the Nation's Resources," p. xiii.

17. Rice, "Shortages and Economic Planning."

18. *Aerospace Daily,* report on 1976 Northrop Corp. stockholders meetings, March 16, 1977.

19. Conference Board, "Report on Investment in the Defense Industry."   ·

20. Some prior sources of this recommendation are the following: M. L. Weidenbaum, "The Military/Space Market: The Intersection of the Public and Private Sectors," U.S. Senate hearings, Subcommittee on Anti-Trust and Monopoly, June 17–21, 1968 (Washington, D.C.: Government Printing Office, 1969); H. P. Spiro, "Optimal Organization of the Military Hardware Industry," Ph.D. diss., University of California, Los Angeles, 1972; R. Perry of Rand Corp. (personal communication).

21. A closely related issue is the question of the "contracting out" to industry of work that is currently done by the government. Here again there is an absence of coordinated government policy (in fact, conflicting guidelines exist). I favor greater use of industry for this work, on criteria of flexibility and economics (again, letting the profit motive work, and achieving quality through competition). As an example of "contracting out," Northrop had a $21 million contract to operate Vance Air Force Base in Oklahoma—to provide services from aircraft maintenance to mowing lawns and running the mess halls. An independent study showed that they were operating the base for 26% less than it cost the DoD to run a comparable base (*Wall Street Journal,* December 26, 1978, p. 24).

22. To quote Thomas Jones of Northrop, "It is wrong to believe that regardless of performance, a defense company has a right to exist, simply because it serves national security; a defense company must earn its way by the manner in which it serves that national security." (Jones, "For a Sound Defense Industry," *New York Times,* 23 November 1976, p. 35.)

23. For example, in 1977 Pratt and Whitney (a division of United Technologies) split its civilian and military aircraft engine business, leaving the former in Connecticut and setting up a new military products operation in Florida.

24. W. J. Sheehan, director of DoD Economic Adjustment Office, personal communication, March 10, 1977.

25. S. Melman, "Twelve Propositions on Productivity and the War Economy," *Challenge,* March–April 1975.

26. C. Shifrin, "Sale of AT&T Subsidiary Pressed," *Washington Post,* February 3, 1976, p. 1.

27. For example, see the recommendations of the Fluke Committee of the Defense Science Board (chaired by John Fluke) on greater use of off-the-shelf commercial test equipment by the DoD, 1976.

28. Even if these people are being paid through the "administrative charge" that is put on foreign military sales, it still means that there are fewer people doing the DoD jobs, because of the manpower ceilings.

29. Refer to chapter 5 for the specific deficiencies of the current program.

30. For an expanded version of these recommendations see J. S. Gansler, "The Expansion Capability of the Defense Industry," paper presented at the American Defense Preparedness Association meeting, Washington, D.C., April 25, 1979.

31. This was also recommended by Chairman Charles Bennett of the House Sea Power and Strategic Materials Subcommittee and Director Les Bray, of the Federal Preparedness Agency.

32. J. S. Gansler, "Cost as a Design Parameter," report to Air Force Systems Command, February 13, 1973 (DoD press release 67-73). For a more detailed discussion see *Defense Management Journal* (Defense Systems Management School, Fort Belvoir, Va.), July 1973.

33. The new profit policy introduced at the beginning of 1977 (see chapter 3 above) was a small step in this direction, but clearly additional actions of this sort are required.

34. A few initiatives in this direction have been taken by the DoD. For example, in a speech in November 1977, Undersecretary of Defense for Research and Development William Perry stated that the DoD "wants to be able to compare [production] costs and determine on a year-to-year basis whether it will be 50-50 or 70-30 division of the two competitors." (Kenneth Bacon, "Pentagon to Try Awarding Contracts for Same Weapon to two Manufacturers," *Wall Street Journal,* November 21, 1977, p. 14.)

35. In 1973 the Army tried buying commercial vehicles in a program called "Project Wheels." It found acceptable performance in vehicles that cost $3,000 to $4,000 each, versus military-unique vehicles that cost $8,000 to $18,000 each. In addition, the military-unique vehicles had R&D costs, and the commercial vehicles came with a one-year warranty. In this same vein, it should be noted that this book focuses on military hardware, rather than "socks, shoes, and underwear" for the troops. But even in the case of such civilian-type items the DoD is inefficient in its procurement practices, since it requires such extreme specialization that it has created a whole unique set of industrial suppliers. This is a different problem, which space did not allow to be addressed in this book. Nonetheless, as the DoD learns to utilize more commercial equipment, commercial specifications, and commercial procurement practices, it will simultaneously be improving its acquisition of civilian-type items.

36. In some areas there once existed groups concerned with the industrial-base perspective. For example, after World War II a Material Securities Resources Board addressed some aspects of the defense industrial base; but gradually this board was phased out. In a meeting

on February 18, 1976, Elmer Staats, head of the General Accounting Office, suggested that perhaps this group should be considered again.

37. Recommended by the National Commission on Supplies and Shortages, "Government and the Nation's Resources," p. xiv. One possible location for this group would be the Bureau of Industry Affairs in the Department of Commerce.

38. Personal communication, May 11, 1977.

Selective Bibliography

Adams, W., "The Military-Industrial Complex and the New Industrial State." *American Economic Review* LVIII, no. 2 (May 1968), pp. 652–665.

Adams, W., *The Structure of American Industry: Some Case Studies.* New York: Macmillan, 1954.

Adams, W., and Gray, H., *Monopoly in America.* New York: Macmillan, 1955.

Aerospace Industries Association of America, Inc., "Monopsony: A Fundamental Problem in Government Procurement." Washington, D.C., May 1973.

Alexander, A. J., "Weapons Acquisition in the Soviet Union, U.S. and France." Rand Corp. report P-4989. Santa Monica, Calif., 1973.

Alexander, A. J., "R&D in Soviet Aviation." Rand Corp. report R-589-PR. Santa Monica, Calif., November 1970.

Alexander, A. J., "The Process of Soviet Weapons Acquisition." Paper presented to the European Study Commission, Paris, April 15–16, 1977.

Alexander, A. J., "Design to Price from the Perspective of the U.S., France and Soviet Union." Rand Corp. report P-4967. Santa Monica, Calif., 1978.

Aliber, R., *The International Money Game.* New York: Basic Books, 1973.

Allison, D., "The Science Entrepreneur." *International Science and Technology,* January 1963.

Amann, R., et al. (eds.). *The Technological Level of Soviet Industry.* New Haven, Conn.: Yale University Press, 1977.

Arms Control and Disarmaments Agency, *World Military Expenditures and Arms Trades 1963-1973.* Washington, D.C., 1974.

Art, R. J., *The T.F.X. Decision: McNamara and the Military.* Boston: Little, Brown, 1968.

Averitt, R. T., *The Dual Economy: The Dynamics of American Industry Structure.* New York: Norton, 1968.

Bain, J. S., "Barriers to New Competition: Their Character and Consequences in Manufacturing Industries. Cambridge, Mass.: Harvard University Press, 1956.

Bain, J. S., *Industrial Organization.* New York: Wiley, 1959.

Baker, R. S., *Woodrow Wilson, Life and Letters,* vol. 8. New York: Doubleday, Doran & Co., 1937.

Baldwin, W. L., *The Structure of the Defense Market, 1955-1964.* Durham, N.C.: Duke University Press, 1967.

Baran, P. M., and Sweezy, P. A., *Monopoly Capital.* New York: Modern Reader Paperbacks, 1966.

Barber, R. J., *The Politics of Research.* Washington, D.C.: Public Affairs Press, 1966.

Barnet, R. J., The Economy of Death. New York: Atheneum, 1969.

Barnet, R. J., and Müller, R. E., *Global Reach: The Power of the Multinational Corporations.* New York: Simon and Schuster, 1974.

Barrett, N. S., *The Theory of Microeconomic Policy.* Lexington, Mass.: Heath, 1974.

Baumol, W. J., *Economic Theory and Operations Analysis.* Englewood Cliffs, N.J.: Prentice-Hall, 1972.

Blair, J. M., *Economic Concentration: Structure, Behavior, and Public Policy.* New York: Harcourt Brace Jovanovich, 1972.

Blair, J. M., "Market Power and Inflation: A Short Run Target Return Model," *Journal of Economic Issues,* VIII, pp. 453–77.

Bleckman, B. M., et al., "Setting National Priorities: The 1976 Budget." Washington, D.C.: Brookings Institute, 1975.

Bohi, D. R., "Profit Performance in the Defense Industry." *Journal of Political Economy,* 1972, pp. 721–728.

Boileau, O. C., "Weapons Acquisition: An Industry View." Procurement Associates, Inc., Covina, Calif., September 1977.

Bray, L. J., testimony before House-Senate Joint Committee on Defense Production, November 24, 1976.

Breckinridge, H., *Preparedness.* New York: Sun, 1916.

Bucy, F. J., "An Analysis of Export Control of U.S. Technology: A DoD Perspective." Defense Science Board report, February 1976.

Bureau of the Census, Department of Commerce, "Concentration Ratios in Manufacturing, 1967." Special reports, 1970.

Burlingame, R., *Machines That Built America.* New American Library, 1955.

Cahn, A. H., Kruzel, J. J., and Dawkins, P. M., *Controlling Future Arms Trade.* New York: McGraw-Hill, 1977.

Canan, J. W., *The Superwarriors: The Fantastic World of Pentagon Superweapons.* New York: Weybright and Talley, 1975.

Carson, R. B., ed., *Government in the American Economy.* Lexington, Mass.: Heath, 1973.

Caves, R. E., *American Industry: Structure, Conduct, Performance.* Englewood Cliffs, N.J.: Prentice-Hall, 1964.

Chandler, A.D., Jr., *Strategy and Structure: Chapters in the History of the Industrial Enterprise.* Cambridge, Mass.: MIT Press, 1962.

Commerce Technical Advisory Board, Dept. of Commerce, "The Role of New Technical Enterprises in the U.S. Economy." Report to Secretary of Commerce, January 1976.

Commission on Government Procurement, "Final Report." Washington, D.C.: Government Printing Office, December 1972.

Comptroller General, "Defense Industry Profit Study." Report to Congress (B-159896), March 17, 1971.

Comptroller General, "Acquisition of Major Weapon Systems." Department of Defense report B-163058, July 1972.

Comptroller General, "Foreign Military Sales—A Growing Concern." June 1976.

Conference Board, "Report on Investment in the Defense Industry." 1976.

Congressional Budget Office, "Budgeting Cost Savings to the DoD Resulting from FMS." Staff report, May 24, 1976.

Corey, E. R. *Procurement Mangement: Strategy, Organization, and Decision Making.* Boston: CBI, 1978.

Danhoff, C. H., "Government Contracting and Technology Change." Washington, D.C.: Brookings Institute, 1968.

Daniels, J., *The Wilson Era: Years of Peace, 1910-1971.* Chapel Hill, N.C.: University of North Carolina Press, 1944.

Defense Science Board, "Industrial Readiness Plans and Programs." Final report, April 15, 1977.

Defense Security Assistance Administration, "F.M.S. and Military Assistance Facts." Data Management Division (Comptroller), 1976.

Defense Supply Agency, "A Study of Increased Procurement Costs and the Industrial Production Base." June 1975.

Department of Defense, Office of the Assistant Secretary of Defense (Comptroller), "100 Top Defense Contractors and Their Subsidiary Corporations." Reports for fiscal years 1945-1975.

Department of Defense, Office of Assistant Secretary of Defense (Comptroller), "Real and Personal Property of the DoD." June 30, 1975.

Department of Defense, Office of the Assistant Secretary of Defense for Installations and Logistics [Procurement], "Profit '76, Summary Report," December 1976.

Drake, H. B., "Major DoD Procurements at War With Reality." *Harvard Business Review,* January–February 1970, pp. 119–141.

Drinnon, J. W., and Gansler, J. W., "Predicting the Costs and Benefits of Competitive Production Sources." Paper presented at Ninth Annual DoD/Federal Acquisition Institute Acquisition Research Symposium, Annapolis, Md., June 1980.

DuBoff, R., "Converting Military Spending to Social Welfare: The Real Obstacles." *Quarterly Review of Economics and Business,* Spring 1972.

DuBoff, R., *Economic Growth and Structural Changes in Western Capitalism.* Andover, Mass.: Warner Modular, 1973.

Eades, G. C., "Achieving 'Appropriate' Levels of Investment in Technological Change: What Have We Learned?" Rand Corp. report P5998. Santa Monica, Calif., November 1977.

Edwards, R.C., Reich, M., and Weisskoff, T. E., *The Capitalistic System.* Englewood Cliffs, N.J.: Prentice-Hall, 1972.

Fassett, F. G., Jr., et al., *The Shipbuilding Business in the United States of America,* vols. 1 and 2. New York: Society of Naval Architects and Marine Engineers, 1948.

Federal Trade Commission, "Economic Report on Corporate Mergers." Staff report, 1969.

Fesler, J. W., *Industrial Mobilization for War*. Washington, D.C.: Government Printing Office, 1947.

Finney, B., *Arsenal of Democracy*. New York: Whittlessey House of McGraw-Hill, 1941.

Fisher, I. N., and Hall, G. R., "Risk and the Aerospace Rate of Return." Rand Corp. report RM-5440-PR. Santa Monica, Calif., December 1967.

Fisher, I. N., and Hall, G. R., "Defense Profit Policy in the United States and the United Kingdom." Rand Corp. report RM-5610-PR. Santa Monica, Calif., October 1968.

Fox, J. R., *Arming America: How the U.S. Buys Weapons*. Cambridge, Mass.: Harvard University Press, 1974.

Friedman, N., and Gray, C. S., "U.S. and U.S.S.R. Mobilization Policies." Hudson Institute, Croton-on-Hudson, New York, May 1979.

Frisch, F. A. P., "Production and Construction: A Comparison of Concepts in Shipbuilding and Other Industries." Paper presented at Fifth Annual DoD Procurement Research Conference, November 1976.

Galbraith, J. K., *The New Industrial State*. Boston: Houghton Mifflin, 1967.

Galbraith, J. K., testimony in hearings on The Military Budget and National Economic Priorities before the Subcommittee on Economy in Government of the House-Senate Joint Economic Committee, June 3-13, 17, 23, and 24, 1969.

Galbraith, J. K., "The Big Defense Firms Are Really Public Firms and Should be Nationalized." *New York Times Magazine,* November 16, 1969.

Galbraith, J. K., *Economics and the Public Purpose*. Boston: Houghton Mifflin, 1973.

Gansler, J. S., testimony concerning embargo of Rhodesia before House Armed Services Committee Subcommittee for Seapower and Strategic and Critical Materials, July 22, 1975.

Gansler, J. S., hearings on Civil Preparedness and Limited Nuclear War before House-Senate Joint Committee on Defense Production, April 28, 1976.

Gansler, J.S., "Lets Change the Way the Pentagon Does Business." *Harvard Business Review,* May-June 1977.

Gansler, J. S., "The U.S. Aircraft Industry: A Case for Sectoral Planning." *Challenge,* July-August 1977.

Gansler, J. S., "The Diminishing Economic and Strategic Viability of the U.S. Defense Industrial Base." Ph.D. diss., American University, 1978. Ann Arbor, Mich.: University Microfilms International, 1978.

Gansler, J. S., "Cost as a Design Parameter." Dept. of Defense Office of Public Affairs press release 67-73, February 13, 1973.

Gansler, J. S. (chairman), "Joint DoD/OMB Study of the U.S. Aircraft Industry." Office of the Secretary of Defense, January 1977.

Gansler, J. S., testimony before House-Senate Joint Committee on Defense Production, May 23, 1975.

Gansler, J. S., statement before House-Senate Joint Committee on Defense Production, November 17, 1976.

Gansler, J. S., "The Expansion Capability of the Defense Industry." Paper presented to The American Defense Preparedness Association, Washington, D.C., April 25, 1979.

Gansler, J. S., and Melman, S., "The Military-Industrial Complex: A Debate." *Defense Management Journal,* March–April 1979.

Gelb, L. H., "Arms Sales." *Foreign Policy,* Winter 1976–1977, p. 8.

Goodhue, L. H., "Fair Profits From Defense Business." *Harvard Business Review,* March –April 1972.

Goure, L., "War Survival in Soviet Strategy: U.S.S.R. Civil Defense." Center for Advanced International Studies, Washington, D.C. 1976.

Gray, H., hearings on Economic Aspects of Government Patent Policies, Senate Select Small Business Subcommittee, March 7, 1963.

Green, M .J., ed., *The Monopoly Makers: Ralph Nader's Study Report on Regulation and Competition.* New York: Grossman, 1973.

Hall, G. R., "Defense Procurement and Public Utility Regulation." Rand Corp. report. Santa Monica, Calif., May 1968.

Hall, G. R., and Johnson, R. E., "A Review of Air Force Procurement, 1962–1964." Rand Corp. report RM-4500-PR. Santa Monica, Calif., May 1965.

Harkavy, R. E., *The Arms Trade and International Systems.* Cambridge, Mass.: Ballinger, 1975.

Harris, S. E., *Economic Reconstruction.* New York: McGraw-Hill, 1946.

Harvey, M. L., and Kohler, F. D., "Soviet World Outlook." Current Affairs Press vol. 1, no. 4. Washington D.C.: Center for Advanced International Studies, 1976.

Heilbroner, R. L., and Thurow, L., *The Economic Problem,* fourth edition. Englewood Cliffs, N.J.: Prentice-Hall, 1975.

Henderson, J. M., and Quante, R. E., *Microeconomic Theory: A Mathematical Approach.* New York: McGraw-Hill, 1971.

Hiller, J. R., and Tollison, R. D., "Incentive vs. Cost-Plus Contracts in Defense Procurement." *Journal of Industrial Economics* XXVI, March 1978, pp. 239–248.

Hirshman, A. D., *Natural Power and the Structure of Foreign Trade.* Berkeley: University of California Press, 1945.

Hitch, C. J., and McKean, R., *The Economics of Defense in the Nuclear Age.* Cambridge, Mass.: Harvard University Press, 1960.

Huston, J. A., *The Sinews of War: Army Logistics 1775–1953.* Washington, D.C.: Government Printing Office, 1966.

Jacquemin, A. P., and DeJong, H. W., eds., *Markets, Corporate Behavior and the State.* The Hague: Martinus Nijhoff, 1976.

Jones, T. K., testimony before House-Senate Joint Production Committee regarding Soviet civil preparedness, May 23, 1975.

Kahn, H., and Schneider, W., Jr., "The Technological Requirements of Mobilization Warfare." Hudson Institute report. Croton-on-Hudson, N.Y., May 1975.

Kaldor, N., and Minlees, J. A., "A New Model of Economic Growth," in *Readings in Microeconomics,* ed. M. G. Mueller. New York: Holt, Rinehart & Winston, 1966.

Kaufman, R. F., *The War Profiteers.* New York: Bobbs-Merrill, 1970.

House Committee on Government Operations, "Inaccuracy of Department of Defense Weapons Acquisition Cost Estimates." Washington, D.C.: Government Printing Office, June 1979 and November 1979.

House Committee on the Armed Services, "Aircraft Production Costs and Profits." 84th Congress, 2nd session, hearings under authority of H.R. 112, February 16–March 22, 1956.

House-Senate Joint Economics Committee, "The Economics of Military Procurement." 91st Congress, 1st session, 1969.

House-Senate Joint Committee on Defense Production, hearings, first session on Defense Priorities System and Associates Special Priorities Assistance Program, May 22–23, 1975.

Kaysen, C., and Turner, D. F., *Antitrust Policy: An Economic and Legal Analysis.* Cambridge, Mass: Harvard University Press, 1959.

Keynes, J. M., "National Self-Sufficiency." *Yale Review,* Summer 1933.

Kindleberger, C. P., *Power and Money: The Economy of International Politics and the Politics of International Economics.* New York: Basic Books, 1970.

Knox, D. W., *A History of the United States Navy,* revised edition. New York: Putnam, 1948.

Kolko, G., *The Triumph of Conservatism.* New York: Free Press, 1963.

Kuhn, T. S., *The Structure of Scientific Revolutions.* University of Chicago Press, 1970.

Kurth, E., "Profit on Capital Employed in Government Contracting, British Style." *Public Contract Law Journal* 9, June 1977, pp. 55–71.

Kurth, J., hearings before the House-Senate Joint Committee on Defense Production, September 29–30, 1977.

Lange, O., and Taylor, F. M., *On the Economic Theory of Socialism.* Minneapolis: University of Minnesota Press, 1948.

Leijonhufvud, A., *On Keynesian Economics and the Economics of Keynes.* New York: Oxford University Press, 1975.

Lens, S., *The Military-Industrial Complex.* New York: Pilgrim, 1970.

Lipsey, R. G., and Lancaster, K., "The General Theory of the Second Best." *Review of Economic Studies* XXIV (1956–57), pp. 11–32.

Lodge, G. C., review of *The Ethical Basis of Economic Freedom. New York Times,* October 24, 1976.

Logistics Management Institute, "Defense Industry Profit Review, 1968 Profit Data." Washington, D.C., March 1970.

Lyons, R. D., "U.S. Arms-Sale Rise Stirs Capitol Concern." *New York Times,* October 19, 1975.

Mahan, Senator G., speech to NSIA, Washington, D.C., January 1976.

Martinson, O. B., and Mayer, S. C., "An Annotated Bibliography of (DoD) Profit Studies, Developed for Profit '76." Logistics Management Institute, Washington, D.C., September 1975.

McKie, J. W., "Concentration in Military Procurement Markets: A Classification and Analysis of Contract Data." Rand Corp. report RM-6307-PR. Santa Monica, Calif., June 1970.

Melman, S., "Twelve Propositions on Productivity and the War Economy." *Challenge,* March–April 1975.

Melman, S., *Pentagon Capitalism: The Political Economy of War.* New York: McGraw-Hill, 1970.

Milward, A. S., *War, Economy and Society: 1939–45."* Berkeley: University of California Press, 1977.

Mitchell, W. C., *Types of Economic Theory.* New York: Kelley, 1967.

Molander, E. A., "Historical Antecedents of Military-Industrial Criticism." *Military Affairs,* April 1976.

Morse, D. L., "Foreign Arms Sales: Two Sides to the Coin." Association of the U.S. Army, vol. 26, no. 1, January 1976.

Morse, R. A., "A Government Takeover of R&D?" *New York Times,* December 19, 1976.

Morse, R. A., "The Role of New Technical Enterprises in the U.S. Economy." Department of Commerce report, April 1976.

Müller, R. E., "Global Corporations and the American Economy." Paper presented to the Industrial College of Armed Forces, March 18, 1975.

Müller, R. E., "Globalization and the Failure of Economic Policy." *Challenge,* May–June 1975.

Müller, R. E., "Global Corporations and National Stabilization Policy." *Journal of Economic Issues,* June 1975.

Müller, R. E., "Macroeconomic Stabilization Policy and Global Corporations," in D. E. Apter and L. W. Goldman (eds.), *The Multinational Corporation and Social Change.* New York: Praeger, 1976.

Nash, R. C., Jr., "Pricing Policies in Government Contracts. Part II: Government Contracts." *Law and Contemporary Problems* (Duke University School of Law, Durham, N.C.), Spring 1964.

National Commission on Materials Policy, Final Report. Washington, D.C.: Government Printing Office, 1975.

National Commission on Supplies and Shortages, "Government and the Nation's Resources." Washington, D.C.: Government Printing Office, December 1976.

Nelson, D. M., *Arsenal of Democracy: The Story of American War Production.* New York: Harcourt, Brace, 1946.

Noll, R. G., et al., "Government Policies and Technological Innovation. Vol. I: Project Summary." Division of the Humanities and Social Sciences, California Institute of Technology, Pasadena, 1976.

Nordhaus, W. D., "The Falling Share of Profits." Brookings Institution Papers on Economic Activity, 1974.

Opinion Research Corporation, "Caravan Survey," November 1970. (Poll of 500 manufacturers and 50 banks on aerospace investments.)

Peck, M. J., and Scherer, F. M., *The Weapons Acquisition Process: An Economic Analysis.* Cambridge, Mass.: Harvard University Press.

Perry, R., et al. "System Acquisition Strategies." Rand Corp. report R-733-PR/ARPA. Santa Monica, Calif., June 1971.

Pipes, R., "Why the Soviet Union Thinks it Could Fight and Win a Nuclear War." *Air Force* Magazine, September 1977, pp. 55–66.

Proxmire, Sen. W., hearings on Civil Preparedness and Limited Nuclear War, House-Senate Joint Committee on Defense Production, April 28, 1976.

Raskin, A. H., "Some Big Companies Have Their Hands Out," *New York Times,* December 20, 1970, sec. 4, p. 3.

Reich, M., and Finkelhor, D., "Capitalism and the Military Industrial Complex," in Edwards et al., *The Capitalistic System.*

Rice, D., "Shortages and Economic Plannings," *Wall Street Journal,* March 14, 1977.

Roberts, E. B., "Questioning the Cost/Effectiveness of the R&D Procurement Process," from *Research Program Effectiveness,* ed. M. S. Yovits et al. New York: Gordon & Breach, 1966.

Robinson, J., *The Economics of Imperfect Competition,* second edition. London: Macmillan, 1969.

Robinson, J., *Economic Heresies: Some Old-Fashioned Questions in Economic Theory.* New York: Basic Books, 1971.

Rogin, L., *Meaning and Validity of Economic Theory.* New York: Harper, 1956; reprinted 1971 by Harper & Row.

Rosen, S., *Testing the Theory of the Military-Industrial Complex.* Lexington, Mass.: Lexington Books (Heath), 1973.

Sampson, A., "Lockheed's Foreign Policy: Who, in the End, Corrupted Whom." *New York Magazine,* March 15, 1976, p. 53.

Sampson, A., *The Arms Bazaar,* New York: Viking, 1977.

Scherer, F. M., *The Weapons Acquisition Process: Economic Incentives.* Cambridge, Mass.: Harvard University Press, 1964.

Scherer, F. M., *Industrial Market Structure and Economic Performance.* Chicago: Rand-McNally, 1970.

Scherer, F. M., *The Economics of Multi-Plant Operation.* Cambridge, Mass.: Harvard University Press, 1975.

Schlesinger, J. R., *The Political Economy of National Security: A Study of the Economics Aspect of the Contemporary Power Struggle.* New York: Praeger, 1960.

Schwartz, C., et al., "Setting National Priorities: The 1973 Budget." Brookings Institution, Washington, D.C., 1972.

Scitovsky, T., et al., *Mobilizing Resources for War: The Economic Alternatives.* New York: McGraw-Hill, 1951.

Searby, F., "Return to Return-On-Investment." *Harvard Business Review,* April–May 1975.

Senate Committee on Foreign Relations, "U.S. Military Sales to Iran." Staff report, July 1976.

Senate Committee on the Judiciary, Subcommittee on Anti-Trust and Monopoly, 9th Congress, 2nd session, hearings pursuant to S.R. 233, June 17 and 21 and September 10, 1968. Washington, D.C.: Government Printing Office, 1969.

Simons, L. M., "Grumman Set to Refund Iran $28 Million." *Washington Post,* February 10, 1976.

Spiro, H. P., "Optimal Organization of the Military Hardware Industry." Ph.D. diss., University of California, Los Angeles, 1972.

Staley, C. E., *International Economics: Analysis and Issues.* Englewood Cliffs, N.J.: Prentice-Hall, 1970.

Stanford Research Institute, "The Industry-Government Aerospace Relationship." Stanford, Calif., 1963.

Stansberry, J., Air Force study of subcontractor management, spring 1972.

Stekler, H. O., *The Structure and Performance of the Aerospace Industry.* Los Angeles: University of California Press, 1965.

Sullivan, W., "Loss of Innovation in Technology is Debated." *New York Times,* November 14, 1976.

Ulsamer, E. E., "The Designers of Dassault: Men Who Take One Step at a Time," *Air Force Magazine,* August 1970.

U.S. Army War College Division, General Staff Corps., "Personnel Versus Materiel in Plans for National Defense." Document NR 526. Washington, D.C.: Government Printing Office, 1916. (Part of a larger study entitled "Statement of Proper Military Policy for the United States.")

Vaitsos, C., *Intercountry Income Distribution and Transnational Enterprises.* Oxford University Press, 1964.

Vernon, R., "International Investment and International Trade in the Product Cycle." *Journal of Economics* 80, May 1966.

Ward, J. W., and Garcia, L. E., "The U.S. Shipbuilding Industry: Structure, Conduct and Performance." Thesis, Naval Postgraduate School, Monterey, Calif., 1975.

Weidenbaum, M. L., "The Effects of Government Contracting on Private Enterprise." *George Washington Law Review,* December 1966.

Weidenbaum, M. L., "Arms and the American Economy: A Domestic Convergence Hypothesis." *American Economic Review,* July 1968.

Weidenbaum, M. L., *The Modern Public Sector: New Ways of Doing the Government's Business.* New York: Basic Books, 1969.

Weidenbaum, M. L., "The Military/Space Market: The Intersection of the Public and Private Sectors." Hearings before the Subcommittee on Anti-Trust and Monopoly of the Committee on the Judiciary, 90th Congress, Second Session, pursuant to S.R. 233, June 17 and 21 and September 10, 1968. Washington, D.C.: Government Printing Office, 1969.

Weidenbaum, M. L., *The Economics of Peace-Time Defense.* New York: Basic Books, 1974.

Westcott, A., et al., *American Sea Power Since 1775.* New York: Lippincott, 1957.

Wilford, J. N., "U.S. Science is Fine, But Could Be Better." *New York Times,* October 24, 1976.

Wilson, G. C., "The Condor Missile and Its Friends." *Washington Post,* November 9, 1976.

Yarmolinsky, A., *The Military Establishment: Its Impacts on American Society.* New York: Harper and Row, 1971.

Index

Accountability
  in civilian vs. defense sector, 86
  public, 72
  of R&D decisionmakers, 105
Adams, Walter, 72, 73, 137, 294n.77
Advertising, 46
  of price competition, 75, 76
Aerojet, 289n.16. *See also* Jet engine
  industry
Aerospace industry. *See also* Aircraft
  industry
  cyclic nature of, 133
  percent utilization in, 293n.54
  rate of return in, 61, 88
  R&D funding in, 98,104
  return on equity of, 87
  turnover in, 291n.37
  workforce in, 103
Aerospatiale, 211
Afghanistan, Soviet move into, 14, 288
Aircraft. *See also* Helicopters
  AWACS, 34, 206, 308n.27
  bombers, 173
  commercial, 15
  concentration ratios, 166
  cost trends for, 16
  drone, 42, 166
  expenditures for, 17, 21
  F4, 130
  F5, 120, 277
  F15, 34, 299n.37
  F16, 158, 206, 255
  F18, 225
  F111, 34, 90
  Mig-25 (Soviet), 251–252
  Mirage 2000 (French), 313n.21
  plants for, 54
  R&D funding for, 98
  Soviet, 25
  U.S. inventory of, 25
  Viggen (Swedish), 245
Aircraft carriers, cost trends for, 16
Aircraft industry, 223. *See also* Aerospace
  industry
  capacity utilization in, 170, 174, 175
  capital-equipment problems in, 56
  characteristics of, 163
  competing firms in, 18
  corrective actions for, 168

  economic efficiency in, 172
  excess capacity in, 176–178
  future trends in, 181–184
  institutional approach of, 183
  labor force in, 54
  lack of capital investment by, 171
  market structure for, 171–175
  nationalization of, 179
  performance of, 174
  planning in, 182
  production facilities in, 183
  production levels in, 121
  reduction of extra capacity in, 181
  turnover rates for, 191
  "uniform procurement practices" in, 11
  wage rates in, 53
Aircraft modification programs, 35
Air Force, U.S.
  and defense industry, 288n.9
  employment history of, 52
  weapons-systems costs in, 34
Air pollution, expenditures for controlling, 59
Air Power Committee, congressional, 80
Allocation, competitive, 311n.31
All-volunteer services, 21
Aluminum
  lead time for, 66
  price increases for, 65
Amana, 289n.17
Antiaircraft systems, attrition rates
  with, 114
Antitank systems
  attrition rates with, 114
  foreign sales of, 208
Appalachian Regional Commission, cost
  overruns of, 91
Armed Services Procurement Regulations,
  172, 238, 242, 262
Armored personnel carriers, foreign sales
  of, 208
Arms control, and U.S.-Soviet parity, 22
Arms-exporting countries, interdepen-
  dence of, 272. *See also* Sales
Army, U.S.
  and defense industry, 288n.9
  weapons-systems costs in, 34
Army Corps of Engineers, U.S., 208
Arsenal Act, 167, 288n.9